Human Behavior AND THE Larger Social Environment

Related books of interest

THIRD EDITION

Human Behavior AND THE Larger Social Environment

CONTEXT FOR SOCIAL WORK PRACTICE AND ADVOCACY

Miriam McNown **Rita**
JOHNSON RHODES

University of South Carolina *University of South Carolina*

LYCEUM
BOOKS, INC.
Chicago, IL 60637

© 2015 by Lyceum Books, Inc.

Published by
LYCEUM BOOKS, INC.
5758 S. Blackstone Avenue
Chicago, Illinois 60637
773-643-1903 fax
773-643-1902 phone
lyceum@lyceumbooks.com
www.lyceumbooks.com

This book was previously published by Pearson Education.

6   5   4   3   15   16   17   18

ISBN 978-1-935871-60-6

Printed in the United States of America.

Library of Congress Cataloging-in-Publication Data

Johnson, Miriam McNown, 1946-
   Human behavior and the larger social environment : context for social work practice and advocacy / Miriam McNown Johnson, University of South Carolina, Rita Rhodes, University of South Carolina.
      pages cm
   Revised edition of the authors' Human behavior and the larger social environment : a new synthesis, 2nd ed.
   "Third edition"—Preface.
   Includes bibliographical references and index.
   ISBN 978-1-935871-60-6
   1. Social ecology.   2. Social psychology.   3. Social institutions—United States.   4. Social structure—United States.   5. Social service—United States.   6. United States—Social conditions—21st century.   I. Rhodes, Rita M.   II. Title.
HM861.J64   2015
302—dc23
                                                        2014017746

To our social work students

Contents

PART III. SOCIAL STRUCTURE IN AMERICAN SOCIETY

Preface to the Third Edition

For the past twenty years we have had the privilege of introducing students in the classroom to content on human behavior and the social environment. When we started there was scant attention to the larger social environment in social work human behavior courses.

Now social work educators are aware that the context of social work practice is both important and constantly changing. For example, attitudes towards LGBT people and legal recognition of the rights of same-sex couples have changed dramatically over the course of just a few months. On the other hand, the country appears to be going backward in other areas; political divisiveness and voter suppression are serious concerns. It is important that students have both a deep understanding and ability to make sense of an evolving social environment, as well as current information and data. We believe that this text helps students meet that challenge.

In writing this text, one of our goals was to make the material useful to beginning social work students without overwhelming them. We made decisions based on our belief that it is not important for students to learn and memorize specific definitions or lists so much as it is imperative that they be able to reflect critically on new ideas and apply abstract concepts to different situations. With this in mind, we have applied the following strategies. First, we have used a limited number of perspectives and theories that students can learn thoroughly and well. Second, although we have explored many sources, we usually offer a single, simple definition of a term. Our definitions may not agree entirely with what other authors have written, but they work well for material presented in this book. Third, we have reduced some concepts, perspectives, or theories to their most essential elements in an effort to make them more understandable. In doing so, we have sacrificed some complexity that might be appropriately incorporated at more advanced levels of study. Finally, we have arranged concepts in ways that are arguably arbitrary; some social work authors and sociologists have organized them differently. We found this arrangement works best for us and for the students and instructors who use this text in their Human Behavior and the Social Environment (HBSE) classes.

We have deleted outdated content and replaced it with material that is the most recent available. In many cases that meant that we used current news sources and websites (from government sources and from respected organizations such as the Economic Policy Institute, the Pew Center, the Kaiser Family Foundation, the Sentencing Project, and the Human Rights Campaign) rather than academic journals. In some instances, the information—such as innovations in social media, immigration reform, efforts to increase the minimum wage, and state laws and court cases related to same-sex marriage—was literally evolving as we wrote. Our goal was to provide examples for which the application of perspectives and theories was current and relevant.

ORGANIZATION OF THE TEXT

Based on the feedback we have received, we believe that this text can be used before, after, or concurrently with a course on individual development. It also provides a broad foundation for courses on policy practice, practice with communities and organizations, and diversity.

The text is composed of four sections and ten chapters. Part I is an introduction to the basic theoretical perspectives that social scientists use.

In addition, we include preferred social work perspectives. Chapter 1 explains the major perspectives that are systematically revisited in the chapters that follow.

Part II presents eight social institutions, beginning in chapter 2 with politics and the economy. Chapter 3 addresses those social institutions that are, for the most part, government-related: education, criminal justice, and the military. This material provides foundation content for students who may enter careers in school social work, work with legal offenders and their families, and members of the military, veterans, and their families. Chapter 4 covers three social institutions that are not, for the most part, government-supported: health care; religion; and mass media, social media, and communications technology.

Part III discusses social structure in American society. Chapter 5 examines social stratification, giving particular attention to the issue of social class and the troubling gap in income and wealth. Chapter 6 considers the role of cultural diversity in influencing individuals and families, and chapter 7 presents information on gender, sexual orientation, and disability. Both chapters also address issues of inequity and oppression.

Acknowledging that human behavior is dependent on context, part IV gives attention to the social settings that individuals and families inhabit. Chapter 8 covers locational communities. Chapter 9 discusses organizations. Chapter 10 presents residential institutions, which are a likely major source of employment for social workers in the twenty-first century.

In summary, this text represents our effort to reinforce the unique social work outlook that human behavior is shaped by systems beyond the intrapsychic and familial domains. It is essential that students recognize the power of large systems to harm the most vulnerable among us. We believe that such an understanding will well serve the next generation of social workers.

Throughout the book, social and economic justice emerges as a constant theme. Students are encouraged to think critically about the mechanisms of oppression and discrimination in both historical and contemporary contexts. We hope that such knowledge would bring students to examine the values of the larger society as well as their own and to become advocates to advance social and economic well-being.

ACKNOWLEDGMENTS

We would like to express our appreciation to the student graduate assistants who helped with this edition: Dan Jensen, Danielle Unkefer, Amy Skinner, Brittany Miller, Pamela Tamowski, Brittany Cintron, and Leya Alderfer. We also want to thank the staff at Thomas Cooper Library, Paul Mendelson, and David Follmer at Lyceum.

Core Competencies Addressed

The Council on Social Work Education accredits programs of social work education in the United States. It requires that students be able to demonstrate core competencies and practice behaviors. This textbook addresses many of these competencies and practice behaviors in depth.

CSWE CORE COMPETENCIES AND PRACTICE BEHAVIORS*
EXAMPLES IN THIS TEXT

Competencies and Practice Behaviors	Chapters
2.1.3—Apply critical thinking to inform and communicate professional judgments.	
• distinguish, appraise, and integrate multiple sources of knowledge, including research-based knowledge, and practice wisdom	1–10
2.1.4—Engage diversity and difference in practice.	
• recognize the extent to which a culture's structures and values may oppress, marginalize, alienate, or create or enhance privilege and power	2–7
• gain sufficient self-awareness to eliminate the influence of personal biases and values in working with diverse groups	5–7
• recognize and communicate their understanding of the importance of difference in shaping life experiences	5–7
2.1.5—Advance human rights and social and economic justice.	
• understand the forms and mechanisms of oppression and discrimination	2, 3–7, 9–10

2.1.7—Apply knowledge of human behavior and the social environment.
- utilize conceptual frameworks to guide the processes of assessment, intervention, and evaluation   1–10
- critique and apply knowledge to understand person and environment   1–10

2.1.9—Respond to contexts that shape practice.
- continuously discover, appraise, and attend to changing locales, populations, scientific and technological developments, and emerging societal trends to provide relevant services   2–4, 8

Adapted with the permission of the Council on Social Work Education

PART I

Conceptual Frameworks

The Council on Social Work Education (2008, pp. 4, 6) requires that social work students be able to "utilize conceptual frameworks to guide the processes of assessment, intervention, and evaluation," and "distinguish, appraise, and integrate multiple sources of knowledge." Chapter 1 introduces students to sociological and social work perspectives that are used throughout the text to promote critical thinking and enhance understanding.

REFERENCE

Council on Social Work Education (2008). *Educational policy and accreditation standards.* Council on Social Work Accreditation, Inc. Retrieved from http://www.cswe.org/File.aspx?id = 41861.

CHAPTER ONE

Introduction to Perspectives and Theories

WHERE WE BEGIN

Abigail Garvey was seeing her last client for the day. Abby guessed that Jennifer Floyd, like many of her recent clients, would be asking for information about the resources that were available for newly unemployed workers in Oak Grove. Abby was already aware of how precarious Jennifer's economic situation was, having made a referral for her to Consumer Credit Counseling for help in managing her family's credit card debt a few months previously.

Jennifer had been a longtime client of Abby's. Jennifer had met with Abby seven years ago, when she graduated from high school, for career planning. Jennifer was undecided on whether to enroll in classes at the local tech school or take a job at the local big box retail store. Jennifer decided to take the job because, as she pointed out, she could begin earning money immediately and marry her high school sweetheart, Zachary Schneider. Jennifer was drawn to Zach as someone who had a strong work ethic and the potential to be a loving, involved father. Zach was already employed at the local electronics manufacturing plant and had a promising future there.

Jennifer was determined to join Zach and her older siblings in the town's typical employment pattern—going straight from high school to working in the community. Abby remembered thinking at the time that she wished that Jennifer, who was bright and seemed ambitious, had considered a wider range of options. Six months later, Jennifer was married. A year later, she had her first child and fifteen months after that, twins. The wages at the plant were not bad, and with Jennifer and Zach working different shifts, obtaining child care was not a problem.

Now the plant was closing. It was being moved to Mexico where local workers would receive $8 per day to do what Zach had done for $11 an hour. Although he would receive temporary unemployment benefits, they would lose their family health insurance. Jennifer was being paid just slightly more than minimum wage and because she worked part-time, was not eligible for benefits.

Jennifer felt overwhelmed—she and Zach had finally made some progress in paying down their credit card bills, but now the children all had ear infections that required doctor visits and prescription medication, and their older model car was becoming increasingly unreliable. Because her family and friends were also facing hard times, Jennifer didn't feel that she could count on them for support.

Abby was not much older than Jennifer. She had forgone four years of salary and had postponed marriage and having children in order to obtain her BSW degree. Despite her training, the words "I told you so" came to mind when she considered Jennifer's predicament. Abby had always thought that the most difficult part of counseling was watching her clients make poor choices. On the other hand, how could anyone have predicted that the U.S. economy would falter so badly and recover so slowly and the plant would close? Blaming Jennifer, or telling her what she should have done seven years ago, obviously wouldn't help now.

Like Abby, some social workers may believe that some clients' problems originate in their own poor choices. But social workers are trained to use more than common sense, instincts, and good intentions in analyzing situations. They are taught to understand that human society and all of its parts interact in complex ways that are not easily reduced to simple, linear, cause-and-effect explanations. Jennifer's decision to terminate her formal education at age eighteen is not necessarily the cause of her family's impending economic crisis. Abby needs to consider that Jennifer is an employee of an organization, a member of a community, and a participant in an economic system that also shaped her life chances.

There are discernable patterns in human behavior and in the social systems that humans create. Jennifer's problems are not unique to her, her employer, or even to her community. Social work courses taught Abby that while she must respect Jennifer's individual choices, there are also other descriptions and explanations of circumstances that will help Abby select an appropriate intervention.

In addition, there are multiple ways of understanding the same events. In counseling sessions, Jennifer will present her view of what is happening and why. Her immediate supervisor, and the executives at company headquarters, might see things quite differently, not to mention the company's stockholders, the town council, her fellow employees, politicians and legislators, and other stakeholders. Abby will review her own perspectives.

Abby will conclude that all of these points of view have elements of truth, but that one or two of them are more useful in understanding Jennifer's situation, in selecting a practice model, and then in formulating a course of action.

SHIFTING PERSPECTIVES IN SOCIAL WORK

A *perspective* is a particular point of view that reflects "taken-for-granted" assumptions or a system of beliefs. Perspectives provide a broad conceptual and value framework within which theory development or selection takes place (Chess & Norlin, 1991). Most people would agree that a perspective is not intended as a guide for practice. Perspectives have strong explanatory power and are thus useful for assessments, but do not prescribe specific forms of intervention. Instead they allow the thoughtful selection of one or more practice theories.

As a profession, social work has borrowed extensively from other disciplines, including the social sciences (e.g., sociology, psychology), the life sciences (e.g., biology, genetics), and the humanities (e.g., religion, philosophy, history). There is no perspective or body of theories that is totally unique to social work, although some perspectives and theories are used more often than others.

Historically, social workers and social work educators have shifted from one perspective to another. During the 1960s and 1970s, the social work profession moved from an emphasis on intrapsychic phenomena to an orientation that also paid attention to social environments and larger social systems (Leighninger, 1978). The systems perspective served as a theoretical bridge to address person *in* environment as a unitary focus rather than the false dichotomy of person *and* environment that had characterized earlier stages (Hearn, 1979).

The systems theory perspective also views behavior patterns as interactional and reciprocal rather than linear. In other words, rather than an explanation that says, in effect, a particular action on the part of A results in a predicable response from B, systems theorists would say that B is influenced by A, but A is at the same time also influenced by B. A and B could be individuals, families, or groups, or an individual in a family, or a group in an organization, and so forth. The limitations of a linear model seemed to be corrected by an emphasis on thinking systemically.

By the 1980s the social system approach, which emphasized system stability, was beginning to be challenged. Although social workers continued to pay attention to person-in-environment concepts, some believed that a clearer understanding of how and why systems change was needed. The ecosystems perspective, which has strong roots in systems theory, replaced the systems perspective with greater attention to process and what happens across encounters, reflecting the reciprocal relationships between organisms and their environments. Both perspectives are described in greater detail next.

PERSPECTIVES USED IN THIS TEXT

Because this text is concerned primarily with the broader contexts of human behavior, it draws heavily on sociological perspectives. In their analyses of macro (large) systems, sociologists predominantly rely on two perspectives: the functionalist perspective and the conflict perspective. Two other perspectives, the social constructionist perspective and the rational/social exchange perspective, are often used in the analysis of smaller systems and individual interactions. We (the authors) believe, however, that the social constructionist perspective and the rational/social exchange perspective offer useful insights in examining some social institutions and social settings. We include the ecosystems perspective because it is especially relevant for social work practice in that it views human behavior as part of reciprocal relationships with and within a context of many levels of systems that are interconnected. Finally, we include both a diversity perspective and a strengths perspective because they are central to the profession's value system.

Two of the perspectives used in this text, the ecosystems perspective and the functionalist perspective, are partially derived from and closely related to the systems perspective. *Systems* are defined as organized wholes comprising component parts that interact in a distinct way and endure over time (Anderson, Carter, & Lowe, 1999, p. 294). The *systems perspective*, also often called *general systems theory* (see von Bertalanffy, 1968), is an interdisciplinary construct developed to identify common principles of organization that can be applied to all phenomena. In other words, this perspective assumes there is a similar underlying order to everything in the universe.

Other basic assumptions of the systems perspective include the following:

- Each system has a structure; the parts have a relationship to each other.
- The whole is more than the sum of its parts.
- Everything is connected; a change in any one part affects the system as a whole.
- All systems are, at the same time, made up of smaller (sub)systems and are parts of larger systems.
- Each system has a boundary that separates it from other systems and helps to give it its identity.
- As systems evolve, they become more complex (i.e., the parts become differentiated and more specialized).

While physical scientists use a systems theory perspective to analyze everything from atoms to galaxies, social scientists use it to analyze social systems and their interactions. A *social system* is a social unit, such as a family, group, organization, or community, comprised of elements that are functionally related and interdependent. The parts of social systems do not need to be in close physical proximity to each other. They may have psychological rather than physical boundaries because they exist in social reality rather than in physical reality. The structure of a social system is determined by social roles and shared expectations; often members share common goals.

The assumptions of the systems and social systems perspectives can be illustrated with a school of social work. The school is more than a collection of individuals and spaces, more than faculty, staff, and students, offices, and classrooms. It is part of a larger system, a department, college, or university. It contains subsystems, such as student associations and faculty committees. Professors relate to students as instructors, advisors, and mentors; they relate to the administration as employees. In a large school, some staff may have specialized functions (e.g., accounting, clerical support, or supervision of other staff). The obvious boundaries of the school not only include building and classroom walls, but also might include psychosocial boundaries such as ID cards, enrollment lists, professional jargon, or a value system that is unique to the profession. It is easy to see how everything is connected and how one part affects the others. For example, if a professor in a foundation course fails to properly prepare students, instructors in subsequent courses will have to change their lessons to accommodate the students' deficiencies.

FIGURE 1.1   CRITICAL THINKING ABOUT SOCIAL SYSTEMS

See if you can apply systems concepts to your family as a social system. What are the parts and how are they interrelated? What larger systems are they a part of? What are the physical and psychosocial boundaries that set them apart from their larger environment? How has your enrollment in school affected other family members? In what ways has your family become more complex since you were born?

The Ecosystems Perspective

One of the common criticisms of the systems perspective stems from the abstract way it conceptualizes phenomena. Because systems concepts literally apply to all phenomena, they do not tell us much about any particular element or interaction. "Ecology, the biological science that studies organism-environment relations, offered concepts of these relations that were less abstract than those offered by systems theories and closer to common human experience" (Germain & Gitterman, 1995, p. 816). The *ecosystems perspective* (also called the *ecological perspective*) was introduced to social work by Carel Germain in 1973. It conceptualized the environment as "more than a static setting" for people's lives (Germain & Gitterman, 1995, p. 816). Concepts from ecology were used to supplement the systems perspective. This was consistent with the person-in-environment worldview of social workers (which Germain and Gitterman wrote as *person:environment* to signify how closely the two are intertwined).

The ecological perspective makes clear the need to view people and environments as a unitary system within a particular cultural and historic context. Both person and environment can be fully understood only in terms of their relationship, in which each continually influences the other within a particular context. Hence, all concepts derived from the ecological metaphor refer not to environment alone, or person alone; rather, each concept expresses a particular person:environment relationship, whether it is positive, negative, or neutral. (Germain & Gitterman, 1995, p. 816)

Another construct of the ecosystems perspective is *adaptation*, or the various processes people use to achieve a better level of fit between themselves and the settings in which they find themselves. Social systems, as well as individuals, are involved in a process of continuous adaptation within and with their larger environments. In our school of social work example, adaptation would occur if the university lost funding for work-study positions and the school developed paid internships in various social service agencies to fill the gap for financially needy students.

Goodness-of-fit is the extent to which there is a match between an individual's or a group's needs, rights, goals, and capacities and the qualities of their physical and social environments (Germain & Gitterman, 1995, p. 817). In our prior example, goodness-of-fit would be achieved if the school recognized that its student body was comprised primarily of full-time workers and changed its course schedule to offer mostly evening and weekend classes.

Other important ecosystems constructs include niche and habitat. Germain and Gitterman (1995, p. 818) define *niche* as the "status occupied by an individual or family in the social structure . . . [often related to] color, ethnicity, gender, age, poverty, sexual orientation, or physical or mental states." *Habitat* is defined as places or settings where individuals can be found. Whereas it is impossible to analyze the natural social and physical environments of humans as distinctly separate from each other, in this text we find it useful to concentrate on niches in part III and discuss settings where people live and work—locational communities, organizations, and residential institutions—in part IV.

The Functionalist Perspective

The *functionalist perspective* (often called *structural functionalism*) also is closely related to the systems perspective. It is used by sociologists, who are less interested in individual adjustment or smaller social systems than in how society works. They use functionalism to understand larger social systems and the functioning of society as a whole. According to this perspective, "a society is composed of interrelated parts, each of which serves a function and (ideally) contributes to the overall stability of the society" (Kendall, 2013, p. 21). Drawing upon systems perspective and social systems theory, one assumption is that large societal systems reflect a general orderliness and that they maintain a balance or stable state. If one part changes, all the other parts are affected and the system may no longer function smoothly. A recent example is the Great Recession that began in 2007, when a history of risky investments led to the financial failure of some major Wall Street firms and the need for government bailouts to keep others operating, so that the entire U.S. economy would not collapse.

Systems, ecosystems, and functionalist perspectives assume that systems are constantly changing, but that these change processes are incremental (slow and in small steps) and are self-correcting when the system gets out of balance. Functionalists believe that all social phenomena serve the purpose of maintaining the social system. Functionalists see a useful function in everything in society, including elements, characteristics, or processes that most people would view as negative, such as poverty or racial inequality (Davis & Moore, 1945). Because maintaining the status quo supports the interests of those who already hold power and wealth, functionalism is often criticized by those who believe the existing system is unfair.

Theorists who espouse a systems-related perspective (ecosystems or structural functionalism) support small, incremental, and self-righting changes. There is little expectation that the environment will be markedly changed. This point of view differs substantially from the position of conflict theorists (discussed next) who routinely call for fundamental structural change.

The Conflict Perspective

The *conflict perspective* is another perspective commonly used by sociologists. It is most often linked with Karl Marx, who wrote about interclass struggle. Unlike the functionalist perspective, conflict theorists argue that social systems are not united or harmonious but are divided by class, gender, race, or other characteristics that reflect differences in social power as much as anything else. According to this perspective, "groups in society are engaged in a continuous power struggle for scarce resources" (Kendall, 2013, p. 23). In the conflict perspective, problems are defined as social and structural rather than individual, meaning that they can be solved only by social change, not by individual adaptation. Conflict theorists would agree that "it's not the fact that there are rich and poor that generates egalitarian struggle, but the fact that the rich grind the faces of the poor. It's always what one group with power does to another group—whether in the name of health, safety, or security—it makes no difference. The aim, ultimately, of the fight for equality, is always the elimination of subordination . . . no more toadying, scraping and bowing, fearful trembling" (Walzer, 1983, p. 13).

Early social workers recognized structural inequality and oppression, but as a profession they have not until recently drawn upon the conflict perspective as a way to conceptualize human behavior in the social environment. The development of empowerment theories (Lee, 2001; Solomon, 1976, 1987), which have their roots in the conflict perspective, has led to a renewed interest in utilizing this perspective as a way to explain social injustice and privilege. *Empowerment* is a proactive response to assist people who experience systematic forms of harassment and oppression through consciousness-raising and enhancing self-efficacy. In Canada the term *anti-oppressive practice* is used for social justice work within the profession. It includes both process and outcome and encompasses a variety of practice approaches.

Critics of the conflict perspective note that, particularly without adoption of an empowerment approach, social workers using this perspective may overemphasize polarization and antagonism, viewing clients simply as victims and their opponents as oppressors (Robbins, Chatterjee, &

Canda, 2006, p. 88). On the other hand, in contrast to other helping professions, social work has a specific commitment to empowerment at both the personal and group levels.

The Rational/Social Exchange Perspective

The *rational/social exchange perspective* is based on the assumptions that human beings have the capacity to reason, make choices based on consideration of available alternatives and anticipated consequences, and act in their own best interest. Human behavior is believed to be purposeful and goal-directed. At the individual level, rational decision-making theories (e.g., rational choice theory, social exchange theory, fair-exchange theory, reciprocity) suggest that people make decisions based on a cost-benefit analysis.

The rational/social exchange perspective has also been applied to larger social systems (groups, organizations, communities, societies) (Kendall, 2008). Nevertheless, beyond the individual level, rational decision making by a collective body encounters many barriers, including lack of agreement on political, social, economic, and cultural values and goals; inability to compare competing costs and benefits; and the fragmented nature of policy making in large bureaucracies (Dye, 1998, pp. 25–27). Often benefits can be identified only for specific groups, and many of those are conflicting. Another barrier is that individual actors may look out for their own interests rather than that of the collective body or their constituency. The reality is that, at the level of larger systems and social institutions (organizations, communities, government), policies that generate the maximum social gain—the most benefits for the most people—are difficult to develop. In fact, Dye argues that rational decision making "rarely takes place at all in government" (1998, p. 25).

The Social Constructionist Perspective

The *social constructionist perspective* emphasizes the role of the human mind and the shared subjective understanding of localized experiences in defining the social world. ("Localized experience" refers to the notion that all people live in a specific cultural and historical setting that shapes their perceptions.) The constructionist perspective is based on the assumption that there is no objective reality; rather reality is defined by perceptions and is, in fact, a social construction (see Schutz, 1967). From a constructionist perspective, sociological phenomena, such as society and social institutions, considered by most people to be elements of objective reality, are no more than creations of human thought processes. Although constructionists do not deny the reality of such social phenomena, they suggest that it is important to study the subjective interpretations of such phenomena made by individuals and groups. In sum, this perspective suggests that reality is socially constructed through social interaction and people act in accordance with their constructed reality. An important concept in this perspective is that of standpoints. "*Standpoints* are truths or knowledge created through awareness of reality gleaned from particular social locations. The concept of standpoint assumes that all people see the world from the place where they are situated socioculturally. What is considered to be real depends on one's standpoint and is grounded in experiences related to one's position within the sociocultural topography" (Van Den Bergh, 1995, p. xxvii). The social constructionist perspective is useful in reminding social work practitioners that members of minority groups or other marginalized people may experience a social reality that is quite different from the one experienced by members of the white middle class.

One criticism of social constructionism is that, if everything is subjective and therefore relative, there is no basis for judging situations or determining preferred outcomes (Robbins, Chatterjee, & Canda, 2006, p. 346). Critics of the social constructionist perspective also worry that if social problems are understood as merely the perceptions and claims of particular groups, then there is no basis for taking action (Best, 1989).

The Diversity Perspective

In the past, the idea that America was a "melting pot" held prominence. Today, most social workers do not accept this as a productive point of view, but rather embrace the notion that celebrating different cultures, as well as other kinds of diversity, is healthy for individuals, families, groups, organizations, communities, and society. Acknowledging and valuing human diversity is central to the profession's value base and essential for culturally competent practice. "Social workers understand how diversity characterizes and shapes the human experience and is critical to the formation of identity" (Council on Social Work Education, 2008, p. 4). Nevertheless, it is important to distinguish between strengths-affirming honoring of differences and recognition of those divisions that are rooted in inequality and facilitate discrimination. Social workers must celebrate diversity while also negotiating resolutions to conflicts in a way that promotes social justice and economic fairness for everyone.

The Strengths Perspective

Another point of view that reflects social work values is the *strengths perspective* (Saleebey, 2002). "While recognizing the fallibilities of people, the strengths perspective brings some balance to the understanding of the human condition" (Saleebey, 2002, p. 265). The strengths perspective views all individuals and groups, regardless of their histories, as having value and capabilities, with resources, skills, motivations, and dreams that must be considered when working with them such that they gain more control over their lives. This perspective offers a basis from which helpers become agents of the client system, which is regarded as having special expertise. Critics of the strengths perspective say that it ignores problems or simply reframes them in a more positive light.

FIGURE 1.2   APPLYING THE PERSPECTIVES

Imagine you have seven friends who have quite different ideas about the community you live in. Read the description of each friend and decide which perspective guides his or her view of the community.

1. Anthony points to the construction of a new shopping mall that the community attracted through the offer of tax breaks for the developer. He notes that although some citizens objected to the project initially, they were persuaded to support it based on a careful evaluation of the potential long-term benefits compared to the short-term costs. Anthony takes pleasure in the observation that the community can usually reach consensus because citizens are willing to take a logical approach to problems.

2. Although some critics of the community point out the absence of cultural events, Yvonne is quick to respond that there is a thriving amateur theater group and community art programs. The community has recently used tax dollars to buy and renovate an old downtown movie theater to host films that are not available to the general commercial market.

3. Michelle takes pride in the community's response to the special needs of both children and older adults. She notes that in developing new neighborhoods, community leaders and members pay attention to the need for adequate green space, sidewalks, and access to public transportation. The community also takes care to screen noise and limit air pollution.

4. James is a big hometown fan. He enjoys the community traditions, such as the annual Fourth of July parade and the community-sponsored Halloween activities for the children. He minimizes any problems the community might have, noting that the City Council, the Chamber of Commerce, the schools, and religious bodies all contribute to the smooth operation of the community as a whole.

5. Marquita experiences the community in a totally different way. It makes her upset to see how children in some neighborhoods attend new schools with computers in every classroom, while those in other neighborhoods have run-down buildings and outdated texts. She notes that some neighborhoods have lots of green space and recreation facilities, while others are strewn with litter and children play in the streets. Marquita believes that the upper-class people who are the leaders in the community government make decisions that ignore the needs of those with limited resources and power.

6. Kim is not surprised to learn that her friends have such different points of view. She is intrigued by how people can view the same community and develop such different evaluations but is comfortable with the idea that even after extensive conversation, her friends may leave with different ideas, all of which have validity.

7. Tom is excited by all of the opportunities in the community to interact with people from different backgrounds, not just in special ethnic celebrations but also in daily encounters. He believes that one of the great assets of the community is the variety of cultures and lifestyles that are found there.

HOW THEORY INFORMS PRACTICE

A *theory* is narrower than a perspective. It is a proposition that explains or predicts something. In other words, it is an educated guess, based on both previous knowledge and observations. Most scientists treat theories as hypotheses to be tested, not as statements of absolute truth. In other words, a theory is provisional; that is, it is used until it is contradicted by objective data supporting a better explanation. A theory may *describe* (how things happen as they do) or *explain* (why they happen as they do). *Prediction* is based on recognizing a recurring pattern so that future events can be anticipated. Prediction may occur without a full understanding or explanation of cause and effect. Usually predictive power alone is not sufficient to develop effective interventions.

Explanatory theories provide a basis for the development or adoption of models of intervention. *Models* provide guidance on how to intervene in a range of situations. They focus on what to do by describing patterns of activities and highlighting certain principles that give professional practice consistency (Payne, 1997, p. 35).

In this text we concentrate on several perspectives and a limited number of related theories that help to describe and explain human behavior. A good understanding of these provides the foundation for selecting appropriate models for intervention. Social work students will spend more time exploring theories of change and models of practice in other courses.

In general we would like to think that models flow neatly from theories and that theories are grounded in coherent perspectives. The reality, however, is that the relationship between these three elements is messy. For example, sometimes an innovative practice intervention precedes the development of a theory that explains why it works, and there are some theories that offer no applications that can be translated directly into interventions. Payne (1997) suggests that when all three elements—perspective, theory, and model—are fully developed and in place, the effective practice of social work is more likely to occur.

REFERENCES

Andersen, M., & Taylor, H. (2013). *Sociology: The essentials* (7th ed.). Belmont, CA: Wadsworth.

Anderson, R. E., Carter, I., & Lowe, G. R. (1999). *Human behavior in the social environment* (5th ed.). New York, NY: Aldine de Gruyter.

Best, J. (1989). Extending the constructionist perspective: A conclusion and introduction. In J. Best (Ed.), *Images of issues typifying contemporary social problems* (pp. 243–252). New York, NY: Aldine de Gruyter.

Chess, W. A., & Norlin, J. M. (1991). *Human behavior and the social environment: A social systems model* (2nd ed.). Boston, MA: Allyn & Bacon.

Council on Social Work Education. (2008). *Educational policy and accreditation standards.* Alexandria, VA: Council on Social Work Education.

Davis, K., & Moore, W. (1945). Some principles of stratification. *The American Sociological Review, 10,* 242–249.

Dye, T. R. (1998). *Understanding public policy* (9th ed.). Upper Saddle River, NJ: Prentice Hall.

Germain, C., & Gitterman, A. (1995). Ecological perspective. In R. L. Edwards and J. G. Hopps (Eds.), *Encyclopedia of social work* (19th ed., Vol. I, pp. 816–824). Washington, DC: NASW Press.

Hearn, T. (1979). General system theory in social work. In F. J. Turner (Ed.), *Social work treatment* (pp. 333–359). New York, NY: Free Press.

Kendall, D. (2008). *Sociology in our times* (7th ed.). Belmont, CA: Wadsworth.

Kendall, D. (2013). *Sociology in our times* (9th ed.). Belmont, CA: Wadsworth.

Lee, J. (2001). *The empowerment approach to social work practice: Building the beloved community.* New York, NY: Columbia University Press.

Leighninger, R. D. (1978). Systems theory. *Journal of Sociology and Social Work, 5,* 446–480.

Payne, M. (1997). *Modern social work theory* (2nd ed.). Chicago, IL: Lyceum.

Robbins, S. P., Chatterjee, P., & Canda, E. R. (2006). *Contemporary human behavior theory: A critical perspective for social work.* Boston, MA: Allyn & Bacon.

Saleebey, D. (2002). *The strengths perspective in social work practice.* Boston, MA: Allyn & Bacon.

Schutz, A. (1967). *The phenomenology of the social work world* (G. Walsh & F. Lennert, Trans.). Evanston, IL: Northwestern University Press.

Solomon, B. B. (1976). *Black empowerment: Social work in oppressed communities.* New York, NY: Columbia University Press.

Solomon, B. (1987). Empowerment: Social work in oppressed communities. *Journal of Social Work Practice, 2,* 79–91.

Van Den Bergh, N. (1995). Feminist social work practice. In N. Van Den Bergh (Ed.), *Feminist practice in the 21st century* (pp. xi–xxxix). Washington, DC: NASW Press.

Von Bertalanffy, L. (1968). *General systems theory: Foundations, development, applications.* New York, NY: George Braziller.

Walzer, M. (1983). *Spheres of justice.* New York, NY: Basic Books.

Social Institutions

Social institutions are among the more abstract notions we present in this book. Social institutions are defined as patterns of human interaction that meet the basic social needs of a society. These needs include reproduction and socialization of the young; establishing a hierarchy of power; producing and distributing goods and services; dealing with questions about meaning, such as the purpose of life, the reason for suffering, and what happens after death; transmitting knowledge and skills across generations; treating the sick and injured; providing for dependent members of society; maintaining social order and defending national interests; and disseminating information. Sociologists recognize several basic social institutions that exist in all societies in addition to the family; among these are government/polity, economy, religion, education, and health care. Some recognize or acknowledge additional social institutions. In this book, we will discuss three additional social institutions: criminal justice; the military; and mass media, social media, and communication technology. These eight social institutions have been selected because they are particularly relevant to social work students. Although social welfare is a social institution that is clearly relevant to social workers and their clients, we are not including it in this book because social work students take complete courses on this topic.

Even though the idea of a social institution might be difficult to grasp, everyone has had experience with the cumulative effects of each of the social institutions discussed in this section. They have as much influence on social work clients as any smaller social system because they provide the context within which families, organizations, and communities operate. The collectivity of social institutions is what constitutes a society.

We restrict ourselves to three or four major perspectives in our discussion of social institutions. These four perspectives are those used by most social scientists/sociologists to explain social institutions: the functionalist perspective, the conflict perspective, the rational/social exchange perspective, and the constructionist perspective. These perspectives were defined and described in chapter 1.

It makes sense that a rational perspective would apply (at least in principle) to the economy and to government-supported social institutions. The reader should not be surprised, however, to learn that the rational perspective is not easily applied to the health care system, mass media, or religion. Although specific organizations within these systems have centralized administrative and decision-making bodies, and there may be alliances and coalitions that act in concert to meet social needs or to promote particular agendas, there are no central coordinating or planning bodies that are charged with (or have the authority for) setting priorities or making policies regarding those systems as a whole.

We believe that social institutions have the capacity to oppress. They also have the capacity to promote well-being, although for many social work clients, that is not what they experience. Thus, we will explore the effects of each social institution as a context for individuals and families, looking in particular at how they obstruct or promote well-being.

In part II, we begin with what we believe are the most significant social institutions, that is, economics and politics, in chapter 2. In chapter 3, government-related social institutions—education, criminal justice, and the military—are examined. In chapter 4, non-government-related social institutions—health care, religion, and mass media, social media, and communication technology—are addressed. These last five social institutions are examined each in its own right and also in relation to the political economy.

The Political Economy

The Economic System

We have devoted an entire chapter to the two most important social institutions in America, that is, the economic system and the political system. We will introduce the two separately, but at the end of the chapter, we will discuss how closely they interact. This interaction is so complete that we will label it the *political economy* and thereafter treat it as a single institution.

THE ECONOMIC SYSTEM

The *economic system* organizes and regulates a society's production, distribution, and consumption of goods and services. The American economic system is based on *capitalism*. In an American context, capitalism is usually understood as being synonymous with the business world. The three basic characteristics of capitalism typically cited by economists are private ownership, unfettered market competition, and pursuit of profit. These present a clear contrast to the characteristics of *socialism*, which are public ownership, central planning, and collective goals. These pure ideological models seldom exist in reality; instead many countries have mixed economic models. Even the United States does not have a "pure" form of capitalism, as the government is actively involved in several aspects of economic control. Recent examples of significant government involvement in the economy include the federal bailouts of large banks and automakers in the Great Recession.

Issues and Trends in the Economic System

Corporate Capitalism

A *corporation* is "an organization with a legal existence including rights and liabilities, separate from that of its members" (Macionis, 2014, p. 471). As one outspoken Native American environmentalist notes,

> Corporations exist beyond time and space. . . . They do not die a natural death; they outlive their own creators. And they have no commitment to locale, employees, or neighbors. This makes the modern corporation entirely different from the baker or grocer of previous years. . . . Having no morality, no commitment to place,

> and no physical nature . . . a corporation can relocate all of its operations to another place at the first sign of inconvenience: demanding employees, too high taxes, restrictive environmental laws. The traditional ideal of community engagement is antithetical to corporate behavior. (Mander, 1991, pp. 133–134)

The "profit imperative" and the "growth imperative" are fundamental corporate drives.

Originally chartered by the British monarchy and created as extensions of the government to "promote the general welfare," over time corporations "changed from temporary creations beholden to the state to permanent businesses with a vested interest in serving private capital" (Palmer, 2003, p. 53). In 1886, the Supreme Court ruled that corporations have many rights similar to individuals, and corporations have since assumed that they can exercise rights to free speech, privacy, and protection against self-incrimination (Hartman, 2002). In fact, in a 2010 landmark decision, the U.S. Supreme Court ruled that the government cannot restrict political contributions made by corporations, suggesting that they have the same free speech rights as individuals under the First Amendment (Liptak, 2010).

While small businesses and individual entrepreneurs are often glorified by politicians, the reality is that contemporary American capitalism is about large corporations; *corporate capitalism* dominates the economic system. There are millions of corporations, but only a small number—fewer than a couple of hundred companies—control the vast majority of economic activity. Starting with a database of 37 million companies and investors worldwide, a team of Swiss researchers pulled out 43,060 multinational corporations and then identified a core of 1,318 companies that appeared to collectively own the majority of the world's large blue-chip and manufacturing firms—60 percent of global revenues (Coghlan & MacKenzie, 2011). Among those, the researchers found 147 even more tightly knit companies—mostly financial institutions—that controlled 40 percent of the entire network.

Sociologists often differentiate between *work establishments*, the actual place where someone works, and *firms*, the parent company or organization. An example of a work establishment would be a local Kentucky Fried Chicken, Pizza Hut, or Taco Bell restaurant. An example of a firm would be their "parent company," Yum! Brands. A majority of workers, especially those in the service sector, go to work in establishments with fewer than 100 employees. A third of all workers, however, are employed by very large firms. Corporations such as automobile manufacturers (e.g., General Motors) and gigantic retailers may employ hundreds of thousands of workers. Wal-Mart is the largest private employer in the world, with more than 11,000 retail units in 27 countries, and 2.2 million "associates" around the world, including 1.4 million in the United States ("Our Business," corporate.walmart.com, 2013). One out of every ten retail workers in the United States is employed by Wal-Mart (Covert, 2013). In 2012 Wal-Mart had revenues of $447 billion, larger than the gross domestic product (GDP) of many countries.

Conglomerates are giant corporations that result from mergers and takeovers of smaller corporations. Beginning in the later 1960s, conglomerates began to appear as a result of the mergers of firms with diverse products and services. For example, Proctor and Gamble, which launched its first branded product, Ivory Soap, in 1879, currently sells many popular items, including Tide, Pampers, Dawn, Crest, Charmin, Oil of Olay, Pantene, Iams, Gillette, Bounty, Duracell, and Tampax.

During the 1980s, many corporations acquired other firms in the same or similar industries. By the late 1990s, this trend involved mergers of more than 5,000 firms a year and transactions of more than $1 trillion, over five times the level of a decade earlier (Stockard, 2000, p. 378). Many of the acquisitions involved "hostile takeovers," that is, the purchase of a company against the wishes of its owners.

At the beginning of the twenty-first century, these merger patterns continued. In the financial arena, many investment banking operations were absorbed into large commercial banking companies. For example, Bear Sterns became a part of JP Morgan Chase in 2008, A. G. Edwards became a part of Wachovia in 2007, and later Wachovia became a part of Wells Fargo. None of this could have happened under the Glass-Steagall Act of 1933, which created the Federal Deposit Insurance Corporation (FDIC) and much of the banking regulation that we rely on today. The Gramm-Leach-Blailey Financial Services Modernization Act of 1999 repealed the language of the Glass-Steagall Act and allowed deregulation in the financial services industry. The following year, passage of the

Commodity Futures Modernization Act made it impossible to regulate credit swaps. The mergers and acquisitions continued even during the federal bailout period of late 2008–2009 (e.g., Merrill Lynch was acquired by Bank of America in late 2008), when some financial corporations were already deemed "too big to fail" (i.e., with so much influence over the national economy that Congress was compelled to use tax dollars to save them from bankruptcy) (Goodman, 2008). Subsequently in 2010, Congress passed the Dodd-Frank Wall Street Reform and Consumer Protection Act. The primary purpose of the Dodd-Frank Act, the most significant financial regulatory reform since the 1930s, was renewed oversight of banks and other financial institutions.

There is probably no entity other than national governments that is big enough to stand up to the power of giant conglomerates. Corporations that are designed to generate profits and that owe allegiance only to their stockholders have less interest in the welfare of employees, consumers, or the environment. "As borderless supercitizens global corporations have changed the international order yet our rules and approaches to governance have remained the same" (Rothkopf, 2010). Multinational corporations "no longer operate in the interest of America *or any country*, while claiming the benefits of being American corporations (when it suits them) . . . or foreign-based when that is what it needs to be [to avoid U.S. tax obligations]" (Johnson, 2013, p. 3).

Corporate power is felt not only within a country, but internationally as well. Corporations may conduct research and development in one country, manufacture component parts in one or several countries (where labor is cheap), assemble the parts in another, have their corporate headquarters in yet another, and sell their products throughout the world. Multinational corporations profess loyalty to no single nation. In fact, many are larger and more powerful than nation-states. For example, the yearly revenues for both BP and Shell are equal to the entire annual gross domestic product of the country of Venezuela (Kendall, 2013).

Changing Patterns of Employment

Today the production economy of the United States has shifted from industrial manufacturing to one that is predominantly service-oriented and information-based. The new economy provides few openings for unskilled laborers in well-paying manufacturing jobs. Employment in the *service sector* is split between positions requiring technical skills (such as computer programmers) and poorly paid jobs requiring minimal skills. For example, in the fast-food industry, cashiers no longer have to enter prices and make change; they simply hit keys with pictures on them and the customer's change is automatically calculated and discharged. Even the interaction with customers is scripted ("Do you want to supersize that?"). Employment in this part of the service sector does not pay enough to support a family and is unlikely to provide benefits such as health care insurance, career advancement, and retirement plans.

The Status of Labor Unions in the United States. The Bureau of Labor Statistics (2013b) reported that in 2012, among full-time workers, union members had median weekly earnings of $943, while nonunion members had median weekly earnings of $742. Unorganized laborers have little bargaining power, either individually or collectively. In search of greater profits, many companies moved manufacturing jobs first to the antiunion South and then overseas to reduce labor costs. In reviewing a history of labor systems in the United States, *Washington Post* opinion writer Harold Meyerson (2013) suggests that declining hourly wages reflect the ongoing "Southern suppression of workers' rights and incomes" as antiunion sentiments migrate to Republican-controlled states in the North.

Another *Washington Post* writer, Robert Samuelson (2014), notes that the eclipse of the unions "has been stunning." Unions are supposed to be able to deliver higher wages and fringe benefits, greater job security (including protection against arbitrary or unlawful management practices), and better working conditions. But, Samuelson says, the system broke down in the 1970s and 1980s under pressure from nonunion domestic companies like Wal-Mart, foreign companies like Toyota, and new technologies. By 2012, only 11.3 percent of workers were union members. According to a report released by the Bureau of Labor Statistics in January of 2013(b), North Carolina (2.9 percent), Arkansas (3.2 percent), and South Carolina (3.3 percent) had the lowest rates of union membership, while New York had the highest (23.2 percent). About half of the 14.4 million union members in the United States lived in just seven states:

California, New York, Illinois, Pennsylvania, Michigan, New Jersey, and Ohio. Men, black workers, and older workers (aged 55–64) are more likely to be union members than their counterparts, and full-time workers were almost twice as likely as part-time workers to be union members.

Again according to the Bureau of Labor Statistics (2013b), government workers are almost five times more likely to belong to a union as are private-sector employees. The union membership rate for public-sector workers was 35.9 percent, and the rate for local government workers (e.g., teachers, police officers, firefighters) was 41.7 percent. This compared to a rate of just 6.6 percent for all private-sector workers. Current political attacks on the collective bargaining rights of public-sector employees (starting in Wisconsin and Ohio in 2011) overlook the fact that many of their unions sought and received better health and pension benefits in lieu of higher salaries (Robinson, 2011).

Loss of Jobs. *Downsizing* refers to large-scale worker layoffs. (Downsizing may also be called "reduction in force" or RIF.) *Outsourcing* means contracting to have tasks normally done within the company performed under a contract with another company. Commonly outsourced jobs include custodial work or payroll functions. *Offshoring* is the term used when the jobs are still controlled by the company itself but are moved overseas. Many of the lost jobs were in manufacturing or in telephone call centers (Uchitelle, 2006). Another example of this trend was the transfer of customer service and tech support jobs to India where English-speaking, college-educated, entry-level recruits earn $3,650 a year—good wages in India but only a fifth of what an American would be paid for similar work (Carmichael, 2003). Even such traditionally American products as Levi's blue jeans are now being manufactured overseas, with the exception of a single line of jeans produced at a factory in Greensboro, North Carolina, that sells for $178 a pair (Winn, 2012). Some highly skilled jobs also are being offshored, including those of aeronautical engineers, software designers, and stock analysts (Uchitelle, 2003). Whereas factory layoffs used to be temporary and related to economic downturns, with employers calling workers back once a recovery began, outsourcing and offshoring practices reflect structural and permanent changes in the broader economy.

So far in the twenty-first century, some 42,000 factories have closed in the United States, and one-third of all manufacturing jobs have disappeared (Granholm & Mulhern, 2011). Although other kinds of jobs have been created, the new jobs tend to pay significantly less—as much as 80 percent less (LaLonde, 2007; Uchitelle, 2006).

Uchitelle (2006) notes the reality is that there are not enough good jobs available to meet the demands of college-educated and well-trained workers in the United States, which is why so many are working in jobs for which they are overqualified. Mid-wage occupations have not recovered from the Great Recession; 58 percent of recovery growth has been in lower-wage occupations, such as food service and retail, where median wages range from about $9 to $11 an hour (National Employment Law Project [NELP], 2012).

While American workers have been losing jobs, corporations are doing well. Since the Great Recession, corporate profits have returned to record levels due to three reasons: (1) with high unemployment rates, American workers have not been able to demand pay increases; (2) U.S. companies have opened offices and factories in China, Brazil, and India where wages are lower; and (3) a growing middle class abroad has provided new markets for American products (Irwin, 2013; Karabell, 2011; Macionis, 2014). "Making and selling their goods abroad, U.S. multinationals can slash their workforces and reduce their wages at home while retaining their revenue and increasing their profits. And that's exactly what they've done" (Meyerson, 2011).

Effect of Unemployment and Underemployment. The long-term joblessness rate in the United States remains at record highs, far higher than at any time since the Great Depression (Lei, 2013). Long-term unemployment particularly affects minorities, unmarried people, persons with disabilities, and people with less education (Lei, 2013). Unemployment benefits are not generous; they pay half of a moderate-income worker's salary and less than half the salary of higher earners.

One child out of six was affected by parental unemployment and underemployment in 2012 (Isaacs, 2013). A large body of research finds evidence of increased parental irritability and depression, higher levels of family conflict, and less supportive and more punitive parenting behaviors when parents are laid off (Isaacs, 2013). The stress on children of jobless parents tends to show up in their schoolwork, with lower math scores, poorer attendance, and a higher risk of grade repetition or even suspension (Isaacs, 2013; Lei, 2013).

Beyond the effects on individuals and their families, unemployment also has larger consequences including community breakdown and a rise in social conflict (Lei, 2013; Uchitelle, 2006). In a poor housing market, it is difficult to sell one's house or qualify for a loan to buy a new one, so that one can relocate to take a new job. Unemployed persons tend to withdraw from social and civic activities and direct their anger at a variety of targets, including immigrants, minorities, welfare recipients, and the very rich (Thio, 1998, p. 405).

Beginning in the 1980s, American companies learned that by using "temps" they could hold down wages, reduce the costs of employee benefits, and lay off surplus staff at any time. Although many people (such as students, homemakers, and older adults) work part-time by choice, a significant number do so only because they cannot find full-time employment or need to supplement the income from their full-time jobs. *Contingent work* is becoming a characteristic of the American workforce (Andersen & Taylor, 2013). The contingent workforce is made up of part-time and temporary employees. Temporary workers are the fastest-growing segment of the contingent workforce (Kendall, 2013, p. 394). About 15 percent of new jobs created since the Great Recession have been in the temporary help services sector, with many of them concentrated in large cities (Fang, 2013). Many contingent workers can be classified as *underemployed*, that is, they are overqualified for the positions they fill. For these workers, job security and employment benefits are an illusion.

Minimum Wage

According to the United States Department of Labor ("History of Federal Minimum Wage Rates," n.d.), the federal minimum wage was established in 1938 under the Fair Labor Standards Act. The original amount was $.25 per hour. Southern members of Congress insisted on excluding farm and domestic workers—mostly African American—from the legislation (Meyerson, 2013). Amendments in 1961 and 1966 extended coverage to employees in large retail and service enterprises; state and local government employees of hospitals, nursing homes, and schools; and to workers in laundries, dry cleaners, and large hotels. Subsequent amendments extended coverage to the remaining federal, state, and local government employees who were not protected in 1966.

The federal minimum wage for American workers as of 2014 was $7.25 per hour. But in about half of states companies can pay workers as little as $2.13 per hour if their wage plus tips equals the minimum. Thus the gratuity he or she receives is really the majority of the server's salary, not an added bonus for good service. The "tipped minimum wage" was last adjusted in 1991. Most of these "tipped minimum wage" workers are employed by restaurants and many are women.

Worker productivity and wages were closely correlated until the 1970s. Since then productivity has kept going up but wages have stagnated (Cooper, 2013). Adjusted for inflation, the current minimum wage is substantially lower than it was in the 1960s. If the minimum wage had stayed coupled to productivity, it would now be $16.50 per hour (Johnson, 2013). The period of 1997 to 2007 was the longest time during which the minimum wage was not adjusted.

U.S. taxpayers are actually subsidizing for-profit companies, such as fast-food chains and giant retailers that pay minimum wage, because their employees qualify for welfare benefits, such as food stamps, Medicaid, the Earned Income Tax Credit, free or reduced-price school lunch programs, and Section 8 housing vouchers (National Employment Law Project [NELP], 2013; Trinko, 2013). McDonald's alone costs American taxpayers an estimated $3.8 billion per year (NELP, 2013). As an occupational group, fast-food workers have the lowest average hourly wage of any of the occupations tracked by the Bureau of Labor Statistics (Trumbull, 2014). At the same time, the CEOs of fast-food companies receive salaries in the tens of millions. According to a recent study, a single Wal-Mart supercenter store with 300 employees likely cost taxpayers at least $904,500 per year (Covert, 2013; Trinko, 2013). The group Americans for Tax Fairness (2014) estimates that Wal-Mart receives a total of $6.2 billion annually in federal taxpayer subsidies (monies paid to its employees through various public assistance programs), while the six Walton heirs have a net worth of $148 billion, making them the wealthiest family in America.

Some states have minimum wage standards that are higher than the federal minimum. As of January 2014, twenty-one states and the District of Columbia have minimum wage rates higher than the federal level (Cooper, 2013; United States Department of Labor, "Minimum Wage Laws," 2013). The state of Washington has the highest minimum wage at $9.19 an hour. When state standards are different from the federal level, the higher rate prevails.

Living wage ordinances have been passed in many communities since the mid-1990s in response to the efforts of community, labor, and religious coalitions, as well as university students (Bernstein, 2004; Karger & Stoesz, 2010). A living wage ordinance establishes a wage floor above that of the minimum wage and commonly covers employers who hold large city or county service contracts or who receive substantial financial assistance from the city.

According to analysis by the Economic Policy Institute (Cooper, 2013), adult workers would be the primary beneficiaries of a higher federal minimum wage. Only 12.5 percent of affected workers would be teens; more employees in the age category of 55 or older would benefit. More than a quarter of those expected to be affected are parents. Low- and minimum-wage workers are often dismissed as "secondary earners," but on average, affected workers typically bring home half their family's total income.

According to government reports summarized by economist Robert Reich (2013), the wages for workers in almost a quarter of all jobs in America are not sufficient to bring a family of four above the poverty line. The Bureau of Labor Statistics estimates that in the next decade seven out of ten new jobs will be classified as low-wage, predominantly in retail and food service industries, with many of them being less than full-time. Although opponents argue that raising the minimum wage would result in job losses, research has shown that this is not the case; in fact it is more likely that new jobs would be created due to increased consumer spending (Harkin, 2013).

Globalization

Another profound change in the economy is the globalization of capitalism. According to some sociologists, its impact is comparable to the

Industrial Revolution (Henslin, 2014). As with the Industrial Revolution, there may be both positive and negative outcomes. One positive consequence for low-income Americans is that their purchasing power may be increased by the availability of inexpensive products made in other countries. An economist suggests that the impact of imports from China alone increases the "real incomes" of such consumers by as much as 5 to 10 percent (Overholt, 2006). Another benefit is the growth in the market for American goods sold overseas. Perhaps the most significant benefit is the improvement in living conditions in countries that are industrializing where hundreds of millions of people were moved "from abject poverty to something that was in some cases still awful but nonetheless significantly better" (Krugman, 2000, p. 18). For instance, life expectancy in China increased by over 30 years in the last half-century (Overholt, 2006) and in Indonesia life expectancy rose from 46 years to 63 years between 1968 and 1990 (Krugman, 2000). The growth of manufacturing has had ripple effects throughout the national economy. In countries where the process has gone on long enough, in South Korea and Taiwan, for example, wages have reached high-income country levels (Krugman, 2000).

On the other side of the globalization trend are threats to the U.S. economy and, in particular, American workers. As noted elsewhere in this chapter, many large corporations have become multinational companies; "they access global markets, easy credit, new technologies, and high quality labor at low prices" (Zakaria, 2010, p. 32). Many large American companies generate half or more of their profits outside the United States. But while capital and technology are mobile, labor isn't. American workers do not benefit from global growth in the same way that corporations do. Developing countries such as China and India add hundreds of millions of jobs and are able to produce the same goods and services at a fraction of the price.

The Great Recession

The immediate causes of the economic crisis that began in late 2007 are complex and difficult to grasp, even by economists. Most agree, however, that one major factor was excessive risk-taking at many levels—from individual home buyers who overextended themselves based on assumptions of ever-increasing home values, to mortgage companies that took on customers with marginal credit ratings, to regulators "asleep at the wheel," to large financial institutions that bought and bundled risky loans relying heavily on borrowed money to do so. More jobs were lost in between 2007 and 2009 than in the previous four recessions combined (Saporito, 2011). The effects of the Great Recession include failing consumer confidence, slowed economic growth, and continuing high levels of unemployment.

As of 2013, the wealthiest as a group gained back all that they lost in the recession, while those in the middle and lower classes were still suffering. An economic recession can lead to "scarring"—long-lasting damage to individual economic situations and the economy in general (Irons, 2009). Extended periods of high unemployment may create special impediments for job recovery; older workers (people over forty-five) and those who have been out of work for more than six months experience great difficulties in finding work (Krugman, 2014). In addition, unemployment and/or income loss can reduce long-term educational achievement by threatening early childhood nutrition, reducing a family's ability to provide a supportive learning environment, and by forcing a delay or abandonment of college plans (Irons, 2009).

According to a report in the *Washington Post* (Fletcher & Cohen, 2011) Latinos and African Americans were most likely to be left broke and jobless by the Great Recession. Nearly four in ten Latinos said their households had suffered job losses. Nearly four in ten African Americans had to adjust their housing situations and nearly one in three borrowed money from friends or relatives to get by. The foreclosure crisis pushed black home ownership rates down to 45 percent, the lowest rate since 1997. The status of many middle-class black families was threatened with the loss of jobs in the auto industry and in government agencies, which employ a disproportionate share of African Americans.

Understanding the Economic System

Functionalist Perspective

Functionalists believe that large systems are self-correcting, for the most part, if change occurs incrementally. Thus they support a "free market economy" that is allowed to respond to fluctuating supply and demand, expecting to see a cyclical pattern of peaks and troughs. When matters get too far out of balance, as in periods of recession or inflation, the government steps in to make minor adaptations by changing interest rates, adjusting trade agreements, and other activities.

Functionalists also believe that the opportunity for everyone to be a stockholder, as well as a consumer, is a major positive feature of the American economic system. In effect, everyone, including workers, can also be "capitalists" and share in the profits and the prosperity of a growing company and a strong economy. On the other hand, while *some* households own *some* stock (usually as part of a retirement portfolio), they do not own enough, as individuals, to exercise any control over the companies that they hold stock in.

Conflict Perspective

The laws of supply and demand and the push for profits are not necessarily consistent with the well-being of workers or consumers. Conflict theorists (including Karl Marx) suggest that those who own the means of production will always exploit the laboring classes. These theorists stress that in order to keep labor costs low and profits high, capitalists view workers as expendable commodities who can be exploited to meet the needs of the company.

One indicator of the exploitation of workers is the enormous disparity between the salaries of workers and those who employ them. (See chapter 5 for a comparison of CEO salaries and a typical worker's pay.) Salaries of company executives grew as downsizing became a management strategy. Despite all of the heated rhetoric about executive compensation and extravagant bonuses that occurred at the beginning of the Great Recession, conflict theorists would argue that the focus should not be solely on the distribution of money, but on the concentration of power—both financial and political—in the hands of a few (Domhoff, 2013; Henslin, 2014; Johnson, 2009).

Rational/Social Exchange Perspective

If the explanation of any social institution can be said to be firmly rooted in a social theory, it is capitalism and social exchange. Adam Smith

(1937/1776), one of the earliest economic theorists, suggested that it is self-interest that makes capitalism—and industrial society—function. In business, managers, workers, and customers make decisions based on their own interests. There is no room for sentimentality or idealism. The "market," acting without interference, will find the correct balance so that consumers get the best value for their money and workers are paid what they are worth. Companies that offer shoddily made products or sloppy service are put out of business as consumers seek better deals elsewhere. Workers who do not contribute a value comparable to their wage are laid off. Efficiency—payback on investments—is the key.

Proponents of capitalism assume that the principle of self-interest operates not just among individuals but also among larger systems. For example, a community or even a state, competing with other localities, might offer tax breaks to entice a corporation to build a new plant within its boundaries, thus creating jobs for its residents.

Constructionist Perspective

Even something that sounds as rational and objective as economics can be partly explained in terms of how members of a society interpret the meaning of work, wealth, and economic exchange. One well-known theorist, Max Weber (1978/1922), suggested that the development of capitalism as an economic system was based on the belief system of early Protestants. The followers of John Calvin believed that worldly success was a sign of one's being in God's favor. According to Weber, Calvinists' religious convictions led them to reinvest their wealth, thus laying the foundations of capitalism.

Later generations of Calvinists retained their personal discipline, and their belief system became a work ethic, wherein hard labor and thriftiness were closely associated with morality. The *Protestant work ethic* is firmly established in the American psyche. It suggests that people should work even under conditions that are unfair and/or harmful. The requirement that welfare recipients accept jobs that will not cover their child-care costs is an example of the power of the belief that working is not simply a means of self-support, it is a moral imperative.

Another point of view that has facilitated the growth of American capitalism is the meaning of thrift and of credit and how it is used (Calder,

1999; Hine, 2002; Ritzer, 2001). Those who study the topic have described this trend as a "profound cultural change" (Yip, 2007). At the beginning of the twentieth century, borrowing was frowned upon (Gibbs, 2008; Lewis, 2008; Yip, 2007). Nevertheless, by the 1950s, there was a definitive change in attitudes, and households took on debt in the pursuit of consumer goods. The quality of acquisitiveness used to be discouraged, if not condemned; now Americans are told that consumption is equivalent to patriotism (Gibbs, 2008; Lewis, 2008; Yip, 2007).

Thus, in terms of the socially constructed meanings of work and wealth, we see both continuity and change. Work is still viewed as having inherent value. Wealth, while no longer seen as a sign of salvation, is highly regarded as an indicator of personal worth.

The meaning of consumption may—or may not—change as a result of the Great Recession: "In hard times, people often rediscover the peace that prudence brings, when you try to spend a little less than you have because tomorrow might be worse. But that feels almost un-American; we're optimists by nature, and we've been living large for so long that solvency feels like a sacrifice" (Gibbs, 2008, p. 96). A 2013 Pew study (Fry) found that there was a significant decline in the share of adults under the age of 35 who carried credit card debt, from 48 percent in 2007 to 39 percent in 2010. This pattern of decreasing debt also reflected smaller numbers who owned homes and cars. Nevertheless, more young adults were carrying student loan debt after the recession—40 percent in 2010, up from 34 percent in 2007 and 26 percent in 2001.

The Impact of the Economic System on Individuals and Families

How the Economic System Deters Well-Being

The role of corporate executives is clear; it is to put the corporation's interests, and those of its stockholders, first (Bakan, 2004). Even the greatest advocates of capitalism acknowledge that it is an unfair system, rewarding some very well and leaving others behind. For those at the bottom of the economic hierarchy, the inequity is especially notable. According to the U.S. Census Bureau, nearly 47 million citizens, 15 percent of the population, live in poverty (Rubin, Altman, & Kearney, 2013).

Nearly 11 million working Americans have an income below the poverty line. (See table 5.3 for an illustration of federal poverty guidelines).

According to an analysis of the 2010 Census Bureau report by the Economic Policy Institute (Shierholz & Gould, 2011), the poverty rate for all children was 22 percent. Over one-third of African American children (39.1 percent) and Hispanic children (35.0 percent) were living in poverty. The poverty rate for families with children headed by single mothers hit 40.7 percent. "The large increase in poverty suggests that as anti-poverty policies have come to depend more on paid work as the main pathway out of poverty, the safety net has become less effective in reducing economic hardship when the economy and job market are underperforming" (Shierholz & Gould, 2011, p. 2).

Social scientists divide the labor market into two categories. The *primary labor market* provides jobs that carry with them many benefits, including career advancement opportunities. Examples of occupations in the primary labor market are management positions and the professions. Jobs in the *secondary labor market* require few skills, provide minimal benefits, involve dirty and/or dangerous conditions, and may offer only part-time or seasonal employment; examples include retail store clerks, fast-food preparers, domestic work, and farm work. People of color and women make up the majority of workers in the secondary labor market. One example of the secondary labor market is the meat-and-poultry packing plants that draw Latinos—some of them undocumented Mexicans—to the Southeast (Herbert, 2006). There they do much of the unpleasant work of transforming hogs into hams and sausages and chickens into breasts and drumsticks—work that Americans prefer not to do. (See chapter 9 for more discussion of the meatpacking industry.)

Capitalism depends on having a large reservoir of unemployed workers who are willing to work for minimum wage whenever such work is available. The "acceptable"—that is, desired—level of unemployment advocated by the federal government has changed from a goal of zero (full employment) after the Great Depression to 2 to 3 percent during the 1960s and then to 5 to 6 percent as of the mid-1980s (Heilbroner, 1993). ("Full employment" means that people who want to work can find jobs.) Reflecting the effects of the Great Recession, in mid-spring 2009 national unemployment rates stood at 8.5 percent, with rates in some states registering in the double digits. As of late 2013, the national rate had fallen to a five-year low of 7 percent, with rates ranging from a low of 2.6 percent in North Dakota and 3.6 in South Dakota to highs of 9.0 percent in Rhode Island and Nevada (Bureau of Labor Statistics, 2013a). Half of the jobs that were added between April and October 2013 were in four low-wage industries: retail; hotels, restaurants, and entertainment; home health care workers; and temp jobs ("November Jobs Report," 2013). Economists worry that because so many jobs were destroyed or exported in the Great Recession, it will be years before the unemployment rate gets below 5 percent again, if ever (Saporito, 2011).

How the Economic System Promotes Well-Being

While it is easy to identify oppressive elements in the modern American capitalist economy, it is important to note ways in which the economy also enhances the well-being of many citizens. The high standard of living in this country, especially in terms of consumer goods (e.g., wall-to-wall carpeting, household appliances, electronics, and automobiles), is undeniable. Even the rapid growth of the service sector and its accompanying low wages and job insecurity presents an opportunity for many of the least skilled workers in American society, including high school dropouts, non-English-speaking immigrants, and people with disabilities.

THE POLITICAL SYSTEM

The *political system* is the social institution that establishes a hierarchy of power and leadership. It is where decisions are made and carried out, either directly or indirectly. The *government* is the formal organization that has the legal authority to maintain social order by resolving conflicts among members of the society, protect citizens from threats that come from outside its borders, and provide for the common good.

The United States is a representative democracy. This means that political decisions are made by bodies of representatives elected by the people (e.g., city or county councils, state legislatures, and, of course, Congress) rather than directly by the people themselves. Traditionally, decisions have been made based not only on what constituents wanted, but also on a complex process of negotiation and trade-offs, as well as the direct and indirect influence of "special interest" groups.

A generation ago, *conservatives* were viewed as being moderate and prudent, and politically linked to fiscal restraint, low taxes, free-market forces, "personal responsibility," and military strength. It may be helpful to think of fiscal (economic) conservatives and social (cultural) conservatives in two categories that only sometimes overlap. In the past several decades, social conservative ideology has embraced "traditional" viewpoints on many cultural issues, including nationalism, abortion, sexual orientation, gun rights, and the exercise of religion.

The idea of conventional conservatives in the Republican Party brings up images of middle-class businessmen from small town Main Streets who were fiscally conservative and socially moderate. Through the decades at the end of the twentieth century, the party changed dramatically. An analysis of official Republican party platforms (written statements of principles and plans developed at the national party conventions) documents the move from socially moderate to far right (Fisher, 2012). For example, in 1960 Republicans gave "firm support" to unions; in 1968 they addressed air and water pollution, slums, and discrimination against minorities; abortion was seen as a matter of personal choice in 1976; tax cuts and opposition to government "overregulation" didn't appear until 1980; matters of faith played almost no role until the 1990s; and antigay rhetoric didn't show up until 1992. The changes occurred at the same time as the Republican base, and its values, shifted southward (Meyerson, 2012).

Historically, political *liberals* have been linked with support for labor unions, economic security, worker safety, civil rights, reproductive freedoms, and an active role for government. More recently, a liberal point of view has included consumer protection, environmental sustainability, and universal access to health care. Since the 1980s, the word *liberal* has been used pejoratively in many political contexts, with a subtext that suggests that liberals are wedded to high-taxing, big-spending, large government, and socialist ways. On the other hand, most liberals would describe themselves as "favoring proposals for reform, open to new ideas for progress, and tolerant of the ideas and behavior of others," a definition found in the third edition of the *American Heritage College Dictionary*. Many liberal ideas that seemed controversial at the time they were introduced—such as Social Security and racial integration—are now so taken for granted that they have "simply been absorbed into the national self-portrait" (Quindlen, 2004).

There is considerable concordance between political ideology (liberal and conservative) and the major political parties, with liberals usually voting for Democrats and conservatives usually voting for Republicans. Citizens' ties to their political parties are stronger than ever, and there are clear divides between the supporters of the two major parties. A major study conducted by the *Washington Post* and the Kaiser Family Foundation (Balz & Cohen, 2012) and based on a poll of 3,000 American adults found that a clear majority of Republicans support limited government and say that regulation does more harm than good. Republicans say that people should take care of themselves while Democrats overwhelmingly say government should do everything possible to improve people's lives. The two parties are "mirror images of each other" on issues of abortion, same-sex marriage, and the role of religion in politics.

Issues and Trends in the Political System

Increasing Divisiveness

Over the last several years, the political landscape in the United States has become increasingly divisive, as we move through a period of high levels of partisan polarization. In a Christmas Eve opinion piece, the editorial board of *USA Today* ("Pope's shift creates a template for U.S. politics," 2013) summarized the situation as follows: "To look at the political scene these days is to see incessant squabbles, partisan gamesmanship, and ultimatums that don't even rise to the level of small-mindedness. Members of Congress and many state legislators spend their days in pointless trench warfare, apparently unaware that the only thing they are accomplishing is undermining the public's faith. They are egged on by special interests, purity enforcement groups, and talk radio and cable TV hosts" (p. 8A). There are several factors that account for the current climate of divisiveness. These include (1) redistricting, (2) a lack of incentives for compromise, (3) messaging, and (4) an angry electorate unhappy about changing American demographics and values.

After every ten-year census, congressional district lines are redrawn based on population shifts. In most states, this is done by the state legislature, which often is controlled by members of one political party. It is in their own interest to draw the lines to create "safe" districts to reelect members of their own party. This means that politicians are choosing their voters, rather than the other way around. The creation of "safe" districts makes these lawmakers less responsive to a broad base of constituents and less willing to compromise with members of the other party when they are serving in Congress. In order to accomplish this, the boundaries of such districts often take on odd shapes, and the process is referred to as "gerrymandering." As the voters in each district become more homogenous, congressional incumbents are less likely to be challenged by candidates from the other party, but more likely to face challenges in party primary elections from members of the same party who are further to the right (for Republicans) or to the left (for Democrats). Since the 2008 elections, incumbents are increasingly worried about being "primaried"—challenged by extreme elements within their own party who demand ideological purity and—as the primary election nears—the candidates abandon moderate positions. If there is no viable candidate from the other party, the primary election in each district determines who will win the general election. Jonathan Alter of *Newsweek* summarized the situation as follows: "The American primary system is disturbingly antidemocratic. It disenfranchises independents, who make up about a third of the electorate and aren't allowed to vote in most party primaries. It pushes the candidates in both parties to the extremes, which polarizes the debate in ways that don't reflect the centrist views of the vast majority of Americans and it allows a tiny handful of activist voters to determine who runs the country" (Alter, 2009b, p. 33).

One of the results of gerrymandering and the creation of "safe" districts is that there is no incentive for politicians to work across party lines. "Compromise is a dirty word in primaries where voters prize philosophical conviction over pragmatic legislating; one man's compromise is another man's concession" (Cillizza , 2013a). Pew Research Center studies have consistently found that, in general, people want political leaders who are willing to compromise to get things done, but on specific issues they are more likely to prefer that their elected officials "stick to their position" (Motel, 2013).

Politicians have contributed to the trend of increasing divisiveness by focusing on messages that "energize their base." Political candidates win by rallying their most intense supporters and getting them to the polls. For example, Jonathan Alter notes that the terms *values* and *values voters* were initially used to describe citizens who were concerned about what's happened to "old fashioned notions of decency" (Alter, 2006, p. 51). He laments that when the expression is claimed exclusively by one side of the political spectrum, it implies that people on the other side not only "do not share our values" but that they are morally inferior. Other phrases like "real Americans," when used by one side, also suggest that others are not simply in disagreement, but that they are unpatriotic or even traitors. Such dialogue sets up imaginary barriers between voters and precludes an honest debate about the issues.

In the last decade, the growth of talk radio and 24-hour cable news and the increased fracturing of the media—conservatives read and listen to conservative pundits and liberals read and listen to liberal pundits—has "played a major role in pushing people deeper and deeper into partisan camps" (Cillizza, 2013b). Cable television imposes entertainment values on politics; conflict prevails because analysis is boring (Samuelson, 2010).

Another reason for the current divisiveness is the lingering anger of those who have been left behind in the historic transformation that has marked the United States in the last several decades (Magstadt, 2013). The Civil Rights Movement, affirmative action, women's liberation, and the recent rapid advancement of gay rights have threatened the status of white men, particularly older, straight white men who a generation ago dominated the home, the professions, business, banking, unions, sports, entertainment, higher education, and the media—not to mention politics. The rhetoric of "take back our country" that often appears in political rallies begs the question of "from whom?" and suggests that there is a significant discomfort with the growing ethnic and racial diversity that will define the future of the nation (Meyerson, 2011; Robinson, 2012). This is illustrated in attacks on President Obama, our first African American president, that accuse him of being a Kenyan, a Muslim, a socialist or a Nazi, and other efforts to define him as an alien, or something other than a regular American.

The major result of this political divisiveness is a dysfunctional governing system. "There is no overlapping set of moderates available to engineer congressional compromises; polarization has resulted in paralysis" (Zakaria, 2011, 26). A small number of extremists control the political agenda. In the House, congressmen "often don't represent their districts; they represent the will of the ideologically driven . . . voters who take part in their party primaries, but whose numbers rarely exceed 20 percent of the district's eligible voters" (Alter, 2009a, p. 29). Using the rules of the filibuster, senators representing at most just 10 percent of the country can block all legislation. The bottom line is that the main aim of politicians in both parties is to win elections, not solve problems. It is easier to engage in a perpetual campaign than it is to govern.

Political Influence

A *special interest group* is an alliance of people concerned about some political issue. Influencing legislation is called *lobbying*. The term often has a negative connotation but lobbying is used, mostly legitimately, by special interests groups of all types. These include the National Association of Social Workers, the American Public Welfare Association, and the Child Welfare League of America as well as better-known groups such as the National Rifle Association, the American Association of Retired Persons, and oil companies and pharmaceutical firms. In addition to contributing to campaigns, special interest groups and their lobbyists may affect legislation by testifying before lawmakers' committees, mobilizing support or opposition to a bill by asking members to call or write letters, and even drafting proposed legislation.

Special interest groups are not allowed to make political contributions directly. Campaign finance reforms enacted in the 1970s set limits on direct contributions to political candidates; this led to the creation of *political action committees* (PACs). PACs are organizations that solicit and distribute political contributions as their primary purpose. PACs have been organized by labor unions, trade associations, environmental groups, and religious groups. Contributors give to PACs rather than to a political party when they want to support a specific political cause. The number of PACs has grown steadily, from 608 in 1974 to more than 5,200 in 2012 (Federal Election Commission, 2012).

For the two-year period of 2013–2014, individuals were limited to a maximum $2,600 contribution to a candidate or candidate's committee per election and \$32,400 to a national party committee per calendar year; the purpose of this policy is to limit the power of rich contributors (Federal Elections Commission). But corporations, labor unions, and issue groups can spend hundreds of millions on commercials *about* candidates—just so long as they do not specifically ask the viewer to *vote* for or against the candidate in the ad. Candidates are not allowed to help prepare these ads, coordinate ad buys or schedules, or even know about them before they air. The candidates are left at the mercy of special interest groups—even when the groups are on their side.

In 2010 the Supreme Court of the United States ruled in Citizens United v. Federal Elections Commission that the amount of money that corporations donate to politicians cannot be limited, based on First Amendment rights to free speech. This diminishes the effects of small donations made by average citizens. As a result of the Supreme Court ruling, "the 2010 midterm election was the first time outside groups were permitted to accept unlimited contributions from corporations, unions, and wealthy individuals to spend on ads supporting or opposing candidates" (Beckel, 2012). This made super PACS possible. A *super PAC* may not make contributions to candidates' campaigns or political parties, but may engage in unlimited political spending that is not coordinated with campaigns. There were 1,310 super PACs in 2012.

Both political parties have embraced the use of super PACS (Miller, 2013). One of the best-known, American Crossroads, a Republican-affiliated group, spent \$175.8 million on the national races (Schouten, 2012b). Individuals, such as casino magnate Sheldon Adelson and his wife, donated more than \$68 million to conservative super PACS supporting Republican candidates (Schouten, 2012a). Nearly two-thirds of the millions that flowed into super PACs in 2012 came from individuals, with more than half of the money coming from just eleven people (Schouten, Schnaars, & Korte, 2012). The unprecedented political giving by Adelson and other wealthy donors reflect the impact of recent court rulings on campaign finance. A Common Cause spokesperson noted that "a huge donation, whether it comes from an individual or a corporation, creates a dynamic where the donors are buying influence and access. These are business people. They want something back" (Schouten, Schnaars, & Korte, 2012, p. 7A).

Another mechanism for political fund-raising is donations from tax-exempt "social welfare" organizations. In fact, these organizations outspent the super PACs by a three-to-two margin in 2012 (Beckel, 2012), spending more than $256 million to influence federal elections (Schouten & Korte, 2013). And unlike super PACs, they are not required to release the names of their donors. Organized under section 501(c)(4) of the Internal Revenue Service (IRS) code, historically these were civic leagues or local volunteer fire departments which, by definition, "operated exclusively for the promotion of social welfare." This changed in 1959 when an IRS interpretation changed "exclusively" to "primarily" and these organizations began dabbling in politics (Shegreen, 2013). Over the years, "primarily" has come to be interpreted as more than 50 percent, so any level below 50 percent is considered an acceptable level to engage in political activity. Between 2010 and 2012, the number of applications to the IRS for 501(c)(4) status more than doubled (Thomas & Peoples, 2013). The combination of an ambiguous rule and political strategists taking advantage of it "has led to massive misuse of the tax laws to hide donors' financing campaign activity" (Shegreen, 2013, p. 4A). Sometimes called sources of "dark money," watchdog groups have asked Congress to pay attention to the IRS's failure to regulate political groups masquerading as social welfare organizations (Schouten, 2013).

Although they usually target national and state elections, some groups also are involved at the local level. For example, Americans for Prosperity, the conservative political advocacy organization funded by the wealthy Koch brothers, has sought to influence mayoral and school board races in Iowa, a food tax in a Nebraska town, and a city zoo levy in Ohio (Gray, 2014).

In April 2014, in McCutcheon v. Federal Elections Commission, the U.S. Supreme Court struck down limits on the aggregate amount of donations that individuals could make to candidates and political parties. The previous limit had been $123,000 per two-year election cycle. (The limit on donations to individual candidates remained in place.) While affecting only a small number of very wealthy individual donors, and potentially diluting the impact of super PACs, Justice Stephen Breyer noted in his dissent that "taken together with Citizens United v. Federal Election Commission, [this] decision eviscerates our Nation's campaign finance laws" (Gershman, 2014).

Election campaigns are increasingly commercialized and expensive. For example, at the national level the average House of Representatives winner in 2012 spent more than $1.5 million in the general election. For Senate candidates, the typical winner spent almost $11.5 million (Center for Responsive Politics, n.d.), which works out to spending, on average, more than $5,000 per day for each day of a six-year term, including Saturdays, Sundays, and holidays. According to a nonpartisan research group that tracks political money (Maplight, 2012), in the 2012 election more than 50 percent of itemized contributions to senatorial campaigns were made by people other than the candidates' constituents; this means that the rest of the country potentially has more influence in selecting a senator than the state's residents do.

Voters and Voter Turnout

Given the situation described above, one is not surprised to find high levels of voter apathy in America. Voter turnout is higher when there is real competition and real choice. In addition, voting conditions can affect turnout. Many other countries allow Sunday voting, multiday voting, and voting by mail. (Some states have made voting easier for their residents by allowing same-day registration and permitting absentee balloting by any voter, not just those who can show they are unable to participate on Election Day.)

Compared to participation rates hovering just above 50 percent in the United States, participation rates in other countries tend to be much higher. Among those thirty countries with participation rates near or above 85 percent in their most recent presidential and/or parliamentary election were Australia, Bahamas, Bangladesh, Belgium, Bolivia, Cuba, Denmark, Ethiopia, Kazakhstan, Kenya, Luxembourg, Malaysia, Namibia, Sierra Leone, Singapore, Sweden, Tunisia, Turkey, and Uruguay (International Institute for Democracy and Electoral Assistance, 2013). In the 2012 U.S. general election, 58.2 percent of eligible voters turned out (McDonald, 2013). Minnesota had the highest rate at 75.7 percent, followed by Wisconsin at 72.5, Colorado at 70.3, and New Hampshire at 70.1; the lowest turnout rates were in Hawaii at 44.2 percent, West Virginia at 46.3, Oklahoma at 49.2, and Texas at 49.7 (McDonald, 2013).

The election systems in most other democracies involve *proportional representation*, rather than "winner-take-all" systems such as the ones in the United States and Canada. In a proportional representation election, there are multiple candidates representing a district. Winning candidates are determined by the proportion of votes a party receives. If, for example, the "Purple Party" wins 50 percent of the votes in a ten-member district, five of the elected officials would be from the Purple Party. The single-member district system, such as we have in the United States, "routinely denies representation to large numbers of voters, produces legislatures that fail to accurately reflect the views of the public, discriminates against third parties, and discourages voter turnout" (Amy, 2005). As noted already, when redistricting is applied to this model, creating "safe" districts for one party or the other, it is clear how some voters might feel that their votes are "wasted" if they are not supporters of the majority party.

Verba, Schlozman, and Brady (1995) note that American politics is prone to "participatory distortion." Citizens with more income, education, and age are overrepresented in almost every political activity, from contacting lawmakers to contributing funds. Populations that have higher-than-average voter participation rates include those 65 and older, women, veterans, married persons, those with higher household income and more education, and Midwesterners. People who hold intense opinions on issues such as Second Amendment gun rights and abortion are also more likely to vote.

In the 2008 and 2012 presidential election years, African American voters turned out at a higher rate than whites (64 percent) or other minorities (62 percent) (Balz & Mellnik, 2013). African American turnout has been steadily increasing since 1996 (Weiner, 2013). Voting rates among Hispanics and Asian Americans is lower than whites and blacks (Balz & Mellnik, 2013). In 2012 only about 48 percent of eligible Hispanics and Asian Americans voted. About 12 million eligible Hispanics did not vote; the unmet potential of the nation's fastest-growing minority group is obvious in these findings (Balz & Mellnik, 2013).

Voter enthusiasm is clearly correlated to perceptions of having a stake in the political system and the outcome of the election. Those who believe they have nothing to gain feel alienated and are unlikely to vote. One example of this is the difference in voter turnout between solidly Democratic or solidly Republican states and "swing" states or "battleground" states—those where the outcomes of national elections are seen as uncertain. Differences in turnout have been steadily widening since 1996, with turnout in the swing states greater than other states by seven percentage points in the 2012 election (Page, 2012).

Given the historic nature of the 2008 presidential election, with the first African American major party candidate and the first female Republican vice presidential candidate, interest from nontraditional voters increased. Continuing a trend that began in 1992, youth voter turnout rose significantly in 2008 to 48.5 percent of the eligible youth voting population, but dropped to 41.2 percent in 2012 (Taylor & Lopez, 2013).

Voter Suppression

Recent events have raised serious concerns among civil rights organizations and other progressive groups about new barriers to voter participation. In 2008 the U.S. Supreme Court ruled that states can require voters to produce photo identification at the polls without violating their constitutional rights (Beaumont, 2014). From early 2011 through mid-October 2012 at least 180 bills making it harder to vote were introduced in forty-one states. Vetoes, referendums, court decisions, and/or the U.S. Department of Justice blocked or blunted restrictive measures in fourteen states (Brennan Center for Justice, 2012). In 2013, thirty-three states introduced at least ninety-two restrictive bills (Brennan Center for Justice, 2013), and the Supreme Court made that easier, as described later in this section. The proposed new laws included voter registration drive restrictions, new requirements for proof of citizenship, limitations on same-day registration, purging voter rolls, shortening the time frame for early voting, and making it more difficult for released felons to regain the right to vote. The Republican legislature and governor in North Carolina instituted the most restrictive new laws, including a new requirement for photo ID, elimination of same-day registration, elimination of pre-registration for 16- and 17-year olds, and reduction of the early voting period, including Sundays. In North Carolina nearly 70 percent of blacks voted early in the 2012 elections ("Efforts to suppress votes pop up in the states," 2013). Other states also moved to eliminate early voting on Sundays, which is when many African Americans vote in church-organized drives called "souls to the polls" (Clement, 2013; Lee, 2013).

New requirements for government-issued photo IDs were proposed in response to alleged threats of "voter fraud" and to "protect the integrity of the election process." But voter fraud is virtually nonexistent in this country (Belec, 2012; Levitt, 2007; Magoc, 2012) and does not affect election outcomes. For example, among nearly seven million votes cast in elections in North Carolina in 2012—where some of the strongest voter suppression laws were passed—there were only 121 cases of alleged voter fraud, amounting to 0.00172 percent of the total votes.

The Brennan Center found that up to 11 percent of voting-age American citizens do not have a government-issued photo ID, and the numbers for some groups are even higher; for example, 18 percent of those over 65, 25 percent of African Americans, and 15 percent of those who make less than $35,000 a year do not have photo IDs (Belec, 2012). Because they often change their names after marrying or divorcing, up to a third of women voters do not have identification that reflects their current name (Baumberger, 2013; Belec, 2012).

The governor of North Carolina and other conservatives argue that requiring a photo ID is not an unreasonable requirement; people must show a government-issued photo ID to cash a check or board a plane. Civil rights advocates counter that check cashing and flying are not among the basic rights of citizenship. Government ID offices are often far from where people live and open at inconvenient times. It may be costly and difficult for older adults to obtain documentation of their date and place of birth.

According to the Advancement Project & Voter Protection Program (2012), although there is little evidence of noncitizens voting, at least sixteen states have initiated voter roll purges targeting naturalized citizens. Florida started a highly controversial voter list purge in the spring of 2012. The state produced a list of 182,000 potential noncitizen voters; the list was eventually reduced to forty, drawing widespread criticism that the effort was designed to intimidate legal Hispanic voters ("Efforts to suppress votes pop up in the states," 2013).

In June 2013, in a 5-4 vote, the U.S. Supreme Court struck down Section 4 of the Voting Rights Act of 1965. The law had applied to nine states, mostly in the South, including Alabama, Georgia, Louisiana, Mississippi, South Carolina, Texas, and Virginia, and also Alaska and Arizona, and to scores of counties and municipalities in seven other states. Section 4 set out the formula to determine which states should be subject to Section 5, which required states to submit any changes to election or voting laws or alteration of legislative or congressional districts to the Department of Justice for preapproval (Cillizza, 2013c; Liptak, 2013). The Court decided that the remedy for past racial discrimination that was the heart of Section 4 was no longer necessary (Wolf, 2013). Within two hours of the Supreme Court ruling, the Texas attorney general announced that a law requiring a photo ID that had been blocked by the Department of Justice in 2012 would immediately go into effect. At least seven other states also passed more restrictive laws. The new policies disproportionately impact minorities, college students, older adults, poor people, and women—groups that tend to vote for Democrats (Beaumont, 2014; Wolf, 2013). Some of these laws have been challenged in court, and outcomes are pending.

Demographics of Officeholders

Elected officials in the United States are predominantly white men. Women and people of color are significantly underrepresented in elective office at all levels in proportion to their numbers in the general population.

Most female and minority members of Congress belong to the Democratic Party. In the 113th Congress (2013–2014), less than 20 percent of members were women or minorities; only 4.2 percent of Republicans in Congress were women (Manning, 2013).

In other countries, women make up a substantial number of officeholders. For instance, if one were to compare national legislatures, seventy-one nations have a greater percentage of females (Wallechinsky, 2007). Lawless and Fox (2010, 2012) suggest that there are fewer women than men in office in this country because women do not run for office. This is less a result of discrimination than a lack of political ambition. Women are less likely than men to be recruited to run for office, and they are less likely than men to think they are qualified for office. They also have more difficulty than men in reconciling family needs with the demands of a political career.

Women in Congress can be expected to bring up "women's issues"—gender equity, day care, flextime, reproductive freedom, minimum wage increases, and the extension of nutrition programs (Burrell, 1996), and women generally run well as agents of change because they are viewed as outsiders (Romano, 2006). Both Democratic and moderate Republican women in Congress are more likely than men to use their bill sponsorship and cosponsorship activity to focus on women's issues (Swers, 2002). Legislators of both genders believe that female lawmakers are likely to focus attention on how bills will affect women, and also that women lawmakers have increased political access for economically disadvantaged groups (Political Parity, 2012). Most women legislators also believe that women lawmakers have been effective in encouraging legislative bodies to conduct their business in public, as opposed to behind closed doors (Political Parity, 2012).

Voters may more easily see women as legislators than as elected executives; collaboration, a traditional female attribute, is more valued in legislative settings (Moore, 2013). In fact, data suggests that women are indeed more likely to be willing to compromise with members on the other side of an issue. Women now chair or sit as ranking members of ten of the Senate's twenty committees; they were responsible for passing the vast majority of congressional legislation in 2013 (Newton-Small, 2013). In a study of Senate voting patterns two women, Senator Susan Collins of Maine and Senator Lisa Murkowski of Alaska, were the only two moderates who were found to bridge the middle ground (Cillizza, 2013b). And it was female senators—Collins and Murkowski, along with three of their female Senate colleagues (Kelly Ayotte of New Hampshire, Barbara Mikulski of Maryland, and Patty Murray of Washington), who successfully negotiated the end of the government shutdown initiated by some of their male colleagues in October 2013 (Newton-Small, 2013).

The longest-serving woman in the U.S. Senate is Barbara Mikulski, a social worker from Maryland. Another social worker serving in the 113th Congress is Senator Debbie Stabenow, of Michigan.

According to the Center for American Women and Politics [CAWP] (2014b), in 2014, nearly a quarter (24.2 percent) of state legislators were

TABLE 2.1
Women in Congress

	110th *2007–2008*	*111th* *2009–2010*	*112th* *2011–2012*	*113th* *2013–2014*
Senate	16	17	17	20
House	74	76	74	81

Sources: Amer, M. (2008, September 3). Membership of the 111th Congress: A profile. Washington, DC: Congressional Research Service; Manning, J. E. (2010, December 27). *Membership of the 111th Congress: A profile.* Washington, DC: Congressional Research Service; Manning, J. E. (2011, March 1). *Membership of the 112th Congress: A profile.* Washington, DC: Congressional Research Service; Manning, J. E. (2013, December 6). *Membership of the 113th Congress: A profile.* Washington, DC: Congressional Research Service.

female; since 1971, when the rate was 4.5 percent, the number of women in state legislatures has more than quintupled. The states with the highest proportion of women serving in their legislature were Colorado (with thirteen out of thirty-five), Vermont (with eight out of thirty), and Hawaii (with eight out of twenty-five). The states with the lowest proportion of women state senators were mostly in the South, including South Carolina (with one out of forty-six), Louisiana (with four out of thirty-nine), and Oklahoma (with four out of forty-eight). There were five female governors in 2013. In November of 2010 the first women of color to serve as chief executives in any states were elected. Susana Martinez, a Latina, became governor of New Mexico, and Nikki Haley, an Asian American, became governor of South Carolina. Both are Republicans. As of January 2014, of the 1,351 U.S. cities with populations over 30,000, 249 (18.4 percent) had women mayors (CAWP, 2014a). Results of national polling have shown that the public's willingness to vote for a woman for president has risen substantially, from 33 percent in 1937 to 88 percent in 2007 (CAWP & Political Parity, 2012).

Members of racial and ethnic minorities are underrepresented in elective offices and are predominantly from one political party. Since 1900, 80 percent of African Americans elected to Congress have been Democrats. Only five Republican African Americans have been elected to Congress in more than a century (Blake, 2013). There were no African

American Republican members of the House of Representatives in the 113th Congress. There were two African American senators in the 113th Congress. Out of the 1,950 senators who served in all of U.S. history, only nine have been African Americans; of those, three were appointed rather than elected. There are seven Republican Hispanics in the House and three in the Senate (Manning, 2013). There are no Asian American Republicans serving in the 113th Congress. Both Native Americans elected to the House are Republicans.

Minorities may be gaining political influence in Washington. Even as their numerical count remains relatively flat, some long-serving minority members of Congress have been appointed to committee chairmanships or other powerful positions.

Understanding the Political System in the United States

Functionalist Perspective

Modern governments perform the necessary societal functions that private enterprise will not or cannot perform because there is no profit to be

TABLE 2.2
Minorities in Congress

	110th 2007–2008	111th 2009–2010	112th 2011–2012	113th 2013–2014*
African Americans	42	42	44	45
Hispanics	30	29	28	37
Asians	8	13	13	13
Native Americans	1	1	1	2

*as of December 2013

Sources: Amer, M. (2008, September 3). *Membership of the 111th Congress: A profile.* Washington, DC: Congressional Research Service; Manning, J. E. (2010, December 27). *Membership of the 111th Congress: A profile.* Washington, DC: Congressional Research Service; Manning, J. E. (2011, March 1). *Membership of the 112th Congress: A profile.* Washington, DC: Congressional Research Service; Manning, J. E. (2013, December 6). *Membership of the 113th Congress: A profile.* Washington, DC: Congressional Research Service.

made. Examples include providing safety and protection (e.g., police services, national defense), building and maintaining infrastructure (e.g., roads, sewage treatment plants), and running public facilities (e.g., schools, courts, prisons, parks, and so forth).

Functionalists espouse the *pluralist model* of politics. They argue that there are many competing interest groups, making the political process necessarily one of negotiation and compromise. Although few groups are powerful enough to force their agenda on others, many groups are able to thwart the plans of their opposition. Thus power is widely dispersed and change is slow.

Conflict Perspective

Some conflict theorists, notably C. Wright Mills (1956) and more recently G. William Domhoff (2013), have argued that most important political decisions are made not by elected officials but by a *power elite*, or ruling class, made up of extremely wealthy individuals who enjoy easy access to the centers of U.S. politics.

Elites come from the upper classes—the wealthy and educated—and are usually white. For the first time in history, as of December 2012, more than half of the members of Congress were millionaires; their median net worth was $1,008,767 (Center for Responsive Politics, 2014). The vast majority hold at least a bachelor's degree (93 percent in the House and 99 percent of the Senate) (Manning, 2013). In the 113th Congress, 211 out of 535 members listed law as their occupation, and 187 listed business; 20 were medical doctors, 10 were former state governors, 7 were former judges, and 13 were former cabinet secretaries (Manning, 2013).

Conflict theorists note that the power elite are not participants in some grand conspiracy, but simply are people of similar backgrounds who share mutual interests and agendas, often involving "the welfare of big business." Nevertheless, those who espouse the *power elite model* say that the concentration of wealth and power in a few hands is so great that the people at the top face little opposition. At the same time, the voices of many of the people in the middle and most of those at the bottom have little chance of being heard (Piven & Cloward, 1997).

Rational/Social Exchange Perspective

Modern Western democracies were conceived in the "Age of Enlightenment," an eighteenth-century movement that celebrated the essential rationality of humankind. Philosophers of the time proposed that the "rule of law" should replace the rule of monarchy. Inherent in this concept was the idea that citizens are capable of making logical choices in governing themselves through processes of deliberation and negotiation.

The founders of the United States did not trust the general populace to make decisions directly. For example, they established the Electoral College to select the president. Most Americans believe that, especially if they have access to accurate and unbiased information, they can and should make many political choices for themselves. Sometimes politicians allow this process of *direct democracy* through the use of *referendums* on the election ballot. This happens at the state or local level.

Constructionist Perspective

The constructed meaning of the United States of America has power to influence and shape political directions. Many Americans believe that their country has been especially chosen and blessed by God to lead the world. In the nineteenth century, this idea was expressed in the concept of "manifest destiny"—the idea that God had provided the North American continent to be developed into a utopian society built upon the principles of capitalism, Protestantism, and democracy (Jansson, 2012, p. 119). (This ignored the fact that indigenous Native Americans had a legitimate claim to the same territory, of course.) A more current term is "American exceptionalism" (Lipset, 1996), which many conservatives use to imply a God-given superiority over other nations.

With the exception of Native American and Alaskan and Hawaiian natives, all residents of the United States, or their ancestors, came from somewhere else. Thus "being an American" in the mind of the general public reflects voluntary allegiance to the United States. Despite support of the idea of freedom of speech, those who challenge mainstream values or criticize national policy run the risk of being labeled unpatriotic if not "un-American" (Alter, 2006). The citizens of other countries derive their sense of themselves from a common history and ancestry; they do not become "un-French" or "un-Korean" by expressing unpopular points of view (Lipset, 1996).

The Impact of the Political System on Individuals and Families

How the Political System Deters Well-Being

As discussed under the conflict perspective, the issues of poor people are not commonly addressed by our political system. The poor are isolated and marked off as deviant by "a predominantly middle-class political culture" (Piven & Cloward, 1997, p. 282). Because they have been left out of the mainstream political process, they have few options to make their voices heard. In the past, these included public demonstrations, sit-ins, boycotts, and rent strikes. "Disruptive and irregular tactics are the only resource, short of violence, available to low-income groups seeking to influence public policy" (Piven & Cloward, 1997, p. 284). A recent example is the one-day labor walkouts staged in early December 2013 by fast-food workers in New York, Washington, DC, Detroit, and other American cities pressing for an increase in the federal minimum wage, higher wages in the industry, and the right to unionize without management reprisals (Bacon, 2013). Fast-food workers demonstrated again on May 15, 2014, across cities in the United States and in thirty-two other countries worldwide, targeting at least seventeen restaurant chains, including McDonald's, Burger King, Wendy's, and KFC (Horovitz, Alcindor, Woodyard, MacLeod, & Hjelmgaard, 2013). Strikes in Japan, New Zealand, the Philippines, South Korea, and Switzerland brought global media attention to the protesters' demands.

How the Political System Promotes Well-Being

The U.S. Constitution and judicial system stand as examples to the rest of the world in their protection of the civil rights and civil liberties of racial, ethnic, and religious minorities; women; sexual minorities; people with disabilities; and older adults. Americans enjoy individual freedoms unknown in many countries.

ECONOMICS AND POLITICS TOGETHER: THE POLITICAL ECONOMY

Political economy is the term used to refer to the pervasive interaction of political and economic institutions. In the United States, politics and the economy are so intertwined that often it is difficult to see them or treat them as separate institutions. Many of this country's laws are based on the ideals of capitalism and much of the "free market" economy is politically supported in one way or another.

The Power of Organizations

Piven and Cloward (1997) suggest that despite political oratory to the contrary, as individuals most Americans have little direct influence on the political process. Instead, political dialogue is carried on between organizations—between government agencies or legislative committees and professional associations, unions, PACs, business groups, and corporations—not individuals. Individuals do not have the time, resources, or the interest to regularly monitor and participate in the political process. The complexities of issues and the intricacies of policy making are simply too much for the average citizen to follow. On the other hand, the focus of organizations—to protect the rights, income, occupational roles, property, or other economic interests of their members—makes ongoing interaction with political processes both necessary and potentially profitable.

One of the ways that organizations exercise political power is through lobbying. Lobbyists are paid to exert pressure on lawmakers on behalf of their clients. In some instances they may help draft the new laws. Some special interest groups retain lobbying firms; others have lobbyists working in-house. Total lobbying spending at the federal level increased from $1.45 billion in 1998 to $2.38 billion in 2013 (Center for Responsive Politics, 2013a). From 1998 through 2013, the top spenders on lobbying categorized by industry included pharmaceuticals/health products ($2.7 billion), insurance ($1.9 billion), electric utilities ($1.8 billion), computers/Internet ($1.5 billion), oil and gas ($1.5 billion), TV, music/movies ($1.2 billion), hospitals/nursing homes ($1.2 billion), securities and investments ($1.0 billion), and civil servants/public officials ($1.0 billion)

(Center for Responsive Politics, 2013b). Among the specific organizations at the top of the list were the U.S. Chamber of Commerce ($1.01 billion), General Electric ($298 million), the American Medical Association ($295 million), the American Hospital Association ($249 million), Pharmaceutical Researchers and Manufacturers of America ($246 million), the National Association of Realtors ($246 million), AARP ($230 million), Blue Cross/Blue Shield ($221 million), Exxon Mobil ($193 million), Boeing Company ($183 million), Verizon Communications ($183 million), and Lockheed Martin ($181 million) (Center for Responsive Politics, 2013c).

Often lobbyists are former advisors to the president, congressmen, or state legislators who have recently left political office. Stronger restrictions on such "revolving door" patterns were part of the Honest Leadership and Open Government Act of 2007, which increased the "cooling off period" (the time between leaving office and active lobbying) for senators and cabinet secretaries from one year to two years. Senate and House staff have a one-year restriction. In fifteen states there are not any laws preventing legislators from resigning one day and registering as lobbyists the next, and the restrictions in the other thirty-five states are filled with loopholes or only loosely enforced (Moyers & Winship, 2013). In 2008 the Canadian Parliament extended their "cooling off" period from two years to five years and increased fines for failing to comply with provisions of the act.

One example of an especially powerful political organization is the American Legislative Exchange Council (ALEC), which is registered as a "public charity" under 501(c)(3) in the federal tax code. It is funded by hundreds of thousands of tax-deductible dollars in annual corporation member dues (Magoc, 2012; McIntire, 2012). Almost 2,000 state legislators are members. The organization advances a pro-business, socially conservative agenda, including efforts to promote smaller government, eliminate capital gains taxes, weaken collective bargaining rights, limit corporate liability, and increase populations at for-profit prisons (Macomber, 2013; Magoc, 2012; McIntire, 2012). At ALEC's annual conferences legislators draft model bills without public input that they then take back to their states. ALEC faced public backlash when it became clear that the organization had drafted restrictive voter ID statutes and "stand your ground" gun rights laws (see chapter 3). As a result of negative media attention, many corporate sponsors, including Kraft, Coca Cola, Pepsi, Intuit, Wal-Mart, and Amazon, announced they would stop funding ALEC (Magoc, 2012).

In the last forty years, special interest groups have increasingly focused on single-issue politics, such as Second Amendment (gun) rights or abortion. They derive their strength from the intensity of their members' beliefs and have little interest in compromise (Kendall, 2013).

We have already mentioned how giant corporations dominate the American economy and discussed Wright's theory of the power elite. Corporations are the major contributors to both political parties, and as already noted, limitations on corporate donations to support or oppose candidates for elective office were lifted in 2010 under the U.S. Supreme Court decision in Citizens United v. Federal Election Commission. In response, much of the activity of politicians is aimed at promoting the economic interests of large corporations. "The . . . claim by corporations that they have the same right as any individual to influence the government in their own interest pits the individual citizen against the vast financial and communications resources of the corporation and mocks the constitutional intent that all citizens have an equal voice in the political debates surrounding important issues" (Korten, 1995, p. 59).

The amazing expansion of the influence of corporations over federal, state, and local governments in the last thirty years has led to acknowledgment and criticism of *corporate welfare*, the direct subsidies and tax expenditures granted to businesses. Corporate welfare includes programs that offer financial compensation, programs that provide research (R & D) for industries, and programs that provide subsidized loans or insurance. Between 1995 and 2013, recipients of funding from one of the biggest direct federal subsidy programs, the one for crops and farms, included fifty billionaires (or the businesses in which they had some form of ownership; Nixon, 2013). During 2013 Congress debated reductions to the SNAP program (food stamps), which is included in the farm subsidy program. According to a report in the *New York Times* (Nixon, 2013, p. A23), one critic noted, "The irony is that farm subsidies are going to billionaires at the same time that there are proposals to kick three to five million people off of food stamps." At the state level, corporations may receive special incentives for "job creation." Good Jobs First, a watchdog group that examined economic development efforts in all fifty states, found that most states fail to disclose the details of subsidy programs (Coppins, 2011); this prevents outsiders from evaluating corporate welfare benefits.

Large organizations also benefit from federal tax policies. Currently the proportion of federal tax revenues that come from corporate income tax is 10 percent; this is a significant decline from the 1950s when 25 percent of federal tax revenues came from corporations (vanden Heuvel, 2011). Although the top corporate tax rate in the United States is 35 percent, one of the highest in the world, the availability of a maze of shelters, loopholes, tax credits, preferences, and subsidies encourages corporations to engage in tax avoidance (Kocieniewski, 2011). Some large corporations pay no taxes at all. According to Citizens for Tax Justice, a quarter of companies pay an effective tax rate of less than 10 percent, and thirty large companies, including DuPont, Verizon, Boeing, and Wells Fargo, paid no taxes at all despite record high profits (McIntyre, 2013). For example, General Electric (GE) in 2010 showed a profit of $14.2 billion; they not only did not pay taxes but claimed a tax benefit of $3.2 billion. GE's tax department "includes former officials not just from the [U.S.] Treasury [Department], but also from the IRS and virtually all the tax writing committees in Congress" (Kocieniewski, 2011).

Most people would be surprised to learn that, along with well-known tax-exempt organizations such as the Boy Scouts and Planned Parenthood, sports leagues such as the National Football League, National Hockey League, or the PGA (golf) Tour are also classified as tax-exempt, not-for-profit organizations. According to Senator Tom Coburn of Oklahoma, "It's one of the striking examples in the tax code where middle- and lower-income Americans are essentially subsidizing salaries for multimillionaires" (Schrotenboer, 2013, p. 2C).

Government Spending

Because of its purchasing power alone, the U.S. government has a huge influence over the nation's economy. Total government spending in 2010 was expected to represent 39.9 percent of the gross domestic product (GDP) (Freedman, 2009). The Great Recession of 2007–2009 has brought renewed discussion about the proper relationship between government and the private sector. In times of economic crisis, the federal government is unique in its ability to engage in deficit spending to create jobs or stimulate a sagging economy.

According to the Urban Institute (Isaacs, Toran, Hahn, Fortuny, & Steuerle, 2012) the largest part (41 percent) of the federal budget goes to the elderly and disabled portions of Social Security, Medicare, and Medicaid; 20 percent goes to defense, 10 percent to children, 6 percent for interest payments on the debt, and 23 percent for all other government functions (e.g., agriculture, commerce, veterans benefits, the environment, transportation). The defense budget of the United States now equals that of the rest of the world's nations combined, costing $534 billion in 2010 *without* including the cost of the wars in Iraq and Afghanistan (Crowley, 2010). Republicans see defense as government's core function and many members of Congress use defense contracts to bring money back to their home districts. Social Security costs about $703 billion a year in payouts. The non-child portions of Social Security, Medicare, and Medicaid have grown from about one-tenth to two-fifths of the federal budget over the past five decades and are projected to grow more rapidly in the next decade, representing half of all federal spending and strongly shaping future budgets (Isaacs et al., 2012). Cuts to such spending face political opposition. Most of the 53 million Americans who collect Social Security payments are older adults who are among the most reliable voters (Crowley, 2010).

Many Americans are *operational liberals*—they want government to provide programs and services, but they are *ideological conservatives*—they do not like "big government," which they view as intrusive and wasteful.

Inequities in Government Benefits

Links between the government and the economy affect every citizen. "All groups benefit from government assistance . . . [but] it can be argued that much of the income redistribution that results from public policy favors the more rather than the less affluent" (DiNitto 2010, p. 29). The rich receive government assistance through various income-tax deductions and government contracts and subsidies to their businesses; individuals in the middle class receive government assistance primarily in the form of home mortgage loans and associated tax deductions, and grants and loans for education. The federal government forgoes more than $130 billion in tax revenues by allowing the home mortgage interest deduction (Crowley, 2010). Americans are allowed to claim the deduction for mortgages of up to one million dollars and they can use it for the purchase of a second, vacation home (Crowley, 2010). (Neither of these allowances is likely to benefit middle-income families.) The poor and near-poor receive government assistance in the form of welfare grants, SNAP (food stamps), Medicaid, and earned income-tax credits.

Federal and state taxes are the major source of funding for social welfare programs. Most (about 82 percent) of the federal government's revenue comes from the individual income tax and the payroll taxes used to finance Social Security, Medicare, and the federal unemployment insurance program (Elmendorf, 2010). The individual income tax has tax rates that rise with income level. This is an example of a "progressive" tax. In addition to the federal government, forty-three states also have income taxes (Karger & Stoesz, 2010). The social insurance (payroll) tax rates vary little across income groups; in fact, the average social insurance tax rate is higher than the average individual income tax rate for all income groups except the highest quintile (Elmendorf, 2010). People with higher incomes do not pay payroll taxes on all of their salaries because there is a built-in maximum. (The maximum taxable earnings level in 2014 was $117,000.) This is known as a *regressive tax*; regressive taxes are those that tax the poor at a higher rate than the rich. Sales taxes are particularly regressive for low-income people. In states where groceries and medicines are not exempted, the poor pay sales taxes on 100 percent of their income because they must spend it all to meet the expenses of daily living.

The median income in America is about $50,000 a year and the typical taxpayer at that level of income pays about 20 percent in taxes (Reich, 2011). Rates in other countries are much higher. For example, the average wage tax burden for childless single workers in 2012 was 56.0 percent in Belgium, 50.2 percent in France, and 49.7 percent in Germany; the comparable rate in the United States was 29.6 percent (Organization for

Economic Co-operation and Development, 2013). The comparable rate in Canada is about 30 percent.

The *marginal tax rate* is the rate applied to the dollars earned above a certain cutoff point or bracket; it affects the wealthiest taxpayers. The highest marginal tax rate used in the United States was 91 percent in the late 1950s and early 1960s and it was as high as 70 percent as recently as 1980 (Elmendorf, 2010). Since 1988, when taxes were slashed under President Reagan, the highest marginal tax rate has ranged from 28 percent to 39.6 percent (Elmendorf, 2010). About 46 percent of Americans do not pay any federal income tax at all; this is because most of them do not make enough money, after taking standard deductions, to owe any income taxes (Johnson, Nunns, Rohaly, Toder, & Williams, 2011).

Politics and Social Workers

Without an awareness of the pervasive influence of the political economy, social workers may be tempted to believe that problems exist solely on the individual or family level. The poor in particular are vulnerable. They lack the resources to use the political system to address their needs. Even skilled social work practitioners cannot counsel their clients out of the difficulties created by the inadequacies and injustice of the larger society.

The National Association of Social Workers' (NASW) Code of Ethics encourages political activity. The organization "reaffirms that participation in electoral politics is consistent with fundamental social work values" (NASW, 2012a, p. 109). Activities can include operating federal and state political action committees, organizing national, regional, and chapter training programs, mobilizing support for political candidates whose stance on issues advances NASW's professional and program agenda, and encouraging social workers to seek public office (NASW, 2012a, pp. 105–106). NASW also supports "continued efforts to reform and modernize voter registration laws that make it easier for people to register and vote" (NASW, 2012b, p. 349).

LOOKING AHEAD

Not only are individuals, families, and communities affected by the political economy, but so are the other social institutions. We will explore these relationships in chapters 3 and 4.

REFERENCES

Advancement Project & Voter Protection Program. (2012, September 24). *Segregating American citizenship: Latino voter disenfranchisement in 2012*. Retrieved from http://b.3cdn.net/advancement/18ff5 be68ab53f752b_0tm6yjgsj.pdf.

Alter, J. (2006, September 15). Packaging patriotism. *Newsweek*, pp. 51–54.

Alter, J. (2009a, September 28). The jackass-reduction plan. *Newsweek*, p. 29.

Alter, J. (2009b, February 23). Poof goes the purple dream. *Newsweek*, p. 33.

Americans for Tax Fairness. (2014). Walmart on tax day: How taxpayers subsidize America's biggest employer and richest family. Retrieved from http://www.americansfortaxfairness.org/files/Walmart-on-Tax -Day-Americans-for-Tax-Fairness-1.pdf.

Amy, D. J. (2005). What is proportional representation and why do we need this reform? Retrieved from http://www.mtholyoke.edu/acad/ polit/damy/BeginningReading/whatispr.htm.

Andersen, M., & Taylor, H. (2013). *Sociology: The essentials* (7th ed.). Belmont, CA: Wadsworth.

Bacon, J. (2013, December 5). Fast-food workers strike, protest for higher pay. *USA Today*. Retrieved from http://www.usatoday.com/story/ money/business/2013/12/05/fast-food-strike-wages/3877023/.

Bakan, J. (2004). *The corporation: The pathological pursuit of profit and power*. New York, NY: Free Press.

Balz, D., & Cohen, J. (2012, August 18). Big gulf between political parties, divisions within. *Washington Post*. Retrieved from http://www .washingtonpost.com/politics/big-gulf-between-parties-divisions -within/2012/08/18/f5ee15d4-e31a-11e1-ae7f-d2a13e249eb2_story .html.

Balz, D., & Mellnik, T. (2013, May 8). Census: Blacks voted at higher rates than whites in 2012. *Washington Post*. Retrieved from http:// www.washingtonpost.com/politics/census-blacks-voted-at-higher -rates-than-whites-in-2012/2013/05/08/7d24bcaa-b800-11e2-b94c -b684dda07add_story.html.

Baumberger, J. (2013, October 30). Voter ID laws pose threat to women's rights. *USA Today*, p. 8A.

Beaumont, T. (2014, March 1). Primaries are key tests of voter ID laws. *The State* [Columbia, SC], p. A6.

Beckel, M. (2012, June 16). *Nonprofits outspent super PAC's in 2010.* Retrieved from http://www.opensecrets.org/news/2012/06/nonpro fits-outspent-super-pacs-in-2.html.

Belec, H. M. (2012, Fall). Protecting our suffrage. *Outlook, The Magazine of AAUW* [American Association of University Women], pp. 8–11.

Bernstein, J. (2004). *The living wage movement: What it is, why it is, and what's known about its impact?* National Bureau of Economic Research. Retrieved from http://www.nber.org/chapters/c9951.pdf.

Blake, A. (2013). African Americans in Congress, by the numbers. *The Washington Post.* Retrieved from http://www.washingtonpost.com/ blogs/the-fix/wp/2013/08/28/african-americans-in-congress.

Brennan Center for Justice. (2012, October 11). *Election 2012: Voting laws roundup.* Retrieved from http://www.brennancenter.org/analysis /election-2012-voting-laws-roundup.

Brennan Center for Justice. (2013, December 19). *Voting laws roundup 2013.* Retrieved from http://www.brennancenter.org/analysis/elec tion-2013-voting-laws-roundup.

Bureau of Labor Statistics. (2013a). *Local area unemployment statistics.* Retrieved from http://www.bls.gov/web/laus/alumstrk.htm.

Bureau of Labor Statistics. (2013b). *Union members—2012.* USDL-13–0105.

Burrell, B. (1996). *A woman's place is in the house: Campaigning for Congress in the feminist era.* Ann Arbor: University of Michigan Press.

Calder, L. G. (1999). *Financing the American Dream: A cultural history of consumer credit.* Princeton, NJ: Princeton University Press.

Carmichael, M. (2003, May 12). Help from far away. *Newsweek*, p. E16.

Center for American Women and Politics (CAWP) (2014a). *Facts.* Retrieved from http://www.cawp.rutgers.edu/fast_facts/levels_of_ office/Local-WomenMayors.php.

Center for American Women and Politics (CAWP) (2014b). *Women in state legislatures 2014.* Retrieved from http://www.cawp.rutgers.edu/ fast_facts/levels_of_office/documents/stleg. pdf.

Center for American Women and Politics & Political Parity (2012, August). *Research inventory: American women and politics.* Retrieved from http://www.politicalparity.org/wp-content/uploads/2012/08/research-inventory.p df.

Center for Responsive Politics. (2013a). *Lobbying database.* Retrieved from http://www.opensecrets.org/lobby/index.php.

Center for Responsive Politics. (2013b). *Top industries.* Retrieved from http://www.opensecrets.org/lobby/top.php?indexType = i&show Year = 2013.

Center for Responsive Politics. (2013c). *Top spenders.* Retrieved from http://www.opensecrets.org/lobby/top.php?indexType = s&show Year = 2013.

Center for Responsive Politics. (2014). Millionaires' club: For first time, most lawmakers are worth $1 million-plus. Retrieved from http://www.opensecrets.org/news/2014/01/millionaires-club-for-first-time-most-lawmakers-are-worth-1-million-plus.html.

Center for Responsive Politics. (n.d.). *Election stats.* Retrieved from http://www.opensecrets.org/bigpicture/elec_stats.php?cycle = 2012.

Cillizza, C. (2013a, June 13). People want Congress to compromise. *The Washington Post.* Retrieved from www.washingtonpost.com/politics/people-want-congress-to-compromise.

Cillizza, C. (2013b, April 8). Senate has become more partisan, less collegial—more like the House. *The Washington Post.* Retrieved from www.washingtonpost.com/politics/senate-has-become-more-partisan-less-collegial.

Cillizza, C. (2013c, June 25). What the Supreme Court's Voting Rights Act decision means for politics. *The Washington Post.* Retrieved from www.washingtonpost.com/blogs/the-fix/wp/2013/06/25/what-the-voting-rights-act-decision-means-for-politics.

Clement, S. (2013, August 14). The next round of the battle over voting rights has begun. *The Washington Post.* Retrieved from http://www.washingtonpost.com/blogs/the-fix/wp/2013/08/14/n-c-voter-id-law suit-highlights-next-phase-of-voter-id-battle/.

Coghlan, A., & MacKenzie, D. (2011). Revealed—the capitalist network that runs the world. Retrieved from http://www.newscientist.com/article/mg21228354.500-revealed—the-capitalist-network-that-runs-the-world.html#.U0Ai4WzD_cs.

Cooper, D. (2013). *Raising the federal minimum wage to $10.10 would lift wages for millions and provide a modest economic boost.* Economic Policy Institute. Retrieved from www.epi.org/publication/raising-federal-minimum-wage-to-$10.10.

Coppins, M. (2011, January 10 & 17). A light on jobs in Illinois. *Newsweek,* p. 6.

Covert, B. 2013. Walmart's low wages cost taxpayers millions each year. Think Progress. Retrieved from http://thinkprogress.org/economy/2013/06/07/2120711/walmarts-low-wages-cost-taxpayers.

Crowley, M. (2010, December 13). The sacred cows. *Time,* pp. 55–58.

DiNitto, D. M. (2010). *Social welfare: Politics and public policy* (7th ed.). Boston, MA: Pearson.

Domhoff, G. W. (2013). *Who rules America? The triumph of the corporate rich* (7th ed.). Boston, MA: McGraw-Hill.

Efforts to suppress votes pop up in the states. (2013, August 29). *USA Today,* p. 6A.

Elmendorf, D. W. (2010). *Trends in federal tax revenues and rates.* Washington, DC: Congressional Budget Office.

Fang, M. (2013). *The rise of temp jobs is driving the sluggish recovery.* Think Progress. Retrieved from thinkprogress.org/economy/2013/07/01/2231821/temp-jobs-recovery/?mobile = nc.

Federal Election Commission. (2012). *Political action committees (PAC).* Retrieved from http://www.fec.gov/rad/pacs/FederalElectionCommission-RAD-PACs.shtml.

Fisher, M. (2012, August 28). GOP platform through the years shows party's shift from moderate to conservative. *The Washington Post.* Retrieved from www.washingtonpost.com/politics/gop-platform-through-the-years-shows-partys-shift.

Fletcher, M. A., & Cohen, J. (2011, February 20). Economy poll: African Americans, Hispanics were hit hardest but are most optimistic. *The Washington Post.* Retrieved from www.washingtonpost.com/wp-dyn/content/article/2011/02/20.

Freedman, M. (2009, February 16). Big government is back—big time. *Newsweek,* pp. 24–28.

Fry, R. (2013). *Young adults after the recession: Fewer homes, fewer cars, less debt.* Pew Research Social & Demographic Trends.

Retrieved from www.pewsocialtrends.org/2013/02/21/young-adults
-after-the-recession.

Gershman, J. (2014, April 2). Highlights from Justice Breyer's McCutcheon dissent. *Law Blog*. Retrieved from http://blogs.wsj.com/law
/2014/04/02/highlights-from-justice-breyers-mccutcheon-dissent/.

Gibbs, N. (2008, October 13). Real patriots don't spend. *Time*, p. 96.

Goodman, P. S. (2008, July 20). Too big to fail? *The New York Times*.
Retrieved from http://www.nytimes.com.

Granholm, J. M., & Mulhern, D. G. (2011, August 15). America's workers
get stiffed again. *Newsweek*, p. 6.

Gray, K. L. (2014, April 25). Columbus Zoo levy slammed by Americans
for Prosperity. *The Columbus* [Ohio] *Dispatch*. Retrieved from http://
www.dispatch.com/content/stories/local/2014/04/25/national-group
-asks-for-defeat-of-zoo-levy.html.

Greeley, B. (2013, January 10). Earmarks: The reluctant case for ending
the ban. *Bloomberg Businessweek*. Retrieved from http://www.bus
inessweek.com/articles/2013-01-10/earmarks-the-reluctant-case-for
-ending-the-ban.

Harkin, T. (2013, February 25). Raise the wage to $10.10 an hour. *USA
Today*, p. 8A.

Hartman, T. (2002). *Unequal protection: The rise of corporate dominance
and the theft of human rights*. New York, NY: St. Martin's Press.

Heilbroner, R. (1993). *21st century capitalism*. New York, NY: W. W.
Norton.

Henslin, J. M. (2014). *Sociology: A down-to-earth approach* (12th ed.).
Boston, MA: Pearson Education.

Herbert, B. (2006, June 20). Possible change on the killing floor. *The
State* [Columbia, SC], p. A9.

Hine, T. (2002). *I want that! How we all became shoppers. [A cultural
history]*. New York, NY: HarperCollins.

History of Federal Minimum Wage Rates. (n.d.). U.S. Department of
Labor. Retrieved from www.dol.gov/whd/minwage/chart.htm.

Horovitz, B., Alcindor, Y., Woodyard, C., MacLeod, C., & Hjelmgaard,
K. (2013, May 15). Fast food workers rally for higher wages. *USA
Today*. Retrieved from http://www.usatoday.com/story/money/busi
ness/2014/05/15/fast-food-workers-strike/9114245/.

International Institute for Democracy and Electoral Assistance (IDEA). (2013). *Voter turnout database.* Retrieved from http://www.idea.int /vt/countryview.cfm?id = -1.

Irons, E. D., & Moore, G. W. (1985). *Black managers: The case of the banking industry.* New York, NY: Praeger.

Irons, J. (2009). *Economic scarring: The long-term impacts of the recession.* Economic Policy Institute. Retrieved from www.epi.org/publi cation/bp243/.

Irwin, N. (2013, April). Who will get the spoils of an improving economy: Shareholders or workers? *The Washington Post.* Retrieved from www.washingtonpost.com/blogs/wonkblog/wp/2013/04/09/who-will -get-the-spoils-of-an-improving-economy.

Isaacs, J. (2013). *Unemployment from a child's perspective.* The Urban Institute. Retrieved from http://www.urban.org/publications/10016 71.html.

Isaacs, J., Toran, K., Hahn, H., Fortuny, K., & Steuerle, C. E. (2012). *The Urban Institute.* Retrieved from http://www.urban.org/publications /412600.html.

Jansson, B. S. (2012). *The reluctant welfare state: Engaging history to advance social work practice in contemporary society* (7th ed.). Belmont, CA: Brooks/Cole.

Johnson, D. (2013). What does it mean to be an "American" corporation? *Nation of Change.* Retrieved from www.nationofchange.org/print /37626.

Johnson, R. M., Nunns, J., Rohaly, J., Toder, E., & Williams, R. (2011). *Why some tax units pay no income tax.* Urban-Brookings Tax Policy Center. Retrieved from http://www.urban.org/uploadedpdf/1001547 -Why-No-Income-Tax.pdf.

Johnson, S. (2009). The quiet coup. *The Atlantic.* Retrieved from http:// www.theatlantic.com/doc/print/200905.

Karabell, Z. (2011, January 17). Where the jobs aren't. *Time,* p. 32.

Karger, H. J., & Stoesz, D. (2010). *American social welfare policy* (6th ed.). Boston, MA: Pearson Education.

Kendall, D. (2013). *Sociology in our times* (9th ed.). Belmont, CA: Wadsworth.

Kocieniewski, D. (2011, March 24). G.E.'s strategies let it avoid taxes altogether. *The New York Times.* Retrieved from http://www.nytimes .com/2011/03/25/business/economy/25tax.html?pagewanted = all.

Korten, D. C. (1995). *When corporations rule the world*. West Hartford, CT: Kumarian Press.

Krugman, P. (2000). *The return of depression economics*. New York, NY: W. W. Norton.

Krugman, P. (2013). Raise that wage. *The State* [Columbia, SC], p. A9.

Krugman, P. (2014, February 12). Writing off the unemployed. *The State* [Columbia, SC], p. A7.

LaLonde, R. (2007, October 17). Helping workers where it hurts. *The Washington Post*. Retrieved from http://www.washingtonpost.com.

Lawless, J. L., & Fox, R. L. (2010). *It still takes a candidate: Why women don't run for office* (Rev. ed.). New York, NY: Cambridge University Press.

Lawless, J. L., & Fox, R. L. (2012). *Men rule: The continued under-representation of women in U.S. politics*. Washington, DC: Women in Politics Institute.

Lee, E. F. (2013, March). *Election legislation 2013: Threats and opportunities assessment*. Washington, DC. Retrieved from http://projectvote .org/research-a-publications.html.

Lei, S. (2013). *27 weeks and counting: Long-term unemployment in America*. Urban Institute. Retrieved from datatools.urban.org/fea tures/longtermunemployment/index.html.

Levitt, J. (2007, November 9). *The truth about voter fraud*. Retrieved from http://www.brennancenter.org/publication/truth-about-voter -fraud.

Lewis, K. R. (2008, January 27). Consumption wasn't always pillar of economy. *The State,* [Columbia, SC], p. D2.

Lipset, S. M. (1996). *American exceptionalism: A double-edged sword*. New York, NY: W. W. Norton.

Liptak, A. (2010, January 21). Justices, 5–4, reject corporate spending limit. *The New York Times*. Retrieved from http://www.nytimes.com /2010/01/22/us/politics/22scotus.html?pagew anted = all&_r = 0.?

Liptak, A. (2013, June 25). Supreme Court invalidates key part of Voting Rights Act. *The New York Times*. Retrieved http://www.nytimes.com /2013/06/26/us/supreme-court-ruling.html?pagewanted = all&_r = 0.

Macionis, J. J. (2014). *Sociology* (15th ed.). Boston, MA: Pearson Education.

Macomber, L. (2013, May 30). Tracking the ALEC law-making machine. Retrieved from http://billmoyers.com/2013/05/30/alec-update/.

Magoc, E. (2012, August 21). Flurry of voter ID laws tied to conservative group ALEC. Retrieved from http://investigations.nbcnews.com /_news/2012/08/21/13392 560-flurry-of-voter-id-laws-tied-to-conser -vative-group-alec.

Magstadt, T. (2013). Angry white guys: The roots of reactionary America. *Nation of Change*. Retrieved from http://nationofchange.org/print /37398.

Mander, J. (1991). *In the absence of the sacred*. San Francisco, CA: Sierra Club Books.

Manning, J. E. (2013). *Membership of the 113th Congress: A profile*. Congressional Research Service. CRS 7–5700, R42964.

Maplight. (2012). *Remote control: U.S. candidates raise 51% of campaign funds from outside their states*. Retrieved from http://maplight .org/remotecontrol12.

McDonald, M. P. (2013, July 22). *2012 general election turnout*. Retrieved from http://elections.gmu.edu/Turnout_2012G.html.

McIntire, M. (2012, April 21). Conservative nonprofit acts as a stealth business lobbyist. *The New York Times*. Retrieved from http://www .nytimes.com/2012/04/22/us/alec-a-tax-exempt-group-mixes-legis lators-and-lobbyists.html?pagewanted = all&_r = 0.

McIntyre, R. S. (2013, May 23). Crack down on offshore schemes. *USA Today*, p. 10A.

Meyerson, H. (2011, January 5). Corporate America, paving a downward economic slide. *The Washington Post*. Retrieved from http://www .washingtonpost.com/wp-dyn/content/article/2011/01/04.

Meyerson, H. (2012, August 28). In modern GOP, the old South returns. *The Washington Post*. Retrieved from www.washingtonpost.com /opinions/haroldpmeyerson-in-modern-gop-the-old-south-returns.

Meyerson, H. (2013, July 1). Start the border fence in Norfolk, Va. *The Washington Post*. Retrieved from http://www.washingtonpost.com /opinions/harold-pmeyerson-start-the-border-fence-in-norfolk.

Miller, Z. (2013, November 25). Dark-money Dems: How liberals learned to stop worrying and love Citizens United. *Time*, p. 20.

Mills, C. W. (1956). *The power elite*. New York, NY: Oxford University Press.

Moore, M. T. (2013, September 19). Few women run big cities. *USA Today*, p. 7A.

Motel, S. (2013, February 15). *Statistical portrait of Hispanics in the United States, 2011*. Retrieved from http://www.pewhispanic.org /2013/02/15/statistical-portrait-of-hispanics-in-the-united-states-2011/.

Moyers, B., & Winship, M. (2013). The revolving door spins from sea to shining sea. *Nation of Change*. Retrieved from www.nationof change.org/print/36578.

National Association of Social Workers (2012a). Electoral politics. In *Social work speaks* (9th ed., pp. 105–110). Washington, DC: NASW Press.

National Association of Social Workers (2012b). Voter participation. In *Social work speaks* (9th ed., pp. 346–350). Washington, DC: NASW Press.

National Employment Law Project (NELP). (2012). *The low-wage recovery and growing inequality*. Author. Retrieved from http://www.nelp .org/page/Job_Creation/LowWageRecovery2012.pdf?nocdn = 1.

National Employment Law Project (NELP). (2013). *Super-sizing public costs: How low wages at the top fast-food chains leave taxpayers footing the bill*. Author. Retrieved from http://www.nelp.org/page /-/rtmw/uploads/NELP-Super-Sizing-Public-Costs-Fast-Food-Reports .pdf.

Newton-Small, J. (2013, October 28). The last politicians: The 20 women in the Senate are cutting deals, passing bills and looking like the only adults left in Washington. *Time*, pp. 23–28.

Nixon, R. (2013, November 7). Billionaires received U.S. farm subsidies, report finds. *The New York Times*, p. A23.

November Jobs Report: U.S. creates 203,000 jobs, unemployment rate down. (2013). *The Huffington Post*. Retrieved from http://www .huffingtonpost.com/2013/12/06/november-jobs.report-unemploy ment-rate.

Organization for Economic Co-operation and Development. (2013, March 26). *Tax burdens on labour income in OECD countries continue to rise*. Retrieved from http://www.oecd.org/newsroom/tax-bur dens-on-labour-income-in-oecd-countries-continue-to-rise.htm.

Our business. (2013). Walmart. Retrieved from http://corporate.walmart .com/our-story/our-business/.

Overholt, W. H. (2006, December 21). Globalization's unequal discontents. *The Washington Post*. Retrieved from http://www.washingtontonpost.com.

Page, S. (2012, December 24). 2012 voting brisk in swing states. *USA Today*, p. 1A.

Palmer, L. D. (2003, September/October). Original intent? How corporations became "people." *Spirituality & Health*, p. 53.

Piven, F. F., & Cloward, R. A. (1997). Low income people and the political process. In F. F. Piven & R. A. Cloward, *The breaking of the American social compact* (pp. 271–295). New York, NY: The New Press.

Political Parity (2012). *Why women*. Retrieved from http://www.politicalparity.org/why-women/.

Pope's shift creates a template for U.S. politics. (2013, December 24). *USA Today*, p. 8A.

Quindlen, A. (2004, August 9). Leap into the possible. *Newsweek*, p. 60.

Reich, R. (2011, September 18). Taxing the rich, the Obama way. *Nation of Change*. Retrieved from http://www.nationofchange.org/print/2043.

Reich, R. (2013, January 30). The non-zero sum society. *Nation of Change*. Retrieved from http://www.nationofchange.org/print/36070.

Ritzer, G. (2001). *Explorations in the sociology of consumption: Fast food, credit cards and casinos*. Thousand Oaks, CA: Sage.

Robinson, E. (2011). Starving Wisconsin's unions. *The Washington Post*. Retrieved from http://www.washingtonpost.com/wp-dyn/content/article/2011/02/21.

Robinson, E. (2012). Republican rhetoric over the top. *The Washington Post*. Retrieved from http://www.washingtonpost.com/opinions/republican- rhetoric-thatdamages-the-nation.

Romano, L. (2006, November 9). Hill demographic goes slightly more female. *The Washington Post*. Retrieved from http://www.washingtonpost.com/wp-dyn/content/article/2006/11/08/AR2006110802171.html.

Rothkopf, D. (2010, January 30). Command and control: Fixing capitalism means taking power back from business. *Time*, pp. 44–45.

Rubin, R. E., Altman, R. C., & Kearney, M. (2013, December 8). Making the poor—and the U.S.—poorer still. *The Washington Post*. Retrieved

from http://www.washingtonpost.com/opinions/making-the-poor
-and-the-us-poorer-still/2013/12/08/cda50c26-5dd1-11e3-95c2-1362
3eb2b0e1_story.html.

Samuelson, R. J. (2010, October 25). The dysfunction of American politics. *The Washington Post.* Retrieved from http://www.washington
post.comwp-dyn/content/article/2010/10/24.

Samuelson, R. J. (2014, February 19). Why the IAW lost. *The Washington Post.* Retrieved from http://www.washingtonpsot.com/opinions.rob
ert-samuelson-why-the-uaw-lost/2014/ 02/19.

Saporito, B. (2011). Where the jobs are. *Time,* pp. 26–35.

Schouten, F. (2012a, December 7). Casino CEO put millions into effort to oust dems. *USA Today,* p. 7A.

Schouten, F. (2012b, November 8). Deep-pocketed donors pay the price. *USA Today,* p. 9A.

Schouten, F. (2013, June 11). Watchdogs on lookout for 'dark money.' *USA Today,* p. 5A.

Schouten, F., & Korte, G. (2013, December 24). Proposed IRS rule could hurt voter registration. *USA Today,* p. 2A.

Schouten, F., Schnaars, C., & Korte, G. (2012, February 2). Individuals, not corporations, drive super PAC financing. *USA Today,* p. 7A.

Schrotenboer, B. (2013, May 30). Tax exempt under fire. *USA Today,* p. 2C.

Shegreen, D. (2013, June 20). 1959 IRS rule at center of tea party flap. *USA Today,* p. 4A.

Shierholz, H., & Gould, E. (2011). *A lost decade: Poverty and income trends continue to paint a bleak picture for working families.* Economic Policy Institute. Retrieved from http://www.epi.org/publica
tion/lost-decade-poverty-income-trends-continue/.

Smith, A. (1937/1776). *An inquiry into the nature and causes of the wealth of nations.* New York, NY: Modern Library.

Stockard, J. (2000). *Sociology: Discovering society* (2nd ed.). Belmont, CA: Wadsworth/Thomson Learning.

Swers, M. L. (2002). *The difference women make.* Chicago, IL: University of Chicago Press.

Taylor, P., & Lopez, M. H. (2013). *Six take-aways from the Census Bureau's voting report.* Pew Research Center. Retrieved from http://

www.pewresearch.org/2013/05/08/six-take-aways-from-the-census-bureaus-voting-report.

Thio, A. (1998). *Sociology* (5th ed.). New York, NY: Longman.

Thomas, K., & Peoples, S. (2013, May 19). IRS probe ignored larger, big budget groups. *USA Today*, p. A5.

Trinko, K. (2013, August 5). Fast-food workers need to flip culture. *USA Today*, p. 6A.

Trumbull, M. (2014, May 15). Why do fast-food workers strike? No occupation is lower paid. *The Christian Science Monitor.* Retrieved from http://www.csmonitor.com/Business/2014/0515/Why-do-fast-food-workersstrike-No-occupation-is-lower-paid. Uchitelle, L. (2003, October 5). U.S. companies 'offshoring' jobs. *The State* [Columbia, SC], p. A14.

Uchitelle, L. (2006). *The disposable American: Layoffs and their consequences.* New York, NY: Knopf.

United States Department of Labor (2013). *Minimum wage laws in the states*. Retrieved from http://www.dol.gov/whd/minwage/america.htm.

vanden Heuvel, K. (2011, July 12). Time for a grand bargain on jobs. *The Washington Post*. Retrieved from http://www.washingtonpost.com/opinions/time-for-a-grand-bargain-on-jobs/2011/07/11/gIQA7ocgAI_story.html.

Verba, S., Schlozman, K. L., & Brady, H. (1995). *Voice and equality: Civic volunteerism in American politics*. Cambridge, MA: Harvard University Press.

Wallechinsky, D. (2007, January 14). Is America still no. 1? *Parade*, pp. 4–5.

Weber, M. (1978/1922). *Economy and society*. G. Roth and C. Wittich (Eds.). Berkeley, CA: University of California Press.

Weiner, R. (2013, April 29). Black voters turned out at higher rate than white voters in 2012 and 2008. *The Washington Post*. Retrieved from http://washingtonpost.com/blogs/the-fix/wp/2013/04/29/black-turnout-was-higher.

Winn, P. (2012, September 10). The true cost of "Made in the USA" Levi's? $178. Retrieved from http://www.globalpost.com/dispatches/globalpost-blogs/america-the-gutted/levis-blue-jeans.

Wolf, R. (2013, August 26). On March's 50th anniversary, voting rights still an issue. *USA Today*, p. 1A–2A.

Yip, P. (2007, November 25). Another day older and deeper in debt. *The State* [Columbia, SC], pp. D1, D4.

Zakaria, F. (2010, November 1). Restoring the American dream. *Time*, pp. 30–35.

Zakaria, F. (2011, August 4). The debt deal's failure. *Time*, pp. 25–28.

CHAPTER THREE

Government-Related Social Institutions

Criminal Justice

Issues and Trends in the Criminal Justice System

Crime Rates and Violence

Incarceration Rates

Privatization

The Death Penalty

Understanding the Criminal Justice System

Functionalist Perspective

Conflict Perspective

Rational/Social Exchange Perspective

Constructionist Perspective

Relationship of the Criminal Justice System to the Political Economy

The Impact of the Criminal Justice System on Individuals and Families

How the Criminal Justice System Deters Well-Being

The Criminal Justice System and Minorities

The Criminal Justice System and Social Class

The Criminal Justice System and Gender

The Criminal Justice System and Children and Youth

The Criminal Justice System and Older Adults

The Criminal Justice System and People with Mental Illness

Diversion of Resources

How the Criminal Justice System Promotes Well-Being

The Military

Issues and Trends in the Military

Women in the Military

Gays in the Military

In this chapter, we present three social institutions that are, for the most part, government supported. These social institutions, education, criminal justice, and the military, are particularly important in the lives of many social work clients. We discuss the relationship of each of these social institutions to the political economy and their impact on individuals and families. Because most social work students take entire courses on social welfare, we will not cover this particular social institution.

EDUCATION

The function of education is to pass along a society's formal knowledge and skills in a systematic way, with emphasis on learning that will contribute to students' futures as workers and as citizens. Typically this involves formal instruction by credentialed teachers, within special organizations (schools) designed for the purpose.

Issues and Trends in Education

Decreasing Tax Support for Public Education at All Levels

In general, funding for K–12 education in the United States has been cut significantly only twice, once during the Great Depression and once during World War II. Nevertheless, according to a 2012 report, "three states—Alaska, Alabama and Washington—cut more than $200 per student between 2011 and 2012 and another three states—Arizona, Alabama and Oklahoma—slashed per-student funding by more than 20 percent since 2008. ("Education funding drops in more than half of states," 2012). Still recovering from the Great Recession, in 2012, thirty-five states were still spending at levels lower than before the Great Recession. Areas that are particularly vulnerable to cuts are early childhood programs; art, music, and physical education; teacher:student ratios; and specialized programs such as sports, science, foreign languages, technology, and advanced placement subjects.

Across the country state legislatures have been cutting funding for higher education. According to the State Higher Education Executive Officers Association (Malcolm & McMinn, 2013), since the Great Recession forty-eight states have cut funding for public colleges and universities while just two have increased it. Between 2007 and 2012 fifteen states cut higher education funding per full-time students by 30 percent or more. As public colleges and universities lose state funding, they have come to rely more and more heavily on income from increased tuition and fees, research grants, lottery funds, and philanthropists, and they cut costs by reducing services, cutting back on scholarships and assistantships, increasing class size, hiring more part-time faculty, and using technology to reach a larger market through online education. They also have recruited more out-of-state and international students—who pay higher tuition.

The costs of attending an institution of higher education have increased faster than the rate of inflation, family income, and student aid funds. According to a report from the College Board summarized in the *Chronicle of Higher Education* (Supiano, 2013), prices have generally risen over the past twenty years and more than doubled at four-year public colleges. The College Board tracks both the published price (or "sticker" cost) and the net price, which is "the average price paid by all fulltime students, on financial aid or not, after subtracting all grant aid and federal tax benefits" (p. A3). For the academic year 2013–2014, the average net price for tuition and fees for in-state students at public four-year colleges totaled $3,120, and it was $12,460 for students at private, nonprofit four-year institutions. Full-time students at public two-year colleges received sufficient benefits to have $1,550 left over after paying tuition and fees to help pay for living expenses.

Seven in ten undergraduate students receive some form of financial aid (e.g., grants, loans, work-study, veterans' benefits, and so forth) (Snider, 2013). For the most part loans are payable in a ten-year period. Repayments begin six months after a student leaves school, and student loans cannot be discharged through bankruptcy. At for-profit colleges 92 percent of students take out loans, compared to 60 percent at private not-for-profit colleges and 27 percent at public schools ("For-profit schools don't hold key to lower college costs," 2012). Most of the schools with the highest average default rate (former students who fail to make on-time repayments for 270 days or more) were those run by for-profit companies (Marklein, 2013).

In 2013 major news outlets described outstanding student loan debt as "massive," with a total exceeding $1 trillion nationwide—more than the nation's combined credit card debt. In 1993, less than half of students graduated with debt (Meyers, 2013).

Special Programs and Schools

Of particular interest to social workers are those schools and programs that were developed to address perceived deficiencies in the public education system. These include Head Start, charter schools, magnet schools, and voucher plans.

In the middle 1960s, the federal government began funding *Head Start*, a remedial program for disadvantaged preschoolers designed to give them the skills they need to be ready for kindergarten and first grade. According to the U.S. Department of Health and Human Services, Head Start is based on a "whole child" model; in addition to education, the program provides medical, dental, and nutritional services and parental guidance. Head Start services are "designed to be responsive to each child's and family's ethnic, cultural, and linguistic heritage" (U.S. Department of Health and Human Services, 2005, p. iii). Whereas "there is some evidence suggesting that positive effects of Head Start may have an impact on participants' later life, such as later school success and early adulthood outcomes," recent studies seem to indicate that most impacts have dissipated by early elementary school (Puma et al., 2012, p. 151).

Charter schools are supported by public funds but operate more like private schools because they do not answer to a local school board. These have been in existence only since the early 1990s. In 1999–2000, there were 1,524 charter schools in the United States, serving 339,678 students; by 2009–2010 there were 4,952 charter schools serving 1,611,332 students (Janssen, 2013). The racial background of children in charter schools is 37.3 percent white, 30.3 percent black, 26.1 percent Hispanic, 3.8 percent Asian, and 2.5 percent other. The majority of public school students in New Orleans attend public charter schools, the highest percentage in the nation (Carr, 2009.)

Magnet schools are public schools that offer special facilities and curricula, focusing on areas such as science or the arts. The term *magnet* refers to the way that these schools draw students from outside usual district lines. They were developed in the 1960s in urban areas to hold onto middle-class students who might have otherwise chosen to attend a private school.

In the fall of 2011, there were 30,861 private elementary and secondary schools in the United States, with almost 4.5 million students; 68 percent of private schools had a religious orientation (Broughman & Swaim, 2013). The proportion of children attending private schools in the United States has ranged between 10 and 14 percent since 1930. Under *voucher plans* (also called *school choice*) parents can send their children to a private school and the government pays part or all of their tuition. The idea is to make public schools improve in order to compete for students. Opponents worry that private schools are not accountable to public scrutiny and that these plans violate the principle of separation of church and state by providing tax-based funding to religious schools. They argue that these plans take much-needed monies away from already underfunded public schools, and they encourage racial and ethnic segregation. In 2011–2012, 71 percent of private school students were white, 10 percent were Hispanic or Latino, 9 percent were African American, 5 percent were Asian, and 3 percent were of two or more races (Broughman & Swaim, 2013).

An increasing number of families in the United States are choosing to *homeschool* their children. In 1999, 850,000 students were homeschooled and in 2007 there were 1,508,000 (2.9 percent of the school age population) (Janssen, 2013). In the early years of the movement, parents reported religious motives for keeping their children at home. In a 2007 national survey, 87.6 percent of homeschooling parents expressed concerns about the public school environment, including safety, drugs, and peer pressure; 83.6 percent expressed a desire to provide religious or moral instruction; and an additional 72.7 percent expressed dissatisfaction with academic instruction in schools (U.S. Department of Education Survey cited in Janssen, 2013, p. 417). Most homeschooled children are involved in various extracurricular activities with same-age peers, including field trips sponsored by homeschooling organizations, sports, Scouting, 4-H, and church activities.

The *World Almanac* (Janssen, 2013) provides the following information about homeschooling. In 2007, 76.8 percent of homeschooled children were white, 9.8 percent were Hispanic, and 4.0 percent were black.

Homeschooling is spread evenly across economic levels. More than one in eight (13.7 percent) of homeschooling parents have not completed education beyond high school; 36.4 percent have some college, 29.4 percent hold bachelor's degrees, and 20.5 percent have some graduate or professional schooling.

Homeschooling is legal in all fifty U.S. states, but in many European countries it is illegal or closely monitored. In Germany, parents can lose custody of their children for homeschooling; in Spain and in the Netherlands, it is allowed only under exceptional circumstances.

Bullying and Violence

Several recent high-profile cases reported in the media have led some to characterize school bullying as a "national epidemic" (Toppo, 2012). Bullying is defined as "behavior that is intended to inflict harm, repeated over time, and characterized by an imbalance of power between the perpetrator(s) and victim(s)" (Calbom, 2012). A national survey found that more than one in four students (28 percent)—mostly middle- and high school age—said they had been bullied at school, with 19 percent reporting being made fun of, called names, or insulted, and 9 percent shoved, tripped, or spit on (Calbom, 2012). Eighteen states have passed laws allowing victims to seek legal remedies for bullying from the bullies and their families, or from schools that do not act, thirty-two states require that schools have procedures for investigating bullying incidents, and nine states require administrators to report bullying to police (Toppo, 2012). A 2005–2009 U.S. Department of Education survey report revealed that almost one in ten seventh-graders reported being bullied every day (Toppo, 2012).

Given the recent history of high-profile school shootings in this country, neither children nor parents believe that schools are safe places. On December 14, 2012, twenty first-graders and six teachers and administrators were shot and killed at Sandy Hook Elementary School in Newtown, Connecticut. In subsequent months Congress was unable to pass new gun control laws, but many school districts have hired additional security, and others are exploring recommendations to arm classroom teachers and other school personnel.

After the 1999 Columbine school shooting, many school districts adopted "zero tolerance" policies. These policies punish any infraction of a rule, regardless of accidental mistakes, ignorance, or extenuating circumstances, often with suspension or expulsion. Egregious examples of overreaction are often found in the popular press, such as when a kindergarten student was suspended for ten days in January 2013 for referring to "shooting" a friend with a plastic Hello Kitty bubble-making gun. In a summary of research studies, an American Psychological Association task force concluded that zero tolerance policies have not been shown to improve school climate or school safety (American Psychological Association Zero Tolerance Task Force, 2008).

Statistics show that the number of violent deaths in K–12 school settings in the United States averaged about 45 per year between 1992/1993 and 2010/2011, varying from a high of 57 in the first year of that period to a low of 31 in the last year (Toppo, 2013). Federal data summaries do not yet include 2011/12 or 2012/2013, when the Newtown shooting occurred.

The U.S. Department of Education reported that about 4 percent of public school teachers were physically attacked during the 2007–2008 school year (Thompson, 2013). A survey conducted in 2011 found that 80 percent of teachers stated that they had been intimidated, harassed, assaulted, or otherwise victimized at least once during the previous year (Thompson, 2013). The American Psychological Association surveyed 3,000 teachers and documented that 44 percent reported physical offenses that included thrown objects, student attacks, and weapons shown (Thompson, 2013).

Growth in Community Colleges

Since the 1960s, community colleges have provided access to higher education for many students. According to the National Center for Education Statistics (2008), the country's 1,844 two-year colleges enroll 39 percent of all undergraduate college students. The advantages of community colleges include low cost, easier access for minority students, and a focus on teaching rather than research (Macionis, 2014; National Center for Education Statistics, 2007). Average annual community college tuition and fees are less than half of those at public four-year colleges and universities and they have larger percentages of nontraditional, low-income, and minority students (National Center for Education Statistics, 2008). Nevertheless, in the past twenty years the number of graduates with associate degrees has increased by only 3 percent (Community College Research Center, 2013).

Resegregation in Public Schools

Due in large part to residential segregation, public schools are increasingly filled with students of the same racial and economic background (Holland & Hefling, 2014; Phillips, 2007; Rothstein, 2013). According to a report from the Civil Rights Project at the University of California at Los Angeles (Orfield, 2009), the most serious segregation affects Latinos and African Americans; in these groups almost two out of five children attend an "intensely segregated" school (90 to 100 percent minority). White students are more likely to be in schools that are middle class, whereas 40 percent of black and Latino students attend schools where 70 to 100 percent of the children are poor (Orfield, 2009).

According to the UCLA study (Orfield, 2009), patterns vary by locale. In metropolitan areas, with few exceptions, public schools are made up of nonwhite and poor student bodies. Of the nearly six million black and Latino suburban students, almost two million are in heavily segregated schools; this suggests that in some suburban areas, there is substantial resegregation. The term *de facto segregation* can be used to describe the pattern of racial segregation in schools that results from segregated housing. On the other hand, the typical white child enrolled in a public school today finds himself or herself in a more diverse classroom environment than white children a generation ago. Both the increased exposure to diversity for white children and the growth in isolation for black and Latino children are due to the decline in the number and proportion of white students and the increase in the number of children of color in public school systems. According to the author of the study, "the U.S. is experiencing the final years of a majority white public school system" and if current trends continue, "segregation will become even more pronounced for black and Latino students" (Orfield, 2009, p. 27).

An example of recent resegregation patterns can be found in North Carolina, where the number of 90 percent minority districts has increased almost fivefold since 1999 (Dokoupil, 2010). The results are mirrored throughout the South. According to an article in *The Hechinger Report* (Richard, 2013), in Mississippi schools are as segregated as they were in the 1960s. In towns where African Americans are in the majority, most white children attend small private schools founded around the time of court-mandated desegregation in the late 1960s. This type of public-private school segregation is commonplace from East Texas through northern Florida up to Virginia and Maryland in majority-black small towns and rural communities. When children are separated, resources are divided and taxpayer support is uncertain. The result is poor-quality education.

Segregation is still common in other areas of the country as well. More than half of African American students in Illinois, New York, Maryland, and Michigan attend schools where 90 percent or more of their peers are minority, and in California, Texas, and New York about 57 percent of Latino children attend schools that are majority Latino (Holland & Hefling, 2014).

Rothstein (2013) says that policy makers should not be focused on the lack of racial and ethnic diversity, or even on improving ghetto schools. Instead he argues that they also should be concerned about impoverished neighborhood environments; "housing policy is school policy," Rothstein notes (p. 19). His recommendation to address poor school performance is that low-income minority families living in concentrated poverty areas in central cities be dispersed through the establishment of subsidized housing in white suburbs.

National Education Standards

The No Child Left Behind Act (NCLB) was signed into law by President George W. Bush in 2002 and reauthorized in 2007. Beginning in academic year 2005–2006, all public schools needed to measure students' achievement in reading and math every year for grades 3 through 8 and once in high school, but since 2007 the Department of Education has issued waivers that have released nearly every state from the law's toughest deadlines.

Common Core was initiated by the bipartisan National Governors' Association and the Council of Chief State School Officers and developed by teachers and researchers (Ripley, 2013). According to a professor in the College of Education at the University of South Carolina, one purpose was to avoid the NCLB problem where some states set low test benchmarks on state-made tests and had nearly all their students meet NCLB expectations, but other states set high benchmarks on their own tests and give the appearance of having a weak education program (personal communication, Edwin M. Dickey, September 1, 2013). The standards also were explicitly designed to reflect what colleges and employers expect high school graduates to be able to do (Ripley, 2013).

As of September 2013, forty-six states had adopted Common Core standards and had agreed to test students on them by 2014–2015 and twenty-eight states and the District of Columbia had fully implemented the standards in reading and math (Konz, 2013; Ripley, 2013). The purpose of Common Core is to diminish the large discrepancy among state and school district standards. Under Common Core, all students would be required to earn the same number of credits and take the same sequence of courses. Thus students moving from one state to another would not have to repeat information they had learned at their previous school or miss information their new peers had covered already. According to an experienced school social worker, this is particularly helpful to children in military families that relocate often (personal communication, Kimberly Fleischer, August 31, 2013). Conservative critics and some state legislators view Common Core as an unwarranted federal influence over education, misreading it as a federal mandate rather than a state-level, voluntary adoption of an alternative to the No Child Left Behind initiative (Konz, 2013; Self, 2013). Common Core is also being attacked by some teachers' unions.

Education in Global Perspective

For years the United States was ranked highest in education outcomes measures. According to a national study (Kielstra, 2012), now Finland, South Korea, Hong Kong, Japan, Singapore, and Great Britain are at the top of the rankings, based on measures that include international test scores, graduation rates between 2006 and 2010, and national scores in terms of student achievement. Canada ranked tenth, and the United States ranked seventeenth out of the top twenty-one developed countries. The study concluded that funding is important, but so is having a culture that is supportive of learning (Kielstra, 2012).

There is growing recognition of the importance of early childhood education, but the United States ranks far behind other industrialized nations in this area. Only about 28 percent of four-year-olds and 4 percent of three-year-olds currently attend public pre-K programs (Kamenetz, 2014). In Germany and Japan more than 95 percent of four-year-olds are enrolled in early childhood education.

In contrast, for countries that are the least industrialized there is continuing concern about basic literacy, even though rates are improving. According to the United Nations Education, Scientific and Cultural Organization (UNESCO, 2012), in half of all countries providing data, the literacy rate is 95 percent, with young women aged 15 to 24 making the strongest improvements. Nevertheless, 775 million adults worldwide cannot read or write and two-thirds of these are women.

Understanding the Education System

Functionalist Perspective

In addition to the function of transmitting knowledge and teaching skills, structural functionalists suggest that the education system sorts children and youth and then trains them to fill positions at different levels in society. These theorists believe that schools fill a gatekeeping function by identifying the most qualified individuals, selecting them for advanced education, and channeling them toward leadership positions.

The education system also socializes the young, instilling values of respect, obedience, punctuality, and perseverance. Particularly in the case of mandatory and free public schooling, education serves the purpose of acculturation for the young children of recent immigrants. This is especially important in a country with as much diversity as the United States.

Social institutions have both manifest and latent functions. *Manifest functions* are those that are intended and obvious. *Latent functions* are unintended side effects, and those functions that are often hidden, or at least not acknowledged by participants. Some of these may be positive and some may be negative. Besides the obvious manifest functions of education, this social institution also has latent functions. These include providing free child care and supervision for a significant part of the day—which is particularly helpful for parents who are employed outside the home. Another latent function is keeping adolescents out of the labor market where they might compete for jobs with unskilled adults.

Conflict Perspective

Social conflict theorists argue that school systems in the United States perpetuate class inequality. This is achieved by *tracking*, or ability grouping, based on standardized tests that magnify small differences (Tobias, 1989). Poor and minority students are assigned to remedial and vocational skills classes where they receive a diluted academic program, making it unlikely that they will ever catch up to their white, middle-class peers (Kozol, 2005; Oakes, 1985; Tobias, 1989).

The financial costs of higher education prevent many people with below-average incomes from enrolling. When only the affluent can afford to attend prestigious colleges or restrictive programs, social and economic privilege is reinterpreted as personal merit (Macionis, 2014). Our society reserves the most desirable occupational opportunities for those who have four-year or graduate degrees, even if educational attainment is unrelated to the demands and responsibilities of a particular job. In this way, credentialism (evaluating a person on the basis of his or her educational background) is used as a strategy to restrict certain careers to a small (and privileged) segment of the population (Collins, 1979).

Gillborn (1992) used the term *hidden curriculum* to describe how schools teach obedience to authority and conformity to cultural norms in addition to the academic curriculum. Learning the student role prepares children for the routines of the work world. Conflict theorists note that middle- and upper-class youth are more likely to be encouraged to think critically and creatively, thus preparing them for leadership roles, while the behaviors of lower-class children are shaped to accommodate the demands of the assembly line and the clerical pool.

Rational/Social Exchange Perspective

Although some property owners complain that they have to pay high taxes even when they have no children in the public school system, most taxpayers understand the need for educated citizens and workers. (One of the authors has a T-shirt with this slogan on the front: IF YOU THINK EDUCATION IS EXPENSIVE, TRY IGNORANCE). As a technologically advanced society, the United States relies on a literate workforce and must provide at least a basic education to all members of society to prepare them for their roles as citizens.

Constructionist Perspective

Social constructionists remind us of the importance of perceptions. Jonathan Kozol, who conducted a study that highlighted the alarming differences in funding levels between affluent suburban schools and inner-city schools, noted the effects of perceptions that "the poorest districts are beyond help" and that resources would thus be "wasted on poor children" (Kozol, 1991, p. 99). He concluded that these "children hear and understand [that] they are poor investments—and behave accordingly . . . . Expectations are a powerful force."

The application of the social constructionist perspective to the education system has focused for the most part on *labeling theory* and *self-fulfilling prophecy* (Merton, 1949). Basically, this suggests two parallel processes. The first affects the students individually. Once labeled "slow" or "a behavior problem," students will come to accept the label and act accordingly. Even when nonpejorative labels are used (e.g., "sharks" or "goldfish"), children know to which level they have been assigned (Tobias, 1989). The second process affects the teachers. Once they believe that a child is "bright" or "struggling," they will respond to the child according to their expectations of how that child will perform—challenging the bright ones and "dumbing down" lessons for the less able children, thus unintentionally creating the results that were predicted. The effects of the labeling process were confirmed in a classic study conducted in the 1960s (Rosenthal & Jacobson, 1968), when elementary teachers were told that certain randomly selected students were "spurters" or "nonspurters," and those in the "spurter" groups subsequently made greater gains.

In another classic study, Ray Rist (1970) observed that after only eight days of class, a kindergarten teacher divided her students into three groups. The "slow learners" were put at a table in the back of the room and the "fast learners" sat at a table next to the teacher's desk. As the year progressed, the fast learners came to think of themselves as smart and the teacher treated them as such. The children in the back of the classroom received little attention. Rist himself concluded that the divisions were based on social class, as there had not been any testing done early in the semester. The same classroom divisions were retained in the first and second grades, thus consigning many students to a long-term negative educational experience based on one teacher's uninformed assessment less than two weeks into their school careers.

Relationship of the Education System to the Political Economy

The education system in the United States reflects the political economy in several ways. Schools foster patriotism by teaching lessons in history, civics, and other social studies. Further, the values of individualism and competition assumed to be crucial to a capitalist economy are promoted in the schools.

Schools also provide captive audiences for advertisers. By accepting corporate donations or sponsorships, brand loyalty is introduced and consumerism is reinforced. Market-driven educational materials are integrated into the school day. For example, Exxon has produced a documentary on the beauty of the Alaskan coastline, McDonald's has created a nutrition chart, and kindergartners are taught to read through a program that uses corporate logos (Kilbourne, 1999, p. 46). While Channel One is offered free to school systems as a teaching tool for current events using a twelve-minute daily broadcast, its corporate parent says that it serves as a direct pipeline for advertisers seeking to reach the teen market (Croteau & Hoynes, 2014, p. 64). A research study (Austin, Chen, Pinkleton, & Johnson, 2006) found that students who watched Channel One were more likely to remember the ads than the news content. According to the Channel One website, the programs are broadcast to almost 5 million children across the United States. In 2010 that included about 8,000 schools (Ford, 2010). Another way that for-profit businesses intrude into the school environment is through placing advertisements on lockers and school buses and paying for naming rights to libraries, computer labs, and cafeterias (Ford, 2010).

Some leading academics (see Bok, 2003; Gould, 2003) are concerned about the increasing commercialization of institutions of higher education. With rising enrollments exceeding revenues, many schools are becoming more entrepreneurial (Raines & Leathers, 2003). Changes in their missions reflect an increasing emphasis on research, particularly in areas expected to produce commercially profitable intellectual property, and less on educating the future citizens of their state. "Hustling for dollars" has become a major focus, with practices ranging from promotion of corporate-academic partnerships to selling naming rights to buildings or even restricting sales of soft drinks to a single brand (Brinson, 2003). Universities are put in the position of marketing themselves in competition against each other, for students as well as for cash (Brewer, Gates, & Goldman, 2002). For example, in order to make profits from their sports programs, universities reschedule major conference games to meet the broadcast demands of television sports executives, even though fans are inconvenienced, student athletes have to miss classes, and midterm exams are disrupted (Morris, 2003). To attract new students, university campuses have added or updated amenities such as elaborate exercise facilities, high-end coffee shops, and more online courses. A prime example of the entrepreneurial spirit in higher education is the appeal of the University of Phoenix, which offers online degrees in business, criminal justice, education, human services, nursing, psychology, and technology. Profits in distance learning are huge because distance learning requires no classrooms or parking lots; the same courses can be updated and repackaged and sold over and over again.

The Impact of the Education System on Individuals and Families

How the Education System Deters Well-Being.

State sources contribute less than half of public elementary and high school revenue, with the rest coming from the federal government and local property taxes, and much of the federal monies go to special programs (Kendall, 2013). Schools in wealthier communities or neighborhoods have more resources, while schools in poorer communities or neighborhoods have fewer resources. The result is great discrepancies in the quality of education provided to children living in different communities.

As discussed under the "Conflict Perspective" section, tracking is usually based on the results of standardized tests. Such tests measure not only intelligence and aptitude but also culturally acquired knowledge. Because IQ tests reflect the dominant culture, members of minority cultures will remain at a disadvantage. African American children are over-represented in special education classes.

African American students are suspended and expelled at rates higher than white students, reflecting different disciplinary responses by teachers and administrators (George, 2011a; George, 2011b). In a statewide analysis of 6.6 million records that examined every Texas seventh-grader from 2000 through 2002 and tracked them for the next six years or more, researchers at Texas A&M University found that African American students had a 31 percent higher likelihood of being disciplined for discretionary offenses, such as disrespect, defiance, insubordination, disruption, and foul language, compared with whites and Hispanics. Such offenses allow educators significant latitude in how they respond.

According to one study (Delpit, 1995), rather than embracing diversity in the classroom, many white teachers, out of misdirected goodwill, make a conscious effort to be "color blind." Insensitivity to cultural differences in learning and communication styles hinders minority children, leading to low self-esteem and negative school experiences. For example, Heath (1982) observed that African American children seemed unresponsive to teachers' questions. She discovered that the students thought that questions such as "What is this?" or "What do you call that?" were silly because obviously the teacher already knew the answer. The children came from communities where people asked open-ended questions about whole events: "What did you do today?" or "What did you like best about your field trip?" In their homes caregivers accepted many different answers and the answers almost always involved telling a story, describing a situation, or making a comparison.

Children from cultural backgrounds with collectivist rather than individualist traditions may go out of their way to help each other; some teachers perceive this as cheating or not "doing their own work" (Gallimore, Boggs, & Jordan, 1974). Because of their strong cultural value of humility, Asian American children may hesitate to ask questions of the teacher or to take credit for, or show pride in, their work. Teachers need to take this into account when evaluating the classroom interaction of these students.

Children and families with limited English face extra challenges in dealing with school systems. Obstacles include the lack of bilingual teachers, the inability to communicate with school personnel, and the inability to understand school correspondence sent to the child's home (Dale, Andreatta, & Freeman, 2001). Some migrant worker parents report being intimidated by the educational system even when language assistance is available. According to Fry (2007), almost half (46 percent) of fourth-grade students in the English language learner (ELL) category scored "below basic" in math and nearly three-quarters scored "below basic" in reading. In middle school, more than two-thirds (71 percent) of eighth-grade ELL students scored "below basic" in math and the same proportion scored "below basic" in reading. The overall result of such factors is that Latino children have a higher dropout rate than other racial and ethnic groups (Janssen, 2013).

Graduation rates vary dramatically by state. For the class of 2009, the average freshman graduation rate ranged from 56.3 percent in Nevada to 90.7 in Wisconsin (Janssen, 2013). Another way to measure dropout rates is to examine the number of 16- to 24-year-olds who are not in school and have not earned a high school diploma or GED. According to the U.S. Census (Janssen, 2013), data for 2010 indicate that 7.4 percent of the young people in this age group fell into this category. Males in this age group are more likely than females to be high school dropouts (8.5 percent versus 6.3 percent). The rate for whites was 5.1 percent, and for blacks the rate was 8.0 percent. Hispanics had the highest dropout rate at 15.1 percent, which was down from 22.4 percent in 2005. (Data for Native Americans and Asian-Pacific Islanders were not included in the report.)

Dropout rates are also related to socioeconomic status. The dropout rate (10 percent) for students in the lowest income quintile (fifth) of the population is six times greater than the dropout rate (1.6 percent) for students in the highest quintile (National Center for Education Statistics, 2007). In other words, students who drop out are more likely to come from families where parents also are likely to have had little schooling.

This pattern perpetuates intergenerational cycles of disadvantage. Data show that there has been little change in dropout rates by income level since 1990.

Dropout rates also vary along urban–suburban dimensions. Only about half (52 percent) of students in the country's 50 largest cities complete high school; in the most extreme cases (Baltimore, Cleveland, Detroit, and Indianapolis), fewer than 35 percent of students graduate with a diploma (Swanson, 2008).

Enrollment in college is affected by family income as well as test scores. Multiple studies have demonstrated that a higher proportion of lower-scoring students from wealthy families attend college compared with those from lower-class families, and high-scoring students from lower-class families are less likely to attend college than their peers from affluent families (Henslin, 2014).

How the Education System Promotes Well-Being

This country has led the world in the proportion of young people completing different levels of mass education, first for elementary and high schools, and later for colleges and graduate schools (Lipset, 1996, p. 21). In 1940, only 24.5 percent of the U.S. population had completed high school; in 2009, that figure had increased to 86.7 percent (Wright, 2010). In 1940, fewer than one in twenty Americans had completed four or more years of college; in 2009, it was almost three in ten (Wright, 2010).

Within the past generation, federal laws have enhanced the opportunities for children with disabilities. The Equal Education for All Handicapped Children Act (PL 94–142) was passed in 1975. Renamed the Individuals with Disabilities Education Act in 1990, it mandates that students with disabilities receive a free and appropriate education. Many schools have *mainstreamed* children with disabilities so that they can attend classes with their nondisabled peers, as well as have access to special education teachers and classrooms, speech therapists, occupational therapists, and physical therapists.

Federal laws have also enhanced opportunities for female athletes in school settings. Historically, most women had little opportunity for involvement in high school and college sports. Title IX of the Educational

Amendments of 1972 prohibited sex discrimination in educational institutions receiving federal funds. This law has led to more funding for women's athletics.

Many schools also go beyond instruction to meet some of the more basic daily needs of poor children. They provide screening for visual and hearing problems, some provide dental and mental health services, and most have school nurses. In 2008, more than 30 million children participated in the national school lunch program (U.S. Department of Agriculture, 2008). The program was established under the National School Lunch Act, signed by President Harry Truman in 1946. Under the Seamless Summer Option, schools can continue to feed children from low-income areas during traditional summer vacation periods. Under the Community Eligibility Option of the Healthy, Hunger-Free Kids Act of 2010, low-income school districts (those with more than 40 percent of students receiving food stamps or other federal aid) can offer free lunches to all children (Murphy, 2013). Currently employed in Boston, Atlanta, Washington, DC, and Grand Rapids, Michigan, the program will be available nationwide starting in the 2014–2015 school year. The program has the effect not only of easing hunger but also of facilitating the handling of paperwork and of erasing the stigma that children of poor families face when they are singled out for reduced-cost or free lunches (Murphy, 2013).

According to the website of the School Social Work Association of America (SSWAA) "school social workers bring unique knowledge and skills to the school system and the student services team. In particular, school social workers are trained in mental health concerns, behavioral concerns, positive behavioral support, academic and classroom support, consultation with teachers, parents and administrators as well as with individual and group counseling techniques. . . . School social workers are hired by school districts to enhance the district's ability to meet its academic mission, especially where home, school and community collaboration is the key to achieving student success" (SSWAA, 2012). Among the services they provide are biopsychosocial assessments, crisis intervention, family counseling, home/school/community liaison, individual therapy and counseling, mediation, small group therapy and counseling, case management, consultation, parent education, referrals, resource procurement, and grant writing (Kontak, 2008).

CRIMINAL JUSTICE

The social institution of criminal justice is America's formal system of social control. It includes a loose confederation of more than 55,000 agencies at the local, state, and federal levels that often operate independently of each other (Kendall, 2013). The criminal justice system represents the parts of government that have the political mandate to protect members of society, but abuses of power can also unfairly strip citizens of their freedoms. The system includes a variety of law enforcement organizations (e.g., local police, county sheriffs, federal marshals, Alcohol, Tobacco, and Firearms [ATF] agents, Immigration and Customs Enforcement [ICE] agents, and the courts and facilities for the incarceration of offenders [e.g., detention centers, jails, and prisons]).

There are many outspoken critics of the American criminal justice system. Currie (1998, p. 8), for example, states, "If we look squarely at the present state of crime and punishment in America . . . it is difficult to avoid the recognition that something is terribly wrong; that a society that incarcerates such a vast and rapidly growing part of its population—but still suffers the worst violent crime in the industrial world—is a society in trouble, one that, in a profound sense, has lost its bearings."

Issues and Trends in the Criminal Justice System

Crime Rates and Violence

There are three major sources of crime statistics in the United States (the FBI's Uniform Crime Reports, the National Incident-Based Reporting System [NIBRS], and the National Crime Victimization Survey), and each uses a different method of collecting and reporting data. Based on these reports, it appears that crime rates have declined in this country since the early 1990s. Since 2008, according to the preliminary 2012 FBI report, there has been a continuing decline in rape, property crimes, burglary, larceny, and arson. Rates for violent crime, murder, aggravated assault, and motor vehicle theft were up in 2012, but by less than 2 percent in each category (Federal Bureau of Investigation, 2013).

Crime rates are affected by a number of factors, including how crimes are defined, how they are reported and tracked, or whether they are reported at all. An apparent increase in burglaries might reflect the fact that more items are insured and the insurance companies require police reports before they will reimburse victims for their losses. Changing population demographics, especially the proportion of people between the ages of 18 and 24, may account for some changes in crime rates (Bohm & Haley, 2014; Cole, Smith, & DeJong, 2013). Adults over the age of 45 make up a third of the population but account for only 7 percent of arrests for serious crime (Siegel & Worrall, 2014). Criminologists attribute lower rates of crime (especially robbery, burglary, and auto theft) in the 1990s to a strong economy and job market. The theory that the crime rate goes up in hard economic times was challenged with data reporting low rates after the Great Recession. Criminologists believe that the lower rates resulted from improved policing practices, such as a focus on high-crime locations, and better precautions taken on the part of ordinary citizens, such as the use of alarm systems (Yost, 2011).

According to Bureau of Justice statistics summarized by Wright (2010, p. 325), victims of crimes are most likely to be single or separated, poor, urban, young people of color. Except for rape and domestic violence, most victims are male. Youths are almost twenty times as likely to be the victims of violent crime as are older adults. Poor people (i.e., those with household incomes of less than $7,500) are the most likely to be victimized by crime, especially violent crime. Separated individuals are about twice as likely as never-married or divorced people, and more than six times as likely as married people to be victims of violent crime (Bohm & Haley, 2014).

Crime rates have fallen for about two decades, and even though they have risen slightly in the last two years, violent crimes remain at a historically low level (Leger, 2013). Nevertheless, the violent crime rate in the United States is several times higher than countries in Europe and even worse when compared to Asian countries, where rates of violent crime are among the lowest in the world (Macionis, 2014). The U.S. firearm homicide rate is twenty times higher than the combined rates of twenty-two countries that are our peers in wealth and population (Brady Campaign to Prevent Gun Violence, n.d.). The gun homicide rate per capita in the United States is thirty times that of Britain and Australia (where there are strong gun control laws) (Zakaria, 2012). (See figure 3.1.) A major contributing factor is the extensive private ownership of guns in the United States. There are 88.8 firearms per 100 people in the United States, almost twice as many as the next three countries on the list (Zakaria, 2012). On the other hand, while the number of guns remains high, the number of individuals and households that own guns has declined sharply since the 1970s, in part due to the aging of the gun-owning population—mostly white males—and the decreasing popularity of hunting (Violence Policy Center, 2011). Male gun ownership hit its peak in 1990, when 52.4 percent of males reported owning a gun; that number had dropped to 33.2 percent by 2010 (Violence Policy Center, 2011). Gun ownership is becoming increasingly concentrated, with an estimated 20 percent of gun owners possessing 65 percent of the nation's guns. Although overall gun violence is down, 70 percent of all homicides in 2011 were committed with a firearm.

FIGURE 3.1 GUN VIOLENCE IN THE UNITED STATES

- One in three people in the United States knows someone who has been shot.
- On average, 32 Americans are murdered with guns every day and 140 are treated for a gun assault in an emergency room.
- Every day on average, 51 people kill themselves with a firearm, and 45 people are shot or killed in an accident with a gun.
- An average of eight children and teens under the age of 20 are killed by guns every day
- Firearm homicide is the second-leading cause of death (after motor vehicle crashes) for young people ages 1–19 in the United States.
- The lifetime medical cost for all gun violence victims in the United States is estimated at $2.3 billion, with almost half the costs borne by taxpayers.
- Nine out of 10 Americans, including three out of four NRA members, agree that we should have universal background checks, but as of late 2013 Congress had not acted to strengthen any gun violence prevention measures subsequent to the Sandy Hook Elementary School tragedy and two other highly publicized mass shootings that occurred in 2012.

Source: Brady Campaign to Prevent Gun Violence, n.d.

According to an article in the *New York Times* (Zernike, 2006), an alarming trend in violent crime is the increase in the number of firearm homicides that are apparently the result of minor disputes—or "stupid arguments over stupid things," as the police commissioner of Philadelphia calls them. Suspects tell police they killed someone who "disrespected" them or a family member or gave them a dirty look. Disagreements that in the past would have led to fistfights or perhaps knives now lead straight to gunfire.

Also contributing to this trend in violence was the passage of "Stand Your Ground" laws in more than thirty states, starting with Florida in 2005. These laws make it legal for individuals to use lethal force outside of their homes if they believe that someone is going to do them great harm. They replaced earlier laws that encouraged people to withdraw from the situation if they could do so safely. "In the five years after the law was passed, the rate of justifiable homicide in Florida tripled" (Sullivan, 2013). Using state-level crime data from 2000 to 2009, researchers at Texas A&M University found that stronger self-defense laws did not deter burglary, robbery, or aggravated assault, but in states with Stand Your Ground laws homicide rates increased by 7 to 9 percent (Cheng & Hoekstra, 2012).

The Florida state Stand Your Ground law received national attention after a self-appointed neighborhood watch coordinator shot and killed an unarmed African American teenager, Trayvon Martin, who was returning to his father's house after buying candy and a soft drink at a nearby convenience store. The shooter, George Zimmerman, initially was not arrested because, according to the police chief, there was no evidence to refute his claim of self-defense (Roig-Franzia & Horwitz, 2013). Six weeks later he was charged with murder. Zimmerman was found not guilty at trial. Although he did not use the Stand Your Ground defense, the judge told the jury that "he had no duty to retreat and the right to stand his ground" (Roig-Franzia & Horwitz, 2013).

Of particular concern to social workers is the problem of *hate crimes*, a criminal act that is motivated by bias against someone's national origin, race, ethnicity, religion, sexual orientation, or disability. Hate crimes were recognized by state governments during the 1980s; by 2005, forty-six states, the District of Columbia, and the federal government had enacted hate crimes legislation (Cole, Smith, & DeJong, 2013). The FBI reports on hate crime incidents each year (see table 3.1). Offenders convicted of hate crimes receive more severe sentences than those who commit the same act but without hatred as the motive. Victims may include businesses, organizations, or institutions, as well as individuals. African Americans, Jews, and gay men are disproportionately the victims of hate crimes. After the terrorist attacks of September 11, 2001, many individuals of Middle Eastern heritage were unfairly targeted in hate crimes because of growing distrust of Muslims and Arabs.

Incarceration Rates

In a shift from earlier approaches that emphasized rehabilitation and deterrence, a new philosophy of criminal justice focusing on incarceration of large numbers of criminal offenders, including drug users and pushers, appeared at the end of the twentieth century. Rather than being a response to an increase in crime or a surge in the population, the increased rate of incarceration reflects policy choices. The United States, with a rate of 716 per 100,000 residents, incarcerates a higher percentage of its population than any other country (Wang, 2013). More than half of federal prison inmates were convicted for drug offenses (Zakaria, 2012).

According to the Sentencing Project, after the previous five decades of stability, the American prison system for the last forty years has been characterized by unrelenting growth. "The culture of punishment, in part

TABLE 3.1
Incidence of Hate Crimes in the United States in 2011

Bias category	Percent of 6,222 incidents reported
Race	46.9%
Religion	19.8%
Sexual orientation	20.8%
Ethnicity/nation origin	11.6%
Disability	0.9%

Source: adapted from Federal Bureau of Investigation, Hate Crime Accounting, December 10, 2012 driven by political expediency with 'tough-on-crime' policies marketed as the solution to 'fear of crime,' has been aggressively implemented at every stage of the criminal justice process: arresting, charging, sentencing, confining, releasing, and supervising" (Austin et al., 2013, p. 2). Between 1980 and 2011, the prison population in the United States grew from 319,598 to 1,504,150 (an increase of 371 percent) and in the same time frame the number of those in jail grew from 182,288 to 735,601 (an increase of 304 percent). If one includes those on probation or parole, the number of individuals under corrections department control totaled just under seven million in 2011. Although prison *admissions* have dropped nationwide since 2008, prison *populations* are down only slightly because there has been very little progress in reducing the average length of stay. Most of the decrease in population reflects significant changes in only four states: New York, New Jersey, Michigan, and California. Although many states have been relaxing mandatory minimum sentencing requirements for drug offenses over the last ten years, such provisions are not retroactive.

"Today, there is general agreement that this vast expansion of correctional control occurred not by accident, but as the result of deliberate policy choices that impose intentionally punitive sentences that have increased both the numbers of people entering the system and how long they remain under correctional control" (Austin et al., 2013, p. 2). When Congress passed the Anti-Drug Abuse Act of 1986, harsh sentences were mandated. These guidelines differentiated between crack (which is used by poor and minority people) and powdered cocaine (which is used predominantly by middle-class and wealthy people). A subject caught with 50 grams of crack faced the same penalty as one with 5,000 grams of powder (Rawe, 2007). In two Supreme Court decisions handed down in late 2007, federal judges were empowered to reject these unfair sentencing guidelines. The U.S. Sentencing Commission voted on December 11, 2007, to allow some 19,500 federal prison inmates to seek reductions in their crack-cocaine sentences (Hajela, 2007).

Some states are trying approaches to reduce the growth of the prison population. Among these efforts are reducing first-time prison admissions through diversion programs that steer selected low-risk offenders to community corrections programs or a continuum of treatment services, reducing recidivism by using short-term residential facilities for persistent parole and probation violators, and reducing the risk of reentry by offering specially designed treatment and education programs to inmates.

Privatization

Another trend in the criminal justice system is the construction and operation of prisons by private companies. The private sector has a long tradition of contracting to provide services to inmates, such as provision of meals, medical or psychiatric care, and education; the private sector also has operated detention facilities for juveniles for many years (Bohm & Haley, 2014). In response to the incarceration boom noted above, many states asked private organizations to build and operate new prisons. In the ten years between 1985 and 1995, the number of prisoners housed in private facilities increased from 935 to 63,595, an increase of almost 7,000 percent (Reiman & Leighton, 2013). The rate of increase has slowed since then, but as of 2010, there were 128,195 inmates housed in private prisons (Reiman & Leighton, 2013).

The Corrections Corporation of America (CCA), a private company founded in 1983, dominates the private prison business. According to the 2012 annual letter to their shareholders, found on their website (Corrections Corporation of America, 2013), CCA is the nation's largest owner and operator of privatized correctional and detention facilities and one of the largest prison operators in the United States, behind only the federal government and three states. The CCA operates more than sixty-seven facilities, including fifty-one company-owned or controlled facilities, with a total design capacity of approximately 92,500 beds in twenty states and the District of Columbia. It also provides transportation, health care (including medical, dental, and psychiatric services), food services, and work and recreational programs. It has more than 17,000 employees.

Criminal justice and policy analysts disagree about whether privatization has been a success. It seems clear that private facilities can be opened more quickly and make changes in programs more easily (Bohm & Haley, 2014). There are claims that they can be built at a cost savings of 25 percent or more, and operating cost savings of 10 to 15 percent, but some studies indicate that the savings are considerably less (Bohm & Haley, 2014; Cole, Smith & DeJong, 2013; Reiman & Leighton, 2013). It may be that savings are realized through lower labor costs and/or tax breaks and infrastructure subsidies. Those who argue against privatization worry that companies in the "prison business" are interested in keeping their facilities full and contribute to political campaigns and use their lobbyists to encourage legislation that will result in even higher levels of incarceration (Bohm & Haley, 2014; Cole, Smith, & DeJong, 2013).

Groups such as the American Civil Liberties Union have criticized conditions in private prisons and the lack of public oversight. Academics who study and teach about the criminal justice system argue that

> there is no evidence that private corrections can solve a correctional institution's fiscal or managerial problems, and this is reason enough not to jump "governmental ship." But it's not the only reason. When people say that they support the privatization of jails, they also say and/or acknowledge a great deal more. They affirm that one of the most important jobs in this country—restricting the freedoms of American citizens—should be taken away from the government and placed in the hands of a corporation whose sole purpose is to generate profits for shareholders. They affirm that profit is an acceptable motive for incarceration and often accept that more inmates equals more profits. They agree that private, for-profit, and often publicly held corporations should be granted the authority to use force, including deadly force. (Territo, Halsted, & Bromley, 2004, p. 509)

The Death Penalty

The U.S. Supreme Court reinstated the death penalty in 1976, making the United States the only Western industrialized nation that still allows capital punishment. (Eighteen states and the District of Columbia do not use the death penalty [Death Penalty Information Center, 2013b]). Between 1976 and 2013, 1,379 individuals were put to death by the criminal justice system in the United States; of these, 771 (56 percent) were white, 474 (34 percent) were African American, 110 (8 percent) were Hispanics, and 24 (2 percent) were "other" (Death Penalty Information Center, 2014).

Amnesty International has been monitoring developments around the use of the death penalty and campaigning for its abolition for more than three decades. According to a report on their website (Amnesty International, 2014), the total number of countries carrying out executions decreased from 37 in 1994 to 22 in 2013. Almost 80 percent of all known executions in 2013 took place in just three countries: Iran, Iraq, and Saudi Arabia, but this figure does not include the thousands secretly put to death in China. "Common to almost all executing countries was again the justification of the use of the death penalty as an alleged deterrent against crime. But this position is becoming increasingly untenable and discredited. There is no convincing evidence that capital punishment is a particular deterrent to crime" (Amnesty International, 2014, p. 4).

Public support for the death penalty has fallen from a high of about 80 percent in the 1980s to between 50 and 66 percent, depending on the poll (Death Penalty Information Center, 2014; Drehle, 2008). In addition to the basic question of whether it is morally acceptable for a government to kill its citizens for any reason, critics of the death penalty argue that it is inherently unfair because poor, uneducated, and minority men are much more likely to suffer this penalty than are more affluent, well-educated, white offenders. One researcher has identified three other factors that contribute to the inequity of capital punishment. According to Haney (2005), the jury selection process screens out opponents of capital punishment; members of juries do not understand the instructions that might lead them to choose an option other than the death penalty; and jurors are over-influenced by media portrayals of violent criminals, leading them to disregard mitigating factors such as poverty and childhood neglect.

Dozens of scientific studies have demonstrated that the death penalty continues to be administered in a fashion that discriminates against poor people and African Americans and killers of whites (Bohm & Haley, 2014). "Over 75 percent of murder victims in cases resulting in execution were white, even though nationally only 50 percent of murder victims are white" (Death Penalty Information Center, 2014). One reason for this is that many poor defendants who end up on death row are assigned inexperienced, unskilled, or unprepared attorneys. Defense lawyers call it "meet 'em and plead 'em" when they are allowed only a few minutes to get acquainted with a client they are seeing for the first time, often in a crowded holding cell, before going into the courtroom where the client will accept a plea agreement (Valentine, 2013). In 1987, the U.S. Supreme

Court ruled "that state death penalty statutes are constitutional even when statistics indicate that they have been applied in racially biased ways" (Bohm & Haley, 2014, p. 328).

The death penalty is also administered unevenly across various regions of the country. Five states (Florida, Missouri, Oklahoma, Texas, and Virginia) have accounted for two-thirds of all executions since the death penalty was reinstated in 1976. Texas completed its 500th execution in June 2013. Virginia has executed a total of 110 prisoners, Oklahoma 104, Florida 77, and Missouri 68 (Death Penalty Information Center, 2013a). Executions are very rare in the rest of the country, even for inmates who have been sentenced to death. As of September, Texas had executed eleven people in 2013, one less than all other states combined (Death Penalty Information Center, 2013a). New Jersey abolished the death penalty through legislation in 2007, the first state to do so in forty years. Another five states have since have taken similar steps to end capital punishment: Connecticut, Illinois, Maryland, New Mexico, and New York (Death Penalty Information Center, 2013b). Delaware and Colorado are considering doing the same. According to the Death Penalty Information Center (2014), enforcing the death penalty costs Florida $51 million a year above what it would cost to punish all first-degree murderers with life in prison without parole. The cumulative cost of imposing the death penalty in California since 1978 has topped $4 billion.

The most powerful rationale for discontinuing the death penalty is that there cannot be certainty that judgment is without error. For instance, between 1973 and 2013, 142 prisoners were released from death row in twenty-six different states because they were either improperly convicted or because documentation of their innocence was presented after sentencing (Death Penalty Information Center, 2013a). These included twenty-four people in Florida prisons and twenty in Illinois.

Reversing its 1989 ruling, in June 2002 the U.S. Supreme Court held that the Eighth Amendment ban on cruel and unusual punishment does indeed prohibit the execution of a capital offender who is mentally retarded. During the intervening time between rulings, sixteen states had enacted laws prohibiting the execution of persons with mental retardation. Many other states are currently developing procedures to implement the Court's decision.

On March 1, 2005, the U.S. Supreme Court ruled (5–4) that it is unconstitutional to sentence to death an individual who committed the crime while under the age of eighteen. This decision was based in part on information provided in a brief submitted by the National Association of Social Workers and six other organizations (Stoesen, 2005).

FIGURE 3.2   CRITICAL THINKING ABOUT THE DEATH PENALTY

Is capital punishment always wrong?
   Many people are opposed to capital punishment on moral grounds. Some people think, however, that perpetrators of particularly heinous crimes deserve the death penalty. One example of this is child rape.
   Can you frame arguments on both sides of this issue?
   You might want to consider the following questions.
   • If you are against capital punishment, should you be consistent and be against it in all cases?
   • Are some criminals beyond rehabilitation?
   • Should some criminals be removed permanently from society?
   • Should we consider the costs of lengthy appeals or lengthy prison sentences?
   • What is the potential effect on crime victims of different kinds of sentencing?

Understanding the Criminal Justice System

Functionalist Perspective

Functionalism is based on the assumption that members of society subscribe to the same values and presumes that the laws of a society reflect that consensus. Punishing deviance reinforces agreement about societal norms. The sociologist Emile Durkheim (1964/1895) argued that instead of disrupting society, deviance serves to produce social solidarity.

Consistent with a functionalist perspective, one response to deviance is to *rehabilitate* (i.e., "correct") offenders. This approach emphasizes constructive improvement not only through external control (i.e., probation or parole, or incarceration) but also by offering skills training, counseling, and treatment for drug and/or alcohol abuse. The goal is for the offender to conform to societal expectations and become a functioning member of society.

Another option is to remove deviants by deporting, incarcerating, or executing them. Currie (1998, p. 30) reports that incarceration is modestly effective with "high-rate" offenses, such as robbery and burglary. It is much less so for violent crimes, such as homicide, because for some offenses, especially murder, the first serious crime may be the only one the offender commits. Both approaches, rehabilitation and removal, have the ultimate goal of keeping society in balance.

Conflict Perspective

Conflict theorists would say that the criminal justice system erroneously defines problems as occurring at the individual, rather than at the societal level, and therefore efforts to address social conditions are rejected (Macionis, 2014). "To look only at individual criminality is to close one's eyes to social injustice and to close one's ears to the question of whether our social institutions have exploited or violated the individual" (Reiman & Leighton, 2013, p. 186).

Conflict theory looks to differences in socioeconomic class to understand and explain both deviant behavior and societal responses to it. Individuals from all class levels break the law, but they commit different kinds of crimes. People from lower socioeconomic class backgrounds are more likely to commit property crimes. Property crime includes robbery, burglary, larceny, and motor vehicle theft. Conflict theorists believe that chronic unemployment inherent in the capitalist system leads poor people to commit property crimes in order to survive (Thio, 2000).

Rational/Social Exchange Perspective

Gordon (1973, p. 174) notes that "nearly all crimes in capitalist societies represent perfectly *rational* [italics in original] responses to the structure of institutions upon which capitalist societies are based." This is because most crimes are motivated by a desire for money or goods and thus are an understandable way of coping with inequity (Reiman & Leighton, 2013). But even individuals who already have much more than they need may engage in illegal activities if they think they can get away with it.

Deterrence theory suggests that people who are rational will refrain from committing crimes if they believe that the "costs" of the punishment will outweigh the "benefits" of the crime (Siegel & Worrall, 2014). Given current rates of recidivism, some criminologists doubt the value of incarceration as a deterrent.

Constructionist Perspective

The definition of *deviance* varies according to cultural norms. No act is criminal or delinquent in and of itself; only the response of the criminal justice system, determined by political processes, makes it so. For example, prostitution is legal in Nevada but not in any other state. Gambling is still illegal in many places, but most states now promote government-sponsored lotteries as a preferred alternative to raising property or income taxes to support education. Even on a much smaller scale, the definition of deviance and labeling of deviants may vary according to circumstance. In a classic study of high school behaviors, Chamblis (2007) found that when two different groups were engaged in the same behaviors (truancy, drinking, vandalism, wild parties, and petty theft), one group was generally viewed positively, while the other was not. Boys from upper-income families were never arrested and were described as "most likely to succeed." The boys in the other group were from lower-income families and were labeled "troublemakers."

Relationship of the Criminal Justice System to the Political Economy

All Americans are constantly bombarded by commercial messages that promote materialism. Sociologist Robert Merton (1949) identified the problem of imbalance between a society's cultural goals and the means that people have to achieve those goals. Cloward and Ohlin (1960) extended Merton's thinking and argued that crime results not only from limited opportunities, but also from the existence of illegitimate opportunities. For example, residents of inner-city slums have the same aspirations for "success" as do middle- and upper-class people. "At the very least overwhelming numbers of the poor give allegiance to the values and principles of the dominant American culture" (Ryan, 1976, p. 134). The problem is that because they lack access to good education, training, and legitimate employment opportunities, they are attracted to alternate opportunities for making money: robbery, burglary, drug dealing, prostitution, pimping, gambling, and other "hustles."

The use of prison labor has produced mixed benefits to the American economy (Cole, Smith & DeJong, 2013). State prisoners are routinely used for cleaning up highways or state parks and other low-skill jobs. Advocates for labor opposed prison-made goods competing with those made in the free market economy, but in 1979 Congress lifted restrictions on the interstate sale of prison-made products. Goods produced include clothing and textiles, cosmetics, and electronics. According to a report cited by *Teamster Nation* ("Corporations using prison labor . . . .", 2013), at least thirty-seven states have legalized the contracting of prison labor by private corporations. The list of companies that use prison labor includes such well-known corporations as IBM, Boeing, Motorola, Microsoft, AT&T, Texas Instruments, Dell, Compaq, Honeywell, Hewlett-Packard, Lucent Technologies, Intel, Northern Telecom, TWA, Nordstrom's, Revlon, Macy's, Pierre Cardin, and Target stores. Inmates who work inside state penitentiaries generally receive the minimum wage. In some states they receive considerably less. For example, in Colorado they get about $2 per hour. In privately run prisons, inmates may receive as little as 17 cents per hour, the equivalent of $20 per month. The highest-paying private prison is run by CCA in Tennessee, where prisoners receive 50 cents per hour. In the federal prison system, the minimum wage is $1.15 (Siegel and Worrall, 2014). According to Cole, Smith and DeJong (2013, p. 641), whereas the idea of using prison labor may appear attractive, the inefficiencies inherent in the system tend to limit its economic value. For example, production needs to be stopped periodically to count heads and make sure that tools have not been stolen. In the two years between 2008 and 2010, the participation declined from 11.5 percent of federal prisoners to 7.6 percent.

As noted already in the "Issues and Trends" section, the construction and operation of prisons have become a big business. This "has created a large and politically potent constituency of those whose jobs and status depend on yet further expansion [of the inmate population]" (Currie, 1998, p. 7). In fact, Dyer (2000, p. 2) suggests that the most plausible explanation for the unprecedented growth in the U.S. prison population is the money that ends up in the bank accounts of the shareholders of some of America's best-known corporations; underwriting prison construction by selling tax-exempt bonds is now estimated to be a $2.3 billion annual industry itself.

Eric Schlosser, in an article in the *Atlantic Monthly*, wrote "The prison-industrial complex is not a conspiracy . . . it is a confluence of interests that has given prison construction in the United States a seemingly unstoppable momentum. It is composed of politicians . . . who have used the fear of crime to gain votes; impoverished rural areas where prisons have become a cornerstone of economic development; [and] private companies that regard the roughly 35 billion spent each year on corrections not as a burden on American taxpayers but as a lucrative market" (Schlosser, 1998, p. 54). In addition, unions representing prison workers have supported the growth of prisons. For example, unions in California make large contributions to political campaigns and have supported tough sentencing laws such as Proposition 184 (three-strikes penalties) that enhance the length of sentences (Segal, 2008)

The Impact of the Criminal Justice System on Individuals and Families

How the Criminal Justice System Deters Well-Being

As noted previously, the United States has the highest incarceration rate of any nation in the world. Over 3 percent of the U.S. population is either in prison (2.3 million) or on probation or parole (4.9 million) (Lindorff, 2013). The rate of incarceration in the United States is six times the average for all industrialized nations (Lindorff, 2013). Despite this, the crime rate in the United States also exceeds that of other industrialized countries.

The Criminal Justice System and Minorities. In contrast to their white counterparts, people of color are disproportionately policed, incarcerated, and sentenced to death. These practices put communities of color at risk. (See figure 3.3).

FIGURE 3.3   RACIAL DISPARITIES IN THE CRIMINAL JUSTICE SYSTEM

- While people of color make up about 30 percent of the United States' population, they account for 60 percent of those imprisoned.
- 1 in every 15 African American men and 1 in every 36 Hispanic men are incarcerated in comparison to 1 in every 106 white men.
- According to the Bureau of Justice Statistics, one in three black men can expect to go to prison in their lifetime.
- Individuals of color have a disproportionate number of encounters with law enforcement, indicating that racial profiling continues to be a problem.
- Harsh school punishments, from suspensions to arrests, have led to high numbers of youth of color coming into contact with the juvenile-justice system and at an earlier age.
- African American youth have higher rates of juvenile incarceration and are more likely to be sentenced to adult prison. According to the Sentencing Project, even though African American youth are about 16 percent of the youth population, 37 percent of the detained population are moved to criminal court and 58 percent of African American youth are sent to adult prisons.
- As the number of women incarcerated has increased by 800 percent over the last three decades, women of color have been disproportionately represented. African American women are three times more likely than white women to be incarcerated, while Hispanic women are 69 percent more likely than white women to be incarcerated.
- The war on drugs has been waged primarily in communities of color where people of color are more likely to receive higher offenses. According to the Human Rights Watch, people of color are no more likely to use or sell illegal drugs than whites, but they have a higher rate of arrests.
- Once convicted, black offenders receive longer sentences compared to white offenders. The Sentencing Project reports that African Americans are 21 percent more likely to receive mandatory-minimum sentences than white defendants and are 20 percent more likely to be sentenced to prison.
- Voter laws that prohibit people with felony convictions from voting disproportionately impact men of color. An estimated 5.3 million felony-disenfranchisement policies have led to eleven states denying the right to vote to more than 10 percent of their African American population.

Source: Center for American Progress (Kerby, 2012)

Given the opportunities for discretionary decision making at various stages of the criminal justice process, there is ample opportunity for discrimination. According to a number of studies cited by Andersen and Taylor (2013), African Americans and Latinos are more likely to be arrested, convicted, and incarcerated for offenses than are whites. Other factors being equal, minorities receive harsher sentences and are less likely to be released on probation. They also are more likely to be victims of excessive use of force by police. The number of blacks behind bars jumped 62 percent between 1990 and 2005 (Wright, 2007); nearly one in nine African American males between the ages of 25 and 34 is in prison (Pew Center on the States, 2008).

Historically, police officers have been white, although equal opportunity and affirmative action programs are changing that. Still, many judges are white, male, and middle, if not upper, class (Kendall, 2008). Using Alabama as an example, Jesse Jackson (2003) noted that the prison population increased by 600 percent in the past thirty years, while the population grew by only 30 percent. Over two-thirds of the prisoners were black. Only 16 of Alabama's 220 judges were black. None of its appellate judges were black. None of the district attorneys were black, and only eight of sixty-seven county sheriffs were black. "The back of the cell has replaced the back of the bus," Jackson argued.

Racial profiling is the term used to describe disproportionate law enforcement activities that target people of color. Several research studies have found that police officers regularly stop or search African American and Latino drivers at a higher rate than white drivers (Cole, Smith, & DeJong, 2013; Siegel & Worrall, 2014). Some states have written laws that require law enforcement personnel to check the immigration status of individuals the officer believes to be in the country illegally; this has led to racial profiling and legal challenges to those laws.

Sometimes members of society see crimes as less socially significant if the victim is viewed as less worthy. This practice is called victim discounting (Schaefer, 2012, p. 211). Although close to half of all homicide victims are African Americans, nearly four out of five of those executed by the justice system had murdered a white person (Wright, 2010).

The Criminal Justice System and Social Class. The FBI does not collect or report data on the socioeconomic class of arrested and convicted persons. Although violent crime is a serious problem among the poor, especially in inner-city neighborhoods, the majority of people who live there have no criminal records. In general, the poorer a person is, the more likely he or she is to be a victim of crime (Wright, 2010).

People from middle- or upper-class backgrounds commit white-collar crimes—income tax evasion, bribery of public officials, embezzlement, fraud, or other crimes committed by people in the course of their employment or financial affairs (Sutherland, 1940). These crimes do not involve violence, but in their efforts to enrich themselves, white-collar criminals may cause significant harm to consumers, investors, or employees.

Critics trace the roots of the Great Recession to the actions of a handful of bank executives and hedge fund managers who stretched the limits of responsible stewardship of their businesses' and clients' finances. Many people lost their homes, jobs, or retirement savings. Five years later, almost no bankers have faced legal sanctions for their part in precipitating the crisis ("Why have so few bankers gone to jail?" 2013). Some lawmakers believed that the gradual erosion and eventual repeal of parts of the banking regulations put in place in 1933 (the Glass-Steagall Act) were an important part of the cause of the Great Recession. In 2010, Congress passed the Dodd-Frank Act, which made significant changes in financial regulations (Sweet, 2010).

The important point is that the laws against white-collar crimes are relatively lenient and seldom enforced (Macionis, 2014). The probability of getting arrested, convicted, and sent to prison is strongly associated with social class. Geis (1999) asks, "Is it fair that a person who steals a television set should do prison time while a person who bilks the government out of millions walks away with a fine or a community service sentence?" (p. 154).

The Criminal Justice System and Gender. In the two decades between 1980 and 1999, the number of women in prisons increased sixfold (Chesney-Lind, 2002). Between 1999 and 2011, the average growth rate for all prisoners in state and federal custody was 17.3 percent; for women, it was 24.2 percent (Carson & Golinelli, 2013). On the other hand, men continue to be incarcerated at a rate thirteen times greater than women.

Female prisoners' past lives put them at particular risk for certain health problems. Mothers in state prison were more likely than fathers to report homelessness, past physical or sexual abuse, and medical and mental health problems (Glaze & Maruschak, 2010). While 5.6 percent of male state prison inmates report having a mental impairment, 11 percent of females report having one (Maruschak, 2008).

Female inmates are more likely than male inmates to have children and to have been living with those children immediately prior to incarceration. Forty-six percent of female prisoners are single parents compared to 15 percent of male prisoners (Mumola, 2000). Women are likely to have their parental rights terminated as they are often the sole guardians of their children (Chesney-Lind, 2002).

At the time of their arrest, 6 to 10 percent of women are pregnant (Centers for Disease Control, 2003). In three quarters of the states, it is legal to shackle women during the third trimester of pregnancy; almost half of states and the Federal Bureau of Prisons allow restraints to be used during labor (Doetzer, 2008). In July 2010 the *Chicago Tribune* ran a front-page story on more than twenty Cook County ex-inmates who said they were handcuffed or shackled during labor (Mastony, 2010). Of pregnant state prisoners in 2004, only 53.9 percent received some type of prenatal care (Glaze & Maruschak, 2010). The provision of residential programs for inmate mothers and their infants is very limited.

The Criminal Justice System and Children and Youth. Most states establish a maximum age under eighteen years, the age of legal majority, for juvenile court jurisdiction. In some states, minors who are charged with certain offenses may or must be prosecuted as adults. In forty-five states, juvenile court judges can transfer cases to adult court; in twenty-nine states, certain types of violent crime such as murder, rape, and armed robbery must be tried in adult court (Cole, Smith, & DeJong, 2013).

An estimated 1.7 million minor children, or about 2.3 percent of the population of the United States under age 18, have one or two parents in prison (Glaze & Maruschak, 2010). Between 1991 and 2007, the number of children with a mother in prison more than doubled. At the time of their initial incarceration, mothers were more likely than fathers to have been the primary caregiver of a child; once mothers were in prison, the child's grandmother was the most common replacement (Glaze & Maruschak, 2008). For male prisoners, the child's mother was the most common current caregiver.

The Criminal Justice System and Older Adults. According to a study by the Pew Charitable Trusts (Vestal, 2013) between 2001 and 2008 the number of prisoners over the age of fifty-five in state and federal facilities nearly doubled, and during that same period health care costs in prisons increased by about 50 percent. The aging of the prison population is the result of a large number of inmates living out longer sentences and an increase in the number of older people who are sent to prison. Although there is a federal program that authorizes early release for older prisoners, Human Rights Watch says the release program "has been bogged down in bureaucracy and that wardens and judges remain reluctant to free inmates" (Serrano, 2013).

The Criminal Justice System and People with Mental Illness. According to a 2006 study, more than half of all prison and jail inmates have mental health problems (Bureau of Justice Statistics, 2006). Research studies document that people with mental illness are overrepresented in the criminal justice system. The level of their impairment may vary, but with proper treatment incarceration could have been avoided in many cases (Horowitz, 2013).

One example of the mistreatment of mentally ill prisoners is documented in a court case in South Carolina (Cohen, 2014). The presiding state judge ruled that the South Carolina Department of Corrections (SCDC) mental health program was "inherently flawed and systemically deficient in all major areas." Key findings included the following.

- The mental health program at SCDC was severely understaffed, particularly with respect to mental health professionals, and impacted the proper administration of services from reception and evaluation through discharge.
- Seriously mentally ill inmates were exposed to a disproportionate use of force and segregation (solitary confinement) when compared with non-mentally ill inmates. These conditions contributed to the

deaths of multiple inmates in segregation, while placing other inmates and staff at risk.

- SCDC's screening and evaluation process was ineffective in identifying inmates with serious mental illness and in providing those it did identify with timely treatment.
- Administration of psychotropic medications was inadequately supervised and evaluated.
- SCDC's current policies and practices concerning suicide prevention and crisis intervention were inadequate and resulted in the unnecessary loss of life among seriously mentally ill inmates.

In his conclusion, the judge noted the eight-year length of the litigation. "Rather than accept the obvious at some point and come forward in a meaningful way to try and improve its mental health system, [the Department of Corrections has] fought this case tooth and nail. . . . The hundreds of thousands of tax dollars spent defending this lawsuit, at trial and most likely now on appeal, would be better expended to improve mental health services delivery at SCDC."

Diversion of Resources. State government funding spent on prisons has risen at six times the rate of spending on higher education in the last twenty years (Zakaria, 2012). Several states, including Michigan and California, spend more on corrections than on higher education (Heinlein & Cain, 2008). According to an article in *Time* magazine (Zakaria, 2012), since 1980 the state of California has built twenty-one prisons and one college campus. It spends about $50,000 per prisoner each year compared to less than $9,000 per college student per year. Across the nation, even a portion of the dollars spent on the criminal justice system could make a big difference in employment, education, housing, and medical treatment for the poor, especially poor children, who are otherwise at risk for becoming the criminals of the future.

How the Criminal Justice System Promotes Well-Being.

In a society that is unable or unwilling to invest in prevention or rehabilitation, incarceration provides short-term security and protection by keeping offenders locked up. Many people believe that as a growing "industry," the building of new prisons offers economic opportunities in rural communities that have no other alternatives for generating new jobs. Prisons offer appealing opportunities because "they don't pollute, they don't go out of business, [and] they don't get downsized" (Lamb, cited in Dyer, 2000, p. 16). (See chapter 10 for further discussion on this topic.)

The authors of this text found it difficult to identify other benefits of the criminal justice system. Perhaps the better strategy to ensure security in this country would be the promotion of fair and equal treatment of all individuals, regardless of their race, class, gender, or age. The rights of the accused are not protected by our current criminal justice system, and it does a poor job of keeping the members of society safe from harm. Van Wormer (2001, p. 227) suggests that "today we face not a crime crisis . . . but a criminal justice crisis. The solution to the problem has become the problem: the war on crime has become a war on people, black people, poor people, drug addicts, and the mentally ill." Perhaps in their roles as probation or parole officers, correctional treatment specialists, juvenile justice counselors, and as social workers in family courts, prisons and jails, and victim assistance programs, social workers can make a positive difference (Ritter, Vakalahi, & Kiernan-Stern, 2009).

THE MILITARY

The military is a social institution that dates from at least the beginning of recorded history. It is designed to protect a society from internal and external threats. The military (National Guard) is used in times of internal danger, such as when armed forces are needed to protect a community during or after a devastating natural disaster. In the past, military troops were used to put down widespread riots (such as the race riots that occurred in major cities after the assassination of Martin Luther King, Jr., in 1968) or to protect vulnerable citizens in extreme circumstances (such as when National Guard troops were called upon to protect African American children as federal court orders for school integration were being carried out in parts of the South in the 1960s).

A rigid hierarchy is an important characteristic of the military. People serving in the military are categorized according to a number of formal levels, or ranks, with those in higher levels enjoying extensive privileges and those in lower levels expected to exhibit strict obedience and conformity. An important distinction between the United States and many other countries is that the head of the military (the secretary of defense) and the commander in chief (the president) are both civilians.

According to the Office of Undersecretary of Defense Personnel and Readiness, (2010) there are about 1,140,000 million enlisted troops and about 237,000 officers serving in the U.S. military. In addition, there are about 850,000 in the reserves. The active duty military workforce is younger than its civilian counterpart. African Americans were equitably represented in the military overall. Proportions of most other minorities also were representative of the civilian population. Women comprise 14.7 percent of active duty troops. Military women are more likely to be members of a racial minority group than are military men. In addition to the growing presence of women in the military, the proportion of married members has also increased, hovering around 50 percent for enlisted personnel and at higher levels for officers. In general, male service members are more likely to be married than are female members. Military personnel are more likely to be high school graduates than their civilian counterparts, and a vast majority of officers hold college degrees. In 1973, the draft (military conscription) ended, and the United States changed to an all-voluntary force. Many people join the military based on a sense of calling, captured in words like "duty, honor, and country," setting aside individual self-interest in favor of a presumed higher good (Moskos, 2000, p. 27). Nevertheless, with the end of conscription, marketplace factors began to play an increasing role. As employment prospects in the civilian job sector diminish, young people find opportunities for specialized training, job security, housing, health care, and travel offered by the military more enticing.

According to summaries presented by Macionis (2014) and Thompson (2011), the members of the military come overwhelmingly from certain regions of the country, with the South greatly overrepresented. More than 40 percent of new recruits are from the South, and half of all active-duty military personnel are stationed in just five states: Virginia, North Carolina, Georgia, Texas, and California. Today's military are from rural areas and small towns and are generally from working-class families. "America's military seems to resemble the makeup of a two-year commuter or trade school outside Birmingham or Biloxi far more than that of a ghetto or barrio or a four-year university in Boston" (Halbfinger and Holmes, cited in Macionis, 2014, p. 498).

Issues and Trends in the Military

Women in the Military

Women have served in the country's armed services dating as far back as the Revolutionary War, when they nursed the ill, laundered clothing, and cooked for the troops (Women in the U.S. Army, 2008). Many of the jobs performed by the women of that time are now known as military occupational specialties. Although they were not allowed to enlist in the Continental Army, women played a vital role by joining their husbands during campaigns. The most famous example of early military service by a woman was Mary Hays McCauley ("Molly Pitcher"), who replaced her fallen husband at his cannon during the Battle of Monmouth in 1778.

Beginning in 1942, women were allowed to formally enlist and separate military units were established. The military services were integrated by gender in 1948 when President Truman signed the Women Armed Services Integration Act. Women were admitted to the military academies in 1976. Beginning in the 1990s, basic training was integrated by gender in all of the armed forces except the Marines (Moskos, 2000).

On October 1, 1994, a new Department of Defense policy stated that dangerous jobs would not be closed to women but it failed to open ground combat assignment jobs to females. Since that time women have served aboard warships and as combat pilots (Moskos, 2000). Operation Desert Storm, popularly known as the first Gulf War (1990–1991), represented another major turning point for women in the military, in that the lines between combat and noncombat zones were blurred. Since the start of the wars in Afghanistan (2001–present) and Iraq (2003–2011) almost 290,000 women have served in those combat zones (Michaels, Brook, & Welch, 2013). The demands of war and an all-volunteer military have required that women fill positions as medics, military police, intelligence officers, and other roles often showing up on the front lines (Michaels, Brook, & Welch, 2013). In early 2013 the secretary of defense officially lifted the ban on women in combat, a policy to be fully implemented by

January 2016 (Michaels, 2013). The new policy will enhance women's opportunities for promotion.

Currently, only males ages 18 to 25 have to register with Selective Service ("the draft"); females do not have to register. That policy is unlikely to survive a legal challenge (Thompson, 2013).

Gays in the Military

In 1994 after much negotiation among the members of the administration, Congress, and service chiefs, a new policy was developed (Moskos, Williams, & Segal, 2000). The Defense Authorization Act, known colloquially as "don't ask, don't tell," forbade the military to inquire about a service member's sexual orientation, but if the individual publicly self-disclosed, he or she was to be discharged. The "don't ask, don't tell" policy was repealed in September 2011. Despite the concerns expressed by some members of the military as well as politicians, no newsworthy incidents followed, and recruitment efforts continued to meet established quotas. Pentagon officials said they found no evidence the repeal disrupted forces or harmed unit cohesion as predicted by opponents (Watson, 2011).

A Growing Gap between Civilians and the Military

According to a Pew Research Center survey (2011), in contrast to previous decades, only about 0.5 percent of the American population has served on active duty in the military. At the height of World War II, the number who had served on active duty was nearly 9 percent. A large majority (84 percent) of veterans who served after 9/11 say that the public does not understand their problems. Most Americans express strong support for the troops, but question the value of both of the post-9/11 wars; only a quarter of respondents said they followed news of the wars closely and half say the wars made little difference in their lives. Only about 2.4 million troops have served in Afghanistan and Iraq since 9/11, exactly one percent of the 240 million Americans over 18 (Thompson, 2011). Many active-duty troops have a sibling or had a parent in uniform and almost 100,000 are married to another service member, further enforcing the idea that the members of the military are a population that is separate and distinct from the rest of society (Thompson, 2011).

Understanding the Military

Functionalist Perspective

The manifest function of the military is to provide security for the members of a society. Historically, on the other hand, the military also was used to expand a country's resources at the expense of other nations through invasion. The military also supports latent functions; these include providing training and employment to young adults and promoting values such as nationalism, patriotism, and obedience to authority.

Conflict Perspective

Conflict theorists would argue that the burden of defending the country falls disproportionately on poor and minority members of society. For example, during the Vietnam War, young men who were enrolled in college were given deferments while their working-class peers were subject to the draft. Although recent data do not reflect a great disparity across race and class in military service, it is reasonable to believe that youth who have limited educational and employment options are more likely to enlist.

Rational/Social Exchange Perspective

At a national level, federal lawmakers argue for a strong military in terms of readiness in case of attack, but also as a deterrent to possible aggression on the part of other nations. At the same time, such support translates into income for their districts for defense-related industries and military bases. At the global level, a rationalist perspective suggests that military intervention in other countries is based, at least in part, on a rational assessment not only of potential threats, but also of potential and real benefits, such as control over oil reserves.

Constructionist Perspective

As with other social institutions, the military has created its own language to shape perceptions of its role and mission. In 1947, the Department of

War became the Department of Defense. Wars are no longer called "wars," but operations: for example, "Operation Urgent Fury" (Grenada, 1983), "Operation Just Cause" (Panama, 1989), "Operation Desert Storm" (Iraq, 1990–1991), "Operation Enduring Freedom" (Afghanistan, 2001–present), and "Operation Iraqi Freedom" (Iraq, 2003–2011). Whereas the term *war* suggests a massive and long-lasting undertaking, "operation" implies a strategic and short-term enterprise. The military also creates euphemisms to describe the more disturbing facets of war, such as "collateral damage" for unintended civilian casualties.

Relationship of the Military to the Political Economy

During World War II, the industry of the country expanded in order to produce military goods, such as airplanes, ships, tanks, and guns. After the war ended, the country had to decide what to do with this large military capacity and determined that if it were to remain a world leader, then national defense needed to be a continuing priority.

President Dwight Eisenhower, in his farewell address to the nation in 1961, both supported and warned the country about what he called the "military-industrial complex":

> We recognize the imperative need for this development.... [but] in the councils of government, we must guard against the acquisition of unwarranted influence, whether sought or unsought, by the military-industrial complex. The potential for the disastrous rise of misplaced power exists and will persist. We must never let the weight of this combination endanger our liberties or democratic processes. We should take nothing for granted. Only an alert and knowledgeable citizenry can compel the proper meshing of the huge industrial and military machinery of defense with our peaceful methods and goals, so that security and liberty may prosper together. (*Public Papers of the Presidents*, 1961)

Despite Eisenhower's concerns, the military budget continued to be a significant part of the country's economy. The United States spends as much on defense ($645.7 billion in 2012) as the next fifteen highest-spending countries combined, but some other countries spend more as a percent of their gross domestic product (GDP) (Heeley, 2013). For example, Afghanistan and countries in the Middle East (e.g., Iran, Iraq, Israel, and Saudi Arabia) spend between 4.95 and 11.28 percent of their GDP on defense, compared to the United States at 4.12 percent of GDP. (Canada spent $18.4 billion in 2012, 1.04 percent of its GDP.)

The military's connection to the economic system is sometimes less obvious than large contracts with companies that build missiles or tanks. For example, military imagery permeates toys, video games, and movies. From G. I. Joe to "First to Fight" to *Blackhawk Down* and "Ironman" children and youth are exposed to combat violence. Civilian gamers are immersed in a virtual world of war, and gaming technology is used by the military to train troops (Jamail & Coppola, 2009).

The Impact of the Military on Individuals and Families

How the Military Deters Well-Being

Other wars have resulted in more deaths (about 750,000 in the Civil War and more than 290,000 in World War II [Department of Veteran's Affairs, 2013]), and recent improvements in battlefield care, including better body armor, forward-deployed surgical teams, and swift medical evacuations mean that significant numbers of troops who would have died have survived. In Afghanistan, the survival rate for wounded troops is now 95 percent (Cullison, 2010). On the other hand, survivors often return home with significant impairments: burns, loss of limbs, and traumatic brain injury. As of September 2013 at least 2,133 members of the U.S. military had died in Afghanistan and 19,200 had been wounded in hostile action ("U.S. Military Deaths in Afghanistan at 2133," 2013). More than 4,300 troops were killed in Iraq, and more than 32,000 wounded.

The large numbers of wounded were unanticipated, and the military health care system has been stretched beyond capacity. In addition to physical wounds, significant numbers of soldiers returned home with mental health diagnoses. Since many Vietnam veterans did not begin showing manifestations of stress disorders until ten years after returning home, it is difficult to estimate the long-term impact and social cost of war experiences for Iraq and Afghanistan vets (McClam, 2008). According to the U.S. veterans health care website (PTSD Resources and Treatment,

2014), experts think post-traumatic stress disorder (PTSD) occurs in about 11 to 20 percent of veterans of the Iraq and Afghanistan wars. Sexual harassment or sexual assault that occurs in the military during peacetime, training, or war may also result in PTSD. Among veterans who use Veterans' Administration (VA) health care, about 23 percent of women reported sexual assault when in the military. Because there are so many more males serving in the military, over half of all veterans with military sexual trauma are men. More than 20 percent of veterans with PTSD also have a substance use disorder; almost one out of every three veterans seeking treatment for substance use also has PTSD. It is common for depression to be associated with PTSD, and also risk for suicide. Based on the most recent data available, in fiscal year 2009, the suicide rate among male VA service users was almost double that for the U.S. male population overall, and among females, it was more than 2.5 times greater. The wars in Afghanistan and Iraq have also resulted in increased numbers of veterans who have been diagnosed with traumatic brain injury (TBI). The Department of Defense estimates that 22 percent of all Afghanistan and Iraq combat wounds are brain injuries. Whereas the effects of TBI can be time-limited, most veterans will still experience symptoms 18–24 months after the incident.

For a long time, the number of mental health and behavioral health professionals available to vets has been "woefully inadequate" according to a Pentagon task force (Isikoff & Reno, 2007, p. 10). In May 2013, the VA, Department of Defense, and U.S. Department of Health and Human Services released an interim report outlining interagency progress on increasing the capacity to respond to veterans in crisis, implementing a national suicide prevention campaign, establishing pilot projects where the VA was working with community-based mental health providers, and hiring nearly 1,400 mental health providers (Interagency Task Force on Military and Veterans Mental Health, 2013).

According to the Department of Veterans Affairs (Zoroya, 2014), in 2013 nearly 48,000 Iraq and Afghanistan veterans were either homeless or enrolled in federal homelessness prevention programs. This was almost triple the number from 2011, and the number does not include veterans from other wars. The three primary causes of homelessness among veterans are mental illness, financial troubles, and the lack of affordable housing (McClam, 2008).

Unlike the draftees of the Vietnam War era when most soldiers were young, single men, half of today's all-volunteer military personnel are older reservists and guardsmen who are married with children, so the burdens of deployment are shared by families (Skipp & Ephron, 2006). Deployment length and frequency are risk factors for both individual mental health and family functioning. Previously, overseas deployments averaged less than twelve months. Today tours of duty in Afghanistan can last as long as fifteen months, and repeated redeployment is not uncommon.

In 2013, two million children under the age of 18 had at least one active-duty parent, and a quarter of those children were under the age of 6 (Murphey, 2013). Nearly half of all active-duty service members have children, and 14 percent of those service members are single parents. In addition to parental separation, another stressor for military families is repeated geographic relocation, which may occur as often as every two to three years (Herzog, 2008). Due to frequent moves, the children experience change in school, loss of friends, and separation from extended family members.

How the Military Promotes Well-Being

Historically, tens of millions of U.S. veterans have received service-related benefits such as training, tuition benefits, housing aid, medical care, employment preferences, and retirement pensions (Campbell, 2004). Following World War II, eight million returned veterans received a college education or vocational training under the GI Bill (the Servicemen's Readjustment Act, signed into law by Franklin D. Roosevelt) (Ephron, 2007). Congress passed an updated version of the GI Bill in 1985. It was designed more as a peacetime recruiting tool than a wartime benefit; it covers average in-state tuition costs at public universities, but does not include housing and other educational expenses (Ephron, 2007).

According to Pentagon officials, bad news for the economy is good news for the military, as retention and recruitment numbers jump (Milburn & Manning, 2008). Military service guarantees a paycheck and benefits, even in bleak economic times. According to the public service website Military-Ranks.org (2014), the Department of Defense pay grade

E-1 (for new recruits) in the Army, Navy, Coast Guard, and Marines shows a monthly salary of $1,468. Levels of military compensation grew by 20 percent on top of inflation between 1998 and 2010; military compensation today is higher than that earned by 80 percent of civilians of comparable age and education (Thompson, 2011). The person who comes into the military as a commissioned officer (pay grade O-1) makes a starting salary of $2,784 per month. Everyone in the active military gets free (or almost free) housing, food, and medical care and an annual clothing allowance.

African Americans have benefitted from a military that was among the first U.S. institutions to become racially integrated after President Truman signed Executive Order 9981 on July 26, 1948 (Borlik, 1998). Compared with an oppressive civilian society at midcentury, the military offered more opportunities for job security and advancement. This more positive feature of the military environment continues to the present day. African Americans report that race relations are better in the military than in civilian life (Moskos & Butler, 1996). The military is the only social institution in the country where white men routinely take orders from black men.

About 70,000 foreigners have won American citizenship through military service since 9/11 (Thompson, 2011).

LOOKING AHEAD

In the next chapter, we will examine social institutions that are not closely associated with government. These social institutions—health care, religion, and mass media—are also an important part of the context of the lives of social workers and those they serve.

REFERENCES

American Psychological Association Zero Tolerance Task Force. (2008). *APA Zero tolerance task force report.* Retrieved from http://www.apa .org/pubs/info/reports/zero-tolerance.aspx.

Amnesty International. (2014). *Death sentences and executions in 2013.* Retrieved from http://www.amnesty.org/en/death-penalty/death-sen tences-and-executions-in-2013

Andersen, M., & Taylor, H. (2013). *Sociology: The essentials* (7th ed.). Belmont, CA: Wadsworth.

Austin, J., Cadora, E., Clear, T. R., Dansky, K., Greene, J., Gupta, V., Mauer, M., Porter, N., Tucker, S., Young, M. C. (2013). *Ending mass incarceration: Charting a new justice reinvestment.* Retrieved from http://sentencingproject.org/doc/publications/sen_Charting%20a%20New%20Justice%20Reinvestment.pdf

Austin, E. W., Chen, Y., Pinkleton, B. E., & Johnson, J. Q. (2006, March 3). Benefits and costs of Channel One in a middle school setting and the role of media-literacy training. *Pediatrics, 117.* Retrieved from http://www.pediatrics.org/cgi/content/full/117/e423.

Bohm, R. M., & Haley, K. N. (2014). *Introduction to criminal justice* (8th ed.). New York, NY: McGraw-Hill Education.

Bok, D. (2003). *Universities in the market place: The commercialization of higher education.* Princeton, NJ: Princeton University Press.

Borlik, A. K. (1998). Military commemorates 50 years of racial integration. American Forces Press Service. Retrieved from http://www.defenselink.mil/utility/printitem.aspx.

Brady Campaign to Prevent Gun Violence (n.d). About gun violence. Retrieved from http://www.bradycampaign.org/about-gun-violence.

Brewer, D. J., Gates, S. M., & Goldman, C. A. (2002). *In pursuit of prestige: Strategy and competition in U.S. higher education.* New Brunswick, NJ: Transaction Publishers.

Brinson, C. S. (2003, December 6). Public colleges' future grows more uncertain as state funding slides. *The State* [Columbia, SC], p. A7.

Broughman, S. P., & Swaim, N. L. (2013). *Characteristics of private schools in the United States: Results from the 2011–12 private school university survey.* Washington, DC: National Center for Education Statistics, U.S. Department of Education.

Bureau of Justice Statistics. (2006, September 6). *Study finds more than half of all prison and jail inmates have mental health problems.* Retrieved from http://www.bjs.gov/content/pub/press/mhppjipr.cfm.

Calbom, L. M. (2012, June 8). School bullying: Legal protections for vulnerable youth need to be more fully assessed. Retrieved from http://www.gao.gov/products/gao-12-785t.

Campbell, A. C. (2004). The invisible welfare state: Establishing the phenomenon of twentieth century veteran's benefits. *Journal of Political and Military Sociology, 32,* 249–267.

Carr, S (2009, December 17). Recovery School District looks at making charters pay rent. *The Times-Picayune* [New Orleans]. Retrieved from http://www.nola.com/education/index.ssf/2009/12/recovery_school _district_looks.html.

Carson, E. A., & Golinelli, D. (2013). *Prisoners in 2012.* U.S. Department of Justice, Office of Justice programs. Retrieved from http://www.bjs .gov/content/pub/pdf/p12ac.pdf.

Centers for Disease Control and Prevention (2003). *Women, injection drug use, and the criminal justice system.* Retrieved from http://www- .thebody.com/cdc/women_idu.html.

Chamblis, W. J. (2007). The saints and the roughnecks. In J. M. Henslin (Ed.), *Down-to-earth sociology: Introductory readings* (14th ed.). New York, NY: Free Press.

Cheng, C., & Hoekstra, M. (2012). Does strengthening self-defense law deter crime or escalate violence? *National Bureau of Economic Research.* Retrieved from http://www.nber.org/papers/w18134.

Chesney-Lind, M. (2002). Imprisoning women: The unintended victims of mass imprisonment. In M. Mauer and M. Chesney-Lind, (Eds.), *Invisible punishment: The collateral consequences of mass imprisonment* (pp. 79–94). New York, NY: The New Press.

Cloward, R. A., & Ohlin, L. E. (1960). *Delinquency and opportunity: A theory of delinquent gangs.* New York, NY: Free Press.

Cohen, A. (2014). Judge rules for better conditions for inmates with serious mental health issues. Retrieved from http://mentalhealth4in mates.org

Cole, G. F., Smith, C. E., & DeJong, C. (2013). *The American system of criminal justice* (13th ed.). Belmont, CA: Wadsworth.

Collins, R. (1979). *The credentialed society: An historical sociology of education and stratification.* New York, NY: Academic Press.

Community College Research Center (2013). *Community College FAQs.* Retrieved from http://ccrc.tc.columbia.edu/Community-College -FAQs.html.

Corporations using prison labor to grab even more cash. (2013, May 17). Teamster Nation. Retrieved from http://teamsternation.blogspot.com /2013/05/corporations-using-prison-labor-to-grab.html.

Corrections Corporation of America (2013). *A new view of corrections: 2012 annual letter to shareholders.* Retrieved from http://cca.com /investors/financial-information.

Croteau, D., & Hoynes, W. (2014). *Media society: Industries, images, and audiences* (5th ed.). Thousand Oaks, CA: Pine Forge Press.

Cullison, A. (2010, April 2). On distant battlefields, survival odds rise sharply. *The Wall Street Journal.* Retrieved from http://online.wsj .com/news/articles/SB1000142405274870465500457511462383793 0294.

Currie, E. (1998). *Crime and punishment in America.* New York, NY: Metropolitan Books.

Dale, J. G., Andreatta, S., & Freeman, E. (2001). Language and the migrant worker experience in rural North Carolina communities. In A. D. Murphy, C. Blanchard, & J. A. Hill (Eds.), *Latino workers in the contemporary South* (pp. 93–104). Athens, GA: University of Georgia Press.

Death Penalty Information Center. (2013a). *Number of executions by state and region since 1976.* Retrieved from http://www.deathpenaltyinfo .org/number-executions-state-and-region-1976.

Death Penalty Information Center. (2013b). *The death penalty in 2013: Year end report.* Retrieved from http://www.deathpenaltyinfo.org/ documents/YearEnd2013.pdf.

Death Penalty Information Center. (2014). *Facts about the death penalty.* Retrieved from http://www.deathpenaltyinfo.org/documents/Fact Sheet.pdf.

Delpit, L. (1995). *Other people's children: Cultural conflict in the classroom.* New York, NY: New Press.

Department of Veteran's Affairs. (2013). *America's wars fact sheet.* Retrieved from http://www.va.gov/opa/publications/factsheets/fs _americas_wars.pdf.

Doetzer, G. (2008). Hard labor: The legal implications of shackling female inmates during pregnancy and childbirth. *William & Mary Journal of Women and the Law, 14.* Retrieved from http://scholarship .law.wm.edu/wmjowl/vol14/iss2/9.

Dokoupil, T. (2010, March 29). North Carolina faces claims of resegregation. *Newsweek*, p. 10.

Drehle, D. V. (2008, January 3). Death penalty walking. *Time*. Retrieved from http://content.time.com/time/magazine/article/0,9171,16998 55,00.html.

Durkheim, E. (1964). *The rules of sociological method.* New York, NY: Free Press. Originally published in 1895.

Dyer, J. (2000). *The perpetual prisoner machine: How America profits from crime.* Boulder, CO: Westview Press.

Education funding drops in more than half of states. (2012, September 5). *Huffington Post*. Retrieved from http://www.huffingtonpost.com /2012/09/05/education-funding-drops-i_n_1855826.html.

Ephron, D. (2007, November 26). A learning disability. *Newsweek*, pp. 40–41.

Federal Bureau of Investigation. (2013). *Preliminary annual uniform crime report.* Retrieved from http://www.fbi.gov/news/stories/2013 /june/preliminary-2012-crime-statistics/preliminary-2012-crime-sta tistics.

For-profit schools don't hold key to lower college costs. (2012, January 27). *USA Today*, pp. A1, 2.

Ford, A. (2010, November 17). Captive audience: Has advertising in school gone too far? *Time*, pp. 63–64.

Fry, R. (2007, June 6). How far behind in math and reading are English language learners? Pew Hispanic Center. Retrieved from http://pew hispanic.org/reports.php?ReportID = 76.

Gallimore, R., Boggs, J. W., & Jordan, C. (1974). *Culture, behavior and education: A study of Hawaiian-Americans.* Beverley Hills, CA: Sage Publications.

Geis, G. (1999). Is incarceration an appropriate sanction for the nonviolent white-collar offender? Yes. In C. B. Fields (Ed.), *Controversial issues in corrections* (pp. 152–158). Boston, MA: Allyn & Bacon.

George, D. S. (2011a, July 19). Study shows wide varieties in discipline methods among very similar schools. *The Washington Post*. Retrieved from http://articles.washingtonpost.com/2011-07-19/local/352673 92_1_juvenile-justice-discipline-gap-high-poverty-schools.

George, D. S. (2011b, December 28). In Washington area, African American students suspended and expelled two to five times as often as whites. *The Washington Post*. Retrieved from http://articles.washing tonpost.com/2011-12-28/local/35285256_1_black-students-white -students-concerns-about-school-discipline.

Gillborn, D. (1992). Citizenship, "race," and the hidden curriculum. *International Studies in the Sociology of Education, 2,* 57–73.

Glaze, L. E., & Maruschak, L. M. (2010). *Parents in prison and their minor children*. U.S. Department of Justice Programs. Retrieved from http://www.bjs.gov/content/pub/pdf/pptmc.pdf.

Gordon, D. M. (1973). Capitalism, class and crime in America. *Crime and Delinquency, 19,* 163–186.

Gould, E. (2003). *The university in a corporate culture*. New Haven, CT: Yale University Press.

Hajela, D. (2007, December 13). Some families in the US rejoice after changes to rules for crack-cocaine sentences. *The State* [Columbia, SC]. Retrieved from http://www.thestate.com/nation-extra/v-print /story/256707.html.

Haney, C. (2005). *Death by design: Capital punishment as social psychological system*. New York, NY: Oxford University Press.

Heath, S. B. (1982). Questioning at home and at school: A comparative study, doing the ethnography of schooling. In G. Spindler (Ed.), *Educational anthropology in action*. New York, NY: Holt, Rinehart, & Winston.

Heeley, L. (2013, April 24). *U.S. defense spending vs. global defense spending*. Retrieved from http://armscontrolcenter.org/issues/security spending/articles/2012_topline_global_defense_spending/

Heinlein, G., & Cain, C. (2008, May 2). Prison costs on agenda: Experts to discuss reforms to help state handle corrections spending. *Detroit News*. Retrieved from http://www.detnews.com.

Henslin, J. M. (2014). *Sociology: A down-to-earth approach* (12th ed.). Boston, MA: Pearson Education.

Herzog, J. R. (2008). *Secondary trauma in family members of combat veterans*. (Unpublished dissertation, University of South Carolina.)

Holland, J. J., & Hefling, K. (2014, May 15). School integration slipping 60 years after Brown. *The State* [Columbia, SC], p. A7.

Horowitz, A. (2013, February 4). Mental illness soars in prisons, jails while inmates suffer. *The Huffington Post*. Retrieved from http://

www.huffingtonpost.com/2013/02/04/mental-illness-prisons-jails
-inmates_n_2610062.html.

Interagency Task Force on Military and Veterans Mental Health. (2013).
2013 interim report. Retrieved from http://www.whitehouse.gov
/sites/default/files/uploads/2013_interim_report_of_the_interagency
_task_force_on_military_and_veterans_mental_health.pdf.

Isikoff, M., & Reno, J. (2007, October 29). "How do you fund a war, but
not the casualties?" *Newsweek*, p. 10.

Jackson, J. (2003, July 27). Old South holds back new South's potential.
The State [Columbia, SC], p. D3.

Jamail, D., & Coppola, J. (2009, August 6). Militarizing the homeland.
Retrieved August 6, 2009 from http://www.truth-out.org/archive
/item/85485:militarizing-the-homeland

Janssen, S. (Ed.). (2013). *The world almanac and book of facts: 2013.*
New York, NY: World Almanac Books.

Jansson, B. S. (2012). *The reluctant welfare state: Engaging history to
advance social work practice in contemporary society* (7th ed.). Belmont, CA: Brooks/Cole.

Kamenetz, A. (2014, May 13). State spots in preschool declining, report
finds. National Public Radio. Retrieved from http://www.npr.org
/blogs/thetwo-way/2014/05/13/312054303/state-spots-in-preschool
-declining-report-finds.

Kendall, D. (2008). *Sociology in our times* (7th ed.). Belmont, CA:
Wadsworth.

Kendall, D. (2013). *Sociology in our times* (9th ed.). Belmont, CA:
Wadsworth.

Kerby, S. (2012). *The top 10 most startling facts about people of color
and criminal justice in the United States: A look at the racial disparities inherent in our nation's criminal-justice system.* Center for American Progress. Retrieved from http://www.americanprogress.org
/issues/race/news/2012/03/13/11351/the-top-10-most-startling-facts-
about-people-of-color-and-criminal-justice-in-the-united-states/.

Kielstra, P. (2012). *The learning curve: Lessons in country performance
in education.* London, UK: Pearson. Retrieved from http://the
learningcurve.pearson.com/.

Kilbourne, J. (1999). *Deadly persuasion: Why women and girls must fight
the addictive power of advertising.* New York, NY: Free Press.

Kontak, D. (2008). *Roles of school social workers.* Retrieved from http://sswaa.org/associations/13190/files/Elements of School Social Work 2012.pdf.

Konz, A. (2013, September 6). More schools roll out tough core standards. *USA Today*, p. 3A.

Kozol, J. (1991). *Savage inequalities: Children in America's schools.* New York, NY: Crown.

Kozol, J. (2005). *The shame of the nation: The restoration of apartheid schooling in America.* New York, NY: Crown Publishers.

Leger, D. L. (2013, October 25). Violent crime rises for 2nd year, but rates are still historically low. *USA Today*, p. 1A.

Lindorff, D. (2013). The united police states of America. Retrieved from http://www.nationofchange.org/print/37137

Lipset, S. M. (1996). *American exceptionalism: A double-edged sword.* New York, NY: W. W. Norton.

Macionis, J. J. (2014). *Sociology* (15th ed.). Boston, MA: Pearson Education.

Malcolm, H., & McMinn, S. (2013, September 3). Tuition rises as state funding sags. *USA Today*, p. 4B.

Marklein, M. B. (2013, August 26). Caution! Student loans must be paid back! *USA Today*, p. 4A.

Maruschak, L. M. (2008). Medical problems of prisoners. Bureau of Justice Statistics. Retrieved from http://www.ojp.usdoj.gov/bjs/.

Mastony, C. (2010, July 18). Childbirth in chains. *Chicago Tribune*, pp. 1, 10.

McClam, E. (2008, January 19) Next wave of homeless vets emerges. *USA Today.* Retrieved from http://usatoday.printthis.clickability.com/pt/cpt?action=cpt&title.

Merton, R. K. (1949). *Social theory and social structure.* Glencoe, IL: Free Press.

Meyers, J. (2013, July 18). Increasing student loan debt having a "ripple effect" on the economy. *USA Today*, p. A1.

Michaels, J. (2013, October 21). Female marines inch closer to ground combat. *USA Today*, p. 4A.

Michaels, J., Brook, T. V., & Welch, W. M. (2013, January 24). Pentagon opens front lines to women. *USA Today*, p. 1A–2A.

Milburn, J., & Manning, S. (2008, December 3). Bad economy good for military. *The State* [Columbia, SC], p. A4.

Miltary-Ranks.org. (2014). Welcome to Military-Ranks.org. Retrieved from http://www.military-ranks.org/.

Morris, R. (2003, October 7). For USC, the show must go on. *The State* [Columbia, SC], pp. C1, C4.

Moskos, C. C. (2000). Toward a postmodern military: The United States as a paradigm. In C. C. Moskos, J. A. Williams, and D. R. Segal (Eds.). *The postmodern military armed forces after the cold war* (pp. 14–31). New York, NY: Oxford University Press.

Moskos, C. C., & Butler, J. (1996). *All that we can be: Black leadership and racial integration in the Army.* New York, NY: Basic Books.

Moskos, C. C., Williams, J. A., & Segal, D. R. (eds.). (2000). *The postmodern military armed forces after the cold war.* New York, NY: Oxford University Press.

Mumola, C. J. (2000, August). *Incarcerated parents and their children.* U.S. Department of Justice, Office of Justice Programs. Retrieved from http://www.ojp.usdojgov/bjs/.

Murphey, D. (2013, July 22) Home front alert: The risk facing young children in military families. Child Trends. Retrieved from http://www.childtrends.org/wp-content/uploads/2013/07/2013-31Military Families.pdf.

Murphy, B. (2013, September 7). Family income not a factor as all students can eat free. *The State* [Columbia, SC], p. A6.

National Center for Education Statistics. (2007). *Digest of education statistics.* Retrieved from http://nces.ed.gov.

National Center for Education Statistics. (2008). *Special analysis 2008: Community colleges.* Retrieved from http://nces.ed.gov/programs/coe/2008/analysis/index/asp.

Oakes, J. (1985). *Keeping track: How high schools structure inequality.* New Haven, CT: Yale University Press.

Office of Undersecretary of Defense Personnel and Readiness. (2010). *Population representation in the military services.* Retrieved from http://prhome.defense.gov/Home.aspx.

Orfield, G. (2009). *Reviving the goal of an integrated society: A 21st century challenge.* Los Angeles, CA: The Civil Rights Project/ Proyecto Derechos Civiles at UCLA.

Pew Center on the States. (2008). *One in 100: Behind bars in America 2008.* Retrieved from http://www.pewcenteronthestates.org/report _detail.aspx?id = 35904.

Pew Research Center. (2011, October 5). *War and sacrifice in the post 9/ 11 era: The military-civilian group.* Retrieved http://www.pewsocial trends.org/2011/10/05/war-and-sacrifice-in-the-post-911-era.

Phillips, M. (2007, September 10). Separation anxieties. *Newsweek,* p. 15.

PTSD resources and treatment. (2014). U.S. Veterans Health Care. Retrieved from www.military.com/benefits/veterans-health-care.

Public papers of the presidents of the United States, Dwight. D. Eisenhower 1960–1961. Retrieved from http://www.gpoaccess.gov/pub papers/index.html.

Puma, M., Bell, S., Cook, R., Heid, C., Broene, P., Jenkins, F., Mashburn, A., & Downer, J. (2012). *Third Grade Follow-up to the Head Start Impact Study Final Report, OPRE Report # 2012–45.* Washington, DC: Office of Planning, Research and Evaluation, Administration for Children and Families, U.S. Department of Health and Human Services.

Raines, J. P., & Leathers, C. G. (2003). *The economic institution of higher education: Economic theories of university behaviour.* Northampton, MA: Edward Elgar.

Rawe, J. (2007, November 19). Congress's bad drug habit. *Time,* p. 60.

Reiman, J., & Leighton, P. (2013). *The rich get richer and the poor get prison* (10th ed). Boston, MA: Pearson Education.

Richard, A. (2013, April 25). *Racial segregation continues to impact quality of education in Mississippi—and nationwide.* Retrieved from http://hechingerreport.org/content/racial-segregation-continues-to-impact-quality-of-education-in-mississippi-and-nationwide_11853/.

Ripley, A. (2013, September 30). The new smart set. *Time,* pp. 33–36.

Rist, R. C. (1970). Student social class and teacher expectations: The self-fulfilling prophecy in ghetto education. *Harvard Educational Review, 40,* 411–451.

Ritter, J. A., Vakalahi, H. F. O., & Kiernan-Stern, M. (2009). *101 careers in social work.* New York, NY: Springer.

Roig-Franzia, M., & Horwitz, S. (2013, July 16). Holder condemns "Stand Your Ground" laws. *The Washington Post.* Retrieved from http://

www.washingtonpost.com/politics/naacp-urges-eric-holder-do-the
-right-thing/2013/07/16/530425da-ee49-11e2-9008-61e94a7ea20d
_story.html.

Rosenthal, R., & Jacobson, L. (1968). *Pygmalion in the classroom: Teacher expectations and pupils' intellectual development*. New York, NY: Holt, Reinhart and Winston.

Rothstein, R. (2013). *For public schools, segregation then, segregation now: Education and the unfinished march*. Economic Policy Institute. Retrieved from http://epi.org/files/2013/Unfinished-March-School-Segregation.pdf.

Ryan, W. (1976). *Blaming the victim*. New York, NY: Vintage.

Schaefer, R. T. (2012). *Racial and ethnic groups* (13th ed.). Boston, MA: Pearson Education.

Schlosser, E. (1998, December). The prison-industrial complex. *The Atlantic Monthly,* pp. 54–57.

School Social Work Association of America. (2012). *About school social work*. Retrieved from http://sswaa.org/displaycommon.cfm?an = 1& subarticlenbr = 1.

Segal, S. P. (2008). Deinstitutionalization. In T. Mizrahi & L. E. Davis (Eds), *Encyclopedia of social work* (20th ed., Vol. 2, pp. 10–20). Washington, DC: NASW Press.

Self, J. (2013, November 19). Foes find common cause in fighting common core rules. *The State* [Columbia, SC], p. A1.

Serrano, R. A. (2013, December 1). Infirm prisoners hope for freedom. *Chicago Tribune*, p. 31.

Siegel, L. J., & Worrall, J. L. (2014). *Introduction to criminal justice* (14th ed.). Belmont, CA: Wadsworth.

Skipp, C., & Ephron, D. (2006, October 23). Trouble at home. *Newsweek*, pp. 48–49.

Snider, J. (2013, September 9). Demand accountability from universities —and borrowers. *USA Today*, p. 10A.

Stoesen, L. (2005, April). Under-18 death penalty struck down. *NASW News*, p. 1.

Sullivan, S. (2013, July 15). Everything you need to know about "stand your ground" laws. *The Washington Post*. Retrieved from http://www.washingtonpost.com/blogs/the-fix/wp/2013/07/15/everything -you-need-to-know-about-stand-your-ground-laws/.

Supiano, B. (2013, November 1). Tuition rises less sharply, and net price goes up again. *The Chronicle of Higher Education*, p. A3.

Sutherland, E. H. (1940). White collar criminality. *American Sociological Review, 5*, 1–12.

Swanson, C. B. (2008, April 1). Cities in crisis: A special analytic report on high school graduation. *Education Week*. Retrieved from http://www.edweek.org/re/articles/2008/04/01cities_in_crisis.html.

Sweet, W. (2010). *Dodd-Frank act becomes law*. (Master's thesis, Harvard University). Retrieved from http://blogs.law.harvard.edu/corp gov/2010/07/21/dodd-frank-act-becomes-law/.

Territo, L., Halsted, J. B., & Bromley, M. L. (2004). *Crime and justice in America: A human perspective*. Upper Saddle River, NJ: Pearson.

Thio, A. (2000). *Sociology: A brief introduction* (4th ed.) Boston, MA: Allyn and Bacon.

Thompson, C. (2013, November 18). Teacher killings bring the profession's risks to light. *The State* [Columbia, SC], p. A5.

Thompson, M. (2011, November 21). The other 1%. *Time,* pp. 34–39.

Thompson, M. (2013, February 11). Army strong. *Time*, p. 15.

Tobias, S. (1989, September). Tracked to fail. *Psychology Today*, pp. 54–58.

Toppo, G. (2013, November 18). Shooting fears blur facts: School is safe. *USA Today*, p. 1A.

Toppo, G. (2012, June 13). Should bullies be treated as criminals? *USA Today*. Retrieved from http://usatoday30.usatoday.com/news/nation/story/2012-06-12/bullying-crime-schools-suicide/55554112/1.

United Nations Education, Scientific and Cultural Organization. (2012). *Literacy and education data for the school year ending in 2010: Literacy rates are rising, but women and girls continue to lag behind*. Retrieved from http://www.uis.unesco.org/literacy/pages/adult-youth -literacy-data-viz.aspx.

U.S. Department of Agriculture. (2008). *National school lunch program: Total participation*. Retrieved from http://www.fns.usda.gov/.

U.S. Department of Health and Human Services (2005). *Headstart*. Retrieved from http://www.hhs.gov/headstart/.

U.S. military deaths in Afghanistan at 2,133. (2013). Retrieved from http://abcnews.go.com/Politics.

Valentine, C. (2013, June). *Meet 'em and plead 'em: Is this the best practice?* Retrieved from http://www.nacdl.org/Champion.aspx?id = 28953.

Van Wormer, K. (2001). *Counseling female offenders and victims: A strengths-restorative approach.* New York, NY: Springer.

Vestal, C. (2013, October 29). *Study finds aging inmates pushing up prison health care costs.* Retrieved from http://www.pewstates.org /projects/stateline/headlines/study-finds-aging-inmates-pushing-up -prison-health-care-costs-85899516112.

Violence Policy Center. (2011). *A shrinking minority: The continuing decline of gun ownership in America.* Retrieved from http://www.vpc .org/studies/ownership.pdf.

Wang, N. (2013, August 14). Here are all of the nations that incarcerate more of their population than the U.S. *The Huffington Post.* Retrieved from http://www.huffingtonpost.com/2013/08/13/incarceration-rate -per-capita_n_3745291.html.

Watson, J. (2011, September 9). Subtle acts reshape military. *The State* [Columbia, SC], p. A4.

Why have so few bankers gone to jail? (2013, May 13). *The Economist.* Retrieved from http://www.economist.com/blogs/economist-ex plains/2013/05/economist-explains-why-few-bankers-gone-to-jail.

Women in the U.S. Army. (2008). Retrieved from http://www.army.mil /women/Women in the Army, 2008.

Wright, J. W. (Ed.). (2007). *The New York Times 2008 almanac.* New York, NY: Penguin Books.

Wright, J. W. (2010). *The New York Times 2011 almanac.* New York, NY: Penguin Books.

Yost, P. (2011, September 20). FBI: Violent crime down 6% in 2010. *The State* [Columbia, SC], pp. A1, A4.

Zakaria, F. (2012, March 30). Zakaria: Incarceration nation. Retrieved from http://globalpublicsquare.blogs.cnn.com/2012/03/22/zakaria -incarceration-nation/.

Zernike, K. (2006, February 12). Violent crime rising sharply in some cities. *The New York Times.* Retrieved from http://www.nytimes.com /2006/02/12/national/12homicide.html.

Zoroya, G. (2014, January 17). Up to 48,000 Afghan, Iraq vets homeless. *USA Today*, p. 1A.

CHAPTER FOUR

Non-Government-Related Social Institutions

In this chapter, we discuss three non-government-related social institutions, their interaction with the political economy, and their impact on individuals and families. Like the social institutions discussed so far, they are also important in the lives of social work clients.

HEALTH CARE

Health care is the social institution whose purpose is dealing with disease and injury and improving health and maintaining wellness, on both an individual and community level. Typically, in the United States, public health officials are concerned with issues of prevention, while medical practitioners are more focused on treatment and/or cure after the fact, even though they might offer advice on healthy living.

Issues and Trends in Health Care

Cost of Health Care

The United States spends almost $60 billion on health care every week; spending has grown by more than 800 percent since 1960 (Brill, 2013). The United States spends more on health care than any other developed country, 17 percent of the gross domestic product; at its current rate of growth health care will constitute a fifth of the total economy by 2015 (Zakaria, 2012). Most of the uncontrolled growth in federal spending comes from Medicare (the federal health insurance program for older adults).

About a third of health care costs are related to hospitals. In March 2013, Steven Brill wrote an exposé published in *Time* magazine that revealed the "outrageous pricing and egregious profits" of American hospitals. He reviewed the hospital bills of several individuals and reported examples of inflated charges for lab tests, medications, and supplies. Examples included a $7 charge for each small cotton square used to apply alcohol to an injection site when a box of 200 can be bought for $1.91, $24 for a niacin pill that costs a nickel at the drugstore, and $18 each for Accu-Chek diabetic test strips that Amazon sells for about 55 cents each. Brill noted that nonprofit hospitals are, in fact, making profits in excess of hundreds of millions of dollars annually and hospital CEOs are paid salaries in excess of a million dollars.

When physicians order tests and procedures, they face no incentive to restrict their choices because most insurance policies will reimburse the costs under the fee-for-service arrangements that cover much of the medical care provided in the United States. If patients were paying out-of-pocket, they might be more likely to question the need for some tests and procedures.

Paying for Health Care

Individuals can subscribe to group health care plans on their own, but more typically they are covered by their employers' plans (or under the family plan of a working spouse or parent). According to the U. S. Census Bureau (DeNavas-Walt, Proctor, & Smith, 2013), 63.9 percent of Americans were covered by private health insurance, almost all through their employers, in 2012. Between 2003 and 2013 average annual health insurance costs rose from $9,068 to $16,351 for family coverage, an increase of 80 percent; the individual's share of the cost of premiums was about 27 percent (Kaiser Family Foundation, 2013a).

Again, according to the U. S. Census Bureau (DeNavas-Walt, Proctor, & Smith, 2013), the proportion of people covered by government health insurance increased to 32.6 percent in 2012. Medicare covers 15.7 percent of the population (mostly individuals age sixty-five and older) and Medicaid, including State Children's Health Insurance Programs, covers another 16.4 percent of the population (primarily children, pregnant women, and elderly and disabled people who qualify due to low income or other circumstances). In 2012, 15.4% of Americans—or 48 million people—were uninsured. The proportion of Hispanics who were uninsured was 29.1 percent, much higher than the comparable rates for blacks (19 percent), Asian Americans (15.1 percent) and non-Hispanic whites (11.1 percent).

Almost 40 percent of low-wage workers have no health insurance coverage from any source, public or private (Schmitt, 2012). According to a Kaiser Family Foundation report (2013b), people go without coverage because of the high cost of health insurance. Many people do not have access to coverage through their own or a spouse's employment. Uninsured workers are likely to be employed by small businesses that do not offer coverage, or to be self-employed service workers, or part-time workers (National Association of Social Workers [NASW], 2012a). Even when employers offer coverage, often low-wage workers cannot afford their share of the premiums, especially for family coverage. In addition, gaps in eligibility for public health insurance programs leave many without an affordable option. Only nine states provide full Medicaid coverage to low-income adults without dependent children. (See the Affordable Care Act below.)

There are several structural factors that help explain the loss in health insurance coverage for low-wage workers. These include "a steep decline in unionization, an erosion of the inflation-adjusted value of the minimum wage, the deregulation of many historically high-wage industries (such as trucking, airlines, telecommunications), and the privatization of many state and local government functions from school cafeteria workers to public assistance administrators (Schmitt, 2012, p. 11).

People who are uninsured face increased risks on several fronts (NASW, 2012a). They do not access medical providers for preventive care, and delays in seeking treatment may result in more serious illnesses. Public clinics do not satisfy the needs of the many Americans without insurance. Children and adults without insurance are more likely to have poor health and die sooner than those with insurance.

The United States is one of the few industrialized nations where illness or injury can lead directly to financial catastrophe. In America, 62 percent of bankruptcies are related to illness or medical bills and 69 percent of those who have experienced medically related bankruptcy were insured at the time of their filing (Brill, 2013). Financial problems included both direct and indirect medical-related costs: medical bills, drugs, and curtailed employment due to personal illness or the need to care for someone else who was seriously ill.

The Patient Protection and Affordable Care Act

In 2010 the U.S. Congress passed the Affordable Care Act [ACA or "Obamacare"] and it was signed into law by President Barack Obama and is to be implemented over several years. It requires most U.S. citizens and legal residents to have health insurance (Kaiser Family Foundation, 2013b). The idea behind the plan is the same as that for all types of insurance—shared risk. Low-income people will receive subsidies or tax credits. Uninsured people who decline coverage will pay a penalty— about $95 per person or 1 percent of annual income, whichever is greater. People who already have insurance through their employer or Medicare are not affected.

Other features of the ACA include:

- Children can remain on their parents' insurance plan until the age of 26
- Insurance companies can no longer drop someone's health insurance if he or she becomes sick
- Insurance companies cannot set a lifetime limit on coverage
- There are also restrictions on insurance companies imposing limitations for preexisting conditions

Since parts of the ACA are just going into effect, it is difficult to judge the effects of the legislation on patients, health care providers, insurance companies, and the economy.

Unhealthy Lifestyles

In the United States chronic diseases—cancer, diabetes, and heart and lung disease—kill nearly nine out of ten people (Marchione, 2011). These diseases have common risk factors, such as smoking, sedentary life styles, and overeating or eating the wrong kinds of food. More than a quarter of Americans do not perform physical activity outside of work, and more than one in five Americans smoke (Healy, 2012). Many Americans eat less than the recommended amounts of fresh fruits and vegetables. Poor people are at increased risk of poor dietary behaviors because stores in low-income neighborhoods offer fewer fresh fruits and vegetables and more processed snack foods.

More than two-thirds (68.5 percent) of American adults are overweight or obese; more than three in ten (34.9 percent) are obese (Ogden, Carroll, Kit, & Flegal, 2014). Childhood obesity has more than doubled in children and tripled in adolescents in the past thirty years; more than a third of children and adolescents in America are overweight or obese (American Psychological Association, 2010; Ogden et al., 2014). Overweight and obese individuals are at increased risk of high blood pressure, osteoarthritis, type 2 diabetes, coronary heart disease, stroke, gallbladder disease, sleep apnea, and some cancers (endometrial, breast, and colon) (Centers for Disease Control and Prevention, 2013).

Mental Health and Mental Illness

According to the National Alliance on Mental Illness (NAMI), a mental illness is

> a medical condition that disrupts a person's thinking, feeling, mood, ability to relate to others and daily functioning. Just as diabetes is a disorder of the pancreas, mental illnesses are medical conditions that often result in a diminished capacity for coping with the ordinary demands of life. . . .
> Mental illnesses can affect persons of any age, race, religion or income. Mental illnesses are not the result of personal weakness, lack of character or poor upbringing. Mental illnesses are treatable. Most people diagnosed with a serious mental illness can experience relief from their symptoms by actively participating in an individual treatment plan. (NAMI, 2013)

According to NAMI (2013) an estimated one in four of Americans ages eighteen and older suffers from a diagnosable mental disorder in a given year. While mental disorders are commonplace, serious mental illness is in a much smaller proportion of the population—about 6 percent, or 1 in 17 people. Mental disorders are the leading cause of disability in the United States and Canada. Many people suffer from more than one mental disorder at a given time. Mental illnesses usually strike individuals in the prime of their lives, often in adolescence and young adulthood. One half of all lifetime cases of mental illness begin by age 14, three-quarters by age 24.

On the other hand, some forms of mental impairment appear in later stages of life. Nearly 15 percent of people aged 71 or older suffer from dementia. In America, that translates to about 3.8 million people, and by 2040 that number will expand to 9.1 million (Belluck, 2013). Medicare costs for seniors with dementias, such as Alzheimer's, are nearly three times higher than for those without it; Medicaid payments are nineteen times higher (Alzheimer's Association, 2014).

Medical research continues to document organic causes for many forms of mental illness—genetic predispositions or chemical imbalances, for example. Environmental factors also play a role. Certain stigmatized statuses, such as being poor or a member of a minority group, can add to a person's stress level. Many adolescents and adults in the mental health system have histories of early trauma, including abuse, neglect, and domestic violence (NASW, 2012b).

According to summaries of government reports (NAMI, 2013), despite their wide prevalence, mental illnesses often go untreated in the United States. Approximately 60 percent of adults with a mental illness, and almost one-half of youth ages 8 to 15, received no mental health services in 2009. Minority populations are less likely than whites to use mental health services. Blacks and Latinos use mental health services at about one-half the rate for whites and Asian Americans.

In October 2008, Congress passed and the president signed the Paul Wellstone-Pete Domenici Mental Health Parity and Addiction Equity Act. This culminated a nearly twenty-year effort to require group health plans to cover treatment for mental illness on the same terms and conditions as all other illnesses. This meant that group health plans are no longer able to impose limits on inpatient days or outpatient visits or require higher deductibles or cost sharing for mental illness or addiction treatment that are not also applied to all other medical-surgical coverage. Such practices had long been commonplace.

Retail Medicine

Retail medicine is a relatively new and rapidly growing trend in the provision of health care services in the United States for patients with a particular set of needs—minor ailments such as sore throats, sprains, bumps and bruises, flu shots and other inoculations, and routine preventive screenings that typically make up 85 percent of trips to a primary care provider but do not require the services of a physician (Faulkner, 2013). Staffed by nurse practitioners and physician assistants and housed in pharmacies or freestanding clinics, these providers are an alternative to emergency room visits which are not only likely to be more expensive but also likely to include lengthy waiting times (Holleman, 2013). They are well designed to serve the newly insured under the Affordable Care Act who do not have regular health care providers. The number of these outlets is projected to double in the next three years (Faulkner, 2013). Some critics argue that retail medicine may lead to "further fragmentation" of care, and lessen opportunities for preventive care and treatment for chronic conditions that are a usual part of an established relationship with a primary care physician (Pollack, Gidengil, & Mehrotra, 2010).

Alternative Medicine and Holistic Health Care

Alternative medicine refers to some experimental drugs and nontraditional practices, such as those used by Native American healers and some imported from Asian cultures, that are not included in the traditional medical curricula taught in the United States and Great Britain. These include acupuncture, yoga, meditation, and tai chi from Asian countries. One of the most common forms of Native American medicine involves the use of herbal remedies, which can include teas, tinctures, and salves. One remedy for pain uses bark from a willow tree, which contains acetylsalicylic acid, also known as aspirin (American Cancer Society, 2008).

In response to patient demands, the U.S. medical establishment has begun to make accommodations to these alternative treatments (Henslin, 2014). What once was "alternative" may become "conventional," suggesting that the use of the term *holistic* may be preferable in some cases. "Holistic medicine is the art and science of healing that addresses care of the whole person—body, mind, and spirit. The practice of holistic medicine integrates conventional and complementary therapies to promote optimal health, and prevent and treat disease by addressing contributing factors" (American Holistic Medical Association, n.d.). One could interpret Native American healing practices as holistic medicine. Traditional healers aim to "make whole" by restoring well-being and harmonious relationships with the community and nature (American Cancer Society,

2008). Native Americans believe that the spirit is an inseparable element of healing.

Care versus Cure

One-quarter of Medicare spending, more than $125 billion, goes for services for the 5 percent of beneficiaries in their last year of life (Wang, 2012). Research suggests that at the very end, neither high spending nor days in the hospital nor intensive care increase the length of life and may make things worse (Bennett, 2012). Most medical professionals have not been trained to deal with end-of-life care; their focus is on the treatment and cure of diseases. According to one nurse, "Our health-care system is really set up to cure the patient, and if we can't cure, then folks sort of get confused about what do we do here. We have nothing in the toolbox, and that's unacceptable" (Bennett, 2012, p. 55). The medical system ensures that physicians and hospitals are paid well for providing extensive treatment; in fact, they may face legal liability for denying care (Doyle, 2012). The hospice movement, on the other hand, provides palliative care (i.e., comfort, pain relief) and "death with dignity." It focuses on quality of life for terminally ill people rather than triumph over disease. "The best care possible . . . reflects both medical choices and personal and emotional ones" (Bennett, 2012, p. 55). Social workers are likely to play a more significant role in hospice care than in hospital care.

Adults can express their preferences about various types of life-extending medical interventions, but also need to take legal steps to protect themselves from unnecessary medical intervention. By writing a living will and giving durable power of attorney for health care to a trusted relative or friend, patients have the opportunity to exercise control over potentially painful and invasive but ineffective medical treatment at a time in the future when they are unable to speak for themselves. A living will allows them to make the decision of whether life-prolonging medical or surgical procedures are to be continued, withheld, or withdrawn, as well as when artificial feeding and fluids are to be provided or withheld. Physicians and health care providers are directed by the living will to follow the patient's instructions. To be valid, the proper form must be used for each state, and it must be executed in compliance with the laws of the state. The living will generally becomes operative when it is provided to the physician or other health care provider *and* the patient is incapable of making health care decisions for himself or herself, such as when he or she is permanently unconscious and unable to communicate. Despite recommendations from many professionals, only about a third of Americans have living wills or health care proxies (Wang, 2012).

Health Care in a Global Perspective

The leading causes of death in the United States and other developed countries are heart disease, cancer, and stroke. In many low-income nations, poor people do not live long enough to develop these chronic diseases; instead they die from malnutrition, dehydration, internal parasites, and diseases such as malaria, influenza, and pneumonia. Risk factors in these countries include deficiencies in micronutrients like iron and zinc, unsafe water, poor sanitation, and indoor smoke from solid fuels (World Health Organization, 2002). In contrast to low-income countries, the United States ranks first in terms of access to clean water and sanitation facilities.

The number of women in poor countries who die in childbirth is almost the same as it was twenty years ago. Women in Afghanistan and in Sierra Leone in West Africa have a one in eight chance of dying in childbirth during their lifetime (Walt, 2008). This rate compares to one in 4,800 in the United States, one in 8,200 in Great Britain, and one in 17,400 in Sweden.

The United States spends far more money per person on health care than any other country. In 2012, the amount averaged $8,233 for every man, woman, and child in the nation, which is more than two and a half times the average of the thirty wealthiest nations in the Organization for Economic Cooperation and Development (Kane, 2012). Nevertheless, it falls behind other nations on a variety of health care measures: the number of physicians per person, the number of hospital beds, and life expectancy at birth (Kane, 2012).

The American health care system is often compared to the single-payer system used in Canada. *Single-payer* means that the government runs the health care system for all citizens, paid for by tax dollars. Advantages include the system's administrative simplicity—the patient simply shows a card at the point of service (Miller, 2013). Another advantage is that when multinational corporations bid on projects they don't have to worry about health costs. There is universal coverage and better outcomes, with less cost (Miller, 2013). In Canada, procedure costs run about half of what they do in the United States: a CT scan costs $122 compared to $510 in the United States; an appendectomy costs $5,606 rather than $13,003 (Brill, 2013). The 2010 Affordable Care Act features a much smaller role for government in U.S. health care than the Canadian system.

Understanding the Health Care System

Functionalist Perspective

Structural functionalists view illness as dysfunctional because it prevents individuals from performing their assigned roles. This point of view was articulated by James Buchanan Duke, a wealthy North Carolina businessman and the founder of the Duke Endowment. He explained his support for the expansion of health care facilities in the Carolinas in a newspaper interview in the 1920s, saying, "People ought to be healthy. If they ain't healthy they can't work, and if they don't work they ain't healthy. And if they can't work there ain't no profit in them" (Goulden, 1971).

A primary function of the U.S. health care system is to maintain a healthy workforce. The fact that the vast majority of those individuals who have health insurance coverage receive that benefit through their employer makes clear the link between financial support for health care and the needs of the economy. Tax-supported government insurance (e.g., Medicaid) for nonworkers tends to be stingy and often stigmatizing.

Conflict Perspective

The medical establishment includes health care providers, laboratories, clinics, pharmaceutical companies, hospitals, medical supply manufacturers, and insurance companies. Through its political and financial clout, the medical establishment has become the most lucrative business in the country. In theory, the supply-and-demand of a capitalist system should keep health care prices competitive, but in reality, the members of the medical establishment, not health care consumers, determine the demand by deciding what kinds of medical services and supplies are needed and then providing them at the prices they set. Often there are inherent conflicts of interest, as when doctors have financial investments in laboratories, pharmacies, hospitals, and medical supply companies. It is difficult to know if a doctor has made a choice based on the needs of the patient or the needs of his or her bank account. For example, according to testimony before a Senate committee, "physicians routinely receive substantial compensation from medical-device companies through stock options, royalty agreements, consulting agreements, research grants and fellowships." The testimony continued, "physician ownership of medical-device manufacturers and related businesses appears to be a growing trend in the medical-device sector. . . . In some cases, physicians could receive substantial returns while contributing little to the venture beyond the ability to generate business for the venture" (Brill, 2013, p. 34).

On an organizational level, many hospitals use a targeting approach called "customer relationship marketing" (Galewitz, 2012). These hospitals mine patient records to find those that have the ability to pay for tests and procedures from which the hospital can earn significant profits. These patients are contacted by mail and offered services such as cardiac screenings, cholesterol tests, and mammograms.

As the gatekeeper of the profession, the American Medical Association (AMA) controls who can provide medical services by controlling who is licensed to diagnose and treat patients and prescribe drugs, effectively eliminating some competitors (such as homeopathic healers) and controlling those who remain (e.g., nurses, social workers, and physical therapists). Early in the twentieth century, physicians expanded their practice opportunities by campaigning against midwifery. Using the power of the AMA, they persuaded many states to make it illegal for anyone but a physician to deliver babies.

In another example of attempted control by the medical establishment, the South Carolina State Board of Dentistry repeatedly challenged the right of dental hygienists to provide teeth cleaning services in schools by demanding that each child first be examined by a dentist (Werner, 2007). The Federal Trade Commission had to step in to enforce state laws supporting access to these services by children, alleging unfair trade practices.

Constructionist Perspective

Both "illness" and "health" are culturally defined. An example is our understanding of pregnancy and childbirth. Pregnancy was once thought of as a normal part of a woman's life. Even though childbirth was often dangerous or even fatal, women delivered their babies at home with the help of female relatives or nurse-midwives. As noted above, physicians redefined pregnancy as a medical condition and delivery as a medical emergency that required the assistance of a specially educated person, usually meaning a male obstetrician. Both the patient and the physician socially reconstructed even routine births as medical crises requiring in-patient hospitalization. Other routine problems and processes that have been medicalized include short stature, menopause, normal hair loss, trouble sleeping, "restless leg syndrome," "low T" (low testosterone), and erectile dysfunction.

Other examples of the social construction of illness are addictions and behavior problems such as overeating, phobias, and adolescent rebelliousness. These were once identified as personal weaknesses or eccentricities, but came to be defined as diseases or mental disorders. Once these problems were medicalized, physicians became the primary supervisors of treatment as well as gatekeepers to those applying for medical benefits. Contextual factors, such as family patterns, poverty, violence, trauma, and oppression are seldom viewed as relevant in explaining or contributing to the disorders.

Relationship of the Health Care System to the Political Economy

Like other American social institutions, health care is highly integrated with the political economy. In contrast to most other countries, in the United States health care is not a right of citizenship, but a commodity that is delivered to consumers through the private market system. The United States is the only industrialized nation that offers neither national health insurance nor guaranteed health services. Conservative politicians and the medical establishment have always campaigned against proposals for the development of government health care programs and also oppose government intervention in the delivery of health care services. For example, between January 2011 and April 2014, Republicans in the House of

Representatives voted more than fifty times to repeal the Affordable Care Act. (These bills never passed the Democrat-controlled Senate.) The health sector (pharmaceutical and health products industry, hospitals and nursing homes, health services and HMOs, and other health-related industries) has spent more than $5.36 billion on lobbying efforts, according to the Center for Responsive Politics (2013), a nonprofit watchdog group.

Sociologists (see Thio, 2000, pp. 388–389, for example) argue that although medical care appears to be organized like any other business in the free market, it is quite different. Consumers do not have much input into purchasing choices because they cannot determine what they need. Sick or injured people are not in a good position to question their doctors' choices. They rely on the medical establishment to tell them what to get and how much they must pay. Most have few incentives to "comparison shop" because they pay only a small share of the costs directly.

An interesting example of the potential conflict between making a profit and offering good health care is the sharp rise in the rate of Caesarean births. Today, about one in three babies is delivered via C-section in contrast to one in five babies in 1996 (Vedantam, 2013). If the change were based on medical need or medical advances, one would expect the rates to be the same across the country, but the C-section rate is twice as high in Louisiana as it is in Alaska (Vedantam, 2013). Obstetricians may be paid a few hundred dollars more for a C-section compared to a vaginal delivery and hospitals may make a few thousand extra dollars (Rehavi & Johnson, 2013). Advocates for natural childbirth say that hospitals that are driven by profits and concerned about malpractice charges guide expectant mothers to choose surgery.

The Impact of the Health Care System on Individuals and Families

How the Health Care System Deters Well-Being

The medical establishment focuses on microorganisms to explain ill health but often does not consider the harmful effects of poverty. From the perspective of the members of the medical establishment, people in the lower economic classes contribute to their own poor health by eating the wrong foods and living in unsanitary conditions. They seldom question the reasons behind these "choices." By not taking context into account, the medical establishment reduces a societal-level issue to an individual one.

Scientific medicine has not done a good job of meeting the needs of women, people of color, poor people, and older adults. Women and members of racial and ethnic minorities are less likely than white males to receive aggressive and sophisticated health care and mental health care. In 1999, Congress directed the Agency for Healthcare Research and Quality (AHRQ) to produce an annual report, starting in 2003, to track "prevailing disparities in health care delivery as it relates to racial factors and socioeconomic factors in priority populations" (U.S. Department of Health and Human Services, 2006). The first National Healthcare Disparities Report (NHDR), released in 2003, was a comprehensive national overview of disparities in health care among racial, ethnic, and socioeconomic groups in the general U.S. population; the 2004 NHDR initiated a second critical goal of the report series—tracking the nation's progress toward the elimination of health care disparities (U.S. Department of Health and Human Services, 2006). More recently, health care data on women, older adults, residents of rural areas, LGBT individuals, and individuals with special health care needs (such as those with disabilities, and those who need chronic care or end-of-life care) were added.

According to the 2012 National Health Care Disparities Report (Agency for Health Care Research and Quality [AHRQ], 2012), for all measures whites continued to have better access to health care delivery than racial and ethnic minorities. For eleven measures, the gaps between blacks and whites grew smaller, while for two measures the gaps grew larger. For American Indians, Alaska Natives, and Latinos the number of measures where the gap increased was greater than the number of measures where the gap grew smaller. For Asians, gaps grew smaller for four measures and larger for three measures. Changes in other measures were not deemed to have changed significantly.

The 2012 National Health Care Disparities Report (AHRQ, 2012) notes that compared with their urban counterparts, rural residents are more likely to be older and to experience chronic conditions. They are less likely than their urban counterparts to receive recommended preventive services. Problems occur when patients do not speak English or come from a cultural background with a uniquely different understanding of illness and medical treatment. Reliance on young children to interpret complex medical explanations for parents or grandparents, or ignoring important cultural and religious beliefs, may compromise the quality of care. There is a shortage of physicians in rural areas (Association of American Medical Colleges, 2012) and many rural residents depend on small hospitals for their care. There are approximately 2,000 rural hospitals throughout the country. Most of these are "critical access hospitals" that have twenty-five or fewer beds (American Hospital Association, 2011). Because of their small size and the variety of patient needs, they face unique challenges.

Among all measures of health care quality and access that are tracked in the National Health Care Disparities Reports (AHRQ, 2012), individuals with disabilities had worse care than individuals without disabilities. Most measures showed no significant change over time.

The National Health Care Disparities Report (AHRQ, 2012) indicates that there is emerging evidence suggesting that LGBT people face significant barriers to obtaining high-quality medical care. Barriers may include disrespectful behavior from staff and providers, and stigma associated with being a sexual minority. Structural barriers include difficulty obtaining health insurance since many employer-sponsored insurance plans do not recognize same-sex unions.

The American Association of Retired Persons reports that older adults are often denied preventive care routinely provided to others, are less likely to be screened for life-threatening diseases, and are "routinely overtreated, undertreated, or even mistreated by health care professionals with little or no training in geriatrics" (Pope, 2003, p. 7).

The issue of paying for health care was discussed earlier. The experiences of poor people in the health care system are quite different from those who are affluent or well-insured. The poor may use public health clinics and emergency rooms for primary care. They are unlikely to receive preventive care or adequate follow-up services. National Public Radio (Rovner, 2007) reported the case of a young African American boy who died from untreated tooth decay when the infection reached his brain. His case caught the attention of the House Oversight and Government Reform Committee, which questioned why one-third of the children on Medicaid fail to be seen by a dentist in any given year. The reason is that

Medicaid reimbursement is so low that few dentists will see Medicaid patients. Many states offer no Medicaid dental benefits to adults, and the remaining states offer a hodgepodge of services that leave many adults without adequate access to dental care. Routine dental care and most dental procedures, such as cleanings, fillings, tooth extractions, or dentures, are not covered by Medicaid. Many adults suffering from serious dental problems go to the emergency room, where treatment for toothache pain costs about twice what it would cost for a dentist office visit.

How the Health Care System Promotes Well-Being

Obviously, the American health care system has been effective in dealing with many health care problems. Immunizations have resulted in a great reduction or total elimination of some infectious diseases, and other advances in health care technology have produced artificial replacements for limbs and organs, innovative fertility treatments, and life-saving treatments for very low-birth-weight babies. The public health system and occupational safety regulations have done much to reduce health risks from many sources (e.g., lead poisoning, asbestos, and on-the-job injuries.)

Despite concerns about health care delivery in this country, the National Center for Health Statistics (NCHS) (MacDorman, Hoyer, & Mathews, 2013) documents a decline in infant mortality and an increase in life expectancy, with stronger gains made by African Americans. In the early years of the twenty-first century, the NCHS (2012) reported declining death rates for all major diseases. Between 2000 and 2010, age-adjusted cancer death rates decreased 13 percent, and the heart disease death rate declined 30 percent.

The Role of Social Workers in Health and Mental Health Care

Social workers provide case management and discharge planning. They also provide psychosocial services (e.g., crisis intervention, support). Emergency room social workers often provide "psychological first aid" to patients and family members (Ritter, Vakalahi, & Kiernan-Stern, 2009). Public health social workers and social workers who specialize in health care policy focus on health promotion and injury/illness prevention efforts (Ritter, Vakalahi, & Kiernan-Stern, 2009). In the field of mental health and addictions, social workers have provided leadership in developing multilevel interventions that target the individual, family, group, community, and policy makers (NASW, 2012b, p. 230).

RELIGION

Religion is the social institution that organizes a system of beliefs and practices related to aspects of life having to do with the supernatural. It involves the things that are sacred in people's lives—those that inspire awe and reverence—as opposed to everyday experiences. Religion as a social institution is not the same thing as denominational theology or personal spirituality. Social scientists are less interested in specific religious doctrines or beliefs than they are in religious groups and organizations, the behavior of individuals within these groups, and on conflicts between religious groups (Roberts, 1995, p. 28). In this chapter, we explore the influence of religion on American society.

Religions typically include three elements: beliefs, practices (rituals), and a community of believers (Durkheim, 1965/1912). Most formal religions also include norms or rules for how people should behave. Many religions, including those of Native Americans, First Nations, Inuit, and other aboriginal groups, also commonly include many of the following elements: one or more important spiritual beings; creation stories; shamans, healers, and/or prophets; rituals for healing or cleansing; recognition of seasonal changes, especially harvest ceremonies; and rites of passage (e.g., birth, naming, puberty, marriage, and death) (see, for example, Davie, 2001).

While many countries have an official "state religion" (examples include Belgium, England, Iran, Ireland, Israel, Italy, Saudi Arabia, Spain, and Sweden), the United States, of course, does not. On the other hand, Americans do not practice the strict "separation of church and state" that many believe is constitutionally required. The government at many levels supports religion through tax policies, publicly supported chaplains, and invocation of God's presence at ceremonial occasions. Polls show that most Americans do not object to the inclusion of religion in the public realm as long as no particular denomination is favored (Wolfe, 1998). In fact, it is considered "un-American to be godless, or worse, to attack religion" (Thio, 2000, p. 329).

Sociologists describe the United States as having a form of civil religion, a kind of hybrid of religion and politics (Bellah, 1967). American civil religion promotes faith in a supreme being (however individuals choose to understand the deity) and the "American way of life," including individual freedom, patriotism, and the moral authority of elected leaders in times of crisis. Civil religion also has its rituals, including singing the national anthem at sporting events and displaying the flag as a sacred symbol on national holidays and other occasions. American presidents, beginning with Ronald Reagan, have concluded their speeches with "God bless the United States of America," which evokes the civil religion of the nation (Schaefer, 2012, p. 135).

Compared to citizens in other high-income countries, religion is more important to Americans. On a global level, faith is negatively correlated with average national income, except in the case of the United States— that is, countries with more wealth tend to be less religious (Macionis, 2014). The religious views of Americans are more closely comparable to those of developing countries. In Africa and Latin America, a majority of citizens see religion as very important.

Agnostics are people who believe that there is no proof of the existence of God but do not deny the possibility that God exists. Atheists are people who deny the existence of God or gods.

Humanism is a "progressive philosophy of life that, without theism or other supernatural beliefs, affirms [the ability of people] to lead ethical lives of personal fulfillment that aspire to the greater good of humanity." They "defend civil liberties and secular governance" and "see reason and science as the best tools for the discovery of knowledge and the achievement of goals" (American Humanist Association, n.d.).

Evangelicals are members of Protestant churches who believe in being "born again" or "saved"; members stress the importance of scripture and converting nonbelievers. Pentecostals, a subgroup of evangelicals, believe in the inerrancy of scripture, and spiritual gifts, such as "speaking in tongues" and faith healing (Schaefer, 2012).

Many theologians divide common world religions into two major groups, "Western" and "Eastern." The three major Western religions (Judaism, Christianity, and Islam) actually originated in what Americans call the Middle East. They are monotheistic religions (espousing belief in one god). Their followers form congregations and worship formally in groups at specific times and in specific places (i.e., in synagogues, churches, and mosques). Other characteristics of Western religious beliefs are a sense of conflict between the spiritual and the secular, the importance of sacred texts, a perception of time as linear, and a view of each person as a unique creation. Major Eastern religions (Hinduism, Buddhism, and Shintoism), on the other hand, have multiple deities and/or subdeities. There is a belief in the harmonious duality or balance of spiritual and worldly elements, time is viewed as cyclical, and souls are believed to transmigrate between beings (reincarnation). Confucianism and Taoism, widely practiced in the Far East, are usually considered to be philosophies rather than religions.

The importance placed on proselytizing (actively seeking converts) varies considerably among religions. Followers of Eastern religions place much less emphasis on proselytizing than do Christians and Muslims. Hinduism, for example, makes no effort to change the beliefs of others but rather finds ways to integrate them under the great umbrella of traditions that comprise the Hindu faith. Judaism is nonproselytizing because to be Jewish typically involves not only a religious commitment but an ethnic heritage as well. (This is discussed further in chapter 6.) Outreach programs are mostly limited to efforts by Reform Jews aimed at non-Jewish partners and children in mixed marriages.

Today, many Americans show tolerance and support for religious diversity. Nevertheless, they may have little knowledge about faith traditions outside their own. The authors of this text believe that it is important for social work practitioners to have a basic understanding of major religions and religious groups. In some types of social work practice, such as crisis intervention, family counseling, or couples therapy, knowledge of religious culture can facilitate treatment. We recommend that students make an effort to expand their knowledge of different religious traditions.

Issues and Trends in Religion

Patterns of Religious Affiliation

Religion is linked to ethnicity and nationality in all parts of the world. Faith communities in America reflect a very high degree of racial and ethnic segregation. This pattern reflects each group's culture, not a history of forced segregation. Latinos are likely to be Catholic, as are people of Irish, Italian, and Polish descent; many people of Greek descent belong to the Greek Orthodox Church, and African Americans are likely to be members of the African Methodist Episcopal (AME) or black Baptist churches. Many Southeast Asian refugees from Vietnam, Cambodia, and Thailand are Buddhist. Recent Arab immigrants are likely to be followers of the Islamic faith (Muslims). Some faiths are much more diverse in their membership than others (Pew Forum on Religion & Public Life, 2008). For example, Muslims in America are 37 percent white, 24 percent black, 20 percent Asian and 15 percent other. Jehovah's Witnesses are 48 per cent white, 22 percent black, and 24 percent Latino. In contrast, 95 percent of Jews are white, and 91 percent of mainline Protestant church members are white.

Patterns of religious affiliation are also strongly related to geographic region in the United States. This has implications for who might be considered a member of a "religious minority" in different parts of the country. Southern Baptists dominate in the Southeast, Catholics in the Northeast and Southwest, Lutherans in the upper Midwest and upper Great Plains, and Latter-Day Saints (Mormons) in Utah, Nevada, and Idaho. Jews once comprised fully one-third of the population of New York City. Many Jews have now left the urban centers of the Northeast to settle in the suburbs and in Florida.

Shifting Demographics

The Pew Forum on Religion & Public Life (2008) describes religious affiliation in America as "both diverse and extremely fluid" (p. 1). If one includes change in affiliation from one type of Protestantism to another, more than four in ten Americans have either switched religious affiliation, moved from being unaffiliated to being affiliated, or dropped any connection to a specific religious faith.

The most recent data on religious affiliation in the United States shows that about half (50.7 percent) of Americans self-identify as Protestants, 24.6 percent as Catholics, and 1.5 percent as Jews (Macionis, 2014). Two-thirds of Canadians identify either as Protestant or Catholic, but numbers are dropping. The fastest-growing religious group in both America and Canada appears to be the category of people who say they have no religious affiliation; their numbers have more than doubled since 1990 to more than 20 percent of the population (Pew Forum on Religion & Public Life, 2012). On the other hand, Pew Center surveys have found that the "unaffiliated people" are, in fact, fairly religious.

Many of the religious denominations remaining stable in population or showing growth in America reflect the arrival of refugees from Asia, the Middle East, and Latin America. Membership levels in the Roman Catholic Church, for example, remain stable because while the church is losing some members, it is gaining others, primarily first-generation immigrants from Mexico and other Catholic countries. Latinos account for more than a third of Catholics in the United States (Schaefer, 2012, p. 255). But the longer they are in the United States, the more Latinos appear to be open to other faiths. Although Latinos remain the fastest-growing ethnic bloc in the Catholic Church, they are also the fastest-growing segment among the Church of Jesus Christ of Latter-Day Saints (Mormons) and United Methodists (Campo-Flores, 2005). The fastest-growing segment of Presbyterian and Methodist faiths are ethnic Korean congregations (Schaefer, 2012, p. 296).

Generally the larger "mainline" Protestant churches (e.g., Baptist, Episcopalian, Lutheran, Methodist, Presbyterian) have lost members or are struggling to maintain the size of their membership rolls. Many members of mainline Protestant faiths have been leaving them for churches that follow strict codes of behavior and rigid interpretations of biblical teachings (Schaefer, 2012).

There is an increasing generation gap in terms of religious conservatism (Dionne, 2013). Among Americans 68 and older, 47 percent are religious conservatives and only 12 percent are religious liberals. Among those 33 or younger, only 17 percent are religious conservatives, 23 percent are religious liberals, and 22 percent are nonreligous.

Religion and Political Office

In the United States, there should be no "religious test" for public offices, meaning that no elected official can be required to espouse any particular religion or belief. The basis for this is found in Article VI, Section 3, of the U.S. Constitution, which states "The Senators and Representatives before mentioned, and the Members of the several State Legislatures, and all executive and judicial Officers, both of the United States and of the several States, shall be bound by Oath or Affirmation, to support this Constitution; but *no religious test shall ever be required as a qualification to any office or public trust under the United States* [emphasis added]."

Eight states (Arkansas, Maryland, Mississippi, North Carolina, Pennsylvania, South Carolina, Tennessee, and Texas) still retain provisions in their constitutions limiting public office to people who believe in God. In 1961 the U.S. Supreme Court ruled that these restrictions can no longer be enforced (Boston, 2010). The use of a "religious test of office" was widely debated in the presidential election of 1960, when John F. Kennedy's Catholic background was a concern to many Protestants who worried that he would be under the control of the pope. Kennedy addressed these concerns in a speech to a gathering of Southern Baptist ministers in September 1960, reassuring his audience that "I do not speak for my church on public matters—and the church does not speak for me" and succeeded, for a time, in removing religion from the scope of legitimate campaign topics (Garnett, 2008). The religious beliefs of presidential candidates came under increasing scrutiny in the 2008 presidential election. Virtually all candidates were challenged during the primary campaigns, and in the presidential debates, to talk about their personal faith. Academic researchers who study religion and politics noted a change in tone, in addition to increasing emphasis on religion, in recent campaigns; "What you see instead [of a ceremonial reference to God] is the use of God as kind of a political weapon that doesn't just celebrate faith, but is used to identify enemies and to try to position ideas against each other" (Kevin Coe, cited by George, 2007). This use of religion to promote divisiveness and engage in political gamesmanship harbors the potential to exploit the beliefs of people of faith for political gain. Controversy over candidates' religious affiliation was sparked once again in the 2012 presidential campaign. The Republican nominee, Mitt Romney, was a member of the Church of Jesus Christ of Latter-Day Saints (Mormons), and many people believed erroneously that the Democratic nominee, Barack Obama, was a Muslim.

Christian Fundamentalism

Some religious scholars (e.g., Hunter, 1991) believe that there is a new realignment of religious difference that is not based on doctrine or denomination; in fact, this realignment sometimes cuts right through the middle of a congregation or denomination. The dividing line is between conservatives/fundamentalists and liberals/interpretationists.

Fundamentalists in Western religious traditions accept the literal meaning of scripture, that is, they believe it is the "inerrant word of God." Their assumption is that a text means whatever it means to somebody who is reading it today (Helminiak, 1994, p. 25). Fundamentalists assert the absolute correctness of their own beliefs and reject religious pluralism. Many fundamentalists endorse conservative political goals. They are "pro-life" and support the traditional two-parent, husband-and-wife family. They reject some commonly held scientific views, such as evolution and climate change. In national surveys, 26 percent of American adults describe their religious upbringing as "fundamentalist" (NORC, 2011).

Interpretationists use a historical-critical approach to reading sacred texts (Helminiak, 1994, pp. 26–27). This approach is called "historical" because it requires that the text be put back into its historical and cultural context before deciding what it means. It is called "critical" because it requires careful thought and detailed analysis. Liberals/interpretationists are likely to be found among United Methodists, Episcopalians, Congregationalists, Presbyterians, and Unitarians, as well as Reform Jews.

Religion-Related Controversies in Social Work

Social workers often experience two different kinds of value dilemmas related to religion. In some agencies, they may feel pressure to use religious beliefs as a context for the provision of services. In other situations, they may find that their personal religious beliefs are in conflict with those of their clients or the profession.

In 2000, presidential candidate George W. Bush proposed the establishment of faith-based social services as an alternative to traditional social service programs and established a White House office of Faith-Based and Community Initiatives. President Obama continued the office. Supporters of this initiative believe that faith-based services supply the moral content that is lacking in secular nonprofit or government agencies (Karger & Stoesz, 2010).

The social work profession and social work practitioners have a long history of providing services under religious auspices and within religious settings. Nevertheless, when the Faith-Based and Community Initiatives Act was passed, the NASW responded on its website with statements of concern about the possibility of (1) government-funded organizations proselytizing to people seeking aid, (2) limiting access to services based on lack of religious affiliation or observation, (3) hindering existing non-profit social services agencies that are not faith-based, and (4) using employment practices that discriminate on the basis of religion (National Association of Social Workers, 2002). When government-supported social service programs are imbedded in faith-based organizations, professional ethics dictate that social workers respect clients' religious preferences (or lack of religious affiliation).

Perhaps more commonly, some practitioners experience dissonance between their own religious beliefs and practices and those of their clients or the values of the social work profession. Typically these conflicts arise in the context of disagreements over gender roles (i.e., patriarchy), the physical discipline of children, homosexuality, and abortion/reproductive rights.

Understanding Religion

Functionalist Perspective

Functionalists believe that the social order is enhanced by the existence of organized religion(s) (Durkheim, 1965/1912) and civil religion. Religion encourages conformity by providing cultural norms or by sacralizing those norms that already exist (i.e., conferring supernatural legitimacy on the norms and laws of society). Religion unites people through shared symbolism and values. Civil religion expressly encourages patriotism and nationalism.

Conflict Perspective

Although clearly religion has been used in many times and many places to justify persecution, violence, and even war linked to terrorism, conflict theorists focus on how the institution of religion supports the existing social hierarchy and the interests of the ruling class. Historical examples include the Christian teaching of the "divine right of kings" in Europe during the Middle Ages and support of the caste system by the Hindu religion in India. In this country, religion has been used to endorse the status quo by legitimating the destruction of Native Americans, the slavery of Africans, and the oppression of women.

Many religions encourage people to focus on "another world to come" rather than working toward change in this one. The most famous critique of religion from a conflict perspective was offered by Karl Marx. In his statement "religion is the opium of the people," he meant that religion is like a drug that causes people to be complacent and docile even when they are exploited.

Constructionist Perspective

Most religious people would argue that their beliefs are the result of divine inspiration, provided indirectly through prophets, clerics, and religious texts or perhaps directly to themselves individually. Social construction theorists say that people construct religious beliefs as a means of responding to life's uncertainties, tragedies, triumphs, and other great questions, trying to explain the unexplainable, find reason in the unreasonable, and perhaps gain the favor or assistance of supernatural forces. Organized religion is based on a shared construction of reality. Because they are matters of faith rather than fact, neither social workers nor scientists in any discipline can prove or disprove specific religious doctrines, such as the nature of God. On the other hand, some issues, such as the age of the planet or climate change, can be and have been fully addressed through scientific inquiry.

Relationship of Religion to the Political Economy

As noted in chapter 2, Max Weber linked the development of capitalism to early Protestant beliefs. The "Protestant work ethic" continues to be touted as the basis of America's prosperity. Because American Catholics and Jews are also prosperous, and because capitalism is flourishing in non-Christian/non-Protestant countries such as Japan, Taiwan, and South

Korea, Weber's theory probably is best used to explain the early emergence of capitalism rather than its continuing success.

In principle, the American people are committed to the "separation of church and state" (meaning a public policy of neutrality toward religion). The Founding Fathers (Thomas Paine, Benjamin Franklin, George Washington, John Adams, Thomas Jefferson, and James Madison), reacting to European state religions were quite clear in their rejection of a theocratic form of government. Their concern about the misuse and abuse of religion was codified in the First Amendment to the U.S. Constitution, commonly called the "establishment clause": *Congress shall make no law respecting an establishment of religion. . . .* The First Amendment prohibits the creation of a national religion and prohibits the government from preferential treatment of one religion over others, or for religion over nonreligion. Despite the apparent clarity of the First Amendment, there are individuals and organizations that insist that the United States was founded as a "Christian nation" and furthermore, that the Constitution does not mandate a "wall of separation" between church and state. The phrase "wall of separation" was first used in a letter written by Thomas Jefferson in 1802; the letter was cited in decisions by the U.S. Supreme Court in 1878 and again in widely publicized decisions in 1947 and 1948 (Hutson, 1998).

FIGURE 4.1   CRITICAL THINKING ABOUT PRAYER AT PUBLIC MEETINGS

Should prayer be offered at the start of government meetings?

Some people would argue that the U.S. Congress always starts its sessions with a prayer, so it should be all right for other government bodies to do the same. There have been many legal challenges when city councils, school boards, and other local public organizations do the same. Do you believe it should be OK to offer prayer under all circumstances, under some circumstances, or not at all? Is offering prayer all right if all denominations in the community are represented at one time or another? What restrictions would you recommend?

After you develop your response you might want to review the May 5, 2014, U.S. Supreme Court ruling in Town of Greece, New York v. Galloway, which addressed this issue. The justices' opinions can be found at http://www.supremecourt.gov/opinions/13pdf/12-696_4f57.pdf.

The United States government not only tolerates but encourages religion in a variety of ways. These include its tax policies (exemptions for religious organizations and contributions to them), laws (including a 1954 law adding "under God" to the Pledge of Allegiance and a 1955 law requiring that "In God We Trust" appear on all U.S. currency), and practices (such as provision of funding for chaplains in Congress, the armed forces, and prisons; use of the Bible or other religious texts for rituals of "swearing in," and formal recognition of some Christian religious holidays). As noted above, recent administrations support the idea of faith-based social services, which blurs the distinction between secular and religious agencies.

Regardless of the intentions of the Founding Fathers, in practice, Americans today not only permit but insist on public manifestations of religiosity on the part of government officials. The power and grace of God (or "Providence," or "the Supreme Being") are regularly invoked. Political leaders may even use religion to shield their choices from criticism by saying that they prayed for divine guidance before reaching a decision, thus suggesting that questioning them is akin to questioning God.

Many have argued that Americans need to be concerned when those in power use their own religious point of view to interpret and judge the actions of others. The endorsement by public officials of a particular religious view, or even of religion in general, suggests that adherence to a religious creed is a prerequisite or an advantage to those seeking justice and fair treatment. "People who govern in the name of God attribute their own personal preferences to God and therefore recognize no limits in imposing those preferences on other people" ("Center Sues to Remove Monument," 2002). Organizations such as the American Civil Liberties Union, Americans United for the Separation of Church and State, the Interfaith Alliance, and the Southern Poverty Law Center work to protect the interests of religious minorities and atheists from overzealous judges and lawmakers.

Religion offers challenges to both the left and the right ends of the political spectrum. Nonreligious Americans are an important constituency of the Democratic Party, but so are African Americans, who are among the most religious people in the country. "For liberalism to thrive, there needs to be acceptance and, even better, some respect across the boundaries of belief and nonbelief" (Dionne, 2013, p. 2). On the other side, when conservatives link religion, and particularly Christianity, to right-wing political causes they may alienate substantial numbers of young Americans. Some pundits have linked the move of the younger generation away from the church directly to the time when conservative Christians made opposition to same-sex marriage their signature political issue (Sessions, 2012).

The Impact of Religion on Individuals and Families

How Religion Deters Well-Being

As mentioned earlier, the Bible has been used to justify slavery and racism (Hill & Cheadle, 1996). The Christian faith, to which slaves were introduced in America, encouraged them to accept their inferior status.

The beliefs, ritual expressions, norms, and organizational structures of many organized religions routinely subordinate women (McGuire, 1997). For example, in Christianity, the Bible was written by men, edited by men, translated by men, and interpreted by men; until recently, most biblical scholars and religious leaders were male. Thus one should not be surprised to see that men receive favorable treatment in Christian religious belief and practice. Traditional religions have placed women in exalted but protected positions. "Protected" often meant protected from becoming leaders (Schaefer, 2008, p. 156). Patriarchal views in sacred texts and many contemporary religious practices continue to reinforce gender inequity (McGuire, 1997). Like other major religions of the world, the three Western religions (Judaism, Christianity, and Islam) are traditionally patriarchal. Orthodox Judaism, Roman Catholicism, and Islam continue to exclude women from the highest spiritual leader roles. On the other hand, growing numbers of Protestant denominations, as well as Reform and Conservative Jews, allow women to lead congregations. Nevertheless, in many of those denominations women are assigned to assistant clergy or co-pastor positions and find it more difficult than men to secure jobs in large, prestigious congregations (Schaefer, 2008). A 2010 national survey found that in only 12 percent of U.S. congregations the senior or sole ordained leader was female (Hartford Institute for Religion Research, n.d.).

In some other countries, where religion and government are intertwined, the power of the state may be used to impose religiously based restrictions on women. One of the most egregious examples was the Taliban rule in Afghanistan, where women could not leave their homes without male chaperones, were denied the right to education and to employment, and could not be properly examined by health care professionals (Roesler, 2005).

In their book, *Half the Sky,* Kristof and WuDunn (2009) address the question of whether Islam is misogynist (characterized by disrespect for women). They note that when Muhammad introduced Islam in the seventh century, it was a "step forward for women" (p. 150). For example, in contrast to repressive gender practices in Christian nations at the time, Muslim women routinely owned property with rights protected by the law. Over the centuries, however, Christianity has moved ahead while Islam has not, although "many modern-minded Muslims are pushing for greater gender equality" (Kristof & WuDunn, 2009, p. 151). These authors also note that sometimes religion is blamed for oppression when, in fact, it is rooted in the culture of a region.

Controversies over "gay rights," "same-sex marriage," and the ordination of openly gay clergy are putting strains on the unity of many religious denominations. In many American churches, the divide is not geographic (as it was over slavery) but over a basic understanding of tradition and scripture. People on both sides of the issue cite Bible verses in support of their respective positions, with conservatives and fundamentalists using a more literal interpretation and liberals arguing that scripture must be understood in context and that one may not choose to believe and follow some verses (e.g., Leviticus, 18:22 and 20:13) and ignore others (e.g., Leviticus 11:10, 15:19–24, 19:19, 19:27, or 25:44) (Hill & Cheadle, 1996). Some religious leaders say that we should insist "that all citizens receive—at the least—the respect that their status as human beings created in the image of God demands. To succumb to—or worse, to incite—fear and hatred of brothers and sisters because of their sexual orientation is to deny both God's love for us and ours for God" (Brill, 2005, p. A9).

Some religious denominations, especially those that are more conservative, appear to promote homophobia (Helminiak, 1994; Hill & Cheadle,

1996). Although the message may be "hate the sin, love the sinner," their rhetoric supports an atmosphere of intolerance toward gay men and lesbians, which can encourage acts of violence. Clearly, not all religious people are homophobic, but when high-profile Christian leaders, such as Cardinal Timothy Dolan, the Reverend Pat Robertson, Baptist pastor Ron Baity (who received the Family Research Council's highest "pro-family" award in 2012), and Focus on the Family's James Dobson oppose basic rights for LGBT people, one can understand why others might believe that Christians are self-righteous and judgmental (Powers, 2013).

When the Boy Scouts of America decided to admit openly gay scouts in 2013, many churches objected and dropped their sponsorship of scout troops. For example, the Southern Baptists voted to support families who left scouting because of the new policy (Hennessy-Fiske, 2013). Recognition of the biological determinants of human sexuality (as supported by numerous research studies) creates a dilemma for religious people who cannot then reconcile their interpretation of the Bible with the idea that people do not choose their sexual orientation (Meyerson, 2007).

America is not a "Christian nation" in an official sense, but because Christians are a large majority, discrimination against members of minority religions and atheists is common (Miller, 2008). This may take the form of the obvious (such as pressure to participate in Christian prayers, or reluctance to make accommodations for non-Christian holy days or rituals) to the simply thoughtless (such as describing any generous or ethical person as an example of "a good Christian," forgetting that other faith traditions also promote moral behavior). Some Christians may ask, "Why can't we have organized prayer in public schools, or the Ten Commandments posted in the courthouse or a nativity scene in the public square? After all, this country was founded on the principle of majority rule," forgetting that in this country religious beliefs and practices are matters of individual discretion and not issues to be debated and decided by the majority.

Overzealous proselytizing can be interpreted as a threat by members of religious minorities. For example, Raspberry (1999) reported that the Southern Baptist International Mission Board urged its denomination members to pray for the conversion of Jews: "Pray each day for Jewish individuals you know by name . . . Love them as you would an unsaved relative." The president of the Union of American Hebrew Congregations, Rabbi Eric Yoffie, responded, "There's a kind of theological arrogance that pervades all of this, a certain willingness to play God, and an absence of awareness that these sorts of statements throughout history are associated with coercion, hatred and violence. . . . We'd like a little less love and a little more respect."

How Religion Promotes Well-Being

Organized religion promotes the well-being of individuals, families, and society in many ways. First, religion establishes values of cooperation, altruism, and often social justice. Second, many congregations provide social services and support for individuals and groups. In addition, many religious organizations, and in particular African American churches, have nourished social movements.

Most great cultures, and all the major religions, have obligated their people to help the less fortunate, including widows, orphans, the sick or disabled, and even traveling strangers (Morris, 1986). The history of social work as a profession is closely linked to Christian traditions of helping the poor (e.g., the Charity Organization Societies). The profession also draws heavily on the Jewish principle of *tzedakah,* which can be translated as a combination of charity and justice. The traditions of Judaism emphasize the goal of promoting self-sufficiency among recipients of charity, and in protecting them from embarrassment or stigma.

One of the five pillars of Islam is *zakat,* or almsgiving. *Zakat* "is a Muslim's worship of God by means of his wealth through an obligatory form of giving to those in need" (Haneef, 1993, p. 48). Although Islam does not factor in the history of Western social work, these values are consistent with those of the profession.

People who attend church, or synagogue, or mosque regularly enjoy better mental health, probably because they have more friends as well as a support system to help them with problems in their lives (Mishori, 2008). Many religious congregations provide information and referral to connect members and other community residents to social services, training opportunities, and jobs, and sometimes grants or other funding. Their facilities also provide some social services and limited financial support to people in crisis. Black churches have historically functioned as social service agencies in the African American community. Congregations often provide meeting space free of charge or for a very small fee for other social organizations within their community. Many denominations support hospitals, nursing homes and retirement centers, children's homes and residential treatment centers, adoption and foster-care agencies, family life education programs, day-care centers for young children and older adults, after-school programs and recreation programs for school-aged children and adolescents, disaster relief, and refugee resettlement—if not with funding then with volunteers or gifts in kind.

Religious organizations can provide continuity for immigrants to this country. Researchers have found that immigrants are closely affiliated with religious organizations because the facilities provide not only a place to worship in their native language, but also a source of psychological, informational, and instrumental social support (Ellison, Boardman, Williams, & Jackson, 2001). The "ethnic church" performs multiple roles for racially and culturally distinct minorities, providing guidance, emotional support, and a broad range of social activities and outlets (Kim, 1999, p. 366). Churches, temples, and mosques help members retain a sense of identity by providing a place for religious and ethnic fellowship.

People who are persecuted and discriminated against in other areas of life find interior strength and external social support in a wide variety of religious beliefs and practices. Religious organizations may offer one of the few welcoming "communities" for specific minorities. For example, the Metropolitan Community Church provides a safe haven and worship experience for LGBT persons.

African American churches served as a cradle for the Civil Rights Movement and a training ground for the development of civil rights leaders. Religion can be the catalyst to those seeking social justice, inspiring individuals to break out of the limited roles prescribed for them by the society (McGuire, 1997). Black congregations continue this tradition of civic participation, frequently serving as platforms for collective mobilization. Religious congregations are especially successful in organizing local residents for political action in part because they "enjoy relations with other community institutions and congregations, larger religious bodies, and specialized, parallel religious organizations or private and public institutions" (Foley, McCarthy, & Chaves, 2001, p. 221).

MASS MEDIA, SOCIAL MEDIA, AND COMMUNICATION TECHNOLOGY

The mass media are "organizations that use print, analog electronic, and digital electronic means to communicate with large numbers of people, often at the same time" (Kendall, 2013, p. 106). The mass media manage the flow of images and ideas across society; they are a common source of information and a source of socialization. The mass media have the potential to present similar depictions of the world to tremendous numbers of otherwise different and unrelated people. The depictions that the media deliver have the power to affect people's attitudes toward social issues, other people, and even themselves. One media expert noted, "everywhere, the media flow defies national boundaries. This is one of its obvious, but at the same time, amazing features. . . . If there is a [global] village, it speaks American, it wears jeans, drinks Coke, eats at the golden arches, walks on swooshed shoes, plays electric guitars, recognizes Mickey Mouse, James Dean, E. T., Bart Simpson, R2-D2, and Pamela Anderson" (Gitlin, 2001, p. 176).

Because it has multiple functions and serves individual needs, it is unclear whether the Internet is a "mass medium"; it does not fit the usual definition as it lacks centralized control that decides what shall be distributed to the general public (Bagdikian, 2004, p. 56). Nevertheless, it appears that the Internet has changed not only the method of delivery, but also the nature of the product that is delivered. Blogs and podcasts present more immediate, individualized, less objective content. In a world with tens of millions of bloggers, the messages received are not only much more numerous and varied but also much less verifiable (Parker, 2006). Each blogger holds a "megaphone" of sorts, but only a very few hold a degree in journalism.

The mass media are what some sociologists call an "emerging social institution." They are relatively new in human history, dating from the invention of movable type in 1436. Not until the 1840s, with the invention of the telegraph, was long-distance communication separated from transportation (Croteau & Hoynes, 2014). The telephone was invented in the 1870s, typewriters became portable in the 1950s, e-mail arrived in the 1990s, and spreading word via social media emerged in the early twenty-first century. The development of newspapers, magazines, radio, movies, network television, cable TV, and the Internet, and the ubiquitous presence of electronic devices, have made the media an increasingly powerful and influential social institution.

One must distinguish, however, between mass media and social media, and between mass media and traditional journalism. Forty years ago, major broadcast networks were bound by the Radio Act of 1927 to work for the "public interest, convenience, and necessity." Journalism professionals served as "gatekeepers, filtering out the defamatory and the false" in the opinion of Mort Zuckerman (2005), owner of *U.S. News & World Report,* and offering "relatively unbiased accounts of information that their respective news organizations believed the public needed to know" (Koppel, 2010, p. 3). The three major television networks were resigned to the fact that their news divisions would operate at a loss or barely break even (Koppel, 2010). What one sees on television today, in contrast, is designed to make money and what draws viewers is controversy. So cable stations, such as Fox and MSNBC, clearly cater to one end or the other of the political spectrum, and major networks present political news as controversy. For example, the Sunday morning news programs feature a Democrat and a Republican talking about the issues of the day, both avoiding answers to the host's questions, instead repeating prepared talking points (Miller, 2010). And "from the mainstream media's [current] standpoint, they've done their job. You've heard different points of view. . . . Now, you decide" (Miller, 2010). In covering political events, it is clear that the media go out of their way to cover the conflict of encounters among politicians and their constituents; a meeting does not get into the news unless it "blows up." The media give voice to the extremes and ignore the middle.

In 1950, only 9 percent of American homes owned a television; by 1955, the percentage had jumped to 64.5 percent and by 1965, it increased to 92.6 percent (Television Information Office, 1985). According to a national Kaiser Family Foundation survey, as of 2009, 99 percent of American households owned at least one TV, and 93 percent owned at least one computer (Rideout, Foehr, & Roberts, 2010). The American home has, on average, 3.8 television sets and 71 percent of 8- to 18-year-olds have a television set in their bedrooms.

The International Telecommunication Union (2012) reports that the world has six billion cell phone subscribers. According to a 2012 national survey conducted by the Pew Research Center, 91 percent of American adults (Rainie, 2013) and 78 percent of children ages 12 to 17 own a cell phone, and nearly half of them are smartphones (Madden, Lenhart, Duggan, Cortesi, & Gasser, 2013). Of those cell phone owners, 80 percent use them to send or receive text messages, and 50 percent use them to send or receive e-mail; 56 percent use them to access the Internet.

According to a study by the Kaiser Family Foundation (Lamontagne, Singh, & Palosky, 2010), young people do not commonly use their cell phones for oral conversations. Instead, they use them for listening to music, playing games, and watching TV. Young people say they feel they have more control when they text, e-mail, use Facebook, or tweet rather than using voice calls. They even complain that phone calls are an intrusion and thus impolite (Shapira, 2010). In 2011, the number of wireless devices (e.g., cell phones, smartphones, and tablets) in the United States outnumbered the people living there for the first time (Goldman, 2011). In addition to cell phones, 57 percent of Americans have a laptop, 19 percent own an e-book reader, and 19 percent have a tablet computer; about six in ten adults (63 percent) go online wirelessly with one of those devices. Gadget ownership is generally correlated with age, education, and household income, although some devices—notably e-book readers and tablets—are as popular or even more popular with adults in their thirties and forties than young adults ages 18–29.

According to U.S. Census data, almost three-quarters (74.8 percent) of American households have Internet access (U.S. Census Bureau, 2014). In a recent Pew Center study researchers found that youth, education, and household income are the strongest predictors of Internet use (Zickuhr & Smith, 2012). Adults living with a disability are significantly less likely than adults without a disability to go online (54 percent versus 81 percent).

Issues and Trends in Mass Media, Social Media, and Communication Technology

Social Media

The term *social media* refers to a group of Internet-based applications and networks that allow individuals to create and exchange content. Reports show that people who use the Internet spend more time with social media sites than any other kind. In July 2012 the total time spent on social media in the United States was 121 billion minutes, an increase of 37 percent compared to 88 billion minutes in July 2011 (Nielsen, 2012). Everyone from President Obama to Pope Francis uses Twitter; and Twitter, which turned seven years old in March 2013, logs more than 400 million tweets per day, up from 5,000 in 2007 (Farber, 2012).

The Internet and social media increase the possibility of democratic participation by citizens in that it enables individuals to send as well as receive messages without the power of traditional gatekeepers (e.g., newspaper editors and television and radio producers) (Livingstone, 2005). The speed of communication across wide geographic ranges permits the free circulation of information and opinion.

Social media have had a growing impact on human behavior. For example, a recent study found that almost 30 percent of married couples met online. Of those, about 45 percent connected on dating sites (Jayson, 2013). Another survey found that mobile technology has "rocked the dating world"; approximately one-third of respondents agreed that it was less intimidating to ask for a date via text versus a phone call and 25 percent of those aged 21 to 26 used their mobile device to search for information about people they are dating or interested in (Jayson, 2013).

Beyond the obvious benefits of staying connected to family and friends, or working together on group school projects, other benefits of using social media for children and youth include opportunities for community engagements (such as raising money for charities or volunteering for local events), enhancing individual and collective creativity, and expansion of experiences through shared interests that include others from more diverse backgrounds (O'Keeffe & Clarke-Pearson, 2011).

Potential drawbacks and risk factors for children and youth using electronic devices and social media include inappropriate peer-to-peer relationships (e.g., cyberbullying, and sexting [sending, receiving, or forwarding sexually explicit messages or pictures]), and loss of personal privacy (O'Keeffe & Clarke-Pearson, 2011). Cyberbullying is when a child, preteen, or teen is tormented, threatened, harassed, humiliated, embarrassed, or otherwise targeted by another child, preteen, or teen using the Internet, interactive and digital technologies, or mobile phone

(STOPcyberbullying, n.d.). In a 2011 survey, the Centers for Disease Control and Prevention asked high school students whether they had been a victim of electronic bullying, including through e-mail, chat rooms, instant messaging, websites, and texting. One in six students reported being electronically bullied within the past twelve months and girls were twice as likely to report being a victim of cyberbullying as boys (22.1 percent vs. 10.8 percent) (Wood, 2013).

A researcher and her students at the University of Maryland's International Center for Media & the Public Agenda (ICMPA) (Moeller et al., 2013) found that 18- to 21-year-old college students use literal terms of addiction to characterize their dependence on media. A class of 200 students was asked to go media-free for 24 hours; a significant number of them failed to last the entire time period.

One National Public Radio (NPR) commentator, David Pell (2013), mused that the Internet leaves him more connected to people he doesn't know, equally connected to people he does know, but less connected to himself; "most of the moments once reserved for a little alone time have been infiltrated by the real time Internet." Time for self-reflection and creativity are replaced by the urge to entertain oneself with something on a mobile device.

Violence in the Media

Probably the most noteworthy issue related to the mass media is concern about the graphic portrayal of violence. The American Medical Association, the American Academy of Pediatrics, and the American Psychological Association have gone on record reporting the negative effects of violence in the mass media, especially on television and in films, based on studies that show correlations between viewing patterns and aggressive behavior. (Documenting correlation is not the same as proving cause and effect; there may be other mitigating factors that make some children more vulnerable to the effects of violence in the media [see figure 4.2].) Research studies on violence on television have documented that children become less sensitive to the pain and suffering of others, are more fearful of the world around them, more likely to behave in aggressive and harmful ways toward others, and more accepting of the use of violence as a way to solve problems (American Academy of Child and Adolescent Psychiatry, 2002; American Psychological Association, 2008; Pozios, Kambam, & Bender, 2013). A review of twenty years of research also indicates that violent video games increase aggressive behavior in children and adolescents; children who play more violent video games also have more arguments with authority figures (American Psychological Association, 2005). The American Academy of Child and Adolescent Psychiatry (2004) reports that common themes in music videos include advocating and glamorizing abuse of drugs and alcohol; pictures and explicit lyrics presenting suicide as an "alternative" or "solution" to problems; sex that focuses on control, sadism, masochism, and incest; and violence toward women, in addition to graphic violence in general.

FIGURE 4.2   CRITICAL THINKING ABOUT VIOLENCE IN THE MEDIA

Research has documented a significant correlation between viewing television violence and aggressive behaviors. Which of these possible explanations of association seems most plausible to you?
- Children who are more aggressive are drawn to aggressive programming.
- Portrayals of violence in the media lead children to be aggressive (by providing models of aggression).
- There is a reciprocal relationship between aggressive behavior and viewing violence (each causes the other to increase).
- Both behaviors are caused by another variable, such as inattentive parents.

Source: Adapted from Kundanis (2003)

Even local news programs tend to focus on violence. For example, one South Carolina newspaper (*The State,* January 2, 2014, p. B4) featured the following headlines for the six stories of news from the local region in one day: "Man Dies after SUV Hits Ditch, Tree"; "Woman Shot to Death after Answering Knock on Door"; "Mother Charged with DUI after Two Young Daughters Die in Crash"; "7-Year-Old Dies in Chester County Dirt Bike Wreck"; "Hunter Shot to Death by Another Hunter";

and "Woman Dies after Being Hit by Two Cars." The newspaper axiom "If it bleeds, it leads" influences the electronic media as well. Sensational violent crimes make up less than one percent of all crimes, but they constitute a majority of crime coverage, leaving viewers and readers with a badly distorted picture of their world (Dyer, 2000, p. 87).

Mass Media and Children

Because of their immature level of social and intellectual development, media use by children is particularly noteworthy. Television was the first mode of mass media to prompt legislation to protect children's interests. The 1990 Children's Television Act, along with the Federal Communication Commission, sets limits on advertising for children's programs. The Telecommunication Act of 1996 required both television and cable operators to provide the V-chip, a mechanism to give parents and other caregivers control over inappropriate programming.

The American Academy of Pediatrics suggests that no child under age two years should watch screen media and that all children over two be limited to one to two hours of educational screen media a day. Nevertheless, "baby videos designed for one-month-olds, computer games for nine-month-olds, and TV shows for one-year-olds are becoming commonplace," according to a Kaiser Family Foundation study of the media (Rideout, Hamel, & Kaiser Family Foundation, 2006, p. 4). In a typical day, 68 percent of all toddlers use screen media; almost six out of ten watch TV, four out of ten watch a video or DVD, and these youngsters will spend an average of two hours in front of a screen.

Another study found that 40 percent of children regularly watch television by three months of age (Jackson, 2007). One in three children six years old and younger has a television set in his or her bedroom (Rideout, Hamel, & Kaiser Family Foundation, 2006). Two-thirds of parents are convinced that the medium is a good source of learning and helps children get along with others (Jackson, 2007). The Kaiser Family Foundation study noted that parents use TV or DVDs as a "safe" activity to entertain their children while they get ready for work or do household chores; as a tool to change the mood of grouchy, hyper, or squabbling children; as a reward for good behavior; to facilitate transitions, such as calming down before bedtime; and as an instructional tool for teaching basic reading and counting skills (Rideout et al., 2006).

Over the past five years, there has been a large increase in media use among youth. Researchers from the Kaiser Family Foundation report that these children pack a total of 10 hours and 45 minutes worth of media content into 7.5 hours a day, often using more than one medium at a time (Rideout et al., 2010). While time spent watching regularly scheduled programming on television declined, 11- to 14-year-olds consumed an average of five hours a day watching TV programs and movies on the Internet or their cell phones and, in addition, spent another hour and a half a day playing video games.

Diversity and the Media

In the United States, the media are extremely powerful simply because they are unavoidable. Either from direct viewing or reading, or from secondhand reports, Americans obtain the vast majority of their knowledge and beliefs about life outside of their direct experience from media sources (Lester, 1996, p. 6). Americans are becoming more comfortable with being a diverse nation, but minority cultures are increasingly defined by advertisers and scriptwriters rather than reflecting genuine ethnic heritage. Unfortunately, portrayals that assume and reinforce negative stereotypes are common (Lester, 1996, p. 7).

Although the proliferation of cable channels has allowed for "niche marketing" and "narrowcasting"—programming directed at specific minorities (e.g., African Americans, Spanish speakers)—studies show that rather than encouraging cultural integration, this pattern may further segregate those populations from the mainstream. Because ultimately the goal of the media is to generate profits, diversification to include underserved audiences is likely to occur only if they are identified as growing consumer markets (Turow, 1997).

Although television has always included unscripted programs such as game shows and sports programs, since the late 1990s "reality television" has become a common fixture on the screen. This genre of programming features a previously unknown cast in competitive situations (e.g., *Survivor, Big Brother*) or in their daily lives (e.g., *Jersey Shore, Myrtle Beach*

Manor)—also known as "docusoaps." Reality TV has been criticized for being inauthentic, staged, scripted, and heavily edited. Writers for reality television (called "story editors" or "segment producers" to disguise their actual roles) do not receive union pay-scale compensation and union representation, which significantly decreases expenditures for producers and broadcasters. In 2001, the Academy of Television Arts and Sciences added the reality genre to the Emmy Awards and subsequently added two subcategories of awards for reality programming.

Many studies have been conducted to analyze how the media present people of different genders, sexual orientations, ages, social classes, physical (dis)abilities, and racial and ethnic backgrounds. A majority of viewers and readers believe that media messages, even advertisements aimed directly at them, have little impact. Media critic Jean Kilbourne (1999, p. 27) notes, however, that "the most effective kind of propaganda is that which is not recognized as propaganda."

Affluent white men have historically controlled the mainstream media, which helps to explain why some groups are virtually invisible and others are presented in a negative light. In fact, the pervasiveness of a white perspective in the media is one of its most powerful characteristics. The media do not talk about "white culture," or "the white community," as they do "Latino culture" or "the black community," suggesting that whiteness is to be taken for granted and the norm against which all other groups are to be measured.

Race and ethnicity. Children who do not have direct experience with racial diversity are more likely to draw on televised representations of majority and minority cultures. Children's perceptions of race and ethnicity are shaped by depictions of social power, defined by comparative visibility, status, and roles assigned to characters in TV ads. (See figure 4.3.)

A content analysis (Monk-Turner, Heiserman, Johnson, Cotton, & Jackson, 2010) of one week of prime-time television programs on the four major networks (ABC, CBS, NBC, and Fox) found that 74 percent of the people shown were white, 16 percent were black, and 5 percent were Latino; fewer than 3 percent were Asian American or another category. White characters and Latino characters were found in primary roles. Whereas African Americans were three times as likely as Latinos to be present, they were delegated primarily to minor roles. White prime-time characters were presented as middle-income and articulate, and devoid of heavy accents.

FIGURE 4.3   CRITICAL THINKING ABOUT RACIAL PORTRAYALS ON TELEVISION

Select one kind of television programming (e.g., network news, situation comedies, dramas, or children's programming). Watch a total of 30 minutes from different episodes. Make a note of the races of the people portrayed and their respective roles (e.g., are they in leadership/supervisory positions? what are their occupations? do they have speaking roles?) Now watch thirty different television commercials and note the race(s) of the people portrayed and the roles they play.

Do you think the images are realistic in today's society, or idealistic? In the commercials, do you think the advertiser is trying to market their product or services to certain populations?

Gender. The family and heterosexual relationships central to the plots of many films, music videos, and television programs ensure that women are regularly included in media roles (Croteau & Hoynes, 2014, p. 206). Nevertheless, women have never achieved 50 percent parity in network broadcast television (Comstock & Scharrer, 2007).

Females are not proportionately represented in family films, children's shows, and prime-time programs despite their numbers in the U.S. population, according to Researchers at the Annenberg School for Communication & Journalism at the University of Southern California (Smith, Choueiti, Prescott, & Piper, 2013). Analysis of 129 family films between 2006 and 2011, 275 prime-time programs in the spring of 2012, and 36 children's TV shows in 2011 indicated that females represented 38.9 percent of characters in prime-time programs, 30.8 percent of characters in children's shows, and 28.3 percent of characters in family films. In the 129 family films analyzed, not one speaking character out of 5,839 portrayed was a powerful American female political figure. On the other hand, men held over forty-five different prestigious political positions including president, vice president, chief of staff, senators, representatives, mayors, and governors, in G, PG and PG-13 movies. The same study (Smith et al., 2013) found that "sexiness" is gendered across films and television. Females are far more likely than males to be depicted wearing sexy attire, and showing some exposed skin. They also were more likely to referenced by another character (verbally or nonverbally) as being physically attractive or desirous.

According to an analysis by the Women's Media Center (Yi & Dearfield, 2013) in news programming in 2011, 40 percent of the television news force was female and 28.4 percent of television news directors were women. Among the participants in the Sunday morning news talk shows, women were about 20 percent of guests. According to an NPR spokesperson interviewed for the study, "admittedly, the relative lack of female voices reflects the broader world. The fact remains . . . men are still largely in charge of government at all levels, in corporations and nearly all other aspects of society. This means, by default, there are going to be more male than female news sources" (Shepard, 2010).

Gender stereotyping is greater in advertising than in programming. Print ads feature pencil-thin female models with large breasts (often computer-enhanced) with implicit subtexts that suggest that women are subservient to men, if not obviously sex objects (Kilbourne, 1999). Even images that magazines present of mothers mask the reality of women's lives. "No one tires, no one frets, no one sweats. Motherhood is presented as a series of appealing snapshots" (Schwartz, 1996, p. 78).

A serious gap in television programming is the lack of coverage of women in sports. Studies conducted for the Associated Press Sports Editors revealed that women still represent a very small minority in sports news (Yi & Dearfield, 2013). The major networks rarely cover women's sports. Because they have to fill twenty-four hours of sports programming, sports cable channels do a little better (Desjardins, n.d.). Subtle differences in language are used to signify that a male perspective is the norm in American society. This is evident in the media coverage of women's sporting events, which includes constant gender marking: announcers make clear it is the NCAA *Women's* National Championship Game, while the men's version is billed simply as the NCAA National Championship Game (Croteau & Hoynes, 2014). Media scholars have noted that sportscasters call female athletes by their first names and use condescending adjectives to describe them (Desjardins, n.d.).

Sexual Orientation. During the twentieth century, LGBT representations in the mainstream media were rare and often controversial, but by the end of the first decade of the twenty-first century, LGBT characters made regular appearances (Croteau & Hoynes, 2014, p. 219).

There were a few positive representations of gay men on television beginning in the late 1970s and early 1980s. The first lesbian female lead in a situation comedy on prime-time network television was Ellen DeGeneres, in *Ellen* in 1997. Although her series was canceled the following year, she is now a successful and popular talk-show host. The first gay male lead of a situation comedy appeared a year later with the introduction of *Will & Grace*. *Will & Grace* was the most successful show with multiple gay characters in lead roles. While other programs did not feature gays in leading roles, there were recurring gay characters on several shows, such as *Friends, Mad About You, Dawson's Creek,* and *The Simpsons*. In 2009 *Modern Family*, a program featuring a committed gay couple, debuted to critical acclaim.

The Gay and Lesbian Alliance Against Defamation (GLAAD) reported that in the 2012–2013 television season there were thirty-one LGBT characters representing 4.4 percent of all scripted series regular characters on the five broadcast networks: ABC, CBS, The CW, Fox, and NBC; this was up from 2.9 percent in 2011 (GLAAD, 2012). In addition, there were thirty-five scripted LGBT series regulars found on mainstream cable channels. In their review of 101 films released in 2012, GLAAD found that only fourteen featured gay or bisexual characters, and only four included such a character in a substantive role (McDonough, 2013). The low visibility of LGBT characters in film and on television contributes to the myth that gay people are scarce in society.

People with Disabilities. People with disabilities are largely absent from the media. When they are presented, their disability is usually the focus of the story. Persons with disabilities very seldom appear as simply another character, either central to the plot or incidental (Makas, 1993; Nelson, 1996). One notable exception was the main character on the Fox network television medical drama, *House*, which ended in May 2013. Another exception is PBS, and in particular Sesame Street, which routinely includes children and adults with disabilities without portraying them as either victims or heroes. The 2013–2014 television season premieres included two series with main characters with disabilities, one on a major network and another on cable. Actor Michael J. Fox was diagnosed with Parkinson's disease in 1991 and semiretired after disclosing his condition to the public in 1999. He returned to television in *The Michael J. Fox Show* for the 2013–2014 season as a news show anchor living with Parkinson's disease and juggling family and career. *Ironside*, a 1960s series about a detective who uses a wheelchair, came back with an African American actor playing the lead. Disabled actors protested that having a walking actor play a paraplegic was offensive (Gilman, 2013). The *Ironside* show was canceled after a few weeks due to low viewership. Returning in 2013 for its second season on the Sundance cable channel, *Push Girls* features five young women who use wheelchairs.

Supporters of people with disabilities note that marketers are ignoring a potentially lucrative opportunity because of their ignorance, caution, or fear. Except for a handful of examples, people with disabilities are largely invisible in media advertising (Ng, 2013).

Social and Economic Class. Media advertisers seek out audiences that have enough disposable income to buy their product. "Simply put, advertisements aimed at selling products do not feature poor people and rarely feature working-class people. Instead, comfortable middle-class and affluent upper class images reign in ads" (Croteau & Hoynes, 2014, p. 211). Upper-class images are the most obvious in advertising but they also are apparent in television programming. Although many of the early television sitcoms featured working-class families (*The Honeymooners, The Andy Griffith Show, The Waltons, Happy Days*) as well as a few of the more recent ones (*Roseanne, All in the Family, Sanford and Son, The Simpsons, Everybody Loves Raymond, The King of Queens, Family Guy*), overwhelmingly the society portrayed in American media is middle or upper class. Early examples of middle- and upper-class TV families included *Father Knows Best, Dallas,* and *Frasier,* and more recently *Desperate Housewives* and *Modern Family.* The current portrayal of working-class people on television is likely to be reflected in individuals in scripted situation comedies or families on "reality TV." The sitcom *2 Broke Girls*, about two waitresses trying to start a cupcake business in Brooklyn, returned for its third season in 2013–2014. Examples of reality shows include *Duck Dynasty* and *Here Comes Honey Boo Boo,* which feature working-class white Southern families. NPR media critic Eric Deggans suggests that such programs portray disgraceful stereotypes of white working-class people, and similar series about other ethnic/racial or social class groups would not be tolerated.

Older Adults. Prime-time television programming presents a world that is also skewed in the representation of the age of the main characters. With the exception of Betty White in *Off Their Rockers* (2012–2013) and *Hot in Cleveland* (2010–present), older adults, and particularly older women, have gone missing since *Golden Girls,* the story of four older women sharing a home in Miami, left the air in 1992. Older adults make up 15 percent of the populations but comprise only about 3 percent of television characters; as is the situation with younger people, older men tend to appear up to ten times more frequently than older women (Garrett, 2011). While younger women are depicted in specific roles, such as wives, mothers, or workers, older women are not presented as having any particular role (Baumann & DeLaat, 2012).

Overrepresentation of characters between the ages of 30 and 50 might be explained by an economic model that suggests that the industry is trying to attract viewers in a prime consumer demographic group, but this model fails to account for an exclusion of those over 60, who have more disposable income (Comstock & Scharrer, 2007; Lauzen & Dozier, 2005). Television executives believe that older adults are loyal to the same products and brands, and hence are less likely to be influenced by television advertising (Garrett, 2011). Media ads in America tend to use older adults to market health care–related products, even if those products are for ailments that are not particularly age-related, such as allergy medications (Garrett, 2011).

The Internet

According to a Pew Internet & American Life Project survey (Zickuhr, 2013), 85 percent of American adults use the Internet or e-mail, including

98 percent of adults between the ages of 18 and 29, 92 percent of those ages 30–49, 83 percent of those ages 50–64, and 66 percent of those older than 64. Among individuals 77 or older, a full 62 percent do not use the Internet or e-mail. In 1995, only 14 percent of American adults used the Internet. Of those who do not use the Internet, 34 percent said they were not interested, found it a waste of time, or were too busy and 32 percent said it was too difficult or frustrating to use, they were physically unable to use it, or were worried about hackers or viruses.

Some older adults find it difficult to use many Internet websites, preferring those that have senior-friendly features, such as simpler layouts, larger type fonts, and higher color contrast between words and backgrounds (Joseph & Stone, 2005). Experts expect that soon mobile devices will be the primary connection tool to the Internet for most people in the world; intellectual property law and copyright protections will be jeopardized by those who find ways to copy and share content without payment; and the divisions between personal time and work time and between physical and virtual reality will be further erased (Pew Internet & American Life Project, 2008).

A threat of a different kind is found in the expansion of the Internet and its uncensored websites that not only dispense inaccurate information but also actively promote discrimination and violence against vulnerable groups. The Southern Poverty Law Center reported that there were 630 active U.S.-based hate sites on the World Wide Web in 2008 ("Hate Websites Active in 2008," 2009). Organizations with websites included groups affiliated with the Ku Klux Klan (52 sites), Neo-Nazis (89 sites), White Nationalists (190 sites), Racist Skinheads (25 sites), Christian Identity (37 sites), Neo-Confederate (25 sites), and Black Separatists (40 sites). The Pulitzer Prize-winning columnist Thomas Friedman wrote, "because the Internet has an aura of 'technology' surrounding it, the uneducated believe information from it even more. They don't realize that the Internet, at its ugliest, is just an open sewer, an electronic conduit for untreated, unfiltered information. Worse, just when you might have thought you were all alone with your extreme views, the Internet puts you together with a community of people from around the world who hate all the things and people you do" (Friedman, 2002, p. A9).

On a more positive note, more and more people are using the Internet for job-related tasks and to inform themselves on a variety of topics such as weather reports, current events, consumer goods, and medical conditions. In academic settings, both students and instructors have come to rely on the resources offered online.

Trends in News Consumption

According to the Pew Research Center for the People & the Press (2008), since 1993, the proportion of Americans who read a newspaper on a typical day had declined by about 40 percent and the proportion who routinely watch nightly network news had fallen by half. Another study showed that just 23 percent of Americans had read a print newspaper the day before they were surveyed in 2012, down from 47 percent in 2000 (Pew Research Center for the People & the Press, 2012). The proportion of young people who get no news on a typical day has increased substantially over the past decade. But 15 percent of Americans have a "smart phone"; more than a third of them report they get news using these devices.

As technology has transformed mass communications, there have been major changes in the print media. Since 1950 there has been a long-term decline in the size of the newspaper market—a decline that was initially related to the growth of television, and is currently related to the growth of the Internet. Between 1950 and 2005, the number of daily newspapers in the United States decreased from 1,772 to 1,425 (Rust & Yoder, 2007). Within the last thirty years, almost half of the afternoon dailies in large cities have either gone out of business or merged with a morning paper (Bagdikian, 2004). Isaacson (2009) suggests that the problem is not that people are no longer reading newspapers, but that the papers are giving away content for free on their websites. He says that newspapers traditionally relied on three revenue sources—newsstand sales, subscriptions, and advertising—and under the new business model, they rely only on the last of these. As long as people can access news and features for free, it will be difficult for newspapers to survive by charging for content and it is possible to imagine that only a few major national newspapers will last.

In a January 2009 interview on NPR, Leonard Downie, Jr., who was executive editor of the *Washington Post* for seventeen years, discussed the financial crisis of the newspaper industry.

> It's definitely the end of an era, but it's not the end of time for journalism. It's the end of . . . the era of the big, strong newspapers. All their staff expanded, they made lots of money, their circulation reached a peak. It was the golden era of American newspapers. [Despite the decline in circulation] we have acquired this huge audience on the Internet of 10 to 20 million unique visitors a month. So more people are reading *Washington Post* journalism than ever before. The series of articles we did on how soldiers were being treated—wounded soldiers were being treated at Walter Reed Hospital had 5 million page views and an extraordinary response from people across the world over the Internet that forced the government to take immediate action to change things at Walter Reed, fire the Army secretary, et cetera. None of that would have been possible without the Internet. So that's the good news. (National Public Radio, 2009)

Downie also expressed concern about newsrooms shrinking due to economic pressures and whether or not some cities around the country are going to have sufficiently large staffs to cover their communities.

In contrast to newspapers, magazine consumption has increased, primarily because of niche marketing (Rust & Yoder, 2007). The proliferation of magazines reflects the increasing variety of consumer goods. When a product has sufficient sales, it can generate a new magazine focusing on that area—everything from motorcycles to bridal gowns.

Technology and U.S. Elections

For the first time in a U.S. presidential election campaign, in 2008 ordinary citizens became active participants by producing their own material on the contenders, putting together countless political ads and mash-ups of video and audio clips and user comments. "The term is 'user-generated content'—a fancy way of saying that anyone with a computer now can become a player in politics" (Alter, 2008, p. 4).

Major political candidates began using the Internet for effective fund-raising in 2004. Barack Obama used technology to great effect during his presidential bid. In his 21-month campaign, he built a list of 3.1 million contributors and more than 10 million supporters (Fouhy, 2008; Murray & Mosk, 2008). Using online social networking, he drew crowds of 75,000 to his campaign speeches in the spring of 2008, 150 times the size of the audiences he saw early in the race (Alter, 2008). Those in his e-mail database made up a volunteer corps that registered millions of voters and served as the backbone of his get-out-the-vote operation on Election Day (Murray & Mosk, 2008). A supporter stated that Obama's use of technology "will reinvent the relationship of the president to the American people in a way we probably haven't seen since FDR's use of radio in the 1930s" (Connolly, 2008). Obama has created the first truly "wired" presidency.

Technology played a large role again in the 2012 presidential election, but for a different reason. Republican candidate Mitt Romney was caught on video at a private fund-raising event saying that 47 percent of the country is dependent on the government. Political pundit Chris Cillizza described this as "the definitive moment of the campaign," noting that the "power of these 'candid candidate' moments is that they present a jarringly different image of a politician than the one he or she is presenting to the public" (Cillizza, 2013).

Changing Patterns of Ownership: Media Mergers

In 1983 there were fifty dominant media corporations. The decade of the 1990s witnessed a concentration of entertainment and news media ownership. In 1990 there were twenty-three companies, and in 1997 the number dropped to ten. Mergers continued into the early part of the twenty-first century; for example, in 2013 the (Chicago) Tribune Company purchased nineteen TV stations, which will give the Tribune forty-two stations in sixteen markets (Yu, 2013). In 2013 there were only six media conglomerates (e.g., Disney, NBC/Universal, Fox/News Corp, Viacom, CBS, and Time Warner) that now own and operate television networks, radio stations, film studios, music studios, book publishing companies, video rental and movie theater chains, and magazine and newspaper outlets. Rather than competing with each other, these corporations cooperate with each other in a way that expands their individual power.

Understanding the Mass Media, Social Media, and Communication Technology

Functionalist Perspective

For most Americans, print, film, radio, music, television, and the Internet are central parts of daily life. These media experiences have the social effect of creating a common frame of reference. Functionalists would say that elements of the popular culture have the effect of strengthening social bonds. Disseminating information and entertainment are clearly the manifest functions of the mass media. Although their function as an agent of socialization is sometimes manifest (as in programs like *Sesame Street*), often people are unaware of how television and other media continue to socialize not only children but also adults. They support mainstream cultural values (e.g., individualism, competition, and patriotism). Another function of the mass media is to promote commerce by marketing goods and services.

Conflict Perspective

Conflict theorists argue that the mass media are controlled by the wealthy and powerful, who use them to mold public opinion and to help preserve their place of privilege. The messages put forth by the mass media reflect the positions of the owners and managers. "Who gets depicted, what about them gets depicted, why, with what consequences, at what time, and in what situation" is determined in the corporate boardroom (Turow, 1992, p. 164).

Many groups in society are losing access to the public sphere through the media as a result of the mergers discussed under the "Issues and Trends" section. There is a "fundamental contradiction between the ideal that public media should operate as a public sphere and the reality of concentrated private ownership" (Murdock & Golding, 2005, p. 67). McChesney (2000, pp. 29–30) argues that such a concentration of economic, cultural, and political power into so few hands—and mostly unaccountable hands at that—threatens the very basis of democracy.

Constructionist Perspective

The messages that the mass media present play a central role in organizing the images and conversations through which people make sense of the world. A vast body of research has demonstrated that media content does not reflect the realities of the social world.

The late George Gerbner and his colleagues at the Annenburg Public Policy Center at the University of Pennsylvania have studied the mass media for many years. They are concerned about television's role as an "electronic storyteller," replacing traditional cultural sources and monopolizing the socialization process. Most of what we know (or think we know) comes from stories in our culture, not from direct personal experience. With the ever-present effects of the mass media, everyone in America views the same images and listens to the same dialogue, defining what is to be valued and what is to be discounted. There is a homogenization of culture, with much of it being presented for the "lowest common denominator" or, at least, at the level that will bring in viewers and attract sponsors. Gerbner's cultivation theory (Gerbner, Gross, Morgan, & Signorielli, 1994) suggests that heavy viewers of television come to develop a common outlook on the world that is consistent with what they see on TV. Because images are similar across television channels, heavier viewers hold more stereotyped views of social groups than do light viewers (Gerbner et al., 1994), they are more sexist (Signorielli, 1993) and racist (Gerbner, Gross, Morgan, & Signorielli, 1982), and they are more likely to believe that the world is a violent and dangerous place (Gerbner et al., 1994).

Relationship of Mass Media, Social Media, and Communication Technology to the Political Economy

The media are often referred to as the "Fourth Estate" or the "fourth branch of government." This designation reflects the idea that the media (originally print journalists or "the press") have an important role in overseeing government functioning and, in particular, in revealing abuses of state authority (Curran, 2005). This "watchdog" role is supposed to override all other functions in importance. One might argue that now the threat to individual freedom lies not so much with government abuse as with corporate oligopoly. One of the consequences of corporate control of the media is that reporters are less likely to investigate the actions of the conglomerates that pay their salaries (Curran, 2005).

Underwood (1993) reported that as marketing became the focus of most newspapers, MBAs with a background in the business world replaced people with journalistic experience in executive positions. The clear goal of media executives is to create steady profits. The easiest approach for audience maximization (and the advertising revenues that follow) is to create a light, entertainment-oriented product, even in news programming. Media analysts Neil Postman and Steve Powers (1992) argued, for example, that television news was primarily "entertainment fodder." Because advertisers, not consumers, are doing the most important buying, the principal product being sold by the media is the *audience* (i.e., consumers), not newspapers, magazines, or programs (Croteau & Hoynes, 2014).

The United States is one of very few countries where the general perception is that the media should be controlled exclusively by market forces rather than being responsible for the public well-being. In fact, there has been increasing deregulation of American broadcasting, prompted in part by a proliferation of cable channels that supposedly allow the presentation of a wide variety of programming and opposing points of view on all topics.

Politics has become inextricably intertwined with the mass media, and in particular, with television. The medium of television has been accused of having negative effects on the American election process, in particular in relation to the increased cost of political campaigns and a focus on candidates' images rather than campaign issues. The soaring costs of modern election campaigns are a direct reflection of the price of airtime. It is now virtually impossible to get elected to national or state office without an effective media campaign.

The media also detract from American politics by treating political life as a "spectator sport." The sports metaphor of "winning" and "losing" dominates media news and discussion (Croteau & Hoynes, 2014). During the 2012 presidential campaign, newspapers and many major TV networks provided almost daily updates on each candidate's standing in a variety of public opinion polls, eliciting images of a slow-motion horse race. Media coverage of campaigns focuses on the comparative electability of the candidates rather than where they stand on issues. In response to media pressure, candidates often are presented as personalities (created through a process called packaging). Instead of studying and taking a position on an issue, politicians may say something that simply reflects the results of a recent poll or focus group. With a growing demand for 24/7 political coverage, news programs resort to broadcasting repetitions of short blips and slips. Of course, citizens need more adequate information to make informed decisions in the voting booth.

The media coverage contributes to the never-ending campaigns of American politics. Whereas in other countries (e.g., Australia) the national election "season" may last a couple of months, in the United States a new campaign begins almost before the final votes are tallied. Within days of when Barack Obama was reelected in 2012, for example, *Time* magazine ran a cover story speculating on who the 2016 front runners would be.

Many users are only recently becoming aware of how social media relate to the economy. Corporate platforms, such as Google and Facebook, regularly collect information that can be sold and used for marketing purposes (van Dijck, 2013). In contrast to its initial promise as an open public forum, the "free" Internet is "paid for" not in fees but in the user's attention to online ads and provision of his or her profiling and behavioral data (van Dijck, 2013, p. 169).

The Impact of Mass Media, Social Media, and Communication Technology on Individuals and Families

How Mass Media, Social Media, and Communication Technology Deter Well-Being

As noted in "Issues and Trends" under "Diversity and the Media," media images can hurt or mislead when they describe vulnerable populations. Film and television media present a biased view of society that critical thinkers need to examine.

Public Health Issues. The content of television programs and commercials may have a negative impact on viewers' health. Sports programming, for example, is flooded with soda, beer, pizza, fast food, and snack food commercials. Similar products, with the omission of beer and the addition of candy and sweetened breakfast cereals, appear in commercials in children's programs. Too often, children's distorted understanding of nutrition comes from Saturday morning television.

The childhood obesity epidemic is a serious public health problem. According to a meta-analysis of research compiled by the American Psychological Association (2010), the rates of obesity in America's young children have more than doubled and for teenagers they have tripled in the last quarter century. Research studies (American Psychological Association, 2010) have demonstrated strong correlations between increases in advertising for junk food and rates of childhood obesity. It is not surprising to learn that most children under age six are not able to distinguish between programming and advertising; older children can recognize ads but those under age eight do not understand that ads are designed to sell something. It appears that content from advertising is readily retained in children's memories. Children easily develop preferences for certain products with as little as a single commercial exposure. Parents notice that children will request products from the advertisements they have seen when they are shopping with their parents. A Kaiser Family Foundation study (2007) pointed out the lack of public service announcements for healthy eating. There is no advertising for fruits and vegetables because there is no "branding" of those products (Comstock & Scharrer, 2007).

In a study funded by Stanford University and the Robert Wood Johnson Foundation (Tanner, 2007), three- to five-year-old children were presented with identical food items in McDonald's and unmarked wrappers; the children always favored the food in the brand-name packaging. According to the researchers, the children's perception of taste was "physically altered by the branding" (Tanner, 2007, p. B7).

Alcohol and tobacco use are commonly associated with exposure to advertisements and to programs that present drinking and smoking as glamorous activities with no consequences (Perse, 2001). Between 2001 and 2009, youth exposure to alcohol advertising on U.S. television increased 71 percent, according to an analysis from the Center on Alcohol Marketing and Youth at the Johns Hopkins Bloomberg School of Public Health (2014). During this same time frame, youth were twenty-two times more likely to see an ad promoting alcohol consumption than an ad warning against underage drinking and/or alcohol-impaired driving. Alcohol is the most frequently advertised beverage in televised sports and the most common type of drink portrayed in programming. Half of the alcohol advertising on radio is aired during youth-oriented programs (Centers for Disease Control and Prevention, 2006). Researchers studied twenty-four G-rated Disney films that contained an animated human character and found eighteen had at least one instance of "alcohol exposure," defined as a "continuous display" of an alcoholic product (e.g., beer, wine) on the screen (Ryan & Hoerrner, 2004).

Tobacco ads were banned from the broadcast media in 1971; however, through print ads and clever product placement tobacco companies are able to effectively target not only adults but also children. Cigarette smoking occurs even in G-rated children's films (Ryan & Hoerrner, 2004) and is frequently portrayed in many popular films (Comstock & Scharrer, 2007).

The mass media also are effective in promoting the idea that casual sexual activity brings no negative consequences. A 2002 study found that "two-thirds of all television shows airing between 7 a.m. and 11 p.m. had some sexual content, and roughly one in seven shows now includes a portrayal of sexual intercourse, either depicted or strongly implied" (Brown, 2002, p. A3). A study analyzing 1,154 programs (excluding newscasts, sports events, and children's shows) from the 2004–2005 television season (Kaiser Family Foundation, 2005) found that seven in ten programs on cable and broadcast networks contained sexual content and the most popular shows with teenagers are more likely than other programs to feature sexual inferences or images. A RAND Corporation study (2004) on the effects of television on teens' sexual activity found that watching TV shows with sexual content apparently hastens the initiation of teen sexual activity, but shows with content about contraception and pregnancy can help to educate teens about the risks and consequences of sex—and can also foster beneficial dialogue between teens and parents.

Repeal of the Fairness Doctrine. The Fairness Doctrine was a federal law, enacted by Congress in 1949, that required radio and television stations to provide a minimum amount of time for discussion of civic issues, allowing equal time for opposing viewpoints. In the mid-1980s, the National Association of Broadcasters launched a successful campaign to repeal the act. In the six months following the repeal in 1987, civic discussion on the air dropped by 31 percent and since then has virtually disappeared in major markets (Bagdikian, 2004).

When programming is determined solely by commercial interest, there is little incentive to offer anything but profitable content (Croteau & Hoynes, 2014). Since the Fairness Doctrine was abandoned, stations can offer a single viewpoint without considering alterative opinions or public interest content.

How Mass Media, Social Media, and Communication Technology Promote Well-Being

Social learning theory suggests that children will imitate behaviors they observe. In addition to the negative effects noted earlier in this section of the chapter, studies have shown that young viewers of programs like *Mr. Rogers' Neighborhood* exhibited prosocial behaviors such as being more cooperative and helpful and talking about their feelings (Friedrich & Stein, 1975). A longitudinal study of the effects of some television viewing by preschoolers was associated with a number of positive characteristics in adolescents: getting higher grades, reading more books, being more creative, valuing achievement, and acting less aggressively (Anderson, Huston, Schmitt, Linebarger, & Wright, 2001).

One of the most positive aspects of the mass media is their potential to capture the nation's attention and support in the struggle against injustice or fraud. The Civil Rights Movement of the 1960s was nurtured through media exposure. The investigative journalism of Bob Woodward and Carl Bernstein of the *Washington Post* led to the resignation of Richard Nixon when they exposed illegal activities related to the Watergate scandal. During the Vietnam War, seeing film footage from the front lines on the evening news was at least in part responsible for a growing antiwar sentiment that shifted perceptions and public support.

Zeynep Tufekci, a professor at the University of North Carolina who studies the role of social media in social and political movements, suggests that social media "can provide a huge advantage in assembling the strength in numbers that movements depend on. . . . That's one reason the same-sex marriage movement, which uses online and offline visibility as a key strategy, has been so successful, and it's also why authoritarian governments try to ban social media" (Tufekci, 2014).

Television offers a cheap source of entertainment for people who cannot afford to go out, or are restricted to home for other reasons. It may be the only connection some older adults or other isolated individuals have to the world outside of their homes. TV viewing may be the only activity that some families are able to share.

The importance of the communication function of the media becomes particularly clear during an emergency situation. Residents of communities that experience natural disasters (e.g., blizzards, hurricanes, floods, earthquakes, and tornadoes), large-scale industrial accidents, or terrorist scares rely on the media for up-to-the minute information. Media coverage may facilitate and reinforce societal cohesion, giving listeners and viewers a sense of connection to others who are sharing a common experience (Perse, 2001, p. 62).

LOOKING AHEAD

In these last three chapters, we have examined eight social institutions. Each social institution helps to organize social relations in a particular sector of social life.

A concept that describes the hierarchical relationships among people in different social status groups is social structure. We examine social structure as it relates to class, race and ethnicity, gender, sexual orientation, and disability in the next three chapters.

REFERENCES

Agency for Health Care Research and Quality. (2012). *National Health Care Disparities Report, 2012*. Retrieved from http://www.ahrq.gov /research/findings/nhqrdr/nhdr12/.

Alter, J. (2008, August 31). Why the 2008 election is bringing power to the people. *Parade,* pp. 4–5.

Alzheimer's Association. (2014). *Alzheimer's facts and figures*. Retrieved from http://www.alz.org/alzheimers_disease_facts_and_figures.asp ?sp = true.

American Academy of Child and Adolescent Psychiatry. (2002, November). Children and TV violence (Issue Brief No. 13). Retrieved from http://www.aacap.org/cs/root/facts_for_Families/children_and_tv_violence.

American Academy of Child and Adolescent Psychiatry. (2004, July). The influence of music and music videos (Issue Brief No. 40). Retrieved from http://www.aacap.org/cs/root/facts_for_families/the_influence_of_music_and_music_videos.

American Cancer Society. (2008, November 1). Native American healing. Retrieved from http://www.cancer.org/treatment/treatmentsand sideeffects/complementaryandalternativemedicine/mindbodyand spirit/native-american-healing?sitearea = ETO.

American Holistic Medical Association. (n.d.). About holistic medicine. Retrieved from http://www.holisticmedicine.org/content.asp?pl = 2& sl = 43&conten tid = 43.

American Hospital Association. (2011, April). The opportunities and challenges for rural hospitals in an era of health reform. *TrendWatch.* Retrieved from http://www.aha.org/research/reports/tw/11apr-tw -rural.pdf.

American Humanist Association. (n.d.). Good without a god. Available from the American Humanist Association, 1777 T Street NW, Washington, DC 20009–7125.

American Psychological Association. (2005). *Review of research shows that playing violent video games can heighten aggression* (Review of the presentation Violence in video games: A review of the empirical research). Retrieved from http://www.apa.org/releases/violentvideo C05.html.

American Psychological Association. (2008). *Violence on television: What can children learn? What can parents do?* Retrieved from http://www.apa.org/pi/vio&tv.html.

American Psychological Association. (2010). *The impact of food advertising on childhood obesity.* Retrieved from http://www.apa.org/topics /kids-media/food.aspx.

Andersen, M., & Taylor, H. (2013). *Sociology: The essentials* (7th ed.). Belmont, CA: Wadsworth.

Anderson, D. R., Huston, A. C., Schmitt, K. L., Linebarger, D. L., & Wright, J. C. (2001). Early childhood television viewing and adolescent behavior. *Monographs of the Society for Research in Child Development, 66*(1), serial number 264.

Association of American Medical Colleges. (2012, October). *Recent studies and reports on physician shortages in the U.S.* Retrieved from https://www.aamc.org/download/100598/data/.

Bagdikian, B. H. (2004). *The new media monopoly* (2nd ed.). Boston, MA: Beacon Press.

Baumann, S., & de Laat, K. (2012). Socially defunct: A comparative analysis of the underrepresentation of older women in advertising. *Poetics, 40*(6), 514–541. Retrieved from http://www.sciencedirect.com/science/article/pii/s0304422x1200052 6.

Bellah, R. N. (1967). Civil religion. *Daedalus, 96,* 1–21.

Belluck, P. (2013, April 4). Dementia cases, cost of care soaring. *The State* [Columbia, SC], p. A4.

Bennett, A. (2012, June). The cost of hope. *Newsweek*, 52–55.

Boston, R. (2010). 'No religious test' tested. Americans United for Separation of Church and State. Retrieved from https://www.au.org/church-state/february-2010-church-state/featur ed/%E2%80%98no-religious-test%E2%80%99-tested.

Brill, A. (2005, March 12). Will love drive out fear, hatred? *The State* [Columbia, SC], p. A9.

Brill, S. (2013, March 4). Why medical bills are killing us. *Time,* pp. 30–38.

Brown, P. L. (2002, July 27). Sex-charged TV steams up airwaves. *Herald-Leader* [Lexington, KY], p. A3.

Campo-Flores, A. (2005, March 21). The battle for Latino souls: Pentecostal churches are using savvy marketing to attract traditionally Catholic Hispanics. A holy struggle in Chicago. *Chicago Tribune*, p. B1.

Canadian Holistic Medical Association. (2008). What is holistic medicine? Retrieved from http://www.holisticmed.com/whatis.html.

Center on Alcohol Marketing and Youth at the Johns Hopkins Bloomberg School of Public Health. (2014). *Youth exposure to alcohol advertising on television, 2001–2009.* Retrieved from http://www.camy.org

/research/Youth_Exposure_to_Alcohol_Ads_on_TVeGrowing_Faster _Than_Adults/.

Center for Responsive Politics. (2013). *Top industries.* Retrieved from http://www.opensecrets.org/lobby/top.php?indexType = i&showYear = 2013.

Center sues to remove monument. (2002, April). *SPLC* [Southern Poverty Law Center] *Report, 32*(1), p. 4.

Centers for Disease Control and Prevention. (2006, September 1). Youth exposure to alcohol advertising on radio. *Morbidity & Mortality Weekly Report, 55* (34), 937–940. Retrieved from http://www.cdc.gov /mmwr/preview.

Centers for Disease Control and Prevention. (2013). Childhood Obesity Facts. Retrieved from http://www.cdc.gov/healthyyouth/obesity/fact /htm.

Cillizza, C. (2013, March 4). Why Mitt Romney's "47 percent" comment was so bad. *Washington Post.* Retrieved from http://www.washington post.com/blogs/the-fix/wp/2013/03/04/why-mitt-romneys-47-percent -comment-was-so-bad/.

Comstock, G., & Scharrer, E. (2007). *Media and the American child.* Burlington, MA: Elsevier.

Connolly, C. (2008, December 4). Obama policymakers turn to campaign tools. *Washington Post.* Retrieved from http://www.washingtonpost .com/.

Croteau, D., & Hoynes, W. (2014). *Media/society: Industries, images, and audiences* (5th ed.). Thousand Oaks, CA: Sage.

Curran, J. (2005). Mediations of democracy. In J. Curran and M. Gure-vitch (Eds.), *Mass media and society* (4th ed.). New York, NY: Oxford University Press.

Davie, M. B. (2001). *Following the Great Spirit: Exploring aboriginal belief systems.* Hamilton, Ontario: Manor House Publishing.

DeNavas-Walt, C., Proctor, B. D., & Smith, J. C. (2013). *U.S. Census Bureau, Current Population Reports, P60–245, Income, Poverty, and Health Insurance Coverage in the United States: 2012.* Washington, DC: U.S. Government Printing Office.

Desjardins, M. (n.d.). *Gender and television.* Museum of Broadcast Com-munication. Retrieved from http://www.museum.tv/eotvsection.php ?entrycode = genderandtelevision.

Dionne, E. J. (2013, August 4). Religion challenges left and right. *The Washington Post*. Retrieved from http://www.washingtonpost.com /opinions/ej-dionne-jr-religion-challenges-left-and-right/2013/08/04 /2b2e7a2e-fb7d-11e2-a369-d1954abcb7e3estory.html?.

Doyle, J. (2012, July 8). Woman lingers, family frets, costs soar. *The State* [Columbia, SC], p. A8.

Durkheim, E. (1965/1912). *The elementary forms of the religious life*. New York, NY: Free Press.

Dyer, J. (2000). *The perpetual prisoner machine: How America profits from crime*. Boulder, CO: Westview Press.

Ellison, C. G., Boardman, J. D., Williams, D. R., & Jackson, J. S. (2001). Religious involvement, stress, and mental health: Findings from the 1995 Detroit area study. *Social Forces, 80*(1), 215–249. doi:org /10.1353/sof.2001.0063

Farber, D. (2012, June 6). Twitter hits 400 million tweets per day, mostly mobile. CNET. Retrieved from http://www.cnet.com/news/twitter -hits-400-million-tweets-per-day-mostly-mobile/.

Faulkner, W. (2013, October 23). Drop-in retail clinics a growing trend in medical care. Retrieved from http://www.starnewsonline.com/article /20131023/ARTICLES/310234003?template=printart.

Foley, M. W., McCarthy, J. D., & Chaves, M. (2001). Social capital, religious institutions, and poor communities. In S. Saegert, J. P. Thompson, & M. R. Warren (Eds.), *Social capital and poor communities* (pp. 215–245). New York, NY: Russell Sage Foundation.

Fouhy, B. (2008, November 10). Obama team works for 'wired' presidency. *The State*, [Columbia, SC], p. A4.

Friedman, T. L. (2002, May 14). Satellites, Internet spread hate, not understanding. *The State* [Columbia, SC], p. A9.

Friedrich, L. K., & Stein, A. H. (1975). Prosocial television and young children: The effects of verbal labeling and role playing on learning and behavior. *Child Development, 46*, 27–38.

Galewitz, P. (2012, February 6). Hospitals mine personal data for customers. *USA Today*, p. 10B.

Garnett, R. W. (2008, January 28). When Catholicism was the target. *USA Today*, p. 9A.

Garrett, M. (2011, November 8). Few older adults in film and television. *UT San Diego*. Retrieved from http://www.utsandiego.com/news /2011/nov/08/few-older-adults-in-film-and-television/all/?print.

George, J. (2007, December 31). Candidates come marching in with religion. *Chicago Tribune*, pp. 1, 8.

Gerbner, G., Gross, L., Morgan, M., & Signorielli, N. (1982). Charting the mainstream: Television's contributions to political orientation. *Journal of Communication, 32*(2), 100–127.

Gerbner, G., Gross, L., Morgan, M., & Signorielli, N. (1994). Growing up with television: The cultivation perspective. In J. Bryant and D. Zillmann (Eds.), *Media effects: Advances in theory and research* (pp. 17–41.) Hillsdale, NJ: Lawrence Erlbaum.

Gilman, G. (2013, May 20). Hollywood's disabled actors protest NBC's Ironside casting—When is it their turn? *The Wrap*. Retrieved from http://www.thewrap.com/tv/article/hollywoods-disabled-react-iron side-casting-all-we-want-chance-91886.

Gitlin, T. (2001). *Media unlimited: How the torrent of images and sounds overwhelms our lives*. New York, NY: Metropolitan books.

GLAAD. (2012). *Where we are on TV report: 2012–2013 season*. Retrieved from http://www.glaad.org/publications/whereweareon tv12.

Goldman, D. (2011, October 12). US cellphones, tablets outnumber Americans. *CNN Money*. Retrieved from http://money.cnn.com/2011 /10/12/technology/cellphones_outnumber_americans/.

Goulden, J. C. (1971). *The money givers*. New York, NY: Random House.

Haneef, S. (1993). *What everyone should know about Islam and Muslims*. Chicago, IL: Kazi Publications.

Hartford Institute for Religion Research. (n.d.). What percentage of pastors are female? Retrieved from http://hirr.hartsem.edu/research /quick_question3.html.

Hate Websites Active in 2008. (2009, Spring). *Intelligence Report*, pp. 59–65.

Healy, M. (2012, December 11). Longevity masks unhealthy lifestyles. *USA Today*, p. 1A.

Helminiak, D. A. (1994). *What the Bible really says about homosexuality*. San Francisco, CA: Alamo Square Press.

Hennessy-Fiske, M. (2013, June 13). Southern Baptists back those who oppose gay Scouts. *The State* [Columbia, SC], p. A4.

Henslin, J. M. (2014). *Sociology: A down-to-earth approach* (12th ed.). Boston, MA: Pearson Education.

Hill, J., & Cheadle, R. (1996). *The Bible tells me so: Uses and abuses of holy scripture.* New York, NY: Anchor/Doubleday.

Holleman, J. (2013, October 20). Once a rarity, walk-in health care now common in midlands. *The State* [Columbia, SC], p. A6.

Hunter, J. (1991). *Culture wars.* New York, NY: Basic Books

Hutson, J. (1998). 'A Wall of Separation:' FBI helps restore Jefferson's obliterated draft. Library of Congress. Retrieved from http://www .loc.gov.

International Telecommunication Union. (2012). *Measuring the information society: Executive summary.* Retrieved from http://www.itu.int /dms_pub/itu-d/opb/ind/D-IND-ICTOI-2012-SUM-P DF-E.pdf.

Isaacson, W. (2009, February 16). How to save your newspaper. *Time,* pp. 31–33.

Jackson, D. (2007, June 2). With children, sound crowds out sense. *The State* [Columbia, SC], p. A9.

Jayson, S. (2013, July 19). How mobile changes dating habits. *USA Today.* Retrieved from http://www.usatoday.com/story/news/nation /2013/07/18/mobile-dating-behavior-technology/2500359/.

Joseph, N., & Stone, B. (2005, April 25). Diagnosis: Internet phobia. *Newsweek,* p. 74.

Kaiser Family Foundation. (2005). *Sex on TV.* Retrieved from http:// www.kff.org.

Kaiser Family Foundation. (2007). *New study finds that food is the top product seen advertised by children.* Retrieved from http://www .kff.org.entmedia.

Kaiser Family Foundation. (2013a). *2013 employer health benefits survey.* Retrieved from http://kff.org/report-section/2013-summary-of-find ings/.

Kaiser Family Foundation. (2013b). *Key facts about the uninsured popu- lation.* Retrieved from http://kff.org/uninsured/fact-sheet/key-facts -about-the-uninsured -population/.

Kane, J. (2012, October 22). *Health costs: How the U.S. compares with other countries.* Retrieved from http://www.pbs.org/newshour/run

down/2012/10/health-costs-how-the-us-compares-with-other-coun tries.html

Karger, H. J., & Stoesz, D. (2010). *American social welfare policy* (6th ed.). Boston, MA: Pearson Education.

Kendall, D. (2013). *Sociology in our times* (9th ed.). Belmont, CA: Wadsworth.

Kilbourne, J. (1999). *Deadly persuasion: Why women and girls must fight the addictive power of advertising.* New York, NY: Free Press.

Kim, K. C. (1999). Koreans. In E. R. Barkan (Ed.), *A nation of peoples: America's multicultural heritage* (pp. 354–371). Westport, CT: Greenwood Press.

Koppel, T. (2010, November 14). Olbermann, O'Reilly and the death of real news. *Washington Post.* Retrieved from http://www.washington post.com/wp-dyn/content/article/2010/11/12/AR2010111202857 _2.html.

Kristof, N. D., & WuDunn, S. (2009). *Half the sky: Turning oppression into opportunity for women worldwide.* New York, NY: Knopf.

Lamontagne, S., Singh, R., & Palosky, C. (2010). *Daily media use among children and teens up dramatically from five years ago.* Kaiser Family Foundation. Retrieved from http://kff.org/disparities-policy/press-release/daily-media-use-among-children-and-teens-up-dramatically -from-five-years-ago/.

Lauzen, M., & Dozier, D. (2005). Recognition and respect revisited: Portrayals of age and gender in prime-time television. *Mass Communication and Society, 8*(3), 241–256.

Lester, P. M. (Ed.) (1996). *Images that injure: Pictorial stereotypes in the media.* Westport, CT: Praeger.

Livingstone, S. (2005). Critical debates in Internet studies: Reflections on an emerging field. In J. Curran and M. Gurevitch (Eds.), *Mass media and society* (4th ed., pp. 9–28). New York, NY: Hodder Arnold.

MacDorman, M. F., Hoyert, D. L., & Mathews, T. J. (2013). *Recent declines in infant mortality in the United States, 2005–2011.* Centers for Disease Control and Prevention. Retrieved from http://www.cdc .gov/nchs/data/databriefs/db120.htm.

Macionis, J. J. (2014). *Sociology* (15th ed.). Boston, MA: Pearson Education.

Madden, M., Lenhart, A., Duggan, M., Cortesi, S., & Gasser, U. (2013). *Teens and technology 2013*. Pew Research Center Internet & American Life Project. Retrieved from http://www.pewinternet.org/2013 /03/13/main-findings-5/.

Makas, E. (1993). Changing channels: The portrayal of people with disabilities on television. In G. L Berry & J. K. Asamen (Eds.), *Children & television: Images in a changing sociocultural world.* Newbury Park, CA: Sage.

Marchione, M. (2011, September 14). Bad habits killing us. *The State* [Columbia, SC], p. A5.

McChesney, R. W. (2000). *Rich media, poor democracy: Communication politics in dubious times.* New York, NY: New Press.

McDonough, K. (2013, August 21). As television gets more diverse, American movies lag behind in LGBT representation. Retrieved from http://www.salon.com/2013/08/21/as_television_gets_more_diverse _american_movies_lag_behind_in_lgbt_representation/ .

McGuire, M. B. (1997). *Religion: The social context* (4th ed.). Belmont, CA: Wadsworth.

Meyerson, H. (2007, March 21). God and his gays. *Washington Post.* Retrieved from http://www.washingtonpost.com.

Miller, L. (2008, February 25). In defense of secularism. *Newsweek,* p. 15.

Miller, M. (2010). Why we need a third party of (radical) centrists. *Washington Post.* Retrieved from http://www.washingtonpost.com/wp-dyn /content/article/2010/11/10/AR2010111003489.html.

Miller, M. (2013, September 27). Canadians don't understand Ted Cruz's health-care battle. *The Washington Post.* Retrieved from http://articles .washingtonpost.com/2013-09-25/opinions/42373230_1_canadians-health-care-debate-lower-costs.

Mishori, R. (2008, December 21). How spirituality keeps you well. *Parade,* p. 14.

Moeller, S. D., Chong, E., Golitsinski, S., Guo, J., McCaffrey, R., Nynka, A., & Roberts, J. (2013). 24 hours-unplugged. Retrieved from http:// withoutmedia.wordpress.com/.

Monk-Turner, E., Heiserman, M., Johnson, C., Cotton, V., & Jackson, M. (2010). The portrayal of racial minorities on prime time television: A replication of the Mastro and Greenberg study a decade later. *Studies in Popular Culture, 32*(2), 101.

Morris, R. (1986). *Rethinking social welfare: Why care for the stranger?* New York, NY: Longman.

Murdock, G., & Golding, P. (2005). Culture, communications, and political economy. In J. Curran and M. Gurevitch (Eds.), *Mass media and society* (pp. 60–83). New York, NY: Oxford University Press.

Murray, S., & Mosk, M. (2008, November 10). Under Obama, web would be the way. *Washington Post.* Retrieved from http://www.washington post.com/wp-dyn/content/article/2008/11/10/AR2008111000013_.

National Alliance on Mental Illness. (2013). *Mental illness: Facts and numbers.* Retrieved from http://www.nami.org/factsheets/mentalill ness_factsheet.pdf.

National Association of Social Workers. (2002). NASW priorities on faith-based human services initiatives. Retrieved from http://www .socialworkers.org/advocacy/positions/faith.asp.

National Association of Social Workers. (2012a). Health care policy. In *Social Work Speaks* (9th ed., pp. 168–171). Washington, DC: National Association of Social Workers.

National Association of Social Workers. (2012b). Mental health. In *Social Work Speaks* (9th ed., pp. 230–235). Washington, DC: National Association of Social Workers.

National Center for Health Statistics. (2012). *Health, United States, 2012.* Centers for Disease Control and Prevention. Retrieved from http:// www.cdc.gov/nchs/data/hus/hus12_InBrief.pdf.

National Public Radio. (2009). Former "Post" editor details the "rules of the game." Retrieved from http://nl.newsbank.com.

Nelson, J. A. (1996). The invisible cultural group: Images of disability. In P. M. Lester (Ed.), *Images that injure: Pictorial stereotypes in the media* (pp. 119–125). Westport, CT: Praeger.

Ng, C. (2013, May 29). Huge demographic virtually impossible in media wants to be seen. Retrieved from http://abcnews.go.com/business/dis abled-community-media-markieting/story?id = 19143489.

Nielsen. (2012). *Social media report 2012: Social media comes of age.* Retrieved from http://www.nielsen.com/us/en/newswire/2012/social -media-report-2012-social-media-comes-of-age.html.

NORC. (2011). *General Social Surveys, 1972–2010.* Chicago, IL: National Opinion Research Center. Retrieved from http://www.norc .org/GSST.

Ogden, C. L., Carroll, M. D., Kit, B. K., & Flegal, K. M. (2014). Prevalence of childhood and adult obesity in the United States, 2011–2012. *Journal of the American Medical Association, 311*(8), 806–814.

O'Keeffe, G. S., & Clarke-Pearson, K. (2011, April 1). The impact of social media on children, adolescents, and families. *Pediatrics, 127*(4), 800–804. Retrieved from http://pediatrics.aapublications.org /content/127/4/800.full.

Parker, K. (2006, January 2). Lord of the blogs. *The State* [Columbia, SC], p. A9.

Pell, D. (2013). Does the internet make you more connected, or less? National Public Radio. Retrieved from http://www.npr.org/blogs/all techconsidered/2011/08/24/139914259/d oes-the-inter net-make-you -more-or-less-connected.

Perse, E. M. (2001). *Media effects and society*. Mahwah, NJ: Lawrence Erlbaum Associates.

Pew Forum on Religion & Public Life. (2008). *U.S. religious landscape survey: Summary of key findings*. Retrieved from http://religions .pewforum.org/reports.

Pew Forum on Religion & Public Life. (2012). *"Nones" on the rise: One-in-five adults have no religious affiliation*. Retrieved from http:// www.pewforum.org/files/2012/10/NonesOnTheRise-full.pdf.

Pew Internet & American Life Project. (2008). *The future of the internet iii*. Retrieved from http://www.pewinternet.org/.

Pew Research Center for the People & the Press. (2008). *Key news audiences now blend online and traditional sources*. Retrieved from http:// www.people-press.org/2008/08/17/key-news-audiences-now-blend -online-and-traditional-sources/.

Pew Research Center for the People & the Press. (2012). *In changing news landscape, even television is vulnerable: Trends in news consumption: 1991–2012*. Retrieved from http://www.people-press.org /2012/09/27/in-changing-news-landscape-even-television-is-vulner able/.

Pollack, C. E., Gidengil, C., & Mehrotra, A. (2010). The growth of retail clinics and the medical home: Two trends in concert or in conflict? *Health Affairs, 29*(5), 998–1003. Retrieved from http://content.health affairs.org/content/29/5/998.full?.

Pope, E. (2003, November). Second-class care. *AARP Bulletin*, pp. 6, 7–8.

Postman, N., & Powers, S. (1992). *How to watch TV news*. New York, NY: Penguin.

Powers, K. (2013, July 31). Pope's gay tolerance no shock. *USA Today*. Retrieved from http://www.usatoday.com/story/opinion/2013/07/31/pope-francis-gay-comments-column/2606583/.

Pozios, V. K., Kambam, P. R., & Bender, H. E. (2013, August 23). Does media violence lead to the real thing? *New York Times*. Retrieved from http://www.nytimes.com/2013/08/25/opinion/sunday/does-media-violence-lead-to-the-real-thing.html?_r = 0.

Rainie, L. (2013). *Cell phone ownership hits 91% of adults*. Pew Research Center Internet & American Life Project. Retrieved from http://www.pewresearch.org/fact-tank/2013/06/06/cell-phone-ownership-hits-91-of-adults/.

RAND Corporation. (2004). *Does watching sex on television influence teens' sexual activity?* Retrieved from http://www.rand.org/.

Raspberry, W. (1999, September 26). Duty bound to pray for the heathen. *The State* [Columbia, SC], p. A6.

Rehavi, M. M., & Johnson, E. M. (2013). *Physicians treating physicians: Information and incentives in childbirth*. NBER Working Paper No. w19242. Available at SSRN: http://ssrn.com/abstracts = 229856.

Rideout, V. J., Foehr, U. G., & Roberts, D. F. (2010). *Generation M²: Media in the lives of 8–18-year-olds*. Kaiser Family Foundation. Retrieved from http://kaiserfamilyfoundation.files.wordpress.com/2013/01/8010.pdf.

Rideout, V. J., Hamel, E., & Kaiser Family Foundation. (2006). *The media family: Electronic media in the lives of infants, toddlers, preschoolers, and their parents*. Kaiser Family Foundation. Retrieved from http://www.kff.org/entmedia/upload/7500.pdf.

Ritter, J. A., Vakalahi, H. F. O., & Kiernan-Stern, M. (2009). *101 careers in social work*. New York, NY: Springer.

Roberts, K. A. (1995). *Religion in sociological perspective*. Belmont, CA: Wadsworth.

Roesler, S. M. (2005). Women's human rights abuses in the name of religion. In A. Barnes (Ed.), *The handbook of women, psychology and the law* (pp. 280–292). San Francisco, CA: Jossey-Bass.

Rovner, J. (2007, May 7). Democrats to push Medicaid for children. National Public Radio. Retrieved from http://www.npr.org/templates /story/story.php?storyId = 10040676.

Rust, M., & Yoder, C. (2007, May 20). From Lucy to Sanjaya: Broadcast TV isn't dead, but an explosion of media choices means it will never be the same. *Chicago Tribune*, p. 6.

Ryan, E. L., & Hoerrner, K. L. (2004). Let your conscience be your guide: Smoking and drinking in Disney's animated classics. *Mass Communications & Society, 7,* 261–278.

Schaefer, R. T. (2008). *Racial and ethnic groups* (11th ed.). Upper Saddle River, NJ: Prentice Hall.

Schaefer, R. T. (2012). *Racial and ethnic groups* (13th ed.). Boston, MA: Pearson Education.

Schmitt, J. (2012, February). *Health insurance coverage for low-wage workers, 1979–2010 and beyond*. Washington, DC: Center for Economic and Policy Research.

Schwartz, D. (1996). Women as mothers. In P. M. Lester (Ed.), *Images that injure: Pictorial stereotypes in the media* (pp. 75–80). Westport, CT: Praeger.

Sessions, D. (2012, October). Losing their religion. *Newsweek*, p. 10.

Shapira, I. (2010, August 8). Texting generation doesn't share boomers' taste for talk. *Washington Post*. Retrieved from http://www.washing tonpost.com/wp-dyn/content/article/2010/08/07/AR201008070284 8.html.

Shepard, A. C. (2010, April 2). Where are the women? National Public Radio. Retrieved from http://www.npr.org/blogs/ombudsman/2010 /04/where_are_the_women.html.

Signorielli, N. (1993). Television, the portrayal of women, and children's attitudes. In G. L. Berry & J. K. Asamen (Eds.), *Children and television: Images in a changing sociocultural world* (pp. 229–242). Newbury Park, CA: Sage.

Smith, S. L., Choueiti, M., Prescott, A., & Piper, K. (2013) Gender roles & occupations: A look at character attributes and job-related aspirations in film and television. Retrieved from http://www.seejane .org/downloads/key-findings-gender-roles-2013.pdf.

STOPcyberbullying. (n.d.). What is cyberbullying, exactly? Retrieved from http://stopcyberbullying.org/what_is_cyberbullying_exactly .html.

Tanner, L. (2007, August 17). Study: Golden Arches beckon preschoolers. *The State* [Columbia, SC], p. B7.

Television Information Office. (1985). *A broadcasting primer with notes on the new technologies.* New York, NY: Author.

Thio, A. (1998). *Sociology* (5th ed.). New York, NY: Longman.

Thio, A. (2000). *Sociology: A brief introduction* (4th ed.). Boston, MA: Allyn & Bacon.

Tufekci, Z. (2014, March 19). After the protests. *New York Times.* Retrieved from http://www.nytimes.com/2014/03/20/opinion/after -the-protests.html .

Turow, J. (1992). A mass communication perspective on entertainment. In J. Curran and & M. Gurevitch (Eds.), *Mass media and society* (pp. 160–177). London, UK: Edward Arnold.

Turow, J. (1997). *Breaking up America: Advertisers and the new media world.* Chicago, IL: University of Chicago Press.

Underwood, D. (1993). *When MBAs rule the newsroom.* New York, NY: Columbia University Press.

U.S. Census Bureau. (2014). *Measuring America.* Retrieved from http:// www.census.gov/hhes/computer/files/2012/Computer_Use_Infogra phic_FINAL.pdf.

U.S. Department of Health and Human Services. (2006, December). *National healthcare disparities report, 2006.* [Electronic version]. Retrieved from http://www.ahrq.gov/qual/nhdr06/nhdr06.htm.

van Dijck, J. (2013). *The culture of connectivity: A critical history of social media.* New York, NY: Oxford University Press.

Vedantam, S. (2013, August 30). Money may be motivating doctors to do more C-sections. National Public Radio. Retrieved from http://www .npr.org/blogs/health/2013/08/30/216479305/money-may-be-motivat ing-doctors-to-do-more-c-sections.

Walt, V. (2008, September 29). Death in birth. *Time,* pp. 48–52.

Wang, P. (2012, December 12). Cutting the high cost of end-of-life care. Retrieved from http://money.cnn.com/2012/12/11/pf/end-of-life-care -duplicate-2.moneymag/.

Werner, B. (2007, June 21). FTC settles board of dentistry case: Dispute reached back to 2001. *The State* [Columbia, SC], p. B.1.

Wolfe, A. (1998, June 14). Religion, with a grain of salt. *New York Times*, p. 15.

Wood, J. (2013, May 6). New study reports one in six students victim of cyberbullying. Psychcentral. Retrieved from http://psychcentral.com /news/2013/05/06/new-study-reports-one-in-six-students-victim-of -cyberbullying/54520.html.

World Health Organization. (2002, October 30). *Years of healthy life can be increased 5–10 years.* Retrieved from http://www.who.int/media centre/news/.

Yi, R. H., & Dearfield, C. T. (2013). *The status of women in the U.S. media 2012.* Women's Media Center. Retrieved from www.womens mediacenter.com.

Yu, R. (2013, July 1). Tribune buys 19 TV stations to broaden its reach. *USA Today.* Retrieved from http://www.usatoday.com/story/money /business/2013/07/01/tribune-to-acquire-19-tv-stations-for-273b/24 78769/.

Zakaria, F. (2012, March 26). Health insurance is for everyone. *Time,* pp. 22–23.

Zickuhr, K. (2013). *Main report.* Pew Research Internet Project. Retrieved from http://www.pewinternet.org/2013/09/25/main-report-2/.

Zickuhr, K., & Smith, A. (2012). *Digital differences.* Pew Research Internet Project. Retrieved from http://www.pewinternet.org/2012/04 /13/digital-differences/.

Zuckerman, M. B. (2005, November 28). Freedom of the press is guaranteed only to the whinging billionaire who owns one. Catbird seat in *U.S. News & World Report.* [Web log comment.] Retrieved from http://moviecitynews.com/2005/11/freedom-of-the-press-is-guaranteed -only-to-the-whinging-billionaire-who-owns-one-zuckerman-slags -blogs/.

PART III

Social Structure in American Society

Society refers to a group of people who occupy a defined territory and share a common culture. Social structure is "the framework that surrounds us, consisting of the relationships of people and groups, which give direction to and set limits on behavior" (Henslin, 2014, p. 96). In explaining how sociologists study social structure, Grusky (1994) suggests that they look at several key concepts. One is how much inequality exists, and another is how rigid the system is, that is, how easily individuals move from one level to another. (In this text, we will use the term *inequality* to refer to numeric differences and *inequity* when inequality appears to be the result of economic or social injustice.) Another concern of sociologists is how traits present at birth, such as sex, race, and ethnicity, influence subsequent social standing. In this section of the text, we discuss social structure in relation to social class, race, ethnicity, and other social statuses (gender, sexual orientation and identity, and disability). The perspectives that were used to explain social institutions will be used again to contribute to a deeper understanding of social structure.

As noted in chapter 1, a niche is defined as a "status occupied by an individual or family in the social structure"; Germain and

Gitterman noted that our society is "studded with marginal, stigmatized, and destructive niches that denigrate human beings" (1995, p. 818). Of particular interest to social workers is the fact that some groups suffer from discrimination and oppression, while others enjoy unearned privilege. Particular statuses, such as being poor, dark-skinned, female, gay, lesbian, or transgendered, old, or disabled are characteristics of "populations at risk." Rather than just viewing these people as victims of oppression, we will identify the diverse strengths that they have.

Chapter 5 covers social stratification (social class). The impact of social class on individuals and families is discussed and special attention is given to the experiences of the poor.

In chapter 6, we discuss racial and ethnic groups and their characteristics, beginning with the American mainstream/dominant culture (white, middle-class) values and continuing with the cultural characteristics of various racial and ethnic minorities. We have tried to avoid stereotyping these groups, and readers should understand that no brief, general description applies to all individuals in a population. Also, students should not expect to become "culturally competent" practitioners based on reading a few paragraphs in an HBSE text. In particular, students and practitioners need to remain aware of the diversity within diversity of many racial and ethnic groups. In other words, there may be as much variability within groups as among them.

In chapter 7, we discuss other social statuses, beginning with gender and sexual orientation and ending with persons with disabilities. Again, experiences of inequity are presented.

Many beginning social work students feel overwhelmed by the issues of social injustice brought to their attention in human behavior courses. Our intention is to make you critical thinkers, not to lead you to despair. As students, as social workers, and as citizens you will have many opportunities to advocate on behalf of vulnerable individuals and populations.

REFERENCES

Germain, C., & Gitterman, A. (1995). Ecological perspective. In R. L. Edwards et al. (Eds.), *Encyclopedia of social work* (19th ed., Vol. I, pp. 816–824). Washington, DC: NASW Press.

Grusky, D. B. (1994). The contours of social stratification. In D. B. Grusky (Ed.), *Social stratification: Class, race, and gender in sociological perspective* (pp. 3–35). Boulder, CO: Westview Press.

Henslin, J. M. (2014). *Sociology: A down-to-earth approach* (12th ed.). Boston, MA: Pearson Education.

C H A P T E R   F I V E

Social Stratification

SOCIAL CLASS IN AMERICA

Sociologists have yet to reach agreement on how many social classes there are in America and what principal "fault lines" should be used to define them (Grusky, 1994, p. 4). Of greater interest to social workers, perhaps, are the issues of how the lifestyles, attitudes, and personalities of individuals are shaped by their class "locations," and what types of social processes and public policies serve to maintain or challenge discrimination (Grusky, 1994, p. 5).

The idea of social class is one way to describe the inequalities that are present in a society. To be a part of a *social class* is to rank with others in terms of wealth, power, and prestige. This ranking separates people into different groups that experience different opportunities in life and different ways of looking at the world. In fact, sociologists argue "no aspect of life goes untouched by social class" (Henslin, 2001, p. 270).

Inequality is most clearly observed in the amount of wealth held by people in different social classes. *Wealth* refers mostly to real estate, stocks and bonds, and unearned income such as capital gains and executive bonuses, while *income* reflects salary and wages. In the United States, inequality in wealth is much greater than inequality in income. Many of the very rich (those whose net worth is in the hundreds of millions) derive their wealth from inheritance or dividends; it does not come from "working." In 2008, only 19 percent of the income reported by the 13,480 individuals or families making over $10 million came from wages and salaries (Domhoff, 2012).

According to the Forbes list of the four hundred richest Americans in 2013, among the top twenty-five, there are fifteen first-generation billionaire entrepreneurs, seven of whom made their money in computers, technology, or the Internet and four who made their money in finances (Kroll & Dolan, 2013). Others, such as members of the Walton family (Wal-Mart) or the Mars family (candy), clearly inherited their wealth.

Class distinctions are often difficult to describe; not all social scientists agree on the categories. The following section will explore the most common criteria: wealth, occupational prestige, and education.

At the very top of the *upper class* are the members of the "upper-upper" class, sometimes called the "blue bloods," "aristocracy," "old money," or "high society." The matter of birth and inheritance separates the "upper-uppers" from the "lower-upper" class, which is also described as "new rich," the "working rich," or the "corporate class." Most upper-class families have enormous wealth. Increasingly the "new rich" may achieve their status through entrepreneurship, or as one of the corporate elite (Karger & Stoesz, 2010), or as one of the rare star athletes or entertainers who command exorbitant salaries, or as winners of the lottery. The upper class is about 5 percent of the U.S. population (Macionis, 2014).

The *middle class*, comprising 40 to 45 percent of the U.S. population (Macionis, 2014), is the one most shaped by education (Henslin, 2014). It also can be broken down into two groups, the "upper middle" and the "average middle." The "upper middle" class is comprised of the "elite" professionals such as physicians, lawyers, and upper-level managers. The "average middle" class, on the other hand, is composed of members of the "minor" professions such as social workers, teachers, and nurses, as well as middle managers and small business owners. Members of the middle class are dependent on salary income rather than inherited wealth and their employment is the source of their status.

We have combined the *lower middle class* and the *working class* because the distinctions between them are often blurred. People in this class may be skilled laborers, firefighters and police officers, and clerical personnel. Many lower-middle-class people who may have been well-paid factory workers in the past have found themselves "downsized" and working several part-time service jobs in order to maintain their lifestyle. This group constitutes almost one-third of the population (Macionis, 2014).

The *working poor* make up about 20 percent of the population (Kendall, 2013). These are people whose income falls below the official poverty line even though they have jobs, at least part of the year. Their jobs are unskilled and include employment such as house cleaning, seasonal farmwork, and fast-food service. These workers typically receive the minimum wage and no employee benefits.

The *underclass/permanent poor* may be found in isolated rural areas or concentrated in urban centers. They have little or no connection with the job market. Those who are employed typically have temporary positions doing menial labor. Public assistance is their main source of support. About 3 to 5 percent of the population falls into this class (Kendall, 2013).

The official *poverty line* is the amount of money required to support the basic needs of a household; with an income below that line an individual or household is considered officially poor. Official poverty measures are based on an assumption using data collected in the 1950s that families spend about 30 percent of their income on food consumption (Bernstein, 2007). Poverty measures look only at pretax cash income and do not count earned-income tax credits, food stamps, housing subsidies, or health insurance coverage (e.g., Medicaid). Critics say the measures fail to take into account expenses associated with work and medical care, and make no adjustment for geographical variations in the cost of living (Bernstein, 2007).

Temporary Assistance for Needy Families (TANF) is the state-administered federal program that is the major source of support for many poor families with children. TANF benefit levels are extremely low. According to the Center on Budget and Policy Priorities (Floyd & Schott, 2013), the current purchasing power of TANF grants is below 1996 levels after adjusting for inflation. As of July 1, 2013 the TANF benefit level in every state for a family of three with no other cash income was below 50 percent of the official poverty line. (See table 5.1 for a comparison of benefit levels across states.)

DISTRIBUTION OF WEALTH AND INCOME IN THE UNITED STATES

One way of examining social class is to look at income. According to the *Statistical Abstracts of the United States*, income inequality decreased between 1935 and 1970 (Henslin, 2014), but has increased since then. An accumulating body of data, reported by the Economic Policy Institute

TABLE 5.1
TANF Maximum Benefits for a Single-Parent Family of Three, July 2013

High-Level States	Monthly Grants ($)	Low-Level States	Monthly Grants ($)
Alaska	923	Mississippi	170
New York	770	Tennessee	185
New Hampshire	675	Arkansas	204
Connecticut	674	Alabama	215
Vermont	640	South Carolina	216

Source: Center on Budget and Policy Priorities. (2013). Retrieved from http://www.cbpp.org/files/3–28–13tanf.pdf

(Mishel, Bivens, Gould, & Shierholz, 2012), documents the growth in inequality between economic classes in the United States. Income and wage inequality have risen sharply over the last thirty years. The pattern in the 1980s was for the top wage earners to pull away from the middle and the middle to pull away from the bottom. In the 1990s, the bottom and middle wage earners grew closer together, while the top pulled even further away from the rest. The past ten years has been a "lost decade" of wage and income growth for most American families. Between 1979 and 2007, the top 1 percent of households claimed almost six times as much of the total income growth as the bottom 90 percent (Mishel, Bivens, Gould, & Shierholz, 2012). Chief executive officers have fared far better than the typical worker, the stock market, or the U.S. economy over the last several decades. From 1978 to 2011, CEO compensation grew by more than 725 percent (Mishel, Bivens, Gould, & Shierholz, 2012). The average CEO salary in 2011 was $9.7 million, with health care and media CEOs making the highest pay (Shen, 2013).

A typical worker's pay is calculated as the average hourly compensation of production/nonsupervisory workers—about 80 percent of payroll employment. In America in 1960 the CEO-to-worker pay ratio was 42:1; at its height in 2000, it was 531:1 (Domhoff, 2012). The ratio in 2012 was 354:1 (Shen, 2013). This is in strong contrast to Europe, where the ratio is about 25:1.

The Great Recession that began in the fall of 2007, along with the federal bailouts that followed, brought to the public's attention not only the high levels of executive compensation, but also the extent to which well-paid CEOs appeared to be out of touch with the economic experience of everyday Americans. One example was when the heads of three Detroit automobile manufacturers, General Motors, Ford, and Chrysler, came to Washington to appear before a congressional committee, seeking billions of federal dollars to keep their companies running. Each traveled in a private company jet, at a cost of roughly $20,000 for each trip. Recognizing the irony of the situation, one congressman asked, "Couldn't you all have downgraded to first class or jet-pooled or something to get here?" (Milbank, 2008).

According to Forbes (Kroll, 2013), five years after the Great Recession, the wealthiest Americans as a group gained back all that they had lost. The 400 wealthiest Americans are worth just over $2 trillion, more than double compared to a decade ago and roughly equivalent to the GDP of Russia.

A usual way to measure inequality is to divide American society into quintiles (fifths) and then make comparisons. For example, those in the fourth (next-to-top) quintile, while doing quite well, had on average less than half the income of those in the top quintile. While incomes at all levels increased between 2006 and 2012, the average income in the lowest quintile increased by only $233, while the increase for the average income in the highest quintile was $17,818. In the same time period, the income for those in the top 5 percent increased by $30,472. (See table 5.2.) This disparity in income is accounted for, in part, by the low wages paid to those at the bottom of the income scale and has the effect of making the rich richer and the poor poorer.

The minimum wage (see chapter 2) has never been sufficient to support a family if only one member of the family is employed. A worker making $7.25 an hour for 40 hours a week for 52 weeks a year earns $15,080. The 2013 federal poverty guidelines list $23,550 as the poverty line for a family of four (see table 5.3).

Many low-income workers in the food service and retail industries are limited not only by their hourly wage, but also by the other constraints

TABLE 5.2
U.S. Income by Quintile
Changes in Average Income for Each Fifth of the
U.S. Population and the Top 5 Percent

	2006	*2012*
Top 5%	289,446	319,918
Highest fifth	163,637	181,455
Fourth fifth	75,257	81,953
Third fifth	48,561	51,590
Second fifth	29,050	30,226
Lowest fifth	11,128	11,361

Sources: Based on the U. S. Census Bureau's American Community Surveys for 2006 and 2012.

TABLE 5.3
2013 Federal Poverty Guidelines

Size of Family Unit	Poverty Guideline	Required Gross Monthly Income	Required Approximate Hourly Income
1	$11,490	$957.50	$5.52
2	$15,510	$1,292.50	$7.46
3	$19,530	$1,627.50	$9.38
4	$23,550	$1,962.50	$11.32
5	$27,570	$2,297.50	$13.25
6	$31,590	$2,632.50	$15.19
7	$35,610	$2,967.50	$17.12
8	$39,630	$3,302.50	$19.05

Source: U.S. Department of Health and Human Services.

connected to their jobs. For example, shifting schedules make it impossible to get a second job or to attend school (Malcolm & O'Donnell, 2012). There are few, if any, benefits or paid time off. Some are classified as managers, even though they have few supervisory functions, so that their employers do not have to pay them overtime (Davidson, 2012).

Class difference is not just about income (wages and salaries). An accurate measure of *wealth* includes all assets (e.g., savings, stocks, bonds, life insurance policies, real estate holdings, fine art, jewelry, antiques, and classic car collections). The wealthiest Americans can live on the dividends from their investments without having to touch the principal or work for a salary.

According to University of California-Santa Cruz sociologist G. William Domhoff (2012), "in the United States, wealth is highly concentrated in a relatively few hands." He reports that as of 2010, the top 1 percent of households owned more than one-third (35.4 percent) of all privately held wealth. The remainder of the top 20 percent had more than half (53.5 percent). That means that just over 10 percent of the wealth was shared by the bottom 80 percent of the people.

POVERTY AS A SPECIAL CONCERN FOR SOCIAL WORKERS

Social workers are particularly interested in the people at the bottom of the socioeconomic scale—those who suffer from poverty. Because of the profession's commitment to social justice, the needs of the poor are a major focus of change efforts.

Deciding what poverty is, is a problem in itself. Americans think of hunger and homelessness as indicators of the existence of poverty. Clearly most people in the world today, and especially people in the United States and other industrialized countries, do not experience deprivation in the same way that the vast majority of people in the world experienced in past centuries or as some people experience today in a few areas of the globe. Nevertheless, there are millions of people in this country who do not have enough to eat or adequate shelter. We call this poverty as deprivation.

Another view of poverty is relative poverty (called subjective poverty by some sociologists). This is the sense of deprivation experienced when people compare themselves to others who have more of a society's resources. In other words, it is the everyday experience of inequality.

The 2010 census data showed that 44 million Americans—one in seven citizens—were living below the poverty line and the poorest poor, defined as those at 50 percent or less of the official poverty level, represented 6.7 percent of the U.S. population, that is, 20.5 million Americans (vanden Heuvel, 2010; Yen & Wides-Munoz, 2011). The 6.7 percent was the highest in the thirty-five years that the Census Bureau maintained such records.

There is no single type of poor person in the United States. The poor include low-wage workers, disabled veterans, immigrants, marginalized factory workers, the severely and chronically mentally ill, the formerly incarcerated, the undereducated, and the fallen middle class. A common misconception is that the poor are primarily people of color and single mothers and their children. Whereas these groups constitute a disproportionate number of those living in poverty, they are not the majority.

As the heads of poor families, women are overrepresented in poverty. The feminization of poverty is related to increases in the rates of divorce, separation, and out-of-wedlock births; fathers not paying child support; and a reduction in government benefits. Women are more likely to bear the costs of raising children and also to provide unpaid care to family members. Even when women are employed, they are more likely to live in poverty than male heads of households because they are more likely to be employed in the secondary labor market (see chapter 2).

According to a recent report from the Center for American Progress (Chu & Posner, 2013) almost three in ten African American women and Hispanic women lived in poverty in 2012. In an examination of data from the 2007 Survey of Consumer Finances, the Insight Center for Community Economic Development (Chang, 2010) found that nearly half of all single black and Hispanic women had zero or negative wealth (i.e., their financial debts exceeded their assets). For those in their prime working years (ages 36 to 49), white women had a median wealth of $42,600 while the median wealth for women of color was only $5.

Although whites make up the majority of people living in poverty in the United States, people of color are overrepresented among the poor, and they are more likely to be among the extremely poor. According to data analyzed by economist Edward N. Wolff (2012), in 2010 the median worth (including home value) for white families was $97,000; this was in contrast to $4,900 household worth for African American families and $1,300 for Latino families. If home values are not considered, the median household worth for African American families was $100 and the median for Latino families was zero.

As a distinct age group, children in the United States are more likely to be poor than adults or the elderly. According to the Children's Defense Fund (2014), based on 2012 data, children were 60 percent more likely to be poor than adults ages 18–64, and nearly two and a half times more likely to be poor than seniors. More than two-thirds of poor children lived in families with at least one working family member. The youngest children are the poorest: more than one in four children under age 5 were poor—nearly 5 million, and almost half of them—2.4 million—were extremely poor. Nearly half of black children under age five and more than one in three Latino children the same age were poor. Poor children are more likely to die in infancy, to be malnourished, and to have health problems; they also are more likely to start school behind their peers, to drop out of school, to be involved in the criminal justice system, to have babies while they are in their teens, and to be poor as adults—thus perpetuating the cycle of poverty (Children's Defense Fund, 2014; Henslin, 2014).

Whereas older adults used to be among the poorest Americans, in 2011 just 8.79 percent of Americans 65 and older were poor, the lowest rate for any age group (Administration on Aging, 2012). This is due in large part to the effects of Social Security retirement payments; in 2010 86 percent of older Americans reported receiving Social Security, and these payments lifted about 14.5 million seniors above the poverty line (Administration on Aging, 2012; Yen, 2012). In 2014 there were 3.7 million seniors living in poverty compared with 5.2 million in 1969 (Armon, 2014).

According to 2010 census data, a growing proportion of the poor live in suburbs—about a third—compared to 28 percent in cities, 21 percent in small metropolitan areas, and 19 percent in rural communities (Kneebone & Berube, 2013). Counties with the highest poverty rates are found in Appalachia, across the Deep South, and in parts of the Southwest.

SOCIAL MOBILITY

About 60 percent of Americans agree that "most people who want to get ahead can make it if they they're willing to work hard"; on the other hand, about the same number say that the economic system unfairly favors the wealthy (Page & Breitman, 2014). Social mobility in the United States is limited; most people remain in the same social class as their parents (Andersen & Taylor, 2013). Whereas individual social mobility is often closely linked to educational attainment, it also is influenced by factors that affect the whole society such as economic cycles and changes in occupational structure. For example, the recent Great Recession at the end of the first decade of the twenty-first century probably had a profound effect on the life prospects for young adults starting their careers at that time, just as the Great Depression affected their great-grandparents' generation.

Structural mobility occurs when significant changes in society propel many people up or down the social class ladder at the same time. Generally, the trend since 1900 has been toward upward mobility, due to the expansion of the economy and a dramatic increase in average educational attainment. One recent change has been the downward mobility of many middle-class and blue-collar workers as a result of the elimination or exportation of manufacturing jobs (discussed in chapter 2).

Beginning in the 1960s, when the economy boomed and civil rights legislation lowered racial barriers, many African Americans moved into the middle class (Beeghley, 2008). There is now a second generation of middle-class, college-educated African Americans; nevertheless, their children continue to be at risk of losing their middle-class status. During the Great Recession, with the auto industry downsizing and federal, state, and local governments, which employ a disproportionate share of African Americans, shedding jobs, some of the main supports that have sustained middle-class black families in past decades collapsed (Fletcher & Cohen, 2011).

According to the United for a Fair Economy website (Sullivan, Ali, Perez De Alejo, Miller, & Baena, 2013), black families experienced an alarming loss of wealth between 2007 and 2010. Black families lost 27.1 percent of their average net wealth compared to a 6.7 percent loss by white families. As of 2013, the average net worth of African American families is only one sixth that of white families.

Whereas strong kinship networks in minority families act as a buffer against the hardships of poverty, the expectations for reciprocity may hinder upward mobility (Stack, 1997/1974). And although generally one thinks of upward social mobility as a good thing, individuals who change their social class, even through the support and sacrifices of their families, may find themselves painfully alienated from their parents and cut off from their cultural roots (Sennett & Cobb, 1973).

Historically, a woman's social ranking was equated with her husband's; research on the social class of married women is in its infancy (Henslin, 2014). Women also have had less opportunity for upward mobility than men because they were limited to occupations that offered little opportunity for career advancement. When marriages end in divorce, women commonly experience downward social mobility.

UNDERSTANDING SOCIAL STRATIFICATION

Functionalist Perspective

Functionalists believe that an unequal class structure is necessary for a successful society (Davis & Moore, 1945). According to this view, people will work hard only if they receive rewards commensurate with their skills and education. Thus, in order to fill the most important positions in society, the system has to provide exceptional rewards to draw talent away from less important and easier work. The Davis-Moore thesis suggests that social stratification mandates meritocracy, a social hierarchy in which positions are awarded based on ability and credentials. Poverty is also "functional" in this view, because it keeps up the demand for low-wage jobs and ensures that the "dirty" work of society gets done, as well as providing a market for cheap goods.

The "rags to riches" myth—the idea that anyone can make it in America—is functional for society because it encourages people to strive for success. It also places blame for failure on the individual. Functionalists are comfortable with the conviction that poor choices, such as dropping out of school or having babies outside of marriage, lead to a life of poverty.

Conflict Perspective

Critics say that the Davis-Moore thesis ignores inequalities based on inherited wealth and other forms of unearned privilege. Conflict theorists argue that inequality is the result of oppression. Social class involves prestige and power, as well as economic inequality. Typically, those with the most prestige, power, and wealth want to protect their privileges, while those without try to get more.

Karl Marx, who developed conflict theory, believed that social class was the most important factor in understanding human behavior. He said that capitalist industrialized societies were composed of two classes: the bourgeoisie, who owned the means of production, and the proletariat, who sold their labor to the owners. Marx saw great inequality in wealth and power arising from the exploitation of the proletariat, which, he argued, made class conflict inevitable. Marx predicted that inequality would result in revolution. Contemporary Marxists believe that a lack of class consciousness precludes this revolution.

Sociologists who subscribe to the conflict theory perspective argue that the structure of society itself keeps some people from moving up in the social hierarchy by limiting access to education or training. These researchers and academics suggest that race, age, and gender discrimination, as well as changes in the job market, restrict the life experiences of many individuals in a capitalist society. Most sociologists and social workers reject individualistic explanations for poverty such as laziness, lack of intelligence, and other stereotypes that appear to blame the victims of class oppression.

Constructionist Perspective

Constructionism is about subjective understanding. Americans have a different understanding of social class than do Europeans (Adler, 2009; Page & Jacobs, 2009). One does not see a strong class consciousness in the United States, particularly among laborers. Workers think of themselves as middle class (or they aspire to being middle class) and hence lack a sense of shared interests with other low-income people. Vanneman and Cannon in their 1987 book, *The American Perception of Class*, suggested the problem is that the United States has no leftist political party to organize the lower classes and express their interests. In addition, racial and ethnic divisions in American society make alliances within social classes less stable (Andersen & Taylor, 2013).

In contrast to Euro-Americans, who see social status as rooted in wealth and prestige, some minorities may have a different understanding of social class. For example, African Americans view class as detached from income and instead based upon identified middle-class behaviors. These behaviors include maintaining good family relationships, participating in the community, and dressing appropriately (Vanneman & Cannon, 1987, p. 227). Some occupational roles, such as teacher or clergy, also contribute to a valued class position. These are examples of how a vulnerable group can set internal community standards for evaluating worth, separate from those of the larger society.

THE IMPACT OF SOCIAL STRATIFICATION ON INDIVIDUALS AND FAMILIES

Human needs can be divided into several categories. The effects of social class are experienced in all of these.

Addressing the Concerns of Daily Life

Finances

No matter what kinds of problems people have, access to money makes it easier to cope. Many problems "go away" if funds are available to fix them—paying for auto or plumbing repairs, for example, or retaining an attorney, hiring a housekeeper, or scheduling a "mental health getaway." People who have disposable income can focus on things other than problems.

FIGURE 5.1   CRITICAL THINKING: THE EXPERIENCE OF GROWING UP IN DIFFERENT SOCIAL CLASSES.

Reflect on your childhood and your family of origin. What were the indicators of social class that were apparent to you as a child (besides your parents'/ caregivers' occupation, education, and income)? For example, what did you own, where did you live, what experiences did you share, and what were your expectations for your future?

Beyond the exorbitant salaries and bonuses that many at the top of the corporate ladder receive, they also enjoy other perks paid for by their companies. These may include memberships at exclusive country clubs, financial/tax planning services, use of the corporate jet, a company car, personal and/or home security, and paid travel for spouses (Strauss, 2012; Strauss, 2013). According to a congressional analysis, more than 1,500 millionaires paid no income taxes in 2010, mainly due to tax breaks and loopholes (Krugman, 2012; Stone & Colarusso, 2011).

Many people in the middle class have savings accounts. Some have enough equity in their homes to be able to borrow against it in case of emergencies. Middle-class parents expect their children to attend college and provide them with "enriching" experiences, such as music lessons or summer camp, and family trips to museums, historic sites, and other educational places.

Most people in the lower middle class/working class do not have savings; they live paycheck to paycheck. A serious illness or injury or temporary layoff (or even a car repair or broken appliance) constitutes a financial crisis. The members of the working class pay 15 to 20 percent more for most goods and services than do the better off, because instead of paying cash they use their credit cards and then are charged interest and late fees. If a family had a $10,000 credit card balance at 18 percent interest and made only minimum monthly payments, it would take fifty-six years to pay off the debt, and the interest cost alone would total $28,079.

The working poor may be described as living on an "economy budget" (approximately 150 percent of the poverty level).

> Members of families existing on the economy budget never go out to eat, for it is not included in the food budget; they never go out to a movie, concert, or ballgame, or indeed to any public or private establishment that charges admission, for there is no entertainment budget; they have no cable television for the same reason; they never purchase alcohol or cigarettes; never take a vacation or holiday that involves any hotel or motel, or again, any meals out; never hire a babysitter or have any other paid child-care; never give an allowance or other spending money to the children; never purchase any lessons or home-learning tools for the children; never buy books or records for the adults or children, or any toys except in the small amounts available for birthday or Christmas presents . . . ; never pay for a haircut, never buy a maga-zine; have no money for the feeding or veterinary care for any pets; and never spend any money for preschool for the children, or educational trips for them away from home, or any summer camp or activity with a fee. (Schwarz & Volgy, 1992, p. 43)

Actually, it is not just the lower classes, but a surprising proportion of all Americans who are at risk for great financial stress. An income at twice the poverty line (roughly $45,000) for a family of four separates those who can and cannot pay their bills; that means that about 100.5 million people or one third of the country is struggling to make ends meet (vanden Heuvel, 2010). A national survey found that almost half of Americans are "financially fragile," or in other words, unable to handle an unanticipated bill (Lusardi, Schneider, & Tufano, 2011). When asked "If you were to face a $2,000 unexpected expense in the next month, how would you get the funds you need?" 46.5 percent either said they would be unable to cope or that they would have to go to extreme measures, such as pawning possessions or taking out a payday loan, to come up with the money. Another study found that many members of the middle and upper middle class (those households earning between $55,465 and $90,000 per year) are "liquid asset poor" and among the 132.1 million Americans who do not have enough savings to sustain them for three months (Brooks & Wiedrich, 2013). The study noted that nearly half of Americans (43.6 percent) do not have enough savings to cover basic expenses if they were to lose their source of stable income and over 30 percent of households do not even have a savings account.

Karger and Stoesz (2010) use the term *functionally poor* to describe those low-income families who rely on the "fringe economy" (see Karger, 2005) to meet their economic needs. These people have no relationship with regular financial institutions like banks and credit unions and they do not have savings or checking accounts. Features of the fringe economy include credit cards secured with collateral from the cardholder, pre-loaded debit cards, prepaid telephone services, pawn shops, car title pawns, payday loans, tax refund anticipation loans, check cashing outlets, the furniture and appliance rental industry, and subprime loans for automobiles. The functionally poor are continuously exploited and the regulation of the fringe economy is an economic justice issue (Karger & Stoesz, 2010, p. 138).

Typically, members of the underclass/permanent poor have no cash reserves and a negative credit history. They rely on friends and relatives, then title loans and pawnshops, for help with short-term financial needs. They may pay interest rates as high as 300, 400, or even 700 percent to get "immediate" tax refunds or to borrow against anticipated paychecks. Average interest rates for payday loans in Delaware, Wisconsin, South Dakota, and Idaho range from 517 percent to 582 percent ("Highest, lowest payday loan rates surprise," 2014). Fifteen states either ban payday loans or cap interest rates at 36 percent. Among the other states that do not regulate rates, the lowest average rates are found in Colorado at 129 percent, Oregon at 156 percent, and Maine at 217 percent.

Often the poor must rely on in-kind trade-offs (an hour of babysitting in exchange for a ride to the clinic) to make ends meet. Even if they receive a windfall, they cannot get ahead financially because they feel obligated to help out those who have helped them in the past (Stack, 1997/1974).

Nutrition

According to the U.S. Department of Agriculture (Coleman-Jensen, Nord, & Singh, 2013), an estimated 14.5 percent of American households (17.6 million) were "food insecure" at least some time during the year in 2012, meaning they lacked access to enough food for an active, healthy life for all household members. In the same year, 5.7 percent of U.S. households (7.0 million households) had very low food security. In this more severe range of food insecurity, the food intake of some household members was reduced and normal eating patterns were disrupted at times during the year due to limited resources. Rates of food insecurity were substantially higher than the national average for households with children headed by single parents, and black and Hispanic households. Food insecurity was more common in large cities and rural areas than in suburban areas and exurban areas around large cities.

The Supplemental Nutrition Assistance Program (SNAP, formerly the Food Stamp Program) is the country's largest domestic food and nutrition assistance program for low-income Americans. One out of seven American households participates in SNAP and working-age people make up the majority of recipients (Yen, 2014). According to the advocacy group Feeding America (2013) in 2011, 76 percent of SNAP households included a child, an elderly person, or a disabled person. More than eight out of ten SNAP households had gross incomes at or below the poverty line and these households receive about 91 percent of all benefits. The average SNAP household has a gross monthly income of $744. The average monthly SNAP benefit per person is $133.85, or less than $1.50 per meal. SNAP benefits do not last most participants through the whole month. About 90 percent of SNAP benefits are redeemed by the third week of the month. More than half (58 percent) of food bank clients currently receiving SNAP benefits turn to food banks for assistance at least six months out of the year.

Many poor people cannot afford to buy fresh fruits and vegetables and other sources of high grade, low-fat nutrition. Diets high in fat and sugars contribute to various health problems, including obesity, high blood pressure, high cholesterol, and diabetes. And it may be more than a matter of having the cash available for groceries. A report provided to

Congress by the Economic Research Service of the U.S. Department of Agriculture (Ver Ploeg et al., 2009) defines *food deserts* as "areas with limited access to affordable and nutritious food." Of all U.S. households, 2.3 million, or 2.2 percent, live more than a mile from a supermarket and do not have access to a vehicle.

Housing

Shelter is a basic human need. Home ownership is the bedrock of the "American dream" but it is difficult for low-income people to pay rent and save for a down payment at the same time. Home equity is an important source of financial security for many low-income and minority households. The bursting of the housing bubble in the Great Recession caused a significant decline in the median net worth of many families; the median wealth of African Americans dropped by over three-quarters, from around $10,000 to around $2,000 (Mishel, Bivens, Gould, & Shierholz, 2012). Many families lost their homes to foreclosure as they were unable to make payments and their homes' value dropped below the amount they owed on their mortgages.

The Joint Center for Housing Studies at Harvard University (2013) reported that the home ownership rate in the United States fell for the eighth straight year in 2012. This was especially significant among African Americans, whose home ownership rate dropped 5.8 percentage points from its peak and is back to its lowest level since 1995. The decline among Hispanics was a more modest 3.3 percentage points.

According to the U.S. Department of Housing and Urban Development (HUD, n.d.), the generally accepted definition of affordability is for a household to pay no more than 30 percent of its annual income on housing. Families who pay more than 30 percent of their income for housing are considered cost burdened. An estimated 12 million renter and homeowner households now pay more than 50 percent of their annual incomes for housing.

The lack of affordable housing is a significant hardship for low-income households, preventing them from meeting their other basic needs, such as nutrition and health care, or saving for their future (Joint Center for Housing Studies at Harvard University, 2013). Providing housing assistance would have the effect of benefiting low-income families in many more areas than just decent and affordable shelter.

According to a study by the National Low Income Housing Coalition it would take a wage of $18.79 per hour to afford "a decent place" in the United States (Freedman, 2013). For those full-time workers who make only the minimum wage, there is no county in the United States where they could afford to rent a two-bedroom apartment. Given these data, it is not surprising to learn that the homeless population in America is growing. According to the National Coalition for the Homeless (2012), as of January 2012, there were 633,782 homeless on a single night; most homeless persons (62 percent) are individuals, while 38 percent are in family households. A U.S. Department of Education study reported that there were 1.1 million homeless children in public schools during the 2011–2012 school year (Bello, 2013). According to the National Alliance to End Homelessness (2013), the national rate of homelessness was 20 homeless people per 10,000 people in the general population. A majority of persons identified as homeless were staying in emergency shelters or transitional housing, but 38 percent were unsheltered, living on the streets or in cars, abandoned buildings, or other places not intended for human habitation. According to the National Coalition for the Homeless (2012), the rural homeless are likely to be undercounted for a variety of reasons. The odds of being poor are between 1.2 and 2.3 times higher for people in nonmetropolitan areas than in metropolitan areas.

Contributing factors for homelessness, in addition to poverty and the cost of housing, include mental illness and addiction. According to the National Coalition for the Homeless (2012), approximately 16 percent of the single adult homeless population suffers from some form of severe and persistent mental illness, and whereas many people who are addicted to alcohol and drugs never become homeless, people who are poor and addicted are clearly at increased risk of homelessness. Other major factors that can contribute to homelessness include domestic violence and lack of affordable health care.

Health

Although white people generally enjoy better health than people of color, the reason appears to be related to socioeconomic status rather than genetic factors. There is a negative correlation between health status and economic class; the lower a person's class, the less likely it is that he or she will enjoy good health at any age. The poor are more likely to suffer from chronic illnesses, such as diabetes, heart disease, renal failure, and cancer. For the very young the disparity is particularly notable. In the United States the children of the rich can look forward to a healthy childhood, while those who are poor are as vulnerable to risk as those in many developing countries.

The *infant mortality rate* is the number of babies who die before reaching one year of age, per 1,000 live births, in a given year. The 2012 infant mortality rate for the United States was 6 deaths per 1,000 births; this was equal to or higher than 35 other countries in the world, including Cuba (4 deaths per 1,000), Estonia (3 per 1,000), and Poland (4 per 1,000) (World Bank, 2013).

Infant mortality rates within the United States vary considerably from one region to another and among racial groups. At 11.42 deaths per 1,000 births, infant mortality rates for African Americans are more than double the 5.11 rate for whites (Hoyert & Xu, 2012). There may be many reasons for this discrepancy, but an important factor is the quality of medical care received by people of different socioeconomic groups.

There are two major sources of health care insurance coverage in the United States: employers and government programs. The United States is the only industrialized country that relies upon private health insurance to cover the majority of its population. Even the recently enacted Affordable Care Act simply directs uninsured individuals to private insurance companies. The nonpoor usually are insured through group policies with their employers. Retirees and older adults are covered by Medicare. The poor are largely covered by the federal/state Medicaid program. (Unfortunately, Medicaid reimburses providers at such a low rate that many clinics and most dentists will not accept Medicaid patients.)

The working poor in American are commonly excluded from common sources of coverage. They earn too much to qualify for government programs like Medicaid. They frequently are not covered by health insurance at work, and they do not earn nearly enough to be able to afford to buy private insurance on their own. The Affordable Care Act addresses the needs of this group with subsidies for purchasing health care insurance; it remains to be seen how effective this will be.

More than half (54.2 percent) of Americans without health insurance had no regular source of health care (Centers for Disease Control and Prevention, 2012). They delay treatment as long as they can, often until there is a crisis, and then must use the emergency room where there are likely to be long waits and no follow-up.

Mental Health

As is the case with physical health, the lower economic classes also suffer more than the wealthy from mental health problems. In 2010, adults living below the poverty level were three times more likely to have serious psychological distress compared to adults with incomes over twice the poverty level (Office of Minority Health, 2013). Anxiety and depression are the two most common illnesses. While these often have a genetic component, they are profoundly influenced by the individual's social class (Mirowsky & Ross, 1989). Clearly stress is related to mental illness. While the well-to-do experience stress, they also have more resources (e.g., money, staff, time, access to professionals) available to deal with it. Access to private mental health practitioners is correlated with economic status. People with Medicaid are seen in public clinics, often by inexperienced staff or student interns. People of lower socioeconomic status not only experience obvious stressors but also must contend with a subjective experience of lack of control over many elements of their lives. A real or perceived sense of control over one's life may be the most important factor in reducing risk for mental illness (Mirowsky & Ross, 1989).

Transportation

Many Americans are dependent on their automobiles because their communities do not provide adequate alternatives. Lack of transportation seriously limits the poor in their efforts to seek and maintain employment. The working poor generally cannot afford cars; even if they can buy a used vehicle, they cannot afford to keep up with insurance and maintenance expenses. They must rely on public transportation, which is nonexistent in rural areas and offers only limited service in many smaller cities and in suburbs. With many jobs moving from the city center to the suburbs, the urban poor are also constrained in their efforts to be self-supporting. One study showed that more than 40 percent of recently hired welfare recipients had absences likely due to transportation problems (Garasky, Fletcher, & Jenson, 2006). In addition to difficulties in getting to work, lack of transportation limits their ability to get to education and training programs, medical appointments, and child care facilities.

Crime

There is an inverse correlation between income and victimization. The most likely crime victims live in households with incomes under $7,500 (Reiman & Leighton, 2013).

A common cliché is that "justice is blind." The reality, however, is that one's chances of getting arrested, convicted, and sent to prison are significantly shaped by class membership. *"For the same criminal behavior* [italics in original], the poor are more likely to be arrested; if arrested, they are more likely to be charged; if charged, more likely to be convicted; if convicted, more likely to be sentenced to prison; and if sentenced, more likely to be given longer prison terms than members of the middle and upper classes" (Reiman & Leighton, 2013, p. 119). When lower-class status is accompanied by membership in a minority group, the probabilities increase.

Of course, the reality is that the rich and powerful also commit crimes. In comparison to the crimes committed by the poor (those included in the FBI Index), white-collar crime is more costly and probably more widespread (Reiman & Leighton, 2013, p. 129). As noted in chapter 3, white-collar crime is defined as crime committed by people of high social position in the course of their employment or financial affairs (Sutherland, 1940). Examples of white-collar crime are embezzlement, business fraud, and antitrust violations. A recent high-profile example is the fraudulent scheme concocted by Bernie Madoff, which cost thousands of investors more than $50 billion; among the losers were well-known individuals such as Steven Spielberg and Larry King, and nonprofit organizations such as Yeshiva University, New York University, the Elie Wiesel Foundation for Humanity, and many charitable organizations and pension funds ("Madoff's victims," 2009).

According to Reiman and Leighton (2013) it is estimated that white collar crimes cost the country $610.3 billion in 2010. They suggest that the criminal justice system often fails to define the unethical and danger-ous acts of those who are well off as crimes. They add that while poverty contributes to crime by creating need, wealth can contribute to crime by unleashing greed.

Belongingness and Connection

Family Life and Child-Rearing

People of similar background tend to intermarry. This is most true for the "upper-uppers." The trend in America in the twentieth century was for religion to become a less important criterion for spouse selection and level of education to become more important (Cherlin, 2013).

Several trends in marriage, childbearing, and divorce are strongly cor-related with education. College graduates, although they delay marriage, have a higher lifetime probability of marrying than do people without college degrees; college graduates are less likely to have a child out of wedlock than noncollege graduates; and the rate of divorce has been declining for college graduates and increasing for those who did not grad-uate from high school (Cherlin, 2013, pp. 114–116).

There are significant differences in child-rearing patterns across social classes. According to Kohn (1977), lower-class parents expect their children to conform and comply. Middle-class parents, on the other hand, encourage creativity and independence in their children and tolerate more individuality. Lareau (2011) proposes that working-class and middle-class families hold different views about how children develop. She suggests that working-class parents think of children as developing naturally, while middle-class parents believe that children need to be cultivated. Given this viewpoint, middle-class parents are likely to provide their children with many organized activities, such as sports, music lessons, and tutor-ing, whereas working-class parents are more likely to let their children choose their own activities at home or in the neighborhood.

When parents cannot provide child care themselves, upper-class fami-lies may hire live-in nannies. Middle-class families use day-care provid-ers. In lower-middle-class and working-class families, parents may seek employment on different shifts to meet child-care needs and/or rely on kin to take care of their children.

Connections to the Community and Beyond

Upper- and middle-class people often socialize with colleagues and coworkers, sometimes using their contacts to advance their careers. Middle-class friendships involve shared interests and leisure pursuits. Working-and lower-class people tend to spend their free time with relatives. Rubin described these extended family contacts as "the heart of working class social life" (1976, p. 191).

Members of the upper class, particularly wealthy women who are not employed outside their homes, may be involved in volunteer work for various nonprofit organizations; in addition to the value of their contribution to the larger community, these activities build important alliances and interpersonal networks (Ostrander, 1980). Many middle-class people are involved in community activities that relate to their children's interests, such as Scouts, PTA, soccer, and neighborhood organizations.

The upper-upper class—the "blueblood" aristocrats of earlier generations—were often raised in a tradition of noblesse oblige, the sense of obligation to provide for those who were less fortunate. The Rockefellers, Carnegies, and Roosevelts all gave generously from their fortunes to make the world a better place (Cheever, 2012). A variation on that theme was business leaders who looked out for their workers or exercised restraint in relation to their own compensation. Henry Ford, for example, paid his workers three times the contemporary factory wage because he thought they should be able to afford to buy the cars they were producing. George Romney, the father of 2012 presidential candidate Mitt Romney and chairman and CEO of American Motors, voluntarily turned down $268,000 (about $1.7 million in today's dollars) in salary over five years because he said that no executive needed to make that much (Miller, 2012).

Values and Attitudes

There is a persistent belief that the poor differ from other Americans in the values that they hold. Probably the most notable proponent of this view was Oscar Lewis (1966), who suggested that it was the values that the poor embraced that kept them in their lower-class status. According to Lewis, those living in this culture of poverty were unable to delay gratification or plan for the future, and these deficiencies were passed from generation to generation. While Lewis blamed the poor for their poverty, other theorists point to structural reasons for their plight. William Julius Wilson (1996), for example, holds that lack of opportunity rather than lack of motivation is the cause of poverty.

Like Lewis, many people believe that poverty is the *result* of negative attitudes and behaviors. Research, however, indicates that poverty may be the *cause* of values and behaviors typically associated with lack of success in American culture. When they have resources available, previously poor people share the same attitudes that other members of society espouse. Even when they are destitute, the poor tend to have the same dreams as the middle class. In his classic 1967 study of "street-corner" men, for example, Elliot Liebow found that his African American male study participants had internalized the values of the majority culture. It was their impoverished environment that prevented their acting on those values.

As noted above, people in the lower economic classes share the same aspirations as those who have more income. They also share the American value of generosity; in fact, they give a higher percentage of their earnings to charity than do more wealthy Americans (Stern, 2012).

POVERTY IN A GLOBAL PERSPECTIVE

Inequality in income and wealth is a global problem. Oxfam, an international confederation of organizations working to find solutions to poverty, reported in early 2014 that just 1 percent of the world's population controls nearly half of the planet's wealth (Neuman, 2014), and at the same time, one person in three in the world lives in poverty. Economist Paul Krugman (2014) notes that income from wages, salaries, and assets is very unequally distributed in almost all countries, but some nations use taxes and transfers (aid in cash or kind) to reduce levels of disparities. Based on studies conducted by the International Monetary Fund, Krugman further asserts that nations with relatively low income inequality are better able to sustain economic growth.

Some sociologists put the world's nations into three categories (see Macionis, 2014). "High-income countries" are those with the highest overall standard of living based on gross national income; they are clustered in North America and Western Europe and also include Australia, New Zealand, Hong Kong, Japan, South Korea, Malaysia, Israel, and Saudi Arabia. "Middle-income countries" are nations with a standard of living about average for the world as a whole; these include most of Latin America and Asia. The remaining "low-income countries" are nations in which most people are poor; they are spread across sub-Saharan Africa.

According to Macionis (2014, pp. 337, 339) low-income countries are home to about 1.2 billion people or 17 percent of the world's population, but they have just 3 percent of global income. Many of the world's poorest countries depend heavily on subsistence agriculture. About one-quarter of all children do not receive enough food to be healthy. The life expectancy of people in low-income nations is about thirty years shorter than those in high-income nations due to high infant mortality rates and a large number of deaths related to AIDS, malaria, tuberculosis, pneumonia, diarrheal diseases, and parasitic infections (Kendall, 2013).

Sociologists explain poverty in poor countries using dependency theory, which assumes that inequality is the result of the exploitation of poor nations by rich nations (Andersen & Taylor, 2013; Kendall, 2013; Macionis, 2014). African countries, in particular, experienced a history of colonial control that lasted into the 1960s. Sociologists suggest that through neocolonialism rich countries continue to exercise economic control over poor countries without direct military or political involvement. Multinational corporations from the West continue to channel wealth and profits to the high-income countries (see chapter 2.)

LOOKING AHEAD

Social class remains a topic that is not easily acknowledged or discussed. By keeping it invisible, the effects of inequality can be attributed to other causes. Americans worry about crime, drug abuse, and family dissolution. It would be a major step toward social justice if the nation's concerns turned to poverty and a host of other problems directly traceable to racism and economic marginality. Racism is addressed in chapter 6. In chapter 7 we discuss other populations at risk.

REFERENCES

Adler, J. (2009, February 16). Why there won't be a revolution. *Newsweek*, pp. 32–34.

Administration on Aging. (2012). *A profile of older Americans: 2012*. Retrieved from http://www.aoa.gov/Aging_Statistics/Profile/2012/docs/2012profi le.pdf.

Andersen, M., & Taylor, H. (2013). *Sociology: The essentials* (7th ed.). Belmont, CA: Wadsworth.

Armon, R. (2014, February 9). War on poverty has worked—for seniors. *The State* [Columbia, SC], p. A11.

Beeghley, L. (2008). *The structure of social stratification in the United States* (5th ed.). Boston, MA: Allyn and Bacon.

Bello, M. (2013, November 21). Fewer living on streets, HUD study finds. *USA Today*, p. 3A.

Bernstein, J. (2007, February 26). *Economic opportunity and poverty in America*. Retrieved from http://www.epi.org/publication/webfeatures_viewpoints_econ_oppty_andepoverty/.

Brooks, J., & Wiedrich, K. (2013, January). *Assets and opportunity scorecard 2013—living on the edge: Financial insecurity and policies to rebuild prosperity in America*. Corporation for Enterprise Development. Retrieved from http://assetsandopportunity.org/assets/pdf/2013_Scorecard_Report.pdf.

Buchheit, P. (2012). More evidence that our middle class is sliding toward the third world. *Nation of Change*. Retrieved from http://www.nationofchange.org/print/38896

Centers for Disease Control and Prevention. (2012, November 7). *American Indian and Alaska natives population*. Retrieved from http://www.cdc.gov/minorityhealth/populations/REMP/aian.html.

Chang, M. (2010). Lifting as we climb: Women of color, wealth, and America's future. Insight Center for Community Economic Development. Retrieved from www.racialwealthgap.org.

Cheever, S. (2012, August 13 and 20). Gin without the tonic. *Newsweek*, p. 5.

Cherlin, A. J. (2013). *Public and private families: An introduction* (7th ed.). New York, NY: McGraw-Hill.

Children's Defense Fund. (2014). *The state of America's children, 2014.* Retrieved from http://www.childrensdefense.org/child-research-data -publications/data/2014-soac.pdf.

Chu, A., & Posner, C. (2013). *The state of women in America: A 50-state analysis of how women are faring across the nation.* Center for American Progress. Retrieved from http://www.americanprogress .org/issues/women/report/2013/09/25/74836/the-state-of-women-in -america/.

Coleman-Jensen, A., Nord, M., & Singh, A. (2013). *Household food security in the United States in 2012.* United States Department of Agriculture, Economic Research Service. Retrieved from http://www .ers.usda.gove/publications/err-economic-research-report/err155/re port-summary.

Davidson, P. (2012, April 16). Overworked and underpaid? *USA Today,* pp. 1A–2A.

Davis, K., & Moore, W. (1945). Some principles of stratification. *The American Sociological Review, 10,* 242–249.

Domhoff, G. W. (2012). Wealth, income, and power. Retrieved from http://www2.ucsc.edu/whorulesamerica/power/wealth.html.

Feeding America (2013). *SNAP (food stamps): Facts, myths and realities.* Retrieved from http://feedingmaerica.org/how-we-fight-hunger/pro gram-and-services/public-assistance.

Fletcher, M. A., & Cohen, J. (2011, February 20). Economy poll: African Americans, Hispanics were hit hardest but are most optimistic. *The Washington Post.* Retrieved from www.washingtonpost.com/wp-dyn /content/article/2011/02/20.

Floyd, I., & Schott, L. (2013, October 21). *TANF cash benefits continued to lose value in 2013.* Center on Budget and Policy Priorities. Retrieved from http://www.cbpp.org/cms/?fa = view&id = 4034.

Freedman, D. (2013, June 17). When rent takes half your income. Retrieved from http://money.msn.com/home-loans/article.aspx?post = ad32dad6-5b6f -4e80-8fb2-170ce44462a3.

Garasky, S., Fletcher, C. N., & Jenson, H. H. (2006, Summer). Transiting to work: The role of private transportation for low-income house-holds. *Journal of Consumer Affairs, 40,* pp. 64–89.

Germain, C., & Gitterman, A. (1995). Ecological perspective. In R. L. Edwards and J. G. Hopps (Eds.), *Encyclopedia of social work* (19th ed., Vol I., pp. 816–824). Washington, DC: NASW Press.

Grusky, D. B. (1994). The contours of social stratification. In D. B. Grusky (Ed.), *Social stratification: Class, race, and gender in socio-logical perspective* (pp. 3–35). Boulder, CO: Westview Press.

Henslin, J. M. (2001). *Sociology: A down-to-earth approach.* Boston, MA: Allyn and Bacon.

Henslin, J. M. (2014). *Sociology: A down-to-earth approach* (12th ed.). Boston, MA: Pearson Education.

"Highest, lowest payday loan rates surprise." (2014, April 21). *USA Today*, p. 1B.

Hoyert, D. L., & Xu, J. (2012, October 10). Deaths: Preliminary data for 2011. *National Vital Statistics Report, 61*(6).

Joint Center for Housing Studies at Harvard University (2013). *The state of the nation's housing 2013.* Retrieved from http://www.jchs.harvard.edu/sites/jchs.harvard.edu/files/son_2013_key_facts.pdf.

Karger, H. J. (2005). *Shortchanged: Life and debt in the fringe economy.* San Francisco, CA: Berrett-Koehler.

Karger, H. J., & Stoesz, D. (2010). *American social welfare policy* (6th ed.). Boston, MA: Pearson.

Kendall, D. (2013). *Sociology in our times* (9th ed.). Belmont, CA: Wadsworth.

Kneebone, E., & Berube, A. (2013). *Confronting suburban poverty in America.* Washington, DC: Brookings Institution Press.

Kohn, M. L., (1977). *Class and conformity: A study in values* (2nd ed.). Homewood, IL: Dorsey Press.

Kroll, L. (2013, September 9). The Forbes 400: Facts and figures on America's richest. *Forbes.* Retrieved from http://www.forbes.com/sites/luisakroll/2013/09/15/inside-the-forbes-400-facts-and-figures.

Kroll, L., & Dolan, K. A. (2013, September 16). The faces of wealth in America. *Forbes.* Retrieved from http://www.forbes.com/forbes-400.

Krugman, P. (2012, January 22). Taxes at the top. *The State* [Columbia, SC], p. D3.

Krugman, P. (2014, March 11). Equality, efficiency. *The State* [Columbia, SC], p. A11.

Lareau, A. (2011). *Unequal childhoods: Class, race and family life* (2nd ed.). Berkeley, CA: University of California Press.

Lewis, O. (1966, October). The culture of poverty. *Scientific American, 215*, pp. 19–25.

Lusardi, A., Schneider, D. J., & Tufano, P. (2011). *Financially fragile households: Evidence and implications.* National Bureau of Economic Research. Working Paper No. 17072. Retrieved from http://www.nber.org/papers/w17072.

Macionis, J. J. (2014). *Sociology* (15th ed.). Boston, MA: Pearson Education.

Madoff's victims. (2009). *Wall Street Journal.* Retrieved from http://s.wsj.net/public/resources/documents/st_madoff_victims _20081215.html.

Malcolm, H., & O'Donnell, J. (2012, June 3). Scraping by at Walmart. *USA Today*, p. 1B–2B.

Milbank, D. (2008). Auto execs fly corporate jets to D.C., tin cups in hand. *The Washington Post.* Retrieved from http://www.washingtonpoost.com.

Miller, M. (2012, January 18). What Mitt Romney's father could teach him about economic fairness. *The Washington Post.* Retrieved from http://www.washingtonpost.com/opinions/what-mitt-romneys-father -could-teach-him-about-economic-fairness.

Mirowsky, J., & Ross, C. E. (1989). *Social causes of psychological distress.* New York, NY: Aldine de Gruyter.

Mishel, L., Bivens, J., Gould, E., & Shierholz, H. (2012). *The state of working America, 12th edition.* (EPI digital edition). Economic Policy Institute. Retrieved from http://stateofworkingamerica.org/subjects /overview/?reader.

National Alliance to End Homelessness. (2013). *The state of homelessness in America 2013.* Retrieved from http://www.endhomelessness .org/library/entry/the-state-of-homelessness-2013.

National Coalition for the Homeless. (2012). *Homelessness in America.* Retrieved from http://nationalhomeless.org/about-homelessness.

Neuman, S. (2014, January 20). *Oxfam: World's richest 1 percent control half of global wealth.* National Public Radio. Retrieved from http://www.npr.org/blogs/thetwo-way/2014/01/20/264241052/oxfam-worlds -richest-1-percent-control-half-of-global-wealth.

Office of Minority Health. (2013). *Mental health data/statistics*. Retrieved from http://minorityhealth.hhs.gov/templates/browse.aspx?lvl = 3& amp;lvlid-539.

Ostrander, S. A., (1980). Upper class women: The feminine side of privilege. *Qualitative Sociology, 3*, 23–44.

Page, B. I., & Jacobs, L. R. (2009). *Class war? What Americans really think about economic inequality.* Chicago, IL: University of Chicago Press.

Page, S., & Breitman, K. (2014, January 23). United we stand on wealth divide. *The Washington Post*, pp. 1A, 6A.

Reiman, J., & Leighton, P. (2013). *The rich get richer and the poor get prison* (10th ed). Boston, MA: Pearson Education.

Rubin, L. B. (1976). *Worlds of pain: Life in the working-class family.* New York, NY: Basic Books.

Schwarz, J., & Volgy, T. (1992). *The forgotten Americans.* New York, NY: Norton.

Sennett, R., & Cobb, J. (1973). *The hidden injuries of class.* New York, NY: Vintage Books.

Shen, A. (2013, May 22). Average CEO salary reached a new record high of $9.7 million in 2012. Think Progress. Retrieved from http://thinkprogress.org/economy/2013/05/22/2049161/ceo-pay-new-record-2012/.

Stack, C. (1997/1974). *All our kin.* New York, NY: Basic Books.

Stern, K. (2012, December 27). Five myths about charitable giving. *The Washington Post.* Retrieved from http://www.washingtonpost.com/opinions/five-myths-about-charitable-giving/2012/12/27/99cde18a-4de6-11e2-839d-d54cc6e49b63_story.html.

Stone, D., & Colarusso, L. (2011, November 21). Welfare for millionaires. *Newsweek*, p. 23.

Strauss, G. (2012, April 26). Many companies still pick up CEOs' country club tabs. *USA Today*, p. 3B.

Strauss, G. (2013, October 23). Crossing line? Spouses go on company dime. *USA Today*, p. 2B.

Sullivan, T., Ali, M., Perez De Alejo, C., Miller, B., & Baena, N. (2013). *State of the dream: A long way from home.* United for a Fair Economy. Retrieved from http://faireconomy.org/sites/default/files/SOD 2013.pdf.

Sutherland, E. H. (1940). White collar criminality. *American Sociological Review, 5,* 1–12.

U.S. Department of Housing and Urban Development (HUD) (n.d.). *Affordable housing.* Retrieved from http://protal.hud.gov/hudportal /HUD?src = /program_offices/comm _planning/affordablehousing.

vanden Heuvel, K. (2010, September 28). As 44 million Americans live in poverty, a crisis grows. *Washington Post.* Retrieved from http:// washingtonpost.com/wp-dyn/content/content/article/2010/09/ 28/.

Vanneman, R., & Cannon, L. W. (1987). *The American perception of class.* Philadelphia, PA: Temple University Press.

Ver Ploeg, M., Breneman, V., Farrigan, T., Hamrick, K., Hopkins, D., Kaufman, P., . . . Tuckermanty, E. (2009). *Access to affordable and nutritious food—measuring and understanding food deserts and their consequences: Report to Congress.* United States Department of Agriculture. Retrieved from http://www.ers.usda.gov/publications/ap -administrative-publication/ap-036.aspx.

Wilson, W. J. (1996). *When work disappears: The world of the new urban poor.* New York, NY: Alfred A. Knopf.

Wolff , E. N. (2012, November). *The asset price meltdown and the wealth of the middle class.* Paper session presented at the meeting of the Association for Public Policy Analysis & Management, Baltimore, MD. Retrieved from https://appam.confex.com/appam/2012.webpro gram/Paper2134.html.

World Bank (2013). *Mortality rate, infant (per 1,000 live births).* Retrieved from http://worldbank.org/ijndicator/SP.DYN.IMRT.IN.

Yen, H. (2012, September 13). Record-high poverty rate unchanged. *The State* [Columbia, SC], pp. B4–B5.

Yen, H. (2014). The new face of food stamps: Working-age Americans. Associated Press. Retrieved from http://bigstory.ap.org/article/new -face-food-stamps-working-age-americans.

Yen, H., & Wides-Munoz, L. (2011, November 3). 1 in 15 among poorest of the poor, a record. *The State* [Columbia, SC], p. A4.

C H A P T E R S I X

American Society and Cultural Diversity

American Society and Experiences of Racial and Ethnic Inequity

The Experience of Native Americans

The Experience of African Americans

The Experience of Asian Americans

The Experience of Latinos/Latinas (Hispanic Americans)

The Experience of White Ethnics and Jews

The Experience of More Recent Arrivals

Looking Ahead

References

THE UNITED STATES AS A MULTICULTURAL SOCIETY

Recognizing the role of the profession in delivering services to diverse populations and advocating for social and economic justice, the Council on Social Work Education, the accrediting body for schools of social work in the United States, requires that students be prepared to practice with, and advocate on behalf of, members of minority groups. Competent social workers "recognize and communicate their understanding of difference in shaping life experiences" and acknowledge the extent to which a society's structures and the values of the dominant culture "may oppress, marginalize, alienate, or create or enhance privilege and power (Council on Social Work Education, 2008, pp. 4–5).

It is important that social work practitioners not only tolerate or accept differences but that they celebrate diversity as a source of strength for individuals, families, and communities and for our society as a whole.

In the United States and Canada, social workers are likely to be professionally involved not only with individuals and families from a variety of social classes, but also with individuals, families, groups, and communities from different ethnic, racial, and cultural traditions. Knowledge of these differences and skill in applying it (referred to as cultural competence) is a prerequisite for professional practice. There are many implications of cultural differences for social work assessment, counseling, intervention, and community organization efforts (Fontes, 2005; McAdoo, 2007b; Sewell, 2009). What is considered normal or even preferred in some cultures may be frowned on or condemned in others. For example, public displays of affection between people of the same sex (such as holding hands) are viewed as a simple reflection of friendship in some cultures while they are viewed as indications of homosexual attraction in others. What is considered appropriate dress in different settings varies greatly in different cultures; revealing attire that is common in the summertime in America may be quite shocking to people from other backgrounds.

Clearly, the United States has a majority, dominant, or mainstream culture, but it supports various minority or subdominant cultures as well. Whereas America has been called a melting pot, meaning that different immigrant cultures become blended into a uniquely "American culture," it really is more like a tossed salad, where diverse groups retain and share their distinctive subcultural flavors while living together in a larger society. Another term for this pattern is *cultural pluralism.*

Obvious elements of culture are those we can directly observe, such as language, clothing, body adornment, music, dance, or architecture. Culture includes shared beliefs as well as behaviors; culture promotes a sense of group solidarity. It is more than simply the history, language, and traditions of a people, however. "It involves a form of self-conceptualization that the individual assumes or others assign" (Lukes & Land, 1990, p. 155).

Identifying the *majority* or *dominant culture* in America is not just a matter of counting members of different racial and ethnic groups. The dominant culture is a reflection of the power of its members as well as their numbers. The dominant culture is supported by a society's social institutions (discussed in chapters 2, 3, and 4). For example, the need to learn and use the dominant language (English) is demanded in public schools and by most employers (acting as agents of the political economy). These are powerful forces of socialization and control.

Cultural patterns set some members of society apart from the mainstream. Typically, when we think of *cultural minorities*, recent immigrant groups with distinct languages and traditions come to mind. Mass migration to the United States in the last decades of the twentieth century, largely from non-European countries, made America far more multiethnic and multicultural than ever before.

The increasing number of minorities is fueled by both immigration and births. According to the Pew Center (Passel, Livingston, & Cohn, 2012), for the first time in our history, non-Hispanic whites account for a minority of births in the United States. In terms of median age, among different ethnic and racial groups, non-Hispanic whites are the oldest, with a median age of 42.3. Hispanics are the youngest (median age of 27.6). Non-Hispanic blacks fall in between (median age of 32.9) and Asians are also younger than whites (median age 35.9).

Census experts estimate that by 2050, the United States will be a "majority-minority" country (i.e., there will be more people of color than whites). Currently four states (California, Hawaii, New Mexico, and Texas) and the District of Columbia are majority-minority (Teixeira, 2013). Within the next twenty years, Nevada, Maryland, Georgia, Florida,

Arizona, New Jersey, and possibly Delaware and New York are expected to join that category. As of 2010 there were twenty-two majority-minority cities in the largest 100 metropolitan areas in the United States, including San Francisco, San Diego, Los Angeles, Las Vegas, Houston, Miami, New York, and Washington, DC. Overall, the minority proportion across large metropolitan areas should be pushing 70 percent by 2050 (Teixeira, 2013).

Cultural minorities also include groups that have lived here for hundreds of years, such as the African Americans whose ancestors arrived in the holds of slave ships. Native Americans (First Nations) have been living on the North American continent for tens of thousands of years, long before any of the "majority" population arrived. Because of their physical characteristics (interacting with the forces of discrimination and oppression), these racial minority groups have not been fully assimilated into the mainstream and have instead retained many unique cultural features.

If culture is about a perception of difference, of separation from the mainstream, of shared language, values, norms, and experiences, then there are gay and lesbian cultures and a disability culture. From this perspective, the notion of homosexuality or disability is one of group belongingness and distinction from other groups who do not share that identity (Cruikshank, 1992; Gilson & DePoy, 2002). We explore this topic further in the chapter 7.

Many minority cultures have recognized communities. The community protects the social identity of its members in the face of stigma. Many minorities, including gay men and lesbians and people with disabilities, as well as racial and ethnic minorities, are enriched by their connections to their identificational community and its shared traditions.

New Arrivals

Since 1970, the foreign-born population has continued to increase in size and as a percentage of the total population. According to the U.S. Census Bureau (n.d.), the foreign-born population represented one in twenty U.S. residents in 1960, mostly from countries in Europe; today's foreign-born population makes up one in eight residents, mostly immigrants from Latin America and Asia. (About one in five of Canada's population was born in another country, with recent immigrants coming from Asia, Africa, and the Middle East). About one in four American children under the age of eighteen has at least one foreign-born parent. California is the state with the highest percentage (27 percent) of foreign-born residents. The largest number of foreign-born residents (11.7 million) came from Mexico, at least five times higher than any other country.

In addition to cultural differences brought with them from their countries of origin, racial and ethnic minorities also differ in terms of the conditions of their arrival and the length of time they have been in the country. There are three categories of new arrivals: refugees, legal immigrants, and undocumented immigrants.

Refugees are people who are forced out of their homes by war or other extreme political conditions and whose lives or liberty would be endangered if they returned. One example is the "boat people" and other refugees who fled Southeast Asia after the end of the Vietnam War in 1975. Other large groups of refugees have included Eastern Europeans, Afghans, Ethiopians, Cubans, and Salvadorans. Recently the United States has accepted refugees from Africa, where wars have displaced millions of people. These have included members of the Somali Bantu tribe. Africans made up only about 3 percent of refugees resettled in 1990; ten years later that had grown to nearly 30 percent (Swarns, 2003).

As a result of their experiences, many refugees suffer from post-traumatic stress disorder. Working with the United Nations High Commissioner on Refugees (UNHCR) and the United States Department of Health and Human Services Office of Refugee Resettlement, faith-based groups and voluntary agencies such as Catholic Charities, Lutheran Immigration and Refugee Services, Church World Service, and Jewish Family Services work to help refugees resettle successfully in their new home country. Social workers are often part of these efforts, guiding volunteers and church and temple committees to help find and furnish apartments, teach refugees to use public transportation, enroll their children in school, and obtain training and employment. Refugees from agrarian backgrounds (such as the Hmong and the Somalis) may be illiterate, even in their own language, and are unfamiliar with the use of electricity, kitchen appliances, and motorized vehicles. Refugees are expected to become self-sufficient within the first year of their arrival in the United States.

Although the United States makes the largest financial contribution of any country to worldwide refugee assistance programs, many nations much smaller than the United States host many more refugees. According to the UNHCR (2011) at the beginning of 2010, for example, developing countries hosted some 8.3 million refugees, equivalent to 80 percent of the global refugee population. Of the ten countries with the largest refugee populations, seven were to be found in Africa, Asia, and the Middle East. According to the International Rescue Committee (n.d.), most refugees return to their homes when turmoil ends, but when conditions remain unstable or there is a danger of persecution, some refugees stay in a refugee settlement in another country. Unfortunately, many host countries are unable to integrate refugees on a permanent basis. Another option is resettlement in a third country, but this occurs only rarely. The United States accepts a limited number of refugees each year, as authorized by Congress.

Immigrants come to their new home country more or less voluntarily, responding to both "pull" and "push" factors. Sometimes the "pull" factor—dreams of joining relatives and achieving success in a new country—is stronger. At other times, the "push" factor—escaping from squalor and starvation—is stronger. Examples of the latter include the Irish fleeing the potato famine in the nineteenth century, or Haitians or Dominicans escaping the pervasive poverty of their island in the twentieth century.

Immigrants are good for the U.S. economy. The most skilled create products and jobs in technology and engineering. For example, according to a study released by Duke University, while only 12 percent of the U.S. population is made up of immigrants, 52 percent of Silicon Valley technology companies were started by immigrants and one in four technology and engineering companies started between 1995 and 2005 had at least one foreign-born executive (Konrad, 2007).

Two-thirds of immigrant visas to the United States are awarded for family reunification and only 13–15 percent for employment purposes (West, 2010; Zakaria, 2012). This ratio is the opposite of most other countries; for example, 62 percent of permanent-resident visas in Canada are based on skills (Zakaria, 2012).

Undocumented immigrants are, typically, unskilled laborers who are in this country without legal permission trying to find work. Certainly, using the term *illegals* as a noun is degrading and dehumanizing. Living in a country without legal permission is a civil, not criminal violation. A majority of Hispanics believe that the word *illegal* is offensive ("In newsrooms, some immigration terms are going out of style," 2013). The Pew Center uses the term *unauthorized immigrant.*

A recent feature story in *Time* magazine (Vargas, 2012) outlined many of the characteristics of undocumented immigrants living in the United States. The states with the highest shares are Nevada (7.2 percent), California (6.8 percent), and Texas (6.7 percent. There are an estimated 11.5 million undocumented immigrants in the United States. More than half (59 percent) come from Mexico. About one million come from Asia and the Pacific Islands, about 800,000 from Latin America, and about 300,000 from Europe. These are almost always people who entered the country legally—as vacationers or on temporary visas—and then overstay the time permitted. Almost two-thirds of undocumented adult immigrants have lived in the United States for at least ten years and 35 percent have lived here for fifteen years or more (Taylor, Lopez, Martinez, Passel, & Motel, 2011).

Everyday life is difficult for undocumented immigrants. Most states will not issue a driver's license (New Mexico and Washington state are exceptions) (Vargas, 2012). The threat of deportation is a constant concern, especially as at least six states have written their own immigration enforcement laws (Gomez, 2012). (Many of these laws have been challenged as unconstitutional and are being reviewed by the federal judicial system.) Some of the laws require local police officers or sheriffs to check the immigration status of suspects if the officer believes the person might be in the country illegally. This often leads to harassment and/or racial profiling by law enforcement officers or also to the refusal by members of the Hispanic community to report crimes for fear that they or members of their families will be arrested on immigration charges (Gomez, 2012). It is a myth that the United States rarely deports undocumented immigrants; the country deports an average of 350,000 annually and in the last decade more than 2.2 million people were deported (West, 2010).

In debates over immigration reform, some critics argue that undocumented immigrants are a drain on federal, state, and local government resources. Households headed by undocumented immigrants paid $10.6

billion in state and local taxes in 2010 (Garcia, 2013; Institute on Taxation and Economic Policy, 2013). Because immigrants, even legal ones, are barred from most social services they pay to support programs that they will never be able to use. One study found that the average immigrant paid $1,800 more in taxes than government benefits received (West, 2010).

If undocumented immigrants were permitted to work in the United States legally their state and local tax contributions would increase by an estimated $2 billion a year. Legalization of low-skilled immigrant workers would yield significant income gains for American workers and households by creating jobs further up the economic ladder (Dixon & Rimmer, 2009).

According to a 2011 Pew Research Center for the People & the Press survey, the American public sees no contradiction in supporting both stepped-up border security and a way for people already in the United States illegally to gain citizenship if they meet certain conditions, such as passing a background check and having a job. The biggest concern (expressed by 40 percent of respondents) was that illegal immigration places a burden on government services, while 27 percent said that it hurt American jobs.

Acculturation and Assimilation of Refugees and Immigrants

Light-skinned newcomers have the advantage of "blending in" with the majority group in America, at least in terms of appearance, so that they have greater freedom of choice in becoming members of the dominant culture. According to a study conducted using an eleven-point scale to describe skin color, immigrants with darker skin received lower wages than those with lighter skin (Hersch, 2006). In an interview with the *Washington Post*, the researcher noted, "I don't think that any explanation other than discrimination is possible—and I am not one to draw such inferences lightly. . . . On average, being one shade lighter has about the same effect as having an additional year of education" (Morin, 2006). Besides physical appearance, other factors that make assimilation easier are youth, education, bilingualism, the degree of similarity of the background culture to the mainstream culture, and the availability of cultural mentors (Queralt, 1996, p. 67).

The result of successful efforts to blend is called *cultural assimilation* (also referred to as *acculturation*). Cultural assimilation means being able to function on equal terms with the rest of society by understanding and following cultural norms. Achieving a higher level of integration is called *structural assimilation*, which means being fully accepted into the institutions and social circles of the mainstream group. Some sociologists argue that marital assimilation (intermarriage between members of different groups) is the highest level of integration. Nevertheless, there are many instances of intermarriage (such as U.S. servicemen bringing home Korean brides) that do not reflect evidence of full acceptance of a minority group into the majority society. Psychological assimilation involves a change in self-identification by a member of a minority group (Kendall, 2013).

Under the 1965 Immigration and Naturalization Act, an individual who is at least 18 years of age, and who has lived legally in the United States continuously for at least five years (three years for spouses of U.S. citizens) is eligible to become a *naturalized* U.S. citizens if he or she can read, write, and speak English, and pass a test on American history and civics. (See figure 6.1.)

FIGURE 6.1   SAMPLE NATURALIZATION TEST QUESTIONS

1. What is the supreme law of the land?
2. The idea of government is in the first three words of the Constitution. What are these words?
3. What do we call the first ten amendments in the Constitution?
4. What is one right of freedom from the First Amendment?
5. How many amendments does the Constitution have?
6. What are two rights in the Declaration of Independence?
7. Name one branch or part of the government.
8. What stops one branch of government from becoming too powerful?
9. We elect a U.S. senator for how many years?
10. The House of Representatives has how many voting members?
11. We elect a U.S. representative for how many years?
12. Who does a U.S. senator represent?
13. Why do some states have more representatives than other states?

14. If the president and the vice president can no longer serve, who becomes president?
15. How many people are on the Supreme Court?
(See end of section, p. 271, for answers)

Source: U.S. Citizenship and Immigration Services. (2008). Civics Flashcards for the new naturalization test. Retrieved from http://uscis.gov.

The price of full assimilation is the disappearance of the ethnic group. Some people instead choose to be bicultural, meaning that as individuals they are able to successfully negotiate more than one culture, usually the dominant one as well as their own. Typically, these individuals are first exposed to socialization within their minority cultural group and later to significant experiences with the majority culture. This is common for children and adolescents of first-generation immigrants and refugees. Another example of biculturalism is the way African American parents and other caregivers prepare their children to deal successfully with the negative encounters they will be exposed to in the majority culture (see, for example, Carothers, 1990).

Ethnicity, Color, and Race

Ethnicity differs from race (and class) in that it is characterized by cultural distinctions—language, customs, values, beliefs, holidays, music, food, dress, and so forth. These are characteristics shared by people with a common history, and at one time, a common geographic location. First-generation immigrants often live in ethnic enclaves, such as Chinatown, Little Havana, or Little Saigon that help them preserve their ancestral culture. Religion is often closely tied to ethnicity (see chapter 4). Membership in a non-Protestant religious group (e.g., Catholic, Eastern Orthodox Christian) has helped to define and preserve the distinctiveness of many white ethnics, such as the Italians, Irish, Poles, and Greeks (Schaefer, 2012).

Many social workers and sociologists use the term *people of color* to refer to nonwhite people in the United States. Martin Luther King Junior used the phrase "citizens of color" in his "I have a dream" speech in

1963 and "people of color" has been widely used since the late 1980s. The term frames the subject more positively than "nonwhite"—which may be interpreted to imply that "white" is the norm or preferred status. It all sounds simple enough, but defining "white," either legally or culturally, has been a lengthy, controversial, and often logically inconsistent process in this country (Rasmussen, Klinenberg, Nexica, & Wray, 2001).

The broad categorizations of "white" and "nonwhite" people is a variant on the questionable practice of identifying and designating different races (Close, 2000; Smedley & Smedley, 2005). Even the U.S. Census Bureau struggles with the notion of race; its instructions to citizens say that they are to classify themselves by race as it "reflects common usage, not an attempt to define biological stock." According to the U.S. Census Bureau (Humes, Jones, & Ramirez, 2011), the 2010 census included six racial categories: white, black or African American, American Indian or Alaska native, Asian, Native Hawaiian or other Pacific Islander, and "some other race" for respondents reporting entries such as multiracial, mixed, or interracial in response to the race question. The overwhelming majority of respondents (97 percent) reported only one race; the people who identified as white were the most likely to report only one race. Among people who reported more than one race in 2010, the vast majority (about 92 percent) reported exactly two races and an additional 8 percent reported three races. In 2010 four groups were, by far, the largest multiple-race combinations in the United States: white and black (1.8 million), white and some other race (1.7 million), white and Asian (1.6 million), and white and American Indian and Alaska Native (1.4 million). Together, these four combinations composed nearly three-fourths of the multiple-race population in the 2010 census.

It was not until European explorers began encountering people who looked quite different from them that the idea of human *races* developed (Begley, 1995). Generally, racial categories are based on physical characteristics, such as hair texture, facial features, skin color, and body build. More than a century ago scientists classified humans into three racial types: people with lighter skin and fine hair were called Caucasoid, people with darker skin and kinky hair were called Negroid, and people with yellow or brown skin and distinctive folds on the eyelids were called Mongoloid (Macionis, 2014). At first glance, the categories appear to be self-evident. Nevertheless, when scientists try to categorize people by various other biological factors, such as blood type or biochemistry, they come up with quite different arrangements. For example, using blood type, Germans would be in the same category as New Guineans, and using lactose tolerance, Norwegians would be lumped together with the Fulani of Nigeria (Begley, 1995). This, and the fact that race is differently defined in different cultures, suggests that racial categories as we use them every day are social constructs rather than biological realities. Many of the nations of Central and South America, for example, including Mexico and Brazil, have complex systems of placing people in a myriad of racial groups using a color gradient along a continuum from light to dark (Schaefer, 2012). The majority of anthropologists today agree that using the concept of race to distinguish among different populations of humans is meaningless. In fact, most scientists (and many social work students) would argue that there is but one "human race."

Scientific biological arguments to the contrary do not keep Americans from using race as a kind of mental shorthand to categorize and stereotype large populations. In fact, being perceived as members of particular races has very real consequences for everyone in American society today. Especially for people of color, race shapes their daily experiences in ways that whites seldom appreciate. The stresses or hassles associated with being a member of a minority group make getting through the day more difficult for many people.

Stress is accentuated by poverty. The dual influence of race or ethnicity and socioeconomic class status is called "ethclass" (Queralt, 1996, p. 3). Ethclass suggests that an individual's life chances, lifestyle, and behaviors are influenced by the interaction of class and race/ethnicity. For example, the life experiences of an African American physician differ substantially from those of an African American nursing aide.

Inequity and Privilege

A *minority* is a population group that shares a distinctive identity and is subjected to stigma, prejudice, discrimination, and oppression. Characteristics (e.g., color, language, religion, national origin) that define minority status vary in different societies (Schaefer, 2012). Minority does not necessarily connote small numbers, but rather refers to a subordinate position in society. For example, women make up a slight numerical majority of the population but are in a subordinate position and therefore are considered a minority. Even when, as a whole, they outnumber whites (as is predicted to occur in this century), people of color will continue to be a minority in the United States.

A stigma refers to any physical or social attribute that so discredits or devalues a person's social identity that it disqualifies that person from full social acceptance in the minds of others (Goffman, 1963). One might argue that having dark skin, kinky hair, and a broad, flat nose is still a stigma in American society. In the case of gay men and lesbians, stigma results from a violation of the mainstream cultural norm of heterosexism. In the case of persons with disabilities, stigma results from a violation of mainstream cultural norms of appearance and ability. For example, being disfigured as a result of an accident or injury or using a wheelchair may be stigmatizing in this society.

Prejudice is a negative attitude, often based on an irrational generalization, about an entire group of people. A prejudice biases someone against another person simply because the second person is identified as a member of a particular group. An example of prejudice is the belief that Arabs are likely terrorists. Discrimination is an unfavorable action, or unfair treatment, directed toward members of a minority group. An example of discrimination is declining to hire someone with a disability even though that disability is unrelated to job requirements. De jure discrimination is discrimination that is supported by the law; an example is the practice of segregation that was enforced in Southern states before the Civil Rights movement brought legislative and judicial changes. De facto discrimination is discrimination that continues to exist although it is illegal; an example would be realtors who purposely steer African American buyers away from white neighborhoods. Discrimination can be a reaction to many characteristics, including not only race or ethnicity, but also religion, national origin, immigration status, class, gender, sexual orientation, gender identity and expression, disability, age, and appearance. Oppression is "a form of discrimination that is long term, systematic, and institutionalized (i.e., embedded within key social structures such as the educational system, the health care system, and the criminal justice system)" (Queralt, 1996, p. 171).

Xenophobia is a fear of, or contempt for, anything foreign, which may or may not be related to race or ethnicity per se. Nativism refers to beliefs and practices that favor native-born citizens over immigrants (Schaefer, 2012, p. 90). Periods of high immigration are typically marked by nativist resistance that characterizes newcomers as a threat to the integrity of national culture (Portes & Rumbaut, 2006, p. 344).

Inequalities of status and opportunity are probably inevitable in most societies. Privilege is a special advantage or benefit enjoyed by a group or population. When some people are oppressed, others enjoy privilege, regardless of whether they actively support or take part in acts of oppression either collectively or individually. This is an idea that makes many privileged individuals uncomfortable.

In her classic essay, "White Privilege and Male Privilege," Peggy McIntosh has listed forty-six situations and describes how her experience is "privileged" because of her white complexion. For example, "I can swear, or dress in secondhand clothes, or not answer letters, without having people attribute these choices to the bad morals, the poverty, or the illiteracy of my race. . . . Whether I use checks, credit cards, or cash, I can count on my skin color not to work against the appearance that I am financially reliable" (McIntosh, 2001, p. 98).

Insensitivity to privilege is common in the mainstream culture. Tropman (1989) notes "the belief that one earns one's status is an important value within American society" (p. 7). To deny the effects of race, to espouse color blindness, works only if one assumes that being white is no different than being any other color (Kincheloe, Steinberg, Rodriguez, & Chennault, 1998). "The post-race, color-blind perspective allows whites to imagine that depictions of racial minorities working in high status jobs and consuming the same products, or at least appearing in commercials for products whites desire or consume, is the same as living in a society where color is no longer used to allocate resources or shape group outcomes" (Gallagher, 2013, p. 93). As noted already, whiteness is a socially constructed and hence arbitrary category; nevertheless, to be white is to escape the real and entirely nonarbitrary prejudice, discrimination, and oppression experienced every day in this country by people of color.

Answers to Sample Naturalization Test Questions

1. Constitution
2. We the people
3. Bill of Rights
4. Freedom of speech, religion, press, assembly and petition the government
5. 27
6. Life, liberty, and the pursuit of happiness
7. Executive, legislative, and judicial
8. Checks and balances
9. 6
10. 435
11. 2
12. All the people of the state
13. More people
14. Speaker of the House
15. Nine

EXPLORING MAINSTREAM/DOMINANT AND MINORITY CULTURES

It is difficult to describe the commonalities of large populations without oversimplifying. We caution readers to be aware that any discussion of cultural values and practices does not imply that every individual in that culture fully subscribes to its values or norms. It is important to remember that there is much within-group variability and that between-group differences are often exaggerated. Particularly for social work practitioners, it is important to explore with the individual client the meaning that culture holds for him or her rather than making assumptions based on group membership.

We will now discuss cultural characteristics, beginning with "mainstream" values. Although a number of mainstream social values were identified and described over fifty years ago (Williams, 1957), discussion of white, middle-class values in American social work texts is a relatively recent development. The earlier omission reflects the arrogance of the white middle class in assuming that while other groups were different, their own ways were already understood and accepted as the norm and the best model for successful life in America, with no further need for elaboration. Many whites do not think of themselves as having race or ethnicity. Because the majority of social work students and instructors were white and middle class, this assumption was not questioned.

We believe that even white, middle-class students need to be given the opportunity to reflect on the characteristics of mainstream culture. A discussion of minority cultures follows.

Social workers should be aware that, in addition to social class and racial/ethnic differences, when discussing cultural values and practices there are likely to be generational differences, urban/rural differences, and, notably, important regional differences (see, for example, Adams, 2003; Arbesman, 2012; Chinni & Gimpel, 2010; Escott & Goldfield, 1991; Garreau,1981; and Woodward, 2011). Garreau (1981) divided North America into nine regions or "nations," noting that each "has a distinct prism through which it views the world" (p. 2). More recently Woodward (2011), starting with a more historical perspective, used eleven divisions to describe the various cultures of North America. These regions vary not only in terms of history, religion, economics, and politics, but also linguistic dialects, folkways, mannerisms, and—more importantly— deeply held values and attitudes. Of course, not all individuals and families within a region share the dominant culture of that region, just as not all members of a racial or ethnic group espouse all of the cultural traits attributed to that population. Nevertheless, values such as religiosity, obedience to authority, patriarchy, traditional family, duty, and formality in relationships vary greatly across different regions of the United States, with the most conservative attitudes expressed in the "old South" and the least in New England. Canadians not only hold more liberal views in general, but also are more consistent across regions (Adams, 2003). Although one would expect that mobility and mass media would lead to a more homogenous national or continental culture, Bishop (2008) argues in his book *The Big Sort* that mobility has reinforced regional differences as lifestyle choices are leading people to live together in like-minded communities where their values are not challenged. Chinni and Gimpel (2010) divide the country into fifteen types of counties (which tend to cluster in larger regions) that also serve to distinguish local cultures. Their categories include "aging farmlands," "evangelical hubs," "Hispanic centers," "LDS [Mormon] enclaves," "military posts," "Native America lands," and "rural middle America."

Mainstream/Dominant American Values

The mainstream or dominant culture in the United States is usually associated with the white middle class. Historically, this group has been further defined as white, Anglo-Saxon Protestants (WASPs)—generally understood to be immigrants from Great Britain. The choice of English as the official language of the country and the predominance of Protestantism as the majority religion, as well as the adoption of a legal system based on English law, reflect the power and influence of early English, Welsh, Scottish, Scots-Irish, and Irish Protestant settlers. The dominance of WASPs in this country is "most evident in the widespread assumption that terms 'race' and 'ethnicity' apply to everyone but them" (Macionis, 2014, p. 407). Gradually, (white) immigrant groups from other parts of Europe have joined the WASP majority. (Some students might be surprised to learn of the historic reluctance of WASPs to accept "undesirable foreigners," such as Germans and Irish Catholics.)

Much of the core of the mainstream American value system has remained intact through its history and continues to receive widespread support (Prigmore & Atherton, 1986) even though some of the values are inconsistent with each other or even contradictory (Tropman, 1989; Williams, 1957). What is thought of as traditional American culture is the legacy of white, middle-class Euro-American descendants of immigrants from Great Britain, Germany, and Ireland, with somewhat less influence from immigrants from other countries in western and eastern Europe and the Mediterranean coast. Because of their white skin color, similar religious background (Christianity), and frequent intermarriage, members of these immigrant nationalities quickly adopted the mantle of the dominant group (Queralt, 1996), shaping and refining U.S. mainstream culture.

Among the values that characterize this culture are (1) work; (2) achievement—especially as it is reflected in economic success and material comfort; (3) self-reliance, independence, freedom, individualism, and competition; (4) equality before the law; (5) science, logic, progress, efficiency, and practicality; (6) geographic mobility; (7) informality and directness in personal relationships; (8) moralism; (9) time awareness; and (10) youthfulness and an orientation to the future. (The descriptions that follow are true for many white, middle- and upper-class Americans, but readers should be aware that there are many variations within this group, just as there are among members of minority/nondominant groups.)

1. The American emphasis on work is derived from a Puritan heritage that valued work for its own sake. The Protestant work ethic is recognized as the moral basis for the American capitalistic economic system and policies in social welfare. Work for economic gain is considered the path to success, a sign of personal morality, and a moral obligation (see detailed discussion in chapter 2). Many Americans, for example, feel uneasy in contemplative or meditative activities and prefer to keep busy and "work hard" even in their leisure pursuits. Only paid employment is considered "real" work. For example, lack of respect for the homemaking and child-care responsibilities of stay-at-home mothers is reflected in welfare reform policies that require poor mothers to leave their young children in day-care centers and seek jobs outside the home.

2. Although education and occupational status are important, achievement and success in America are often measured in terms of income and wealth. Conspicuous consumption—the purchase of showy automobiles, large houses, fashionable clothing, flashy jewelry, and expensive electronic goods, whose primary purpose is not utilitarian but to impress others—is a modern American characteristic. This trend toward ostentation is a cultural trait promoted even further by a continual stream of media advertising that tells potential customers "you are what you own."

3. Linking the values of work and individualism is the American myth of self-reliance. The tendency of Americans to overestimate what they have accomplished on their own and deny how much they owe to others began with the fiction that colonial Europeans built a land of plenty out of nothing. In reality, however, the abundant concentrations of game and edible plants they found were not natural but had been developed by the stewardship of Native Americans (Kehoe, 1999). Research demonstrates that as they moved westward across the continent, American pioneers were dependent on a large network of kin, neighbors, religious

institutions, and government programs (especially the availability of free or low-cost land).

Belief in the importance of individual rights over those of the family, the collective, or community life is a particularly American characteristic, although its roots can be found in the emergence of capitalism in seventeenth-century Europe. Neither contributing to the group's well-being nor placing the group's well-being first are fully appreciated in American mainstream culture; this contrasts markedly with cultures where the extended family or group is more valued than the individual, as is common in many minority communities (Ewalt & Mokuau, 1996).

Closely linked to the values of achievement and individualism is the American value of competition. This competition occurs not just between sports teams or business enterprises, but also among individuals in groups and even within families. Americans tend to have a dichotomous point of view: if you are not a winner, you must be a loser. There is little sense that with less competition and more cooperation, everyone could "win."

4. The Constitution of the United States was written by men who deliberately rejected the traditional social stratification of Europe; consequently, Americans have a formal commitment to equality before the law (Prigmore & Atherton, 1986). Over time, this concept has been extended to mean an equality of opportunity for social and economic rewards. Nevertheless, for many years, rewards not resulting from achievement, such as those associated with being white or male, were considered the natural order of things. Unfortunately, the continuing prevalence of sexism, heterosexism, institutional racism, nativism, and other group superiority themes mars the American societal ideal of true equality.

5. Perhaps because they live in a relatively young society, Americans tend to value science, logic, progress, efficiency, and practicality. Technical efficiency tends to be valued for its own sake, rather than for what it serves to accomplish (Prigmore & Atherton, 1986). There is a belief that all problems can be solved by science, eventually if not right away. Aesthetics, sentimentality, spirituality, mysticism, rituals and ceremonies, and reverence for the past are often viewed with skepticism.

6. Americans have always valued geographic mobility. Historically, they pressed toward new frontiers. Now individuals and families move far away from home to take advantage of educational or career opportunities,

or simply to seek adventure and change. Adults are often separated from their families of origin by thousands of miles. Even married partners sometimes work and live in different communities or even different states.

The profusion of private automobiles reflects a uniquely American obsession with being able to go where and when one wants, without having to rely on or to consider anyone else. In the 1950s and 1960s, public financing in America was gradually redirected from the streetcars and trolleys that served urban and poor families and was used instead to provide new roads for suburban commuters and their cars, promoting urban sprawl, traffic congestion, and pollution. (This is discussed further in chapter 8.)

7. Americans prefer informality and directness in personal relationships. With its emphasis on equality, American society downplays the use of honorifics and formal titles ("your majesty," "your lordship"). Americans in the mainstream culture often ignore both age and occupational or social status, addressing relatives, close friends, and distant acquaintances, or even strangers by their first names (although this is less common in the South). Direct confrontations about misunderstandings and frank discussion of feelings are not uncommon. There is a sense that "honesty" in relationships is more important than diplomacy.

8. As a group, mainstream Americans have traditionally expressed their morality by responding promptly to calls for help and giving generously to victims of disease and natural disasters. Typically, this humanitarianism is expressed in organized and impersonal ways through large charities such as the Red Cross or the United Way. To most Americans, humanitarianism means private, nongovernment support for those who are in trouble "through no fault of their own" (Prigmore & Atherton, 1986).

On the other hand, many members of the American mainstream are quick to blame chronically poor people, minorities, and other client populations for causing their own problems and are reluctant to support them through government programs or direct subsidies, even though the country as a whole possesses enormous wealth (Jansson, 2012; Prigmore & Atherton, 1986; Ryan, 1976). The American cultural obsession with self-reliance and independence may come at a significant cost to others in the family, group, organization, or community. A narrow Puritanism that seeks reasons for disapproval of others leads to viewing the dependent state of the poor and unsuccessful as immoral rather than simply unfortunate. The core value of individual responsibility exonerates society and confirms personal failure for those who cannot or do not reach success.

9. The American mainstream group puts a premium on time, which they schedule, regulate, and measure exactly (Queralt, 1996, p. 76). In fact, involvement in friendships, and religious or other community activities are often evaluated in terms of the time investments they require. (Minority groups in America tend to be much more flexible in their use of time.)

10. Whereas minority groups in the United States value and respect the aged, mainstream America has had a long-standing infatuation with youth. In a quickly changing society, the aged often have not been appreciated for their wisdom and experience.

African Americans

African Americans are the now the second largest minority group in the United States (ranking just below Hispanics/Latinos in the 2010 census). The ancestors of most African Americans came to this country not as immigrants or refugees but as slaves. Scholars disagree about the relative impacts of the cultural practices of their West African homelands, the slave experience, and more recent oppression as victims of institutional racism, on their current condition. Recent black immigrants have come from Haiti, Jamaica, Trinidad, and Tobago in the Caribbean and from Nigeria, Ethiopia, Ghana, and Kenya in Africa. This influx of immigrants in the last decade of the twentieth century accounted for a quarter of black America's population growth (Berlin, 2010).

Beginning in 1910 and lasting through the 1920s, there was a Great Migration of African Americans from the rural South to northern industrial cities such as Chicago, New York, Philadelphia, St. Louis, and Detroit (Berlin, 2010), where they were employed in meatpacking, automaking, and steel-manufacturing plants. Nevertheless, the majority of African Americans still live in the South.

Clear vestiges of African-based folklore, religion, language, and music remain despite the passage of generations and the historic slave experience of African Americans (Schaefer, 2012). Strong kinship bonds are the most enduring cultural strength that black Americans brought with them from the African continent (Hill, 1999). "Blacks are more likely than whites to care for children and older adults in an extended family network" (Schaefer, 2012, p. 240). According to a Pew Center analysis of U.S. Census data (Pew Research and Social & Demographic Trends, 2010), Hispanics (22 percent), blacks (23 percent) and Asians (25 percent) are all significantly more likely than whites (13 percent) to live in a multigenerational family household. Among blacks, 40 percent are in a three-generation household and 13 percent (the highest share for this category) are in a skipped-generation household. A skipped-generation household is one with grandparents and grandchildren, but neither parent present. The African American family remains a resilient and adaptive social institution despite threats of poverty and discrimination (Billingsley, 1992).

The percentage of family households headed by a single parent among African Americans increased from 36 percent in 1970 to 54 percent in 2007 (Cherlin, 2013). William Julius Wilson (1978, 1996), among others, has argued that a decline in the rate of marriage among African Americans is closely linked to the economy, and particularly the loss of semi-skilled and skilled blue-collar jobs in urban areas. In an interesting study, Lundquist found that there were no significant differences in marriage patterns for blacks and whites in the military. She explains these findings by noting that the military "provides stable employment and offers opportunities for educational and career mobility, particularly for those with fewer opportunities in civilian society" and an "overall social milieu" devoid of much of the racial discrimination present in civilian society (Lundquist, 2004, p. 752). Such an analysis supports the thesis that racial differences in African American family formation trends in U.S. society result not from cultural norms, but are a response to economic and social limitations and opportunities.

Social work scholar Harriette Pipes McAdoo reports that African American parents promote "respect for authority figures, a work ethic, achievement, a sense of duty, obligation to kin, and a strong religious sense" (2007a, p. 165). An increasing number of African American families are less active in the church than their extended family has been in the past; nevertheless, church attendance continues to be an important part of African American family life (McAdoo, 2007c). African Americans are more likely than whites to attend church, with most of them affiliated with Protestant churches and the majority being members of historically black churches (Schaefer, 2012). For more than 300 years, African American churches have served as community centers, promoting the rights of black Americans and providing both informal and formal social services (Walker, 1999; Wilson, 1996). A variety of non-Christian groups have also exerted a great influence on African Americans. Between 1.6 and 1.7 million or about 5 percent of all African Americans are Muslims and between 20 and 40 percent of American Muslims are African Americans (Schaefer, 2012).

Hill (1999) also makes a strong case for both achievement and work orientation being central to African American culture. He argues that the majority of low-income African Americans prefer work to welfare, and that black parents at all income levels hold high educational aspirations for their children. Schaefer (2012) reports that working-class blacks indicate a greater desire for their children to attend college than do working-class whites and that poor blacks are more likely to be working and have more than one wage earner in a family.

As with all minority groups, one has to consider the effects of class, as well as race, in understanding African American culture. In his book *The Declining Significance of Race* (1978), sociologist William Julius Wilson stated that while racism remains an important factor, social class is becoming more central to understanding the African American experience. He suggests that there are two quite different African American worlds: one that is located in the inner city where joblessness and violence define everyday life, and the other located in the middle-class suburbs where good jobs, good schools, and opportunity prevail (Wilson, 1996).

The black middle class in the United States has grown substantially since the 1960s, due in large part to increasing levels of education. In 1964 just 25 percent of African Americans had received a high school diploma; by 2012 that had increased to 85 percent (Eilperin, 2013). The proportion of African Americans aged 25 and over who completed at least four years of college increased from about one out of twenty-five (3.9 percent) percent to more than one out of five (21.2 percent) between 1964 and 2012 (Eilperin, 2013). According to census data, the poverty rate for African Americans in 1966 was 41.8 percent; by 2010 the poverty rate had declined to 27.6 percent (Eilperin, 2013).

Arab Americans and Middle Eastern Americans

There have been several waves of Arab immigration to the United States, the first beginning around 1875. Arab Americans trace their ancestry to twenty-two countries in the Middle East (Arab American Institute, 2009). Most Arab countries are predominantly Muslim, but not all people from the Middle East are Arabs, nor are all Arabs Muslims. An Arab American is a person descended from people whose native tongue was Arabic and who lived by Arab cultural traditions and values; a Muslim is a follower of the Islamic religion and may or may not be Arab (Banks, 1997). The majority of Arab Americans are Christian; 35 percent are Catholic, 24 percent are Muslim, 18 percent are Eastern Orthodox, and 10 percent are Protestant (Arab American Institute, 2009). Recent Arab immigrants are more likely to be Muslim, but only about one-fourth of the Muslims in the United States are Arabs (Banks, 1997).

The U.S. Census does not have an Arab American classification. In terms of racial classification, the government has at different times considered Arab immigrants to be Asians, "other Asians," Caucasian, white, black, or "colored" (Suleiman, 1999). Socially, Arabs are treated as "honorary whites" or "white but not quite" (Samhan, 1999). They are not considered a minority for purposes of legal protection against discrimination in employment or housing. Most Arab Americans identify themselves by national origin rather than by ethnicity. Because there is so much diversity among Middle Eastern immigrants, they lack a sense of solidarity (Walbridge, 1999).

There are about 3.5 million Arab Americans in the United States, living in all fifty states and the District of Columbia. Most live in metropolitan areas; the areas with the most Arab Americans are Detroit, Los Angeles, Chicago, New York (Brooklyn), and Washington, DC (Arab American Institute, 2009). Arab Americans operate small stores in central cities, following the footsteps of Jewish and Korean entrepreneurs (Schaefer, 2008). On average, Arab Americans are better educated and have higher median incomes than other Americans (Arab American Institute, 2009).

Asian Americans and Pacific Islanders

Asian women married to American servicemen account for some of the Asian immigration after 1950. The Immigration and Naturalization Act of 1965, which came into full effect in 1968, abolished discrimination based on national origin and ended forty years of Asian exclusion. Min (1995a) reports that the proportion of immigrants from Asia, as a percent of all immigrants increased from 9 percent in 1960 to 25 percent in 1970, and then to 44 percent in 1980.

According to the 2010 U.S. Census (Hoeffel, Kastogi, Kim, & Shahid, 2012) a total of 17.3 million people in the United States described themselves as Asian or part Asian. Nearly three-fourths of all Asians lived in just ten states. Asian Americans were the fastest-growing group, in terms of rate of growth, between 2000 and 2010. California and Texas had the largest numeric growth of Asians. Asians constituted more than 25 percent of the population in the San Francisco area and in Hawaii.

In the 1980 census, 3.4 million Americans identified themselves as Asians and Pacific Islanders. This was a doubling of the 1970 census figures due primarily to the influx of Southeast Asian/Indochinese refugees (Vietnamese, Laotians, and Cambodians) after the Vietnam War ended in 1975. By 1990, the numbers had doubled again. The breakdown of Asian Americans by major nationality groups in 2010 were Chinese (22.8 percent), Asian Indian (19.4 percent), Filipino (17.4 percent), Vietnamese (10.6 percent), Korean (9.7 percent), and Japanese (5.2 percent) (Hoeffel, Kastogi, Kim, & Shahid, 2012).

Asian Americans are probably the most internally diverse American minority group, representing immigrants from many different nations and cultural traditions. Unlike Latinos, the majority of whom are Catholic and Spanish-speaking, Asian Americans represent a wide variety of religions and languages. Asian Americans also experience diversity related to generational differences (Min, 1995a). Japanese Americans, for example, distinguish among the *Issei* (first generation), the *Nisei* (second generation), the *Sansei* (third generation), and the *Yonsei* (fourth generation) and their experiences in this country (Nishi, 1995; Schaefer, 2012). Koreans distinguish the *Ichomose* or "1.5 generation"—the middle-aged, bilingual and bicultural adults who accompanied their parents to the United States when they were young (Schaefer, 2012).

South Asians—people from India, Pakistan, Bangladesh, and other South Asian countries—are culturally similar to one another and distinct from other Asian groups (La Brack, 1999; Min, 1990). South Asians experienced British colonization and thus many of these immigrants grew up speaking English, at least in school. Typically, those who arrived in America since 1995 are educated, wealthy, and urban. Many are professionals in the health care field; more than 25 percent of foreign-born dentists and more than 20 percent of foreign-born doctors in the United States are from India (Sweis & Guay, 2007). Others are employed in service industries as cabdrivers, motel managers, and convenience store clerks (La Brack, 1999; Mogelonsky, 1995). Most South Asian immigrants share a religious identity either as Hindus or as Muslims (Min, 1990).

The most recent wave of Asian arrivals—the Southeast Asian/Indochinese refugees who arrived in the late 1970s and early 1980s—included not only Vietnamese, Cambodian, and Laotian nationals, but also many ethnic Chinese from all three countries and various highland tribal peoples such as the Lao Hmong and Yao and the Vietnamese Montagnards. These refugee groups had a wide range of educational and economic backgrounds and a variety of language and cultural traditions. Unlike immigrants who move voluntarily, most of the Indochinese refugees survived a stressful, frightening, and often traumatic escape to freedom. Whether they left their homeland by sea or by land, the casualty rate en route was high; this was followed by months or even years of waiting in overcrowded refugee camps in Thailand or Malaysia. Many of those who had education and high-status occupations in their native countries had to accept menial jobs in America due to language differences or lack of formal credentials. Those whose background was agrarian also had to struggle to adjust to modern urban American society.

An additional difficulty for this refugee population resulted from their initial dispersal across every state in the country. They were spread out because they had no previous family ties, there were no established ethnic communities, and per federal policy, they had to be "matched" with congregational sponsors who agreed to take responsibility for them. Refugees later moved on (secondary migration) to areas where the climate was more familiar and other members of their nationality had gathered. Thus, many Indochinese are now found in California, where more than half of Vietnamese Americans, Cambodian Americans, and Hmong Americans live (Gold, 1999). There are also settlements of Vietnamese in Texas and Louisiana. On the other hand, many refugees remain closer to their original sponsors; for example, there are large groups of Cambodians in Massachusetts, Rhode Island, and Washington, and Hmong in Minnesota and Wisconsin.

Many of the cultural values of immigrants from East Asia (i.e., people from China, Japan, and Korea) are derived from Confucianism. This philosophy promotes filial piety and other strong family-centered values. For example, one value is to bring honor to the family, or at least to avoid bringing it shame—in fact, this is a central tenet of Asian cultures (Ho, 1987). Confucianism also teaches the importance of maintaining social harmony. Harmony in interpersonal relationships is accomplished through tact, delicacy, and politeness. Contributions to unity and harmony are more valued than are competitive success or self-satisfaction. Confucianism emphasizes a hierarchical or vertical ordering of society on the basis of age, gender, and social position, specifically in the relationships between father and son, husband and wife, older brother and younger brother, "ruler" (e.g., teacher, employer) and "subject" (e.g., student, employee). These prescribed roles suggest formal styles of interpersonal interaction and contribute to the smooth interaction of individuals in different social roles.

Although they have many cultural similarities, because of the brutal acts of occupying Japanese forces in Manchuria and Korea before World War II, Chinese and Korean Americans may limit their contact with Japanese American communities (Min, 1995a). Also, because most Korean Americans are Christians, their communities are often united through congregational connections, unlike Chinese Americans who are more likely to follow traditional Asian religious practices.

Many Confucian values are shared by refugees from Vietnam, Laos, and Cambodia. Buddhism has also shaped Asian values across the centuries. Buddhism stresses the values of self-control, humility, generosity, mercy, and of cultivating a correct lifestyle. People from many Asian backgrounds are exceedingly reluctant to brag, or even to claim individual credit for their accomplishments. Westerners may be surprised at this level of humility.

Asian Americans are often called the "model minority" since they seem to have succeeded economically, socially, and educationally without significant confrontations with the white majority. Asian American children are more likely than any other ethnic group to grow up with both parents (Henslin, 2014; Wu, 2002). Some sociologists contend that the economic success of Asian Americans can be attributed to cultural values: self-discipline, an emphasis on formal education, and a strong entrepreneurial spirit. Asian Americans are well-represented in professional occupations and in the small business sector (Min, 1995b). Many new Asian immigrants have accepted menial jobs and lived as groups in tight quarters until they saved enough to buy a small business such as a gas station, green grocery, convenience store, laundry, or restaurant where all members of the family helped out. Although family income for Asian Americans is higher than whites, this reflects larger household size and the fact that more family members are employed.

According to the 2010 census briefs (Hixson, Hepler, & Kim, 2012), the term *Pacific Islanders* refers to a person having origins in any of the original peoples of Hawaii, Guam, Samoa, or other Pacific islands. Hawaiians were listed as a separate category on the 1960 census survey, the year after Hawaii became a state. Other island categories were added in 1980 and they were separated from the Asian race category in 2000. Altogether there were 1.2 million Native Hawaiians and other Pacific Islanders counted in the 2010 census. This represented only 0.2 percent of the entire U.S. population, but this populations increased at three times the rate of the total U.S. population between 2000 and 2010, growing by 35 percent. Most Pacific Islanders live in Hawaii or in cities on the West Coast of the United States. As with many other minority cultures, there is a common theme of group affiliation, collective effort, and commitment to family (which is broadly defined, and may be as large as a whole village) (Mokuau & Tauili'ili, 1992).

Filipinos are the third largest Asian American group (behind Chinese and South Asians) in the United States. The Philippines is the most Westernized country in Asia (Min, 1995a). A Spanish colony beginning in the middle of the sixteenth century, the Philippines came under the control of the United States in 1898, after the Spanish-American War. The earliest Filipino immigrants arrived as American nationals. In 1934, the islands gained commonwealth status and gained full independence in 1946, when residents lost their unrestricted immigration rights. America maintained a large naval base and airfield in the Philippines until the 1990s and more than 100,000 Filipino women married American military servicemen and immigrated to the United States. Filipinos learn English in public schools and immigrants to the United States adjust easily because of the strong American cultural influence in their homeland. For example, American-style training prepared many Filipino nurses, physicians, dentists, technologists, paramedics, and pharmacists to move to the United States to practice their professions here (Reimers, 2005). Unlike Chinese and Korean immigrants, Filipinos are less likely to run ethnic businesses (Reimers, 2005; Schaefer, 2012). About a quarter of all Filipino Americans live in southern California (Kendall, 2013). After Japanese Americans, Filipinos have the highest intermarriage rate of Asians (Hoeffel, Kastogi, Kim, & Shahid, 2012), approaching half in some communities (Reimers, 2005). Like many other ethnic groups, there are strong regional, linguistic, and religious differences among Filipino immigrants; these differences tend to hinder the development of intra-ethnic ties (Schaefer, 2012).

Latinos/Latinas (Hispanic Americans)

According to the U.S. Census Bureau, "Hispanic" or "Latino" refers to a person of Cuban, Mexican, Puerto Rican, South or Central American, or other Spanish culture or origin regardless of race (Ennis, Rios-Vargas, & Albert, 2011). *Hispanic* is the term that has been used by the federal government for this minority group since 1978. The terms *Latino* or *Latina* are preferred by some academics. They are geographically more accurate because they refer to people from Central and South America rather than to people from Spain. In this text, we use the terms *Latino* and *Hispanic* interchangeably. Neither Latino nor Hispanic is a racial classification. Latinos may identify themselves racially as white, Native American, black, or a mix of two or more of these. The terms *Chicano* or *Chicana* are commonly used in the West and Southwest for Latinos of Mexican descent who were born in the United States. La Raza (which literally means "the people") connotes pride in pluralistic Spanish, Native American, and Mexican heritage (Schaefer, 2012, p. 240). A slim majority (51 percent) of Latinos prefer to self-identify by their family's country of origin (Taylor, Lopez, Martinez, & Velasco, 2012b).

According to the U.S. Census Bureau (Ennis, Rios-Vargas, & Albert, 2011) Latinos are the fastest-growing minority group, in terms of total numbers, in the United States. The Hispanic population increased by 15.2 million between 2000 and 2010, accounting for over half of the 27.3 million increase in the total population of the United States. Between 2000 and 2010, the Hispanic population grew by 43 percent, which was four times the rate of growth in the total population at 10 percent. Population growth between 2000 and 2010 varied by national origin. Mexicans accounted for about three-quarters of the 15.2 million growth in the Latino population from 2000 to 2010. The increase in the Latino population in the United States was related to both immigration rates and high birth rates. Overall, Hispanics who live in the United States have higher rates of fertility than do whites, blacks, or Asians; the fertility rate for all Americans is about 2.1 children per woman; the rate for American-born Latina women is 2.6; and the rate for foreign-born Latina women living in the United States is 3.1 (Passel & Taylor, 2010). Eight states—California, Texas, Florida, Arizona, New Mexico, New York, New Jersey, and Illinois—account for three-quarters (74 percent) of the U.S. Latino population (Brown & Lopez, 2013). Hispanics made up almost half (47 percent) of the population of New Mexico in 2011, and almost four out of ten (38 percent) of the residents of California and Texas (Brown & Lopez, 2013). According to the 2010 census (Ennis, Rios-Vargas, & Albert, 2011), there were 50.5 million Hispanics living in the United States, or 16 percent of the total population. The Hispanic share of the overall U.S. population is projected to be as high as 29 percent by 2050 (Passell & Cohn, 2008). (The black population is expected to rise slightly to 13 percent, and the Asian share is expected to increase to 9 percent.)

Latinos can be divided along lines of class, race, and culture. The dominance of the Spanish language, however, as well as a growing political awareness, is a unifying force among Latinos. Most Latinos in the

United States speak Spanish; others speak Portuguese, French, Dutch, English, and Native American languages such as Quechua, Mayan, Aymara, and Guarani, and Creole dialects (Castex, 1994). Although Spanish-language television and periodicals help to promote a pan-ethnic identity among Latinos, many still identify primarily with their country of origin (e.g., *Cubano*, *Mejicano*) (Schaefer, 2012).

According to the Pew Hispanic Center (Gonzalez-Barrera & Lopez, 2013), the majority (64 percent) of Latinos in the United States trace their roots to Mexico. The next most numerous in terms of national origin are Puerto Ricans (9 percent) and Cubans (4 percent) (Ennis, Rios-Vargas, & Albert, 2011). These proportions are quite different in different parts of the United States; for example, more than half of Mexican-origin Hispanics live in the West—mostly in California—or the South—mostly in Texas (Gonzalez-Barrera & Lopez, 2013). Cuban Americans tend to live in the Southeast, especially Florida, while Puerto Ricans have settled in New York and New Jersey (Kendall, 2013). The 11.4 million Mexican immigrants living in the United States are by far the single largest country of origin group among the nation's 40 million immigrants.

Latino immigrants tend to maintain ties with their country of origin. The proximity of Mexico encourages immigrants to maintain strong cultural and social ties with their homeland. All Puerto Ricans are U.S. citizens and as such move back and forth freely between their island and cities on the U.S. mainland. More so than other Latinos, they sustain multiple familial, economic, and social relations that span geographic borders (Falicov, 1998, p. 40). Colombians and Dominicans also maintain a high level of contact with their countries of origin (Waldinger, 2007). Many scholars (see Mazzucato & Schans, 2011) use the term *transnational families* to describe families that maintain high levels of contact with both their country of origin and their country of current residence. Most Cuban Americans came to this country as refugees, either as a result of the Cuban Revolution in 1959, during the program of "freedom flights" between 1965 and 1973, or as part of the Mariel boatlift in 1980. Until recently, due to politically imposed barriers, Cuban Americans had the least contact with their native country of all Hispanic immigrants (Waldinger, 2007).

The church is the most important formal organization in the Latino community (Schaefer, 2012, p. 254). According to the Pew Research

Hispanic Trends Project (Martinez & Velasco, 2012) overall, more than six in ten (61 percent) of Latinos say that religion is very important in their lives and Hispanics are more likely than the general public to attend religious services weekly or more often—43 percent versus 36 percent. A growing number of Latinos in the United States are joining Protestant churches. One in five (19 percent) of Latinos report that they are Protestant and twice as many say that they are "born again" or evangelical as say they are mainline Protestants (Taylor, Lopez, Martinez, & Velasco, 2012a). Many of the churches are small, often with Spanish-speaking leadership, and most Latino congregations offer a strong sense of community (Schaefer, 2012, p. 255). Nevertheless, the majority of Latinos (62 percent) remain committed to Catholicism, and Latinos account for over a third of Roman Catholics in the United States (Martinez & Velasco, 2012). Traditional Catholic rituals continue to be practiced in Latino homes. A particular focus of devotion is the Virgin of Guadalupe, the patron saint of Mexico. Falicov (1998, p. 146) describes her as "the perfect fusion of indigenous Aztec and Catholic European elements, the only brown-skinned virgin who validates the promise of Catholicism for indigenous persons [throughout Latin America]. In fact the Virgin of Guadalupe has many Indian names."

Most Latinos embrace familism, or pride and closeness in their families. Familism is generally seen as a good thing, as extended families provide support throughout an individual's lifetime. On the other hand, it may have the negative effect of discouraging youths from taking advantage of opportunities that would separate them from their families (Schaefer, 2012, p. 252). Hispanics, including Mexican Americans, more frequently live in extended families than non-Hispanic whites (Cherlin, 2013). These households are likely to include brothers, sisters, or cousins of the household head, and also members of the generation preceding the household head.

Latino immigrants contribute much to the U.S. economy (Maciel & Herrera-Sobek, 1998). Undocumented workers in particular take jobs that are unattractive to most American citizens (Portes & Rumbaut, 2006). Their work is critical to American agriculture and they also contribute to the construction, meatpacking, restaurant, and textile industries. The American rich probably benefit the most from Latino immigration through the services of underpaid gardeners, maids, cooks, and nannies. Undocumented Latino workers pay local (e.g., sales) and federal (e.g., FICA) taxes for which they will never claim any benefits (Maciel & Herrera-Sobek, 1998, p. 6).

Latinos have earned a reputation as employees who are hardworking and less likely to complain about poor working conditions or low wages than native-born workers (Engstrom, 2001). The commitment of Latinos to work differs from that of middle-class Anglos who are likely to be motivated by individual achievement. Latinos are more likely to toil because they firmly believe they have to for the survival and well-being of their children and other loved ones. On behalf of their families, they are willing to work overtime and/or "moonlight," and accept grueling, exploitative working conditions (Falicov, 1998, p. 124).

Like African American families, Latino families experienced a significant decline in wealth between 2007 and 2010 during the Great Recession. The average net wealth of white families decreased by 6.7 percent, while Latino families lost 41.3 percent of their net wealth (Sullivan, Ali, Perez De Alejo, Miller, & Baena, 2013). As of 2013, the average net worth of Latino families is only one-sixth that of white families.

Latinos in the United States routinely send remittances back to family members in their country of origin. Hispanic immigrants sent approximately $41 billion to Spanish-speaking Latin American countries in 2012; overall remittances to Mexico were estimated to total $22 billion in 2013 (Cohn, Gonzalez-Barrera, & Cuddington, 2013). Remittances are Mexico's third-largest source of income, after oil exports and tourism (Bada, 2003). According to the World Bank (2013), remittances to Latin America in 2011 amounted to more than eight times the total of foreign aid to the region. Nevertheless, the vast majority of Latinos' earnings are put back into the U.S. economy through the purchase of work-related expenses and living essentials.

Another way that Latino Americans support the towns and villages in their home countries is by creating and supporting *clubes de oriundos* (hometown clubs, or hometown associations [HTAs]) (Bada, 2003). "HTAs are developed from the social networks that migrants from the same town in Mexico maintain in their new U.S. communities. These groups raise monies to fund public works and social projects in communities in rural Mexico, as well as other Latin American countries" (Bada,

2003). There are about 3,000 hometown clubs in the United States (Schaefer, 2012).Although many think of Latinos as politically conservative, a recent Pew Center survey (Taylor et al., 2012a) found that whereas they generally oppose abortion (58 percent of immigrant Hispanics and 40 percent of second-generation immigrants), they support a larger government that provides more services rather than a smaller government with fewer services. A majority of Latinos say that homosexuality should be accepted.

Native Americans

In this text, we will use the term *Native Americans* to refer only to those indigenous peoples who are native to the North American continent. (Thus American Indians and Alaskan Natives are included, while Hawaiians, and natives of Guam and Samoa, who also are indigenous peoples, are covered under the Pacific Islander category.) Although some Native Americans prefer the term *American Indian* (Lewis, 1995), because of the many legitimate objections to its use (see Herring, 1999) we will use the former term. The term *First Nations* is widely used in Canada. They also use the term *aboriginal* to include First Nations; Inuit, who were formerly called "Eskimos"; and the Métis, who are descendants of European fur traders and settlers who married First Nations women (Aboriginal Affairs and Northern Development Canada [AANDC], 2014).

According to the U.S. federal Bureau of Indian Affairs (2014) there is no single federal or tribal criterion or standard that establishes a person's identity as American Indian or Alaska Native. The 2010 census defined American Indian or Alaska Native as "a person having origins in any of the original peoples of North and South America (including Central America) and who maintains tribal affiliation or community attachment" (Norris, Vines, & Hoeffel, 2012, p. 2). According to the 2010 census, there are 5.2 million American Indian and Alaska Native (reported alone or in combination with other races) residents in the United States (Norris et al., 2012).

At the time of their arrival in the Americas, European immigrants confronted hundreds of Native American tribes speaking over 700 different languages (Schaefer, 2012). Many of the indigenous cultures were quite advanced, incorporating agricultural practices such as irrigation and crop rotation, ceramic and metallurgical crafts, networks of roads and bridges, and democratic forms of governance. Because of a lack of natural immunity to European diseases, as well as the genocide perpetrated by European invaders, their numbers were reduced to about one-twentieth of the original population, yet more than 300 distinct Native American tribes survive in the lower forty-eight states and more than 200 in Alaska (Lewis, 1995).

According to the 2010 census (Norris et al., 2012), 20 percent of Native Americans and Alaskan natives reside on reservations and designated "American Indian areas" (e.g., trust lands). Native American and Alaska Native populations were highly concentrated in Oklahoma, the upper Midwest, the "four corners" area of the Southwest (where Arizona, Colorado, New Mexico, and Utah meet), and in Alaska. Significant reservation populations include the 169,321 Native Americans on the Navajo Nation reservation (in Arizona, New Mexico, and Utah), and the 16,906 on the Pine Ridge reservation (in South Dakota and Nebraska). The states with the highest proportion of Native American citizens are Alaska (14.8 percent), New Mexico (9.4 percent), South Dakota (8.8 percent), Oklahoma (8.6 percent), Montana (6.3 percent), North Dakota (5.4 percent) and Arizona (4.6 percent). Cities with significant Native American populations include Anchorage, Alaska (with 12.4 percent), Billings, Montana (6.0 percent), Albuquerque, New Mexico (6.0 percent), and Tulsa (9.2 percent), Norman (8.1 percent), and Oklahoma City (6.3 percent) in Oklahoma. Outside of Alaska, Native Americans can be considered an "invisible" minority because they are concentrated in so few states and because many live on reservations (Norris et al., 2012).

According to the 2010 U.S. Census (Norris, Vines, & Hoeffel, 2012), the largest tribes are the Navajo (with 287,000 individuals who identified with one tribal grouping and no other race) and the Cherokee (284,000 individuals). For the Cherokee, if one counts tribal grouping alone or in any combination, the population is above 800,000; for the Navajo the number rises above 332,000.

According to the Aboriginal Affairs and Northern Development Canada office (AANDC, 2014), there were 1,836,035 aboriginals living in Canada in 2011, or 5.6 percent of the population. There were 617 First

Nation communities spread across the provinces and territories, with the largest numbers in Ontario and British Columbia.

After legal victories in the 1960s, Native Americans gained some control over reservation lands in the United States. Beginning in the middle 1970s and into the 1980s, reservation Indians took advantage of their legal status as "domestic dependent nations" to open gaming (gambling) halls and casinos. Indian gaming operates in twenty-eight states.

According to the National Indian Gaming Commission, as reported by the 500 Nations (2012), tribes receive $4 of every $10 that Americans wager at casinos (and 44 percent of all U.S. casino gaming revenue). Another $3.3 billion was earned in restaurants, hotels, and entertainment services. Indian gaming provides 628,000 jobs nationwide (both direct and indirect jobs). Especially for those casinos located near other tourist attractions or major population centers, this economic endeavor provides cash income to support schools, housing, day-care centers, health clinics, community recreation centers, nursing homes, industrial parks, convenience stores, museums, and hotels (Bartlett & Steele, 2002; Kehoe, 1999; C. Wilson, 2013). While the majority of Native Americans continue to live in poverty, profits from casinos are going to many non-Indian investors, including foreigners. Only a quarter of gaming tribes distribute cash directly to their members, and most members receive no more than a few thousand dollars each (Bartlett & Steele, 2002).

Although tourism and the sale of crafts are important sources of employment on many reservations, they do not improve the tribal economy significantly (Schaefer, 2012). Many Native Americans also work for the government, especially in the Bureau of Indian Affairs, but also in state and local governments and for the military.

Native Americans are the most disadvantaged minority in the United States. They rank behind others in income, employment, housing, nutrition, and health, and ahead of others in alcoholism, school dropout rates, infant mortality, delinquency, and mental illness (Andersen & Taylor, 2013). In 2011 more than one in four (26.4 percent) American Indians and Native Alaskans lived in poverty (Austin, 2013b). In the first half of 2013, the rate of unemployment for Native Americans was 11.3 percent; it was highest in the Midwest (16.8 percent) and Northern Plains (15.0 percent) (Austin, 2013a). Even if factors such as age, sex, education level, marital status, and state of residence are controlled, the odds of their being employed are 31 percent lower than that of whites (Austin, 2013a). High educational attainment is the factor most likely to increase Native Americans' odds of securing employment.

According to a press release from the United States Senate Committee on Indian Affairs ("Senate Committee on Indian Affairs Approves Reauthorization of Key Tribal Housing Bill," 2013), approximately 90,000 Native American families are homeless or inadequately housed. While they make up less than one percent of the general population they comprise 8 percent of the country's homeless. Almost half (46 percent) of Native American households are overcrowded and a quarter (25 percent) lack adequate plumbing and kitchen facilities.

Native Americans are a heterogeneous population. They vary in terms of their language, residence (rural, urban, reservation), level of acculturation, and socioeconomic status (Herring, 1999). Even though there are differences among tribes, including the degree of acculturation to the mainstream, there are some common characteristics of most Native American cultures. For example, Native Americans, like many other minorities, take a more collective view of society than the white middle-class mainstream culture. This includes emphasis on the importance of the family, group primacy, and noncompetitiveness. Individual achievement is not valued. Other important Native American values include sharing, cooperation, noninterference, harmony with nature, a present (and cyclical rather than linear) time orientation, and a deep respect for elders (Herring, 1999, p. 72).

Although many Native Americans have been converted to Christianity, many continue to embrace elements of their traditional religions as well (see chapter 4). Native American groups have tried without success to limit tourist access to numerous sacred sites that are located on public lands, such as the Grand Canyon, Zion, and Canyonlands National Parks.

According to the Department of Defense (U.S. Department of Defense, n.d.), American Indians have participated with distinction in United States military actions for more than 200 years. More than 44,000 Native Americans, out of a total population of less than 350,000, served in both the European and Pacific theaters during World War II. Hundreds of members of the Navajo tribe were employed as "code talkers" for the military in the Pacific to provide secure communication (Naval History and Heritage Command, n.d.). The code talkers' primary responsibilities were to transmit information on tactics and troop movements, orders, and other vital battlefield communications over telephones and radios. The Japanese were never able to crack the code. More than 40,000 Native Americans left their reservations to work in war-related industries and they invested more than $50 million in war bonds (U.S. Department of Defense, n.d.).

Native Americans, like other minority groups, are reasserting pride in their ancestry. This is reflected in a surge in self-identified membership (almost quadrupling between the 1960 census and the 1990 census) and interest in restoring native languages to daily use (Kehoe, 1999). Although it has meant the loss of better-educated Indians from the reservations, the movement of Native Americans to urban areas has contributed to the development of intertribal networks. Pan-Indianism refers to intertribal social movements in which several tribes unite in common identity (Schaefer, 2012, p. 157). Powwows, featuring dancing, singing, and competitions, are organized events that celebrate Native American culture and educate the general public (Parfit, 1994). On the other hand, despite the attractiveness of pan-Indianism, many Native Americans resist movement toward a common identity in favor of primary identification with their own tribes (Schaefer, 2012).

White Ethnics and Jews

The term *white ethnics* refers to immigrants from Europe whose language and culture have differed from white Anglo-Saxon Protestants. About half of the U.S. population falls in this category, although many of the earlier arrivals have intermarried and now describe themselves as having a mix of ethnic/national backgrounds—or simply as "white" or "American."

Many early European immigrants (the Dutch, Germans, Scandinavians, and Scots-Irish) spread out across the frontier and became farmers and landowners. Later immigrants were more likely to stay in large cities on the East Coast and in the Midwest, where the first generation or two remained in ethnic enclaves with people from similar backgrounds. There are still high concentrations of Poles in the Chicago and the Milwaukee areas, for example (Pacyga, 1999). The country experienced a surge of immigration from Europe between 1880 and 1914. Immigrants comprised 40 percent of the population of the twelve largest cities in the country, and another 20 percent were second-generation descendants; 60 percent of the industrial labor force was foreign-born (Brody, 1980). Living conditions were abysmal: wages were below subsistence level, working conditions were hazardous, crowded tenements were firetraps, and food poisoning was common (Jansson, 2012). Even with the movement of white ethnics to the suburbs, full assimilation into the mainstream culture was curtailed by the revival of ethnic pride in the 1970s (Radzilowski & Radzilowski, 1999). On the other hand, Schaefer (2012) reports that the ethnicity currently embraced by English-speaking whites is typically symbolic. Symbolic ethnicity does not influence what people do or say, or whom they befriend or marry. It may, in fact, be more a result of experiences in the United States than practices brought from the home country. Some "ethnic" foods and "ethnic" celebrations actually began in the United States. Participating in boisterous St. Patrick's Day parades and drinking green beer, for example, is not how March 17 is observed in Ireland.

Jews are considered by some sociologists to be another white ethnic minority group. They entered America in several waves, beginning before the Revolution, peaking with the immigration of German Jews between the 1820s and 1870s, and again with Jews from Poland, Russia, Romania, and other parts of eastern Europe between 1880 and 1924 (Shapiro, 1999). Despite a long history of anti-Semitism in Europe, most Jews who migrated to the United States came voluntarily until the early 1930s when the tyranny of the Third Reich in Germany drove many from Germany, Austria, Poland, and Hungary (Schaefer, 2012). Another wave of immigration, particularly from Eastern Europe, occurred after World War II. In the 1960s and 1970s, many Jews came from Israel, the Soviet Union, and Iran. From the beginning, Jewish immigrants settled in eastern port cities, including Newport, Philadelphia, Charleston, and Savannah. In the early twentieth century, approximately half of America's Jews lived in New York City (Shapiro, 1999). Currently, the United States ranks second (behind Israel) among nations in the number of Jewish citizens, accounting for 39 percent of the world's Jewish population (Schaefer, 2012). Based on an aggregate of sample community surveys, Jewish organizations estimate that there were 6.7 million American Jews in 2012, with the largest number living in New York (Dashefsky, DellaPergola, & Sheskin, 2013).

There are three major divisions of Jews in the United States: Orthodox (the most traditional), Conservative, and Reform (the most liberal).
Differences are reflected in how traditional rituals are accepted and practiced. Many Jews tend to identify themselves as a cultural or ethnic minority rather than as a religious one (Lipset & Raab, 1995). They express
their identity through a variety of political, cultural, and social activities.
For observant Jews, acts of fasting, eating only permitted foods, and the
study of the Torah and the Talmud assume more importance.

The acculturation pattern of Jews has been an exception to the general
American pattern of success partnering with conservative political values.
Although on the whole Jews are prosperous, they are politically liberal
rather than conservative (Chanes, 2008; Shapiro, 1999). This political orientation may derive from their own long history of oppression that leads
them to empathize with other disadvantaged groups. Another explanation
is the Jewish religious principle of *tzedekah*, the obligation of the fortunate to help individuals and communities in difficulty (Chanes, 2008).

The tendency of young Jews to marry outside their faith community
(at a rate of about half of all marriages) and the reluctance of their non-
Jewish partners to convert are contributing factors to the numeric decline
of this ethnic group; this trend is also hastened by low fertility rates (Wertheimer, 2005). One major exception to the general rule are Orthodox
Jews who experience many fewer losses from intermarriage, and also
have fertility rates far above the Jewish—and overall American—norm.
Almost all children whose parents are both Jews are being raised Jewish,
compared to one-third of the children who have only one Jewish parent.
For children raised in families where there has been intermarriage, almost
three-quarters grow up to marry non-Jews themselves, and only 4 percent
of these bring up their own children as Jews (Wertheimer, 2005).

Jewish sense of family, community, and heritage remains strong.
According to Chanes (2008), Jews connect to their community, traditions,
and other Jews in a variety of ways. Most Jews participate in selected
holidays and forms of cultural involvement, maintain strong social connections to other Jews, and regard being Jewish as very important.
Smaller proportions of Jews—ranging from a quarter to a half—are vari-
ously engaged in other aspects of Jewish life as well, such as synagogue
affiliation, charitable giving, volunteering, and many ritual observances.

Today a greater proportion of Jewish children attend Jewish day schools than ever before, and a greater proportion of Jewish college and graduate students take Jewish studies courses than in earlier years.

UNDERSTANDING RACIAL AND ETHNIC INEQUITY

Discrimination against minorities is no longer legal in this country. While overt expressions of blatant racial and ethnic prejudice diminished considerably in the last half of the twentieth century, prejudice has not disappeared. Modern prejudice is more subtle, more diplomatic, less conscious (Myers, 2012). It may be that people have learned when and where prejudicial talk is not acceptable.

Myers (1999) summarizes how social psychologists explain prejudice using social identity theory. A number of experiments have supported the basic assumptions of this theory: (1) we find it useful to put people into categories, (2) we associate ourselves with certain groups (in-groups), and (3) we compare our group to other groups (out-groups) with a built-in bias favoring our own group. When resources are scarce and people feel insecure and frustrated, prejudice and discrimination toward out-groups is more common. Members of out-groups may be scapegoated for negative social and economic conditions over which they have no control, because it is safer to blame them than to confront people in power.

Functionalist Perspective

Functionalists believe that society works smoothly when everyone shares the same culture. Particularly in times of scarcity or external threat, a sense of "we-ness" (in-group membership) promotes social solidarity. Functionalists therefore are apt to support strict limits on immigration and encourage minorities to pursue cultural assimilation. That is, they encourage minorities to adopt the dominant group's language, values, and norms and stifle their own.

The functionalist perspective emphasizes how the parts of society are structured to maintain its stability. Schaefer (2012, p. 16) notes that, from a functionalist point of view, racist ideologies provide a moral justification for maintaining a society that routinely deprives certain groups of their rights; racist oppression discourages subordinate people from questioning their lowly status; racist myths encourage support for the existing order; and racist beliefs relieve the dominant group from having to address the economic and educational problems faced by subordinate groups.

Conflict Perspective

The conflict perspective often is used to examine relationships among racial and ethnic groups because it readily accounts for the presence of tensions and competition (Schaefer, 2012, p. 17). Conflict theorists argue that powerful people use prejudice and discrimination to hold onto their status in society by exploiting minorities. This is especially true in economic arenas. Elites benefit when inter-group racial or ethnic prejudices keep non-elites from recognizing the interests they share in common. Capitalists exploit racial and ethnic strife to produce a split labor market, that is, workers are divided by race and ethnicity across job statuses (Bonacich, 1972; Henslin, 2014; Roediger, 2002). For example, in some places, higher status (and cleaner) jobs such as driving trucks or other pieces of equipment, are reserved for whites, while people of color pick up the trash, spread the asphalt, or shovel the dirt. There is an implied threat, held over the heads of white workers, that should they strike, minority workers would be called upon to fill their positions. The consequence, according to conflict theorists, is that the working class is divided, and white workers perceive the source of their insecurity in minority workers rather than in the capitalist owners of the company (Henslin, 2014).

Portraying the problems of racial and ethnic minorities as their fault rather than recognizing the role of the dominant majority in developing and/or maintaining the system is sometimes listed as an example of blaming the victim (Ryan, 1976). Conflict theorists remind policy makers that the ultimate responsibility for social problems must rest with those who possess the power and authority to change them (Myrdal, 1944; Southern, 1987).

Some conflict theorists also are concerned about the role of wealthy countries in promoting a brain drain, or the immigration of well-educated skilled technicians and professionals away from their homes in developing nations where their talents are needed. For example, 42 percent of Asian Indians age 25 and older in the United States have postgraduate degrees while only 20 percent of Indians in India have graduated from high school; 27 percent of Nigerians age 25 and older in the United States have postgraduate degrees but 39 percent of Nigerians over the age of 15 in Nigeria are illiterate (Mehta, 2014). The percentage of physicians recruited from abroad ranges between 21 to 34 percent of the total number of doctors in the United States and countries in the British Commonwealth (Shah, 2006). Wu (2002) notes the high proportion of health care professionals among Asian and South Asian immigrants. In addition, when immigrants from other countries are recruited to fill prestigious and financially rewarding positions in America, the United States can continue to ignore native-born members of subordinate groups who could be trained to enter these fields (Schaefer, 2012).

Constructionist Perspective

Our discussion about the difficulty of defining *race* should make clear the role of social construction in race and ethnic relations. Constructionists focus on how labels produce prejudice. Labels lead to selective perception or filtering; that is, they cause people to pay attention to certain things and ignore others (Henslin, 2014). For instance, if you believe that all Asian American students are good at math, you may fail to take note of one who excels in art.

"Racial and ethnic labels are especially powerful. They are shorthand for emotionally-laden stereotypes. The term *nigger*, for example, is not neutral" (Henslin, 2014, p. 335). Neither is "honky," "chink," "spic," "kike," or "wetback." (Scornful terms are also applied to other minority groups: "slut," "fag," "dike," "cripple," and "retard" are examples of other hurtful labels.) Such words arouse powerful emotions and get in the way of rational discourse. Even terms that are intended to promote team identity and pride among fans, such as the Washington Redskins or the Atlanta Braves or the Florida State University Seminoles, are often considered offensive by Native Americans.

Constructionists stress that people are not born with prejudices. Instead children are socialized to be prejudiced through interaction with others, particularly those who hold strong prejudices themselves (Southern Poverty Law Center, 1995). Americans live in a society where racial and ethnic stereotypes abound.

AMERICAN SOCIETY AND EXPERIENCES OF RACIAL AND ETHNIC INEQUITY

All racial and ethnic minorities have been victims of discrimination and oppression at some time in American history. This continues today, most notably in underrepresentation in elective office, discrimination in housing and employment, lack of access to medical care, overrepresentation in the criminal justice system, and everyday hassles. Historically, the experiences of minority groups may have been different but all suffered tremendously. Social cohesion within these populations, including the development of mutual aid organizations and advocacy groups, has greatly facilitated their advancement in American society. The populations are presented below, roughly in chronological order in relation to when they arrived in North America.

The Experience of Native Americans

Although the United States never had an official policy of deliberate extermination of Native Americans, use of the term *genocide* is not inappropriate in describing the actions of many white settlers (invaders) and their government that decimated the populations of indigenous people on the North American continent. The nature of the violence perpetrated against Native Americans (see Bordewich, 1996) as well as the total disregard for human life might bring one to question which people were more deserving of the label "savage." The U.S. government broke treaty after treaty as it forced Indian nations to move westward to clear land for white settlers. Over half of the Cherokee Nation (4,000 individuals) died on the Trail of Tears, the path of their forced removal from the southeastern United States to Indian Territory (Oklahoma). Native Americans were not granted U.S. citizenship until 1924 and could not vote in Arizona or New Mexico until 1948. Until 1930, Native American children were separated from their families and sent to special Indian boarding schools where they were forced to wear Anglo-style clothing and punished when they used their native languages. Many schools serving Native American children today fail to meet their needs; there are few Native American teachers and the curriculum is presented from a Euro-American perspective. *Internal colonialism* is the term used to describe treatment of subordinate groups like colonial subjects by those in power (Henslin, 2014; Kendall, 2013). In the last several decades, however, many federally recognized tribes have established Native American studies and language retention programs and tribal schools and universities on their reservations.

A bit more than 2 percent of the landmass of the United States is designated as reservations or trust lands. Reservations range in size from less than 100 acres to the 16 million acres of the Navajo reservation that covers parts of Arizona, Utah, and New Mexico (Snipp, 1999). Historically, reservations have been marked by severe economic distress. Although the federal government has always encouraged Indians to support themselves through agriculture, less than 1 percent of all reservations lands is highly productive farmland (Snipp, 1999). Native Americans living on reservations experience poor health, unmet medical needs, and high rates of crime; many children never attend school or drop out of school (Schaefer, 2012). According to the Centers for Disease Control (2012), in 2007 American Indian and Alaska Native populations (combined) had the highest rate of motor vehicle–related deaths, one of the highest rates of suicide, and the second-highest death rate due to drugs (includes illicit, prescription, and over-the-counter) compared with other racial/ethnic populations. In 2009, they were among those with the highest prevalence of smoking and binge drinking.

The Experience of African Americans

Between 1619 and the 1860s, more than 500,000 Africans were brought to America as slaves (Kendall, 2013). At the beginning of the Civil War, only 10 percent of blacks in America were free (Walker, 1999). Although not all slaves were brutally treated, most lived under barely subsistence conditions, and it was not uncommon to separate slave families at the auction block. The slave family had no standing in law; marriages between slaves were not legally recognized. Slave codes, laws developed to restrict the rights of slaves, varied from state to state, but there were common themes (Schaefer, 2012, p. 177). For example, it was against the law to teach slaves to read or to give them books, including the Bible. Slaves could not buy or sell anything except by special arrangement. Slaves could not testify in court except against another slave. Slaves could not leave their owners' property without a pass indicating destination and expected time of return. Violators of slave codes were whipped, mutilated, or killed. Female slaves were routinely raped by their masters.

Slavery ended in the South with the Emancipation Proclamation in 1863. The Thirteenth Amendment to the Constitution, ratified in 1865, permanently abolished slavery and the Fourteenth Amendment, ratified in 1868, further protected the rights of former slaves. Nevertheless, African Americans soon lost ground. In 1896, the Supreme Court ruled in Plessy v. Ferguson that "separate but equal" treatment was acceptable. Jim Crow laws in the South enforced segregation in housing, employment, education, and all public accommodations and severely limited independent African American economic initiatives. Lynching (executing someone without a legal trial, usually by hanging) was a mechanism of terror used to keep black citizens from challenging the status quo. There may have been as many as 6,000 lynchings in this country between 1892 and 1921 (Feagin & Feagin, 2012). Another mode of control was arbitrary arrest and imprisonment; often black convicts were used to provide free labor for both public and private enterprises. African Americans were denied the right to vote through a series of quasi-legal obstacles, such as poll taxes and literacy tests.

Even when they were treated as noncitizens or second-class citizens, African Americans have always participated in the defense of this country. The first casualty of the American Revolution was a black man, Crispus Attucks. Five thousand African Americans served continuously during the Revolutionary War; African Americans made up 10 percent of the Union forces and 25 percent of the Union Navy in the Civil War and some 500,000 African Americans served overseas in World War II. African Americans in the U.S. military were assigned to segregated units until the middle of the twentieth century.

In 1954 in Brown v. Board of Education, the Supreme Court voted unanimously that "separate but equal" was unconstitutional under the

Fourteenth Amendment. The following year, blacks in Montgomery, Alabama, launched a boycott against that city's segregated bus system, led by Dr. Martin Luther King, Jr., a key event in the Civil Rights Movement in the United States. Some of the organizations involved were the NAACP, CORE (Congress of Racial Equality), and the SCLC (Southern Christian Leadership Conference). They were supported, in turn, by African American churches and black colleges. Churches provided leadership and opportunities for recruitment of new participants, and added the fervor and conviction of the faith community. The collective identity of the African American community, born of centuries of oppression, was melded with the ideals of social justice—values that invited solidarity with whites and non-Christians alike. Because they were denied conventional access to political power through the vote, black participants in the Civil Rights Movement were forced to rely on unconventional means, such as protests. Largely in response to the massive demonstrations, marches, sit-ins, and boycotts that followed, Congress passed the Civil Rights Act of 1964, the most far-reaching legislation to protect the rights of African Americans since the abolition of slavery.

Although legally protected from discrimination, African Americans still suffer from the effects of prejudice. Examples of mistreatment include the deliberate burning of African American churches and racial profiling (individuals targeted for unfair treatment by law enforcement personnel because of the color of their skin). As noted in chapter 4, African Americans receive less adequate medical care than do whites. Some argue that stress resulting from racism and suppressed hostility exacerbates hypertension (high blood pressure) among African Americans, a critical factor in higher mortality rates from heart disease, kidney disease, and stroke (Schaefer, 2012).

Polling shows that many Americans do believe racial discrimination in housing is a thing of the past (Dewan, 2013). Forty years ago, black renters were frequently denied access to advertised units that were available to equally qualified whites. This kind of "door slamming" discrimination had declined dramatically by 1989 and has continued to decline since. Nevertheless, a recent study commissioned by the U.S. Department of Housing and Urban Development (Turner et al., 2013) found that home buyers who were African American or Asian American were shown fewer homes than whites with the same qualifications. The same study found that for individuals who wanted to rent, those whose ethnicity was more readily identifiable experienced more discrimination than those who might pass as white. There were no substantial differences in the level of discrimination across regions of the country, suggesting that housing discrimination remains a national problem.

When elected to office, African Americans serve predominantly black districts and communities; they hold a disproportionately small share of elective and appointive offices in the United States. For many citizens, the election of an African American president in 2008 marked the beginning of a new era in American politics. Nevertheless, although Obama was born in Hawaii to a U.S. citizen, some high-profile critics questioned his eligibility for office and continued to portray him as less than fully American (see chapter 2).

The Experience of Asian Americans

More than 300,000 Chinese migrated to California between 1850 and 1880, where most performed manual labor for the railroads, and for farmers and miners (Yung, 1999). As "aliens" and persons of color, they had no legal rights and could not become citizens. They were often the target of mob violence—beaten, burned, shot, and lynched (Yung, 1999; Wu, 2002). In the worst of the confrontations, 200 armed white mine workers in Rock Springs, Wyoming, drove out 600 Chinese mine workers, killing twenty-eight of them; all of the whites were acquitted in subsequent trials (Reimers, 2005). Racism, and fears on the part of white laborers that they would lose their jobs to Asian immigrants led to the passage of the Chinese Exclusion Act in 1882 (Andersen & Taylor, 2013; Yung, 1999). This legislation was repealed in 1943, probably because the Chinese were American allies in World War II.

The need for cheap laborers was soon filled with Japanese immigrants, who began coming to the West Coast somewhat later than the Chinese. As they became more successful, they faced similar legal restrictions on their rights. California passed legislation (the Alien Land Laws) in 1913 and 1920 that prohibited Japanese residents from purchasing land (Jansson, 2012). In 1922, the U.S. Supreme Court ruled that foreign-born

Japanese could not become American citizens because they were not Caucasians.

Early in World War II, Japanese Americans, including many who were born in this country, were rounded up and moved to ten internment camps located in remote rural areas in seven states, taking only what they could carry with them (Tamura, 1999). All people on the West Coast of at least one-eighth Japanese ancestry were taken to assembly centers for transfer to evacuation camps; two-thirds of the evacuees were U.S. citizens (Schaefer, 2012). This has been described as "one of the most vicious forms of discrimination ever sanctioned by U.S. laws" (Kendall, 2013, p. 302). Italian Americans and German Americans faced no similar persecution, even though the United States was at war with Germany and Italy as well as Japan. After a Japanese American challenged the constitutionality of the process, the U.S. Supreme Court ruled the detainment unconstitutional on December 18, 1944 (Schaefer, 2012). The last Japanese internment camps were closed in 1946. Four decades passed before the American government issued an apology to those Japanese Americans and their descendants and paid $20,000 to each internment camp survivor, beginning in 1990 (Takaki, 1993).

Asian Americans remain underrepresented in politics, far below the level for blacks and Latinos, but their influence is growing with their overall increase in population numbers and the proportion with citizenship status. Hawaii, where Asian Americans make up the majority of voters, has elected Asian American governors and U.S. senators. Daniel Inouye, a decorated World War II combat veteran, served almost fifty years as a U.S. senator from Hawaii. A Japanese American, he was the highest-ranking Asian American politician in U.S. history. Gary Locke, a Chinese American, was governor of Washington from 1997 to 2005 and Piyush "Bobby" Jindal, an Indian American, was elected governor of Louisiana in 2007 after serving in the U.S. House of Representatives. Nimrata Nikki Haley, another Indian American, was elected governor of South Carolina in 2010. (There has been just one other person of color elected governor of a Southern state—Douglas Wilder of Virginia.)

Although in comparison to other groups, Asian Americans appear to be doing well financially, there are several arguments that this is not an accurate reflection of their true economic status. They are concentrated in large cities such as San Francisco, Los Angeles, New York, and Honolulu, where living expenses are much higher than in the rest of the country on average. Asian Americans live in larger households than do white Americans and a slightly higher proportion of Asian American women work outside the home compared with white women. It is not fair to compare the household family income of an Asian American family which may pool the wages of a husband, wife, grandparent, child, and cousin with a white household with a similar income derived from the work of just one family member (Wu, 2002). Asian Americans are also more likely to be self-employed than white Americans; they put in longer hours and have fewer benefits than employees of large companies (Wu, 2002).

Evidence that Indian Americans still struggle to be fully accepted in society was clear in the nasty racist comments that appeared on Twitter after Nina Davuluri won the Miss America crown in 2013 (Judkis, 2013). Even though she was born in Syracuse, New York, and attended the University of Michigan, some viewers mistakenly thought she was of Middle Eastern origin and labeled her Miss 7-11 (the convenience store), Miss Terrorist, and Miss Al Qaeda (Karim, 2013).

The Experience of Latinos/Latinas (Hispanic Americans)

Mexican immigrants were able to move freely across the U.S. border until 1924 when the Border Patrol was created. While many employers welcomed them, in many southwestern states racist sentiments prevailed. Public schools were segregated and Mexican barrio schools received less funding than schools serving white students (Reimers, 2005). Other public institutions were also segregated, often by "custom" rather than law. In Texas restaurants, movie theaters, and swimming pools either refused to accommodate Mexican immigrants or kept them separate from whites (Reimers, 2005).

During various times in the twentieth century the United States needed labor and many Mexicans have come to work in the fields and orchards, canneries, and meatpacking plants, performing tasks that did not appeal to locals. Living conditions for migrant workers were deplorable, and due to the racism and the power of landowners, attempts to unionize farmworkers failed (Reimers, 2005). Many years later, Cesar

Chavez successfully developed and led the United Farm Workers in the 1960s to demand legislation that would protect agricultural workers from work-related hazards, as well as promoting their right to unionize (Reimers, 2005). Nevertheless, across the nation, on-the-job deaths of foreign-born workers have been increasing and overall death rates for Latinos are consistently higher than those of white and African American workers (Phillips, 2008). (See chapter 9 for a discussion of injuries in the meat-packing industry where many Latinos are employed.)

According to the Federation for American Immigration Reform (FAIR) (2013), 75 percent of farm sales in the United States comes from just 5.7 percent of U.S. farms. These large-scale farming operations enjoyed a nearly 80 percent annual increase in profits between 1997 and 2007. American agribusiness employs more than a million people and half of these workers are undocumented immigrants, according to the Department of Agriculture (Gomez, 2013). The farming sector has grown increasingly dependent on a steady supply of undocumented workers over the past several decades (FAIR, 2013). Although there are an unlimited number of H2A visas for foreign agricultural guest workers, corporate farms organizations complain that the system is too expensive and too cumbersome to use (Gomez, 2013).

Increasing numbers of Spanish-speaking immigrants and their growing political, social, and cultural visibility has led to a resurgence of anti-Latino sentiment. This has been reflected in welfare reform legislation at both national and state levels that led to drastic cuts in benefits previously available to immigrants (Gutierrez, 1999). In 1996, Congress passed the Personal Responsibility and Work Opportunity Reconciliation Act, which gave states the option of ending Medicaid coverage for legal immigrants and excluding legal immigrants who had worked for less than ten years in the United States from SSI and SNAP (Food Stamp) eligibility (U.S. Department of Health and Human Services, 2011). Efforts to make English the "official language" of the country and many states were initiated in the early 1980s. As of 2008, there were twenty-six states with active "English-only" laws. Ironically, the vast majority of first-generation immigrants (from all countries) who come to the United States as children speak English well and English-only is the predominant pattern by the third generation, with the exception of American communities along the Mexican border and in areas of high ethnic density, such as among Cubans in Miami, where bilingualism is more common (Portes & Rumbaut, 2006, pp. 229–230).

According to the National Immigration Law Center (2011), the DREAM (Development, Relief, and Education for Alien Minors) Act is bipartisan legislation that would address the needs of an estimated 1.4 to 2 million young people who were brought illegally to the United States as children under the age of sixteen. It would provide a mechanism for them to apply for temporary legal status that would allow them to work, drive, and go to school, and eventually obtain permanent legal status. They would become eligible for U.S. citizenship if they went to college for at least two years or served in the U.S. military for at least two years (National Immigration Law Center, 2011). These young adults have lived in the United States for most of their lives and view themselves as Americans. As of early 2014, Congress had yet to pass comprehensive immigration reform legislation, which would include the DREAM Act and other provisions.

The Experience of White Ethnics and Jews

The National Origins Quota Act of 1924 established ethnic quotas allowing immigrants to enter the country only in proportion to their numbers already living in the United States. Thus ethnic groups who were already present in large numbers (i.e., people from northern and western Europe) were allowed to immigrate in greater numbers than were those from southern and eastern Europe (e.g., Italians, Poles, Czechs, Romanians, Lithuanians, and Greeks) (Andersen & Taylor, 2013). European immigrants coming through Ellis Island during this period were subjected to literacy tests and even IQ tests, given *in English*. Based on this clearly biased testing, more than three-quarters of eastern European Jews, Hungarians, and Italians were classified as "feeble-minded" (Kamin, 1974).

Although most were fair-skinned, immigrants from Ireland, Italy, Greece, Russia, and eastern Europe faced discrimination based on their religion (Catholicism, Eastern Orthodoxy, and Judaism). Strong anti-Catholic sentiment had already developed in the mid-nineteenth century when roughly one and one-half million Irish peasants immigrated to America to escape the 1845–1848 "potato famine" in their homeland. Mob violence directed against Catholic individuals and their property was common across the country between 1834 and 1854 (Schaefer, 2012). By the 1850s, nativism, especially in opposition to Roman Catholics, became an open political movement in America. Anglo-Americans believed they were being overrun and anti-Catholic, anti-Irish, and anti-immigrant sentiment often merged. Nevertheless, it was not until Congress put up barriers in the 1920s that the flow of immigrants from Europe diminished (Reimers, 2005).

Both Irish Americans and Italian Americans have been subjected to institutionalized discrimination in employment, with "swarthy" Italians being perceived as "not white" (Gambino, 1975; Sensi-Isolani, 1999). More than thirty Italians were lynched in the South between 1890 and 1910 (Sensi-Isolani, 1999). Anti-Catholic suspicion was clearly still an issue in the 1960 presidential election when John F. Kennedy ran for office.

The civil rights of Jews were affected by the "blue laws" enacted by states and cities forbidding a variety of activities on Sunday. (Jews celebrate the Sabbath from sundown Friday to sundown Saturday.) Eastern European Jews who immigrated in the early twentieth century were associated with Marxist politics and hence faced discrimination on that account. Jews were excluded from many premier colleges and universities, as well as clubs, hotels, and some residential neighborhoods, and they also faced discrimination in employment (Selzer, 1972). Prejudice and discrimination against Jewish people is called anti-Semitism. The most virulent and overt anti-Semitism in the United States occurred in the 1920s and 1930s. Well-known American leaders, such as Henry Ford and Charles Lindbergh, contributed to anti-Jewish sentiment by lending credence to fraudulent conspiracy theories (Schaefer, 2012).

In past centuries, Jews were often used as scapegoats and blamed for all kinds of problems, including plagues; at one time, they were expelled from the nations of Spain, France, and England. For nearly 2,000 years, various Christian groups argued that all Jews share in the responsibility of the Jewish elders who condemned Christ to death and used that to justify anti-Semitism. According to a recent national survey of Americans conducted by the Anti-Defamation League (2013), 26 percent of Americans believe that Jews were responsible for the death of Christ. In addition, much anti-Semitism is related to negative stereotypes of Jews as being overly clannish and financially shrewd (Wilson, 1996), and feeling more loyalty toward Israel than the United States (Anti-Defamation League, 2013). Between 14 and 24 percent of survey respondents believe that Jews have too much control on Wall Street, that Jews are "more willing to use shady practices" in their business dealings, that Jews have too much influence over the American news media, and that the movie and television industries are pretty much run by Jews.

The Holocaust refers to the state-sponsored systematic persecution and annihilation of Jews by Nazi Germany and its collaborators. Between 1933 and 1945, two-thirds of Europe's total Jewish population was killed, including 90 percent of the Jewish population of Germany, Austria, and Poland (Schaefer, 2012). Despite irrefutable evidence and the testimony of eyewitnesses and survivors, a very small but vocal group of people called Holocaust revisionists claim that the events of the Holocaust never happened.

Jews have been, and continue to be, targeted by the Ku Klux Klan and neo-Nazi skinheads. The Anti-Defamation League tracks reported anti-Semitic incidents, which include harassment, threats, assaults, and vandalism. A chilling recent development is the use of the Internet to spread hatred toward Jews. In spite of persistent discrimination, Jews have achieved substantial success in the areas of business, education, law, medicine, and the arts.

The Experience of More Recent Arrivals

Among the problems facing many immigrants and refugees in the United States today are language barriers, lack of employment opportunities and/or labor market exploitation, lack of educational attainment, lack of access to health care, racism, and religious intolerance. Those who lack immigration documents are particularly likely to experience problems.

Many Middle Eastern immigrants and American citizens of Middle Eastern descent experience unwarranted prejudice, suspicion, and discrimination (McCarus, 1994). More than a third of Arab Americans report that they or their family members experienced discrimination because of their ethnicity, both before and after the events of September 11, 2001 (Telhami, 2002). After the bombing of the Murray Federal Office Building in Oklahoma City in 1995, some media officials were quick to blame Muslim-Arab extremists, even though the perpetrators were soon identified as two American-born white men (Reimers, 2005). Soon after the tragedies of September 11, at least five individuals were killed just because they appeared to be Arab or Muslim (Ahmad, 2002). (Two of the victims were Sikh Indians, one was an Indian Hindu, one was Pakistani, and one was an Egyptian Coptic Christian). Another 1,000 physical and verbal attacks on Middle Easterners and South Asians were reported in a period of eight weeks.

During this period of strong anti-Muslim sentiment, Congress passed the Patriot Act of 2001. This law gave the government unprecedented powers with regards to detaining, denying entry, and searching immigrants (Brazeal, 2004) and was followed by acts of racial profiling of "Muslim-looking" individuals at airports, and the detention or deportation of immigrants from Muslim countries. The Department of Justice required that all foreign-born Muslim men report to the Bureau of Citizenship and Immigration Services. In a five-month period ending in 2003, 144,513 Muslim men from twenty-five countries were questioned and about 13,000 faced deportation; eventually only eleven remained in custody because of suspected terrorism (Schaefer, 2012).

Over the years and across the country, there has been widespread opposition to the building of new mosques. A professor of Islamic studies at the University of Kentucky told the *New York Times* (Goodstein, 2010), "What's different is the heat, the volume, the level of hostility. . . . it's different when [critics] say these mosques are going to be nurturing terrorist bombers, that Islam is invading, that civilization is being undermined by Muslims." A 2010 Pew Research Center Survey found 25 percent of respondents said that "local communities should be able to prohibit construction of mosques if they do not want them" (Pew Research Center, 2010). The *New York Times* (Goodstein, 2010) reported, however, that in each community where mosques were threatened, interfaith groups led by Protestant ministers, Catholic priests, and rabbis have stepped up to defend them. A two-year study conducted by Duke University's Sanford School of Public Policy and the University of North Carolina concluded that local mosques are actually a deterrent to the spread of militant Islam and terrorism. The study noted that many Muslim leaders invested significant efforts into countering extremism by building youth programs, sponsoring antiviolence forums, and scrutinizing teachers and texts. Radicalization of alienated Muslim youths is a real threat, the University of Kentucky professor said. "But the youth we worry about," he concluded, "are not the youth that come to the mosque."

Negative media portrayals of Arabs and Muslims and omissions or inaccuracies in history and social science texts in North American schools have contributed to perceptions of these peoples as inferior, uncultured, threatening, anti-American, anti-Christian, anti-Semitic, greedy, cruel, and barbaric (Banks, 1997; Muscati, 2002). After 9/11, some Americans felt hostile toward all people of Middle Eastern backgrounds; many people now are careful to draw distinctions between members of whole cultures and a small number of extremists. Nevertheless, a 2010 survey by the Pew Research Center for the People & the Press and the Pew Forum on Religion & Public Life found "that far less than half (30 percent) of respondents said they had a favorable opinion of Islam while slightly more (38 percent) had an unfavorable view."

LOOKING AHEAD

While members of ethnic and racial minorities often grow up in supportive communities, members of other minority populations do not have that advantage. In chapter 7, we will examine the experiences of women, sexual minorities, and persons with disabilities. Each of these populations has found ways to cope and succeed despite experiences of discrimination and oppression.

REFERENCES

500 Nations (2012). 2011 Indian gaming revenues increased 3%. Retrieved from http://500nations.com/news/Indian_Casinos/20120717.asp.

Aboriginal Affairs and Northern Development Canada (AANDC). (2014). *First Nations people in Canada*. Retrieved from http://www.aadnc-aandc.gc.ca/eng/1303134042666/1303134337338.

Adams, M. (2003). *Fire and Ice: The United States, Canada and the myth of converging values*. Toronto, Canada: Penguin Group.

Ahmad, M. (2002). Home insecurities: Racial violence the day after September 11. *Social Text, 20,* 101–115.

Anderson, M., & Taylor, H. (2013). *Sociology: The essentials* (7th ed.). Belmont, CA: Wadsworth.

Anti-Defamation League. (2013, October 28). *ADL poll: Anti-Semitic attitudes in America decline 3 percent.* Retrieved from http://www.adl.org/press-center/press-releases/anti-semitism-usa/adl-poll-anti-semitic-attitudes-america-decline-3-percent.html.

Arab American Institute. (2009). Arab Americans. Retrieved from http://www.aaiusa.org/arab-americans/22/demographics.

Arbesman, S. (2012, April 26). The invisible borders that define American culture. *The Atlantic Cities.* Retrieved from http://www.theatlanticcities.com/arts-and-lifestyle/2012/04/invisible-borders-define-american-culture.

Austin, A. (2013a). *High unemployment means Native Americans are still waiting for an economic recovery.* Economic Policy Institute. Retrieved from http://www.epi.org/publication/high-unemployment-means-native-americans/.

Austin, A. (2013b). *Native American and jobs.* Economic Policy Institute. Retrieved from http://www.epi.org/publication/bp370-native-americans-jobs.

Bada, X. (2003, September 2). Mexican hometown associations. Retrieved from http://www.pbs.org/pov/thesixthsection/special_mexican.php

Banks, J. A. (1997). Arab Americans: Concepts and materials. In J. A. Banks, *Teaching strategies for ethnic studies* (6th ed., pp. 489–510). Boston, MA: Allyn and Bacon.

Bartlett, D. L., & Steele, J. B. (2002, December 16). Indian casinos: Wheel of misfortune. *Time,* pp. 44–58.

Begley, S. (1995, February 13). Three is not enough: Surprising new lessons from the controversial science of race. *Newsweek,* pp. 67–69.

Berlin, I. (2010). *The making of African America: The four great migrations.* New York, NY: Viking.

Billingsley, C. A. (1992). *Climbing Jacob's ladder: The enduring legacy of African-American families.* New York, NY: Simon & Schuster.

Bishop, B. (2008). *The big sort: Why the clustering of like-minded America is tearing us apart.* New York, NY: Houghton Mifflin.

Bonacich, E. (1972). A theory of ethic antagonism: The split labor market. *The American Sociological Review, 37,* 547–549.

Bordewich, F. M. (1996). *Killing the white man's Indian: Reinventing Native Americans at the end of the twentieth century.* New York, NY: Doubleday.

Brazeal, J. Y. (2004). *Discrimination in the new millennium: Terrorizing Middle-Easterners, retraction of civil liberties, and the USA Patriot Act.* Retrieved from http://digitalcommons.law.msu.edu/king/43.

Brody, D. (1980). *Workers in industrial America: Essays on the twentieth-century struggle.* New York, NY: Oxford University Press.

Brown, A., & Lopez, M. H. (2013, August 29). *Mapping the Latino population, by state, county and city.* Retrieved from http://www.pewhispanic.org/2013/08/29/mapping-the-latino-population-by-state-county -and-city/.

Bureau of Indian Affairs. (2014). *Frequently asked questions.* Retrieved from http://www.bia.gov/faqs/index.htm.

Carothers, S. C. (1990). Catching sense: Learning from our mothers to be black and female. In F. Ginsberg & A. Lowenhaupt Tsing (Eds.), *Uncertain terms: Negotiating gender in American culture* (pp. 232–247). Boston, MA: Beacon Press.

Castex, G. M. (1994). Providing services to Hispanic/Latino populations: Profiles in diversity. *Social Work, 39,* 288–297.

Centers for Disease Control and Prevention. (2012, November 7). *American Indian and Alaska natives population.* Retrieved from http://www.cdc.gov/minorityhealth/populations/REMP/aian.html.

Chanes, J. (2008). *A primer on the American Jewish community* (3rd ed.). New York, NY: American Jewish Committee.

Cherlin, A. J. (2008). *Public and private families: An introduction.* New York, NY: McGraw-Hill.

Cherlin, A. J. (2013). *Public and private families: An introduction* (7th ed.). New York, NY: McGraw-Hill.

Chinni, D., & Gimpel, J. (2010). *Our patchwork nation: The surprising truth about the "real" America.* New York, NY: Gotham Books.

Close, E. (2000, September 18). What's white anyway? *Newsweek,* pp. 64–65.

Cohn, D., Gonzalez-Barrera, A., & Cuddington, B. (2013). *Remittances to Latin America recover—but not to Mexico: Remittance trends.* Pew Research Hispanic Trends Project. Retrieved from http://www.pewhispanic.org/2013/11/14/2-remittance-trends/.

Council on Social Work Education. (2008). *Educational policy and accreditation standards.* Alexandria, VA: Council on Social Work Education.

Cruikshank, M. (1992). *The gay and lesbian liberation movement.* New York, NY: Routledge.

Dashefsky, A., DellaPergola, S., & Sheskin, I. (2013). *Jewish population in the United States, 2012.* Mandell L. Berman Institute-North American Jewish Data Bank, University of Connecticut. Retrieved from www.jewishdatabank.org.

Dewan, S. (2013, June 11). Discrimination in housing against nonwhites persists quietly, U.S. study finds. *The New York Times.* Retrieved from http://www.nytimes.com/2013/06/12/business/economy/discrimination-in-housing-against-nonwhites-persists-quietly-us-study-finds.html?_r=0.

Dixon, P. B., & Rimmer, M. T. (2009). Restriction or legalization? *Measuring the economic benefits of immigration reform.* Cato Institute. Retrieved from http://www.cato.org/publications/trade-policy-analysis/restriction-or-legalization-measuring-economic-benefits-immigration-reform.

Eilperin, J. (2013, August 22). What's changed for African Americans since 1963, by the numbers. *The Washington Post.* Retrieved from http://www.washingtonpost.com/blogs/the-fix/wp/2013/08/22/whats-changed-for-african-americans-since-1963-by-the-numbers/.

Engstrom, J. D. (2001). Industry and immigration in Dalton, Georgia. In A. D. Murphy, C. Blanchard, & J. A. Hill (Eds.), *Latino workers in the contemporary South* (pp. 44–56). Athens, GA: University of Georgia Press.

Ennis, S. R., Rios-Vargas, M., & Albert, N. G. (2011, May). *The Hispanic population 2010.* U.S. Department of Commerce, U.S. Census Bureau. Retrieved from http://www.census.gov/prod/cen2010/briefs/c2010br-04.pdf.

Escott, P. D., & Goldfield, D. R. (1991). *The South for new southerners.* Chapel Hill, NC: University of North Carolina Press.

Ewalt, P., & Mokuau, N. (1996). Self-determination from a Pacific perspective. In P. L. Ewalt, M. Freeman, S. A. Kirk, & D. L. Poole (Eds.), *Multicultural issues in social work* (pp. 255–268). Washington, DC: NASW Press.

Falicov, C. J. (1998). *Latino families in therapy: A guide to multicultural practice.* New York, NY: Guilford Press.

Feagin, J. R., & Feagin, C. B. R. (2012). *Racial and ethnic relations* (9th ed.). Upper Saddle River, NJ: Prentice Hall.

Federation for American Immigration Reform. (2013). *Illegal immigration and agribusiness.* Retrieved from http://fair.thinkrootshq.com /publications/illegal-immigration-and-agribusiness .

Fontes, L. A. (2005). *Child abuse and culture: Working with diverse families.* New York, NY: Guilford Press.

Gallagher, C. A. (2013). Color-blind privilege: The social and political functions of erasing the color line in post-race America. In M. L. Andersen and P. H. Collins (Eds.), *Race, class and gender: An anthology* (8th ed., pp. 91–95). Belmont, CA: Wadsworth.

Gambino, R. (1975). *Blood of my blood.* New York, NY: Doubleday/ Anchor.

Garcia, A. (2013, April 3). *The facts on immigration today.* Retrieved from http://www.americanprogress.org/issues/immigration/report /2013/04 /03/59040/the-facts-on-immigration-today-3/.

Garreau, J. (1981). *The nine nations of North America.* Boston, MA: Houghton Mifflin.

Gilson, S. F., & DePoy, E. (2002). Theoretical approaches to disability content in social work education. *Journal of Social Work Education, 37,* 153–165.

Goffman, E. (1963). *Stigma: Notes on the management of spoiled identity.* Englewood Cliffs, NJ: Prentice Hall.

Gold, S. J. (1999). Southeast Asians. In E. R. Barkan (Ed.), *A nation of peoples: America's multicultural heritage* (pp. 505–519). Westport, CT: Greenwood Press.

Gomez, A. (2012, July 24). Hispanics, police at odds in Ala. *USA Today,* p. 3A.

Gomez, A. (2013, March 18). An immigration food fight. *USA Today,* pp. 1A, 2A.

Gonzalez-Barrera, A., & Lopez, M. H. (2013). *A demographic portrait of Mexican-origin Hispanics in the United States.* Pew Research Hispanic Center. Retrieved from http://www.pewhispanic.org/2013/05 /01/a-demographic-portrait-of-mexican-origin-hispanics.

Goodstein, L. (2010, August 7). Across nation, mosque projects meet opposition. *New York Times.* Retrieved from www.nytimes.com/2010 /08/08/us08mosque.html.

Gutierrez, D. G. (1999). Mexicans. In E. R. Barkan (Ed.), *A nation of peoples: A sourcebook on America's multicultural heritage* (pp. 373–390). Westport, CT: Greenwood Press.

Henslin, J. M. (2014). *Sociology: A down-to-earth approach* (12th ed.). Boston, MA: Pearson Education.

Herring, R. D. (1999). *Counseling with Native American Indians and Alaska natives: Strategies for helping professionals.* Thousand Oaks, CA: Sage.

Hersch, J. (2006, April 14). *Skin color and wages among new U.S. immigrants.* Cambridge, MA: Society of Labor Economists.

Hill, R. B. (1999). *The strengths of African American families: Twenty-five years later.* Lanham, MD: University Press of America.

Hixson, L., Hepler, B. B., & Kim, M. O. (2012, May). *The native Hawaiian and other Pacific Islander populations: 2010.* U.S. Department of Commerce, U.S. Census Bureau. Retrieved from http://www.census.gov/prod/cen2010/briefs/c2010br-12.pdf.

Ho, M. K. (1987). Family therapy with Asian/Americans. In M. K. Ho (Ed.), *Family therapy with ethnic minorities* (pp. 24–38). Beverly Hills, CA: Sage.

Hoeffel, E. M., Kastogi, S., Kim, M. O., & Shahid, H. (2012). *The Asian population: 2010.* U.S. Department of Commerce, U.S. Census Bureau. Retrieved from http://www.census.gov/prod/cen2010/briefs/c2010br-11.pdf.

Humes, K. R., Jones, N. A., & Ramirez, R. R. (2011). *Overview of race and Hispanic origin: 2010.* U.S. Department of Commerce, U.S. Census Bureau. Retrieved from http://www.census.gov/prod/cen2010/briefs/c2010br-02.pdf.

In newsrooms, some immigration terms are going out of style. (2013). National Public Radio. Retrieved from http://www.npr.org/templates/transcript/transcript.php?storyId = 182637402.

Institute on Taxation and Economic Policy. (2013). *Undocumented immigrants' state and local tax contributions.* Author. Retrieved from http://www.itep.org/immigration/.

International Rescue Committee. (n.d.). *Frequently asked questions about refugees and resettlement.* Author. Retrieved from http://www.rescue.org/frequently-asked-questions-about-refugees-and-resettlement.

Jansson, B. S. (2012). *The reluctant welfare state: Engaging history to advance social work practice in contemporary society* (7th ed.). Belmont, CA: Brooks/Cole

Judkis, M. (2013, September). Miss America fights post-pageant racism with a beauty queen's poise. *The Washington Post.* Retrieved from http://www.washingtonpost.com/lifestyle/style/miss-america-fights -post-pageant-racism-with-a-beauty-queens-poise/2013/09/22/.

Kamin, L. J. (1974). *The science and politics of IQ.* Potomac, MD: Lawrence Erlbaum.

Karim, R. (2013, October 22). Dark skin = un-American? *The Huffington Post.* Retrieved from http://www.huffingtonpost.com/reef-karim-do /dark-skin-unamerican_b_3958179.html.

Kehoe, A. B. (1999). American Indians. In E. R. Barkan (Ed.), *A nation of peoples: A sourcebook on American's multicultural heritage* (pp. 48–74). Westport, CT: Greenwood Press.

Kendall, D. (2013). *Sociology in our times* (9th ed.). Belmont, CA: Wadsworth, Cengage Learning.

Kincheloe, J., Steinberg, S., Rodriguez, N., & Chennault, R. (Eds). (1998). *White reign: Deploying whiteness in America.* New York, NY: St. Martin's Press.

Konrad, R. (2007, January 3). Immigrants behind 25 percent of startups. *Washington Post.* Retrieved from http://www.washingtonpost.com /wp-dyn/content/article/2007/01/03/AR200701030140 2.html.

La Brack, B. (1999). South Asians. In E. R. Barkan (Ed.), *A nation of peoples: America's multicultural heritage* (pp. 482–503). Westport, CT: Greenwood Press.

Lewis, R. G. (1995). American Indians. In R. L. Edwards et al. (Eds.), *Encyclopedia of social work* (19th ed., Vol. 1, pp. 216–225). Washington, DC: NASW Press.

Lipset, S. M., & Raab, E. (1995). *Jews and the new American scene.* Cambridge, MA: Harvard University Press.

Lukes, C. A., & Land, H. (1990). Biculturality and homosexuality. *Social Work, 35,* 155–161.

Lundquist, J. H. (2004, December). When race makes no difference: Marriage and the military. *Social Forces, 83*(2), 731–757.

Maciel, D. R., & Herrera-Sobek, M. (1998). Introduction. In D. R. Maciel & M. Herrera-Sobek (Eds.), *Culture across borders: Mexican immigration and popular culture* (pp. 3–26). Tuscon, AZ: University of Arizona Press.

Macionis, J. J. (2014). *Sociology* (15th ed.). Boston, MA: Pearson Education.

Martinez , J., & Velasco, G. (2012). *Politics, values, and religion.* Pew Research Hispanic Trends Project. Retrieved from http://pewhispanic .org/2012/04/04/v-politics-values-and-religion/.

Mazzucato, V., & Schans, D. (2011). Transnational families and the well-being of children: Conceptual and methodological challenges. *Journal of Marriage and the Family, 73*(4), 704–712.

McAdoo, H. P. (2007a). African American demographic images. In H. P. McAdoo, *Black families* (4th ed., pp. 157–171). Thousand Oaks, CA: Sage.

McAdoo, H. P. (2007b). *Black families* (4th ed.). Thousand Oaks, CA: Sage.

McAdoo, H. P. (2007c). Religion in African American families. In H. P. McAdoo, *Black families* (4th ed., pp. 97–100). Thousand Oaks, CA: Sage.

McCarus, E. (Ed.). (1994). *The development of Arab-American identity.* Ann Arbor, MI: University of Michigan Press.

McIntosh, P. (2001). White privilege and male privilege: A personal account of coming to see correspondences through work in Women's Studies. In M. Anderson & P. H. Collins (Eds.), *Race, class, and gender: An anthology* (pp. 95–105). Belmont, CA: Wadsworth Publishing.

Mehta, S. (2014, February 3). The "Tiger Mom" superiority complex. *Time*, pp. 35–39.

Min, P. G. (1990). Ethnicity: Concepts, theories and trends. In P. G. Min and R. Kim (Eds.), *Struggle for ethnic identity: Narratives by Asian American professionals* (pp. 16–46). Walnut Creek, CA: Altamira.

Min, P. G. (1995a). An overview of Asian Americans. In P. G. Min (Ed.), *Asian Americans: Contemporary trends and issues* (pp. 10–37). Thousand Oaks, CA: Sage.

Min, P. G. (1995b). Major issues relating to Asian American experiences. In P. G. Min (Ed.), *Asian Americans: Contemporary trends and issues* (pp. 38–57). Thousand Oaks, CA: Sage.

Mogelonsky, M. (1995, August). Asian-Indian Americans. *American Demographics, 17*, 32–39.

Mokuau, N., & Tauili'ili, P. (1992). Families with native Hawaiian and Pacific Island roots. In E. W. Lynch and M. J. Hanson (Eds.), *Developing cross-cultural competence* (pp. 301–318). Baltimore, MD: Paul H. Brookes.

Morin, R. (2006, October 18). Immigrants and the whiter-shade-of-pale bonus. *The Washington Post.* Retrieved from http://www.washington post.com.

Muscati, S. A. (2002). Arab/Muslim "otherness": The role of racial constructions in the Gulf War and the continuing crisis in Iraq. *Journal of Muslim Minority Affairs, 22*, 131–148.

Myers, D. (1999). *Social psychology* (6th ed.). Boston, MA: McGraw-Hill.

Myers, D. (2012). *Social psychology* (11th ed.). Boston, MA: McGraw-Hill.

Myrdal, G. (1944). *An American dilemma: The Negro problem and modern democracy.* New York, NY: Harper.

National Immigration Law Center. (2011, May). *DREAM act: Summary.* Retrieved from http://nilc.org/dreamsummary.html.

Naval History and Heritage Command. (n.d.). *Navajo code talkers: World War II fact sheet.* Retrieved from http://www.history.navy.mil/faqs /faq61-2.htm.

Nishi, S. M. (1995). Japanese Americans. In P. G. Min (Ed.), *Asian Americans: Contemporary trends and issues* (pp. 95–133). Thousand Oaks, CA: Sage.

Norris, T., Vines, P. L., & Hoeffel, E. M. (2012, January). *The American Indian and Alaska population: 2010.* Retrieved from http://www.cen sus.gov/prod/cen2010/briefs/c2010br-10.pdf.

Pacyga, D. A. (1999). Poles. In E. R. Barkan (Ed.), *A nation of peoples: A sourcebook on America's multicultural heritage* (pp. 428–445). Westport, CT: Greenwood Press.

Parfit, M. (1994, June). Powwows. *National Geographic*, pp. 85–113.

Passel, J. S., & Cohn, D. (2008). *Population projections.* Pew Research Hispanic Trends Project. Retrieved from http://www.pewhispanic .org/2008/02/11/ii-population-projections/.

Passel, J. S., Livingston, G., & Cohn, D., (2012). *Explaining why minority births now outnumber white births.* Pew Research and Social & Demographic Trends. Retrieved from http://www.pewsocialtrends .org/2012/05/17/explaining-why-minority-births-nowoutnumber -white-births.

Passel, J. S., & Taylor, P. (2010, August 11). *Immigrants, parenthood and fertility.* Pew Research Hispanic Trends Project. Retrieved from http:// www.pewhispanic.org/2010/08/11/ii-immigrants-parenthood-and -fertility/http://www.pewhispanic.org/2010/08/11/ii-immigrants-par enthood-and-fertility/.

Pew Research Center for the People and the Press. (2010). *Public remains conflicted over Islam.* Retrieved from http://www.pewforum.org /2010/24/public-remains-conflicted-over-islam/.

Pew Research and Social & Demographic Trends. (2010). *The return of the multi-generational family household.* Retrieved from http://www .pewsocialtrends.org/2010/03/18/the-return-of-the-multi-generation al-family-household.

Pew Research Center for the People & the Press. (2011). *Public favors tougher border controls and path to citizenship.* Retrieved from http://www.people-press.org/2011/02/24/public-favors-tougher-bor der-controls-a nd-path-to-citizenship/.

Phillips, N. (2008, June 6). SC first in on-job deaths of Hispanics. *The State* [Columbia, SC], p. A1.

Portes, A., & Rumbaut, R. G. (2006). *Immigrant America* (3rd ed.). Berkeley, CA: University of California Press.

Prigmore, C. S., & Atherton, C. R. (1986). *Social welfare policy: Analysis and formulation.* Lexington, MA: Heath.

Queralt, M. (1996). *The social environment and human behavior: A diversity perspective.* Boston, MA: Allyn and Bacon.

Radzilowski, T. C., & Radzilowski, J. (1999). East Europeans. In E. R. Barkan (Ed.), *A nation of peoples: A sourcebook on America's multi-cultural heritage* (pp. 174–199). Westport, CT: Greenwood Press.

Rasmussen, B. B., Klinenberg, E., Nexica, I. J., & Wray, M. (Eds.). (2001). *The making and unmaking of whiteness.* Durham, NC: Duke University Press.

Reimers, D. M. (2005). *Other immigrants: The global origins of the American people.* New York, NY: New York University Press.

Roediger, D. R. (2002). *Colored white: Transcending the racial past.* Berkeley, CA: University of California Press.

Ryan, W. (1976). *Blaming the victim.* New York, NY: Vintage.

Samhan, H. H. (1999). Not quite white: Race classification and the Arab-American experience. In M. S. Suleiman (Ed.), *Arabs in America: Building a new future* (pp. 209–226). Philadelphia, PA: Temple University Press.

Schaefer, R. T. (2008). *Racial and ethnic groups* (11th ed). Upper Saddle River, NJ: Prentice Hall.

Schaefer, R. T. (2012). *Racial and ethnic groups* (13th ed.). Boston, MA: Pearson Education.

Selzer, M. (1972). *"Kike"—Anti-Semitism in America.* New York, NY: Meridian.

Senate Committee on Indian Affairs approves reauthorization of key tribal housing bill. (2013). Retrieved from http://www.indian.senate .gov/news/press-release/senate-committee-indian-affairs-approves -reauthorization-key-tribal-housing-bill.

Sensi-Isolani, P. A. (1999). Italians. In E. R. Barkan (Ed.), *A nation of peoples: A sourcebook on America's multicultural heritage* (pp. 294–310). Westport, CT: Greenwood Press.

Sewell, H. (2009). *Working with ethnicity, race and culture in mental health: A handbook for practitioners.* Philadelphia, PA: Jessica Kingsley Publishers.

Shah, A. (2006, April 14). *Brain drain of workers from poor to rich countries.* Global Issues. Retrieved from http://www.globalissues.org /article/599/brain-drain-of-workers-from-poor-to-rich-countries.

Shapiro, E. S. (1999). Jews. In E. R. Barkan (Ed.), *A nation of peoples: America's multicultural heritage* (pp. 330–353). Westport, CT: Greenwood Press.

Smedley, A., & Smedley, D. (2005). Race as biology is fiction, racism as a social problem is real: Anthropological and historical perspectives on the social construction of race. *American Psychologist, 60,* 16–26.

Snipp, C. M. (1999). The first Americans. In N. R. Yetman (Ed.), *Majority and minority: The dynamics of race and ethnicity in American life* (6th ed., pp. 131–143). Boston, MA: Allyn & Bacon.

Southern, D. (1987). *Gunnar Myrdal and black-white relations.* Baton Rouge, LA: Louisiana State University.

Southern Poverty Law Center (1995, Spring). The ages of intolerance. In *Teaching Tolerance*, p. 27.

Suleiman, M. S. (1999). Introduction: The Arab immigrant experience. In M. S. Suleiman (Ed.), *Arabs in America: Building a new future* (pp. 1–21). Philadelphia, PA: Temple University Press.

Sullivan, S. (2013, July 15). Everything you need to know about "stand your ground" laws. *The Washington Post.* Retrieved from http://www .washingtonpost.com/blogs/the-fix/wp/2013/07/15/ everything-you -need-to-know-about-stand-your-ground-laws/.

Sullivan, T., Ali, M., Perez De Alejo, C., Miller, B., & Baena, N. (2013). *State of the dream: A long way from home.* United for a Fair Economy. Retrieved from http://faireconomy.org/sites/default/files/SOD 2013.pdf.

Swarns, R. L. (2003, July 20). U.S. a place of miracles for Somali refugees. *The New York Times.* Retrieved from http://www.nytimes.com /2003/07/20/us/us-a-place-of-miracles-for-somali-refugees.html.

Sweis, L., & Guay, A. (2007). Foreign-trained dentists licensed in the United States: Exploring their origins. *Journal of the American Dental Association, 138,* 219–224.

Takaki, R. (1993). *A different mirror: A history of multicultural America.* Boston, MA: Little, Brown.

Tamura, E. H. (1999). Japanese. In E. R. Barken (Ed.), *A nation of peoples: A sourcebook on America's multicultural heritage* (pp. 311–329). Westport, CT: Greenwood Press.

Taylor, P., Lopez, M. H., Martinez, J., Passel, J. S., & Motel, S. (2011). *Unauthorized immigrants: Length of residency, patterns of parenthood.* Pew Research Hispanic Trends Project. Retrieved from http:// www.pewhispanic.org/2011/12/01/unauthorized-immigrants-length -of-residency-patterns-of-parenthood/.

Taylor, P., Lopez, M. H., Martinez, J., & Velasco, G. (2012a, April 4). *Politics, values and religion.* Pew Research Hispanic Trends Project. Retrieved from http://www.pewhispanic.org/2012/04/04/v-politics -values-and-religion/.

Taylor, P., Lopez, M. H., Martinez, J., & Velasco, G. (2012b, April 4). *When labels don't fit: Hispanics and their views of identity.* Pew Research Hispanic Trends Project. Retrieved from http://www.pew

hispanic.org/2012/04/04/when-labels-dont-fit-hispanics-and-their -views-of-identity/.

Teixeira, R. (2013, May 8). When will your state become majority-minority? Think Progress. Retrieved from http://thinkprogress.org/election /2013/05/08/1978221/when-will-your-state-become-majority-minority/.

Telhami, S. (2002, Winter). Arab and Muslin America: A snapshot. *Brookings Review, 20,* 14–15.

Tropman, J. E. (1989). *American values and social welfare: Cultural contradictions in the welfare state.* Englewood Cliffs, NJ: Prentice Hall.

Turner, M. A., Santos, R., Levy, D. K., Wissoker, D., Aranda, C., & Pitingolo, R. (2013). *Housing discrimination against racial and ethnic minorities, 2012: Executive summary.* Washington, DC: U.S. Department of Housing and Urban Development. Retrieved from http:// www.huduser.org/portal/Publications/pdf/HUD-514_HDS2012_ex ecsumm.pdf.

UN High Commissioner for Refugees (UNHCR) (2011). *The role of host countries: The cost and impact of hosting refugees.* Retrieved from http://www.refworld.org/docid/520b3fa24.html.

U.S. Census Bureau. (n.d.). *The size, place of birth, and geographic distribution of the foreign-born population in the United States: 1960 to 2010.* Retrieved from http://www.census.gov/population/foreign /files/WorkingPaper96.pdf .

U.S. Department of Defense. (n.d.). *20th century warriors: Native American participation in the United States military.* Retrieved from http:// www.defense.gov/specials/nativeamerican01/warrior.html.

U.S. Department of Health and Human Services. (2011). *Summary of immigrant eligibility restrictions under current law.* Retrieved from http://aspe.hhs.gov/hsp/immigration/restrictions-sum.shtml.

Vargas, J. A. (2012, June 25). Not legal, not leaving. *Time,* pp. 35–43.

Walbridge, L. S. (1999). Middle Easterners and North Africans. In E. R. Barkan (Ed.), *A nation of peoples: A sourcebook on America's multicultural heritage* (pp. 391–410). Westport, CT: Greenwood Press.

Waldinger, R. (2007). *Between here and there: How attached are Latino immigrants to their native country?* Pew Hispanic Center. Retrieved from http://www.pewhispanic.org/reports/.

Walker, J. E. K. (1999). African Americans. In E. R. Barkan (Ed.), *A nation of peoples: America's multicultural heritage* (pp. 19–47). Westport, CT: Greenwood Press.

Wertheimer, J. (2005). Jews and the Jewish birthrate. AISH.com. Retrieved from http://www.aish.com/jw/s/48899452.html.

West, D. M. (2010, September 1). 7 myths that have clouded the immigration debate. *USA Today*, p. 9A.

Williams, R. (1957). *American society: A sociological interpretation* (2nd ed.). New York, NY: Alfred Knopf.

Wilson, C. (2013, February 21). Native American tribes venture out of casino business. National Public Radio. Retrieved from http://www .npr.org/2013/02/21/172630938/native-american-tribes-venture-out -of-casino-business.

Wilson, T. C. (1996). Compliments will get you nowhere: Benign stereotypes, prejudice and anti-Semitism. *Sociological Quarterly, 37*, 465–479.

Wilson, W. J. (1978). *The declining significance of race.* Chicago, IL: University of Chicago Press.

Wilson, W. J. (1996). *When work disappears: The world of the new urban poor.* New York, NY: Alfred A. Knopf.

Woodward, C. (2011). *American nations: A history of the eleven rival regional cultures of North America.* New York, NY: Viking.

World Bank. (2013) *Developing countries received about $401 billion in remittances during 2012.* Retrieved from http://siteresources.world bank.org/INTPROSPECTS/Resources/334934-1288990760745/Mi grationandDevelopmentBrief21.pdf.

Wu, F. H. (2002). *Yellow: Race in America beyond black and white.* New York, NY: Basic Books.

Yung, J. (1999). Chinese. In E. R. Barkan (Ed.), *A nation of peoples: America's multicultural heritage* (pp. 119–137). Westport, CT: Greenwood Press.

Zakaria, F. (2012, June 18). Broken and obsolete: An immigration deadlock makes the U.S. a second-rate nation. *Time*, pp. 24–25.

CHAPTER SEVEN

Other Social Status Groups

In this chapter, we introduce the concept of social statuses and examine how they apply to three disadvantaged groups: women; lesbians, gay men, bisexual, and transgender individuals; and people with disabilities. Social workers often join with these populations in advocacy efforts toward social justice.

SOCIAL STATUS

"A *status* is a socially defined position in a group or society characterized by certain expectations, rights, and duties" (Kendall, 2013, p. 121). The term *status* is commonly associated with high or prestigious positions in society, but sociologists use the term to describe any specific position. For example, each year college students preparing for professions begin internships with different organizations. They are expected to be prompt, dress appropriately, pay attention to their supervisor or mentor, and bring what they learn back to the classroom for discussion. The status of "student intern" is similar across many disciplines. While "student intern" is a temporary status, many other social statuses are long-term or permanent.

Ascribed statuses are social positions that are conferred at birth or assigned later in life, based on characteristics over which an individual has little or no choice or control. Sex and race are good examples of ascribed statuses. Other kinds of statuses are more within the control of the individual; they are assumed voluntarily as a result of personal choice or direct effort. These are called achieved statuses. Being a college graduate is a good example of an achieved status. Some statuses in American society carry more power and privilege than others. These include being white, male, heterosexual, and nondisabled. In America, other valued statuses are afforded to those people who belong to Christian religious denominations, are youthful, attractive, tall and slim, professionally employed, articulate, wealthy, and famous.

The concepts of prejudice, discrimination, oppression, and privilege that were discussed in relation to race and ethnicity in chapter 6 also apply to the ascribed statuses of gender, sexual orientation, and disability. Nevertheless, the experiences of women, gay men, lesbians, bisexual, transgendered, and questioning (LGBTQ) persons, and people with disabilities may be quite different from those of racial and ethnic minorities. Members of racial and ethnic minorities have the advantage of being part of families and communities that can help them in the process of developing a positive self-identity and in negotiating the demands of the dominant culture (Carothers, 1990; Lukes & Land, 1990). It is highly unlikely, on the other hand, that a gay man or a person with cerebral palsy will grow up in a family and community made up of other gay men or people with cerebral palsy. For these individuals, the first part of the socialization process will come from the dominant culture, complete with negative stereotypes. They are not isolated from society, but they are isolated from each other. Although there are supportive identificational communities of sexual minorities and people with various types of disabilities, most individuals must seek them out as they become adults. (The deaf community is an exception, as you will see later in this chapter.) The situation for women, for the most part, is even more complex. They live in a society that is *patriarchal*—meaning that, by and large, men hold the power to make formal decisions and determine policies. Although women may join together for support and advocacy, many of them owe at least a part of their social standing to the efforts of their fathers and husbands. Just as homosexuals must interact with heterosexuals, and people with disabilities must interact with the nondisabled, women interact daily with males, both in formal situations and also in intimate relationships as partners and caregivers, as daughters, sisters, wives, and mothers.

GENDER

The terms *sex* and *gender* are often used interchangeably. In our discussion, *sex* will refer to biological differences and *gender* will refer to those differences that are culturally constructed and socially transmitted.

Among the real biological differences between the sexes are chromosomal, hormonal, and brain-structure dissimilarities that determine primary and secondary sex characteristics (such as reproductive organs, breast size, and facial hair) and instinctive behaviors. Among biologically supported behavior differences are physical aggression, visual-spatial ability, and sexual behavior (Lippa, 2002).

Although biology determines many aspects of sex-related behaviors, society and culture define gender. The significance of gender is that "it is a device by which society controls its members. Gender sorts us, on the basis of sex, into different life experiences. It opens and closes doors to property, power, and prestige" (Henslin, 2014, p. 289).

Children are socialized by their families, schools, peers, and the mass media to conform to culturally approved gender expectations (*gender roles*). Even in this age of increasing attention to gender equality, girls are still encouraged to look pretty, nurture others, play cooperative games, and be "nice." Boys are encouraged to be tough, competitive, independent, and achievement-oriented.

It is often difficult to separate out what is biological from what is cultural. No human being has ever been raised without the presence of gender socialization and therefore purely biological influences on behavior cannot be isolated for study. While the possibility for a biological explanation of some behaviors cannot be ignored, these behaviors are always expressed in a social environment. Research on sex and gender differences is still being conducted; what is clear, however, is that the context of women's lives is different from that of men's. As already noted, the United States (like virtually all other societies) is patriarchal. Just as racial and ethnic minorities experience inequities in a society that is dominated by whites, women experience inequity in a society dominated by males.

Understanding Social Stratification and Gender

Functionalist Perspective

From a functionalist perspective, a division of labor between men and women, particularly in the family, is the natural order of human society. A complementary set of roles, with men providing economic support and making decisions and women providing care and emotional support, ensures that important societal tasks will be fulfilled (Parsons & Bales, 1955). Some conservative politicians and their supporters and fundamentalist religious leaders promote this traditional interpretation of "the family" as essential to the stability of society.

Conflict Perspective

Conflict theorists remind us that, in most societies, differences exist between men and women in the areas of physical, economic, and political power. A colleague of Karl Marx, Friedrich Engels (1902/1884), said that capitalism intensifies male domination because it creates more wealth, which in turn gives greater power to men as owners of property or primary wage earners. Evidence of male domination in contemporary society is reflected in economic and political-related inequities, and gender-related violence. This is discussed further in the section that follows.

Constructionist Perspective

As noted previously, gender is socially constructed. Language and concepts of gender are intertwined. For example, not long ago the term *mankind* was used to refer to all members of the human race, leaving many women feeling excluded. The use of inclusive language is now encouraged in professional writing and public discourse. See for example "General Guidelines for Reducing Bias" in the *Publication Manual of the American Psychological Association* (2010). Many formerly sexist terms have been replaced (e.g., the traffic caution sign "Men Working" now reads "People Working," and "postman" has been replaced by "mail carrier"). While some people consider this overzealous political correctness, language shapes our view of reality.

The social construction of appropriate gender roles has been in flux over the past forty or fifty years in this country. Especially as more women have entered the paid workforce in large numbers, including leadership roles, assumptions about women's capabilities have changed dramatically. Also, a perception that only men were "family breadwinners" and women were working by choice (i.e., just for supplemental income) has changed.

American Society and the Experience of Inequity Related to Gender

Although not a numerical minority, women are considered a minority in the sense that they exercise less power than men in American society. In the past, laws prevented women from voting, holding property, establishing credit in their own names, serving on juries, and entering certain professions while other laws subjugated them to the control of their fathers and husbands. Whereas this is no longer the case and much progress has been made, there remain significant areas of gender inequality.

"Gender-segregated work" refers to a pattern of employment wherein men and women are found in different occupations (Padavic & Reskin, 2002). Examples would be dental hygienists, secretaries, and flight attendants (female-dominated) and dentists, business executives, and airplane pilots (male-dominated). These occupational choices reflect gendered expectations—that women will nurture and provide assistance and men will take charge and make decisions. Many of the occupations with the highest concentrations of women (e.g., nursing and child care) reflect this. Women were well-represented in several industry sectors, including education and health services, leisure and hospitality, and other services (Bureau of Labor Statistics, 2013b). They were underrepresented in agriculture, mining, construction, manufacturing, and transportation (Bureau of Labor Statistics, 2013b) (see table 7.1).

Women typically hold lower-status, lower-paying jobs than men with similar educational backgrounds. Cross-cultural and historical research has shown that the status given an occupation is higher when most jobs in it are filled by men and lower if those same jobs are filled by women. For example, a hundred years ago, most secretaries (clerks) were men and the job had relatively high prestige. Now that 95.3 percent of all secretaries and administrative assistants are women (Bureau of Labor Statistics, 2013b), the job is accorded lower esteem. In short, it is not the work that provides the prestige, but the gender with which the work is associated.

A majority of women in contemporary American society actually fill two roles, as paid and unpaid workers, and are easily exploited in both. Padavic and Reskin (2002) suggest that the burden of the second shift will probably preserve women's inequity at home and in the workplace for another generation. The *second shift* refers to the child care and housework responsibilities that women assume after returning home from their paid employment (Hochschild, 1989). Women still do more housework than men and they are more likely to perform time-consuming and routine household tasks such as cooking and housecleaning, whereas men's

TABLE 7.1

Concentration of Women in Different Occupations, 2011

Occupation title	Percent women
Speech-language pathologist	95.6
Elementary and middle school teachers	81.7
Social workers	81.6
Tailors, dressmakers, and sewers	74.9
Psychologists	71.2
Accountants and auditors	61.3
Retail salespersons	51.2
Postal service mail carriers	36.0
News analysts, reporters, and correspondents	34.1
Computer system analysts	33.9
Physicians and surgeons	33.8
Lawyers	31.9
Chief executives	24.2
Chefs and head cooks	18.7
Architects and engineers	13.6
Firefighters	4.5
Aircraft pilots and flight engineers	4.3
All occupations	*46.9*

Sources: U.S. Department of Labor, U.S. Bureau of Labor Statistics (May 1, 2012). *Women as a percent of total employed in selected occupation*, 2011. Retrieved from http://www.bls.gov/opub/ted/2012/ted_20120501.htm#bls-print; U.S. Department of Labor, U.S. Bureau of Labor Statistics (2008, Report 1011). *Women in the Labor Force: A databook,* Table 11.

chores involve fixing things and yard work. A recent survey reported by the Bureau of Labor Statistics (2013a) found that on an average day, 82 percent of women and 65 percent of men spent some time doing household activities such as housework, cooking, lawn care, or financial and other household management; on the days they did housework, women spent an average of 2.6 hours on such activities, while men spent 2.0 hours; and on an average day, 20 percent of men did housework compared with 48 percent of women. Only 39 percent of men did food preparation or cleanup, compared with 65 percent of women.

Even when women hold the same positions as men and have comparable skills and training, they tend to earn less. According to the Institute for Women's Policy Research (2013), in the United States in 2012 women who worked full-time had median weekly earnings of $691; this amount represents 80.9 percent of men's median weekly earnings of $854, a drop from 82.2 percent in 2011. Average earnings of Asian ($770) and white ($710) women were substantially higher than the earnings of their black ($599) and Latina ($521) counterparts; for all racial/ethnic groups women earned less than men, but the gap was smallest for African American women (90.1 percent) and greatest for Asian American women (73.0 percent). Only 7.9 percent of the 2,500 highest-paid executives at Standard and Poor's 500 Index companies were female; on average they earned 18 percent less than the men (Hymowitz & Daurat, 2013). The gender gap pattern does not hold true for large cities, however.

There are three arguments presented for why most women earn less than their male counterparts (Macionis, 2014.) First, the type of work that women do tends to pay less; the four most common female professions today are secretary, registered nurse, teacher, and cashier (Bennett, Ellison, & Ball, 2010). Second, women may compromise their careers for family responsibilities, taking time off to care for children or elderly parents, or accepting lower-paying jobs that offer shorter commutes or more flexible hours. Women who take advantage of flexible working conditions (e.g., telecommuting, compressed workweeks, and job sharing) are often viewed as less competent and less committed to their work (Bernard, 2013). The third reason is gender discrimination; in support of this argument is the fact that just one year out of college, women graduates are paid 82 cents for every dollar paid to men (Davidson, 2013). This holds true even though women received higher GPAs than their male colleagues and "while motherhood has been blamed for the persistent pay gap, a decade out of college full-time working women who hadn't had children still made 77 cents on the male dollar" (Bennett, Ellison, & Ball, 2010).

According to a Pew Research Center analysis of census data (Wang, Parker, & Taylor, 2013) for 40 percent of all households with children under the age of eighteen, mothers are either the sole or primary source of income for the family. The study of "breadwinner moms" found two very different groups: 5.1 million married mothers who have a higher salary than their husbands, and 8.6 million single mothers. The married mothers earned $80,000 on average in 2011, while the single mothers earned only $23,000 (Wang, Parker, & Taylor, 2013).

According to the U.S. Equal Employment Opportunity Commission (2008), "unwelcome sexual advances, requests for sexual favors, and other verbal or physical conduct of a sexual nature constitute *sexual harassment* [italics added] when this conduct explicitly or implicitly affects an individual's employment, unreasonably interferes with an individual's work performance, or creates an intimidating, hostile, or offensive work environment." In 1986, the U.S. Supreme Court declared that sexual harassment violates the federal law against sex discrimination as outlined in the 1964 Civil Rights Act. Women's groups applauded the Court's decision in identifying harassment as a source of discrimination. Sexual harassment has come to be understood more recently as an abuse of power (by a person of either sex) to force unwanted attention on a subordinate. According to the US Equal Employment Opportunity Commission, sexual harassment can occur in a variety of circumstances, including but not limited to the following:

- The victim as well as the harasser may be a woman or a man. The victim does not have to be of the opposite sex.
- The harasser can be the victim's supervisor, an agent of the employer, a supervisor in another area, a coworker, or a non-employee.
- The victim does not have to be the person harassed but could be anyone affected by the offensive conduct.
- Unlawful sexual harassment may occur without economic injury to or discharge of the victim.
- The harasser's conduct must be unwelcome. (U.S. Equal Employment Opportunity Commission, 2008)

Employment is not the only area where men exercise power over women. Sexual violence should be understood as a dimension of gender stratification; it is fundamentally about power, not sex (Herman, 2001). According to the National Center for Victims of Crime (2012), in 2010 violent crimes by intimate partners (both male and female) accounted for

13 percent of all violent crimes. Women were three to four times more likely than men to become victims of domestic violence, and almost four in ten (37.5 percent) female murder victims in the United States were killed by their husbands or boyfriends. The violence perpetrated against women by their partners is a reflection of a sexist, patriarchal society that treats women as if they were property.

Young women ages 18 to 24 are more likely to be victims of intimate partner violence than older women, with rates almost triple the national average (Duret, 2012). This victimization typically begins between the ages of 12 and 18; these experiences of violence in relationships can put victims at higher risk for substance abuse, eating disorders, risky sexual behavior, and further domestic violence (Duret, 2012).

"Sexual assault is a form of abuse that involves one or more people forcing, coercing, and/or manipulating another person in order to gain sexual contact. Sexual assault can include rape (a forced sexual act that includes oral, anal or vaginal penetration); unwanted touching, fondling, or kissing; forcing someone to look at or pose for pornographic material; or forced oral sex" (South Carolina Coalition Against Domestic Violence and Sexual Assault, 2002). In the United States someone is sexually assaulted on average every two minutes (approximately 237,800 victims per year) according to the Rape, Abuse, and Incest National Network (RAINN) (2013a). According to RAINN, 73 percent of sexual assaults were perpetrated by a nonstranger, and more than 50 percent of all rape/ sexual assault incidents were reported by victims to have occurred within one mile of their home or at their home. It is estimated that one of every six women has been the victim of an attempted or completed rape in her lifetime (RAINN, 2013a). Approximately 15 percent of sexual assault and rape victims are under age twelve.

Marital rape occurs when a spouse forces his wife to take part in certain sex acts without her consent. Research shows that it can be equally, if not more, emotionally and physically traumatizing than rape by a stranger (RAINN, 2013b). Until the late 1970s, most states did not consider spousal rape a crime (National Center for Victims of Crime, 2004). Currently, rape of a spouse is a crime in all fifty states and the District of Columbia. While spousal rape is now considered a crime, victims often have to overcome additional legal hurdles to prosecution not present for other victims of rape. These include time limits for reporting the offense and a requirement that force or threat of force be used by the offender (RAINN, 2013b).

According to the Rape, Abuse, and Incest National Network (2013b), victims of marital rape face special challenges, including

- Higher likelihood of repeated assaults. Research shows that women who are marital rape victims are more likely to experience repeated assaults than other rape victims; in fact, among battered women, sexual assault may be a routine part of the pattern of the abuse.
- The married perpetrator is more likely to use anal and oral rape to humiliate, punish, and take "full" ownership of their partners.
- Pressure to stay with perpetrator. A victim with children who lacks outside employment may be financially dependent on the spouse and feel there is no way to leave the situation, and the victim may face additional pressure from family members or friends to remain with the perpetrator.
- Difficulty identifying what happened as a crime. A victim may find it difficult, for cultural reasons, to define the other spouse's conduct as rape or identify someone she married and loves as a "rapist."

Some victim advocates argue that the term *marital rape* needs to be expanded to include sexual assault by cohabiting partners, including same-sex partners. According to the Council on Criminal Justice, a victim's advocacy group located in Minnesota (Taranto, 2014), within the last ten years many states have altered their domestic violence laws to be more gender-neutral. Nevertheless, only in Hawaii does the law mention same-sex couples, while some other states have laws that protect only heterosexual couples. A few states, including Arizona, South Carolina, and Virginia, have laws that specifically prevent same-sex victims from obtaining a civil protection order. The majority of states have laws written in gender-neutral language, which means that the courts have the latitude to get involved in cases on behalf of victims in same-sex couples.

Date rape/acquaintance rape is relatively common but underreported on most college campuses. A study funded by the U.S. Department of Justice estimated that one out of five college women is sexually assaulted.

Usually—in 50 to 90 percent of cases—there is alcohol involved and 80 percent of victims stay silent (Krebs, Lindquist, Warner, Fisher, & Martin, 2007).

Partner abuse can also include psychological abuse, such as intimidation, public humiliation, and intense criticism. Examples of intimidation include threats to harm children or pets, or to "out" a same-sex partner.

Male power is also demonstrated in the pornography industry. Pornography is material that appears to endorse, condone, or encourage sexual abuse or degradation. Feminists suggest that the objectification and control of women's bodies portrayed in pornography contributes to violence against women, in part by reinforcing rape myths (e.g., that women secretly want to be raped). Pornography is not limited to adult bookstores; it is a big business that includes Internet sites easily accessible to children. Music videos, while not legally pornographic, commonly include content that is misogynistic (demeaning of females).

Men also experience issues of gender inequity. The gender roles that men labor under are much more constraining than those available for women. For example, a man is expected to be his family's "breadwinner"; being a "stay-at-home dad" may bring social ostracism. About one out of fifteen men in the United States are primary caregivers for their children, perhaps a reflection of the fact that women now outnumber men in receiving college degrees at all levels (bachelors, masters, and Ph.D.) (Paglia, 2013; Yen, 2011). When employers offer flexible work arrangements, men may be penalized more severely than women for taking advantage of them (Bernard, 2013).

Men are also expected to hide their feelings and, in comparison to women, to have a less nurturing relationship with children and friends. Perhaps the most noteworthy inequity is the societal expectation that males go into combat when needed.

Gender around the World

The Global Gender Gap Report (Cann, 2012) ranks countries on their ability to close the gender gap in four key areas: access to health care, access to education, political participation, and economic equality. Over the long term there has been improvement in women's economic status and education, while significant gaps remain in health and political participation. European countries fill ten of the top thirteen ranks, with Iceland in first place, and the United States twenty-second. Canada ranked twentieth. The lower ranking of the United States is due to a smaller percentage of women in political decision-making positions.

Women in Positions of Political Leadership

Within the last fifty years, a number of countries have had female heads of state and leaders of government. These include Australia, New Zealand, South Korea, Thailand, and Liberia and Rwanda (in Africa), Indonesia and the Philippines (in the Asian Pacific islands), Bangladesh, India, Pakistan, and Sri Lanka (in the Asian subcontinent), Bosnia, Croatia, Denmark, Finland, France, Germany, Great Britain, Herzegovina, Iceland, Ireland, Kosovo, Latvia, Norway, Poland, Portugal, Slovakia, Switzerland, Turkey, and Ukraine (in Europe), Israel (in the Middle East), Canada (in North America), and Argentina, Bermuda, Bolivia, Brazil, Chile, Costa Rica, Ecuador, Guyana, Haiti, Jamaica, Nicaragua, Panama, Trinidad, and Tobago (in South and Central America). In countries with parliamentary forms of government, women hold 20 percent of seats and in only twenty-four countries do women represent at least one-third of the members of parliament (Macionis, 2014).

Health Issues

According to the World Health Organization (WHO; 2012), the global maternal mortality rate in 2010 was 210 maternal deaths per 100,000 live births, down from 400 maternal deaths per 100,000 live births in 1990, a decline of 47 percent. With approximately 245,000 maternal deaths in 2010, sub-Saharan Africa and Southern Asia accounted for 85 percent of the global total.

The United States is the only industrialized country not to mandate paid maternity leave for new mothers (Zaino, 2013). In 178 countries working mothers are guaranteed paid leave, and at least 50 countries provide benefits for new fathers ("Maternity leaves around the world," 2012). Four states in the United States mandate paid maternity leave, but the 1993 federal Family and Medical Leave Act policy requires only that companies with fifty or more employees guarantee twelve weeks of unpaid leave for new mothers. Many countries provide for at least fourteen to fifteen weeks of paid leave, and even relatively poor countries, such as Croatia and Serbia, offer a full year of leave at 100 percent of wages ("Maternity leaves around the world," 2012).

A concern that has received worldwide attention is the practice of female genital mutilation. According to the WHO (2013), female genital mutilation is defined as "all procedures that involve partial or total removal of the external female genitalia, or other injury to the female genital organs for non-medical reasons." The WHO reports that about 140 million girls and women are estimated to have undergone this procedure. The practice is most prevalent in western, eastern, and northeastern regions of Africa, some countries in Asia and the Middle East, and among migrants from those areas. The procedure is thought to inhibit sexual desire and ensure marital fidelity. Beside the intense pain, female genital mutilation "can cause severe bleeding and problems urinating, and later cysts, infections, and infertility as well as complications in childbirth and increased risk of newborn deaths" (WHO, 2013). The UN Committee on the Elimination of All Forms of Discrimination against Women, the UN Committee on the Rights of the Child, and the UN Human Rights Committee have been active in condemning the practice and recommending measures to combat it, including criminalization.

Literacy and Education

According to data released by the Education for All Global Monitoring Report and the United Nations Education, Scientific and Cultural Organization (UNESCO) Institute for Statistics (2013), literacy rates for adults and youth continue to rise. Young women aged 15–24 are making the strongest gains, but still lag behind young men. Despite these gains, 774 million adults (15 years and older) still cannot read or write—two-thirds (64 percent) of them are women.

There were more than 57 million out-of-school children in the world in 2011 (Education for All Global Monitoring Report and UNESCO Institute for Statistics, 2013). While access to education has been improving globally, there has been little progress in reducing the rate at which children leave school before reaching the last grade of primary education. Sub-Saharan Africa and South and West Asia have the highest rates of early school leaving. Across these regions, more than one in every three students who started primary school in 2011 will not make it to the last grade. In sub-Saharan Africa, primary-school-age girls were 1.3 times more likely to be out of school than boys, and in South and West Asia the ratio was about 1:2. In the rest of the world, there was no difference by gender.

In some countries, girls may be barred altogether from attending school. In Afghanistan, for example, in areas controlled by the Taliban, girls' schools were shut down. In Pakistan, Malala Yousafzai, an outspoken advocate for girls' education at the young age of fifteen, was shot in the head as she boarded her school bus. She survived the assassination attempt and moved to England with her family to continue her studies. In 2013 she was nominated for the Nobel Peace Prize.

Even when there are no political or legal barriers to school attendance for girls, because school fees are required in many countries and families have limited resources, they may decide to invest in their sons' educations rather than their daughters'. Girls are also more likely to be victims of sexual harassment and violence in schools, which leads to high dropout rates.

Sex Trafficking

According to the National Human Trafficking Resource Center (2013), *sex trafficking* includes commercial sexual exploitation of children, as well as every instance where an adult is in the sex trade as the result of force, fraud, or coercion. Commercial sexual exploitation may include prostitution, pornography, stripping, live-sex shows, and "sex tourism." Sex tourism is a practice whereby people travel to particular parts of the world specifically to engage in commercial sexual activity. Sex tourism is such a profitable enterprise that the International Labour Organization estimates that somewhere between 2 and 14 percent of the gross domestic product in Thailand, Indonesia, Malaysia, and the Philippines is derived from sex tourism (Andersen & Taylor, 2013, p. 286).

Victims of sex trafficking can be women or men, girls or boys, but the majority are women and girls. According to the Office of Refugee Resettlement (2012), victims of sex trafficking are subjected to starvation, confinement, beatings, rape and gang rape, forced drug use, and threats of violence to their families. Victims face numerous health risks such as physical injuries, traumatic brain injury, sexually transmitted diseases, sterility, miscarriages, and forced or coerced abortions. Psychological harms include shame, grief, fear, self-hatred, post-traumatic stress disorder, and suicide.

Feminism and Women's Movements

The first wave of the women's movement began in the United States, Canada, and parts of western Europe in the late nineteenth century. Initially focused on suffrage (the right to vote), it faded after the 1920s. A second wave emerged in the 1960s with broad goals related to legal rights, access to jobs, equitable wages, and reproductive freedom. A third wave emerging in the 1990s brought greater attention to the conditions of women living in the least industrialized countries. The life experiences of these women are shaped by both gender stratification and their location in exploited regions of the world. Women's movements in developing countries are increasingly influenced by globalization, international funding for nongovernmental organizations, and transnational advocacy groups (Kimball, 2012). Although there are significant cultural differences between the countries in which these different women's movements are taking place, they have seen some success in exposing patriarchal structures and in addressing health care, violence against women, and human rights. There has been less success in resolving the issue of poverty.

SEXUAL ORIENTATION AND IDENTITY

Sexual orientation is defined as a person's preference of partners in emotional-sexual relationships: same sex, other sex, or both sexes. Homosexuality (attraction to members of the same sex) and heterosexuality (attraction to members of the other sex) are not mutually exclusive; sexual orientation lies on a continuum rather than being a dichotomy (either/or). This understanding of sexual orientation leads us to other categories of sexuality, which include bisexual and transgendered individuals. *Bisexuality* refers to sexual attraction to people of either sex. According to the American Psychological Association (2011), *transgender* is an "umbrella term for persons whose gender identity, gender expression, or behavior does not conform to that typically associated with the sex to which they were assigned at birth."

It has always been difficult to get accurate information on the number of people who are sexual minorities. One of the few researchers who made an effort was Alfred Kinsey (1948, 1953), who estimated that 4 percent of males and 2 percent of females are exclusively homosexual. A 2012 Gallup phone survey of more than 120,000 randomly selected adults found that 3.4 percent of respondents self-identified as lesbian, gay, bisexual, or transgender (Gates & Newport, 2012). Broken down by race and ethnicity, 4.6 percent of blacks identified at LGBT, 4.3 percent of Asians, and 4.0 percent of Hispanics, compared to 3.2 percent of non-Hispanic whites. Women are more likely (3.6 percent) than men (3.3 percent) to identify as LGBT. In terms of age, younger adults are more likely to identify as LGBT than older adults; 6.4 percent of those aged 18 to 29 identified as LGBT while only 1.9 percent of those 65 and older identified as LGBT. LGBT identification is highest among those with some college education (4.0 percent) but not a college degree (2.8 percent). More than 5 percent of those with incomes of less than $24,000 a year identify as LGBT, a higher proportion than among those with higher incomes—including 2.8 percent of those making $60,000 a year or more.

According to a study by the Williams Institute (Badgett, Durso, & Schneebaum, 2013), in contrast to conventional wisdom, there is evidence that LGBT individuals are more likely to be poor than heterosexual people. Families headed by same-sex couples are significantly more likely to be poor than are heterosexual married couple families.

It should be noted that homosexual activity or experiences are not the same thing as homosexual identity. Many heterosexuals have had homosexual encounters. According to a 2008 nationwide survey (Chandra, Mosher, Copen, & Sionean, 2011), 12.7 percent of women and 5.6 percent of men between the ages of 15 and 44 reported having at least some homosexual activity at some time in their lives.

Many research studies have linked homosexuality to biological factors, such as brain structure, hormonal influences, and genetics (King, 2005). Others suggest that sexual orientation is a product of society (Foucault, 1990), both society and biology (Bailey & Dawood, 1998), or simply a personal choice.

Sexual Orientation as Community and Culture

Generally gay men and lesbians find large urban centers to be more hospitable to sexual diversity than rural areas. In some large cities, there are identifiable gay neighborhoods such as the Castro district in San Francisco, but even some smaller cities such as Asheville, North Carolina, Key West, Florida, Provincetown, Massachusetts, and Santa Fe, New Mexico have substantial gay populations.

As noted in chapter 6, there are also gay and lesbian communities that are not geographically anchored (Cruikshank, 1992). The creation of these gay and lesbian identificational communities resulted from both experiences of discrimination and a sense of commonality. Without a strong gay community, the gay liberation movement would not have come into existence; the existence of that movement, in turn, helped to expand gay communities (Cruikshank, 1992). Stigmatization and social rejection prompted a sense of solidarity in response to isolation from mainstream American society, but Queralt (1996) argues that there would be a gay community even without elements of oppression.

"Even if sexual minorities do not have a culture in the traditional sense, in the process of accepting a homosexual identity, they are socialized into a new set of norms and values" (Lukes & Land, 1990, p. 156). Not all gay men and lesbians belong to or participate in an identifiable culture related to their sexual orientation; nevertheless, there are elements of a common cultural experience that include pairing behavior; definitions of family; the time, place, and reason for celebrations; and religious services (Lukes & Land, 1990, p. 156). Cruikshank (1992) argues that, in its broadest terms, the essence of gay and lesbian cultures is self-determination. "To follow a different path openly and wholeheartedly rather than furtively, [lesbians and gay men] have created a culture in which homosexuality is the norm" (p. 139).

Understanding Social Stratification and Sexual Orientation

Functionalist Perspective

Because functionalists assume a complementary set of roles for men and women, they do not see a legitimate place for LGBT people in society; in fact, they perceive them as a threat to traditional family arrangements. This perspective tends to support the status quo and the view that a stable society is one wherein members share a common set of values, beliefs, and behavioral expectations. Thus there is an absence of widespread support for civil rights for lesbians and gay men. Although LGBT people have advocated for themselves and experienced success in a variety of venues, they continue to experience discrimination in many areas.

Conflict Perspective

Sexual minorities are routinely oppressed in American society. Social conflict theorists believe that, in defense of their idea of "the family," conservatives are willing to sacrifice the individual rights of gay men and lesbians in order to preserve their own social standing.

Founded in 1973, Lambda Legal is the oldest national organization pursuing litigation, public education, and advocacy on behalf of equality and civil rights for lesbians, gay men, bisexuals, transgender people, and people with HIV. This organization helps individuals secure their rights by providing legal information about federal laws and the laws in their state (Lambda Legal, 2013). The Human Rights Campaign is the largest national lesbian, gay, bisexual, and transgender civil rights organization, with 1.5 million members and supporters (Human Rights Campaign, n.d.).

Constructionist Perspective

Just as gender is a social construction, so are sexual orientation and socially approved sexual relationships. A variety of sexual expressions have been found in almost all societies, but different cultures tend to privilege one orientation (usually heterosexism) over others. While in the United States homosexuality is often viewed as a deviant lifestyle, other countries and cultures are or have been more accepting of same-sex attraction (Gramick, 1983). In ancient Greece and Japan, male-male relationships were held in higher esteem than male-female relationships (Gramick, 1983; Greenberg, 1988). In Brazil and some other Latin American countries, labeling of homosexuality depends upon whether the male takes an active penetrating role, in which case he would be considered heterosexual regardless of the sex of his partner (Cherlin, 2008, p. 190). By calling homosexual behavior an "abomination," and labeling gay men and lesbians "sinners," religious conservatives impose a moral judgment that justifies and encourages discrimination against this at-risk population.

American Society and the Experience of Inequity Related to Sexual Orientation

Heterosexism is the view that heterosexuality is "normal" and that any other pattern of intimate interpersonal relationship is inherently abnormal or wrong. It was not until 1973 that homosexuality was eliminated as a mental disorder from the *Diagnostic and Statistical Manual of Mental Disorders* (*DSM*) of the American Psychiatric Association. Homophobia is the unreasonable fear of homosexuals and homosexuality. Gay men and lesbians may be accused of seeking "special" rights when in fact they simply want the same basic civil rights and liberties available to heterosexual citizens. Unlike racism and sexism, heterosexism is widely tolerated in our society, legally supported under many circumstances, and even encouraged in some sectors.

Workplace Discrimination

In a summary of research studies, the American Association of University Women (Belec, 2014) reported that 42 percent of LGBT workers have experienced discrimination on the job. The situation is worse for LGBT people of color and for transgendered people. In one survey, 97 percent of transgender respondents reported harassment at work and 27 percent reported that they were fired. Currently there is no federal-level protection against discrimination against LGBT people in the workplace.

Attitudes toward Same-Sex Couples

Gay men and lesbians may face ridicule or social ostracism when they live with a partner and do so openly, express affection toward a partner in public, or talk about their weekends, vacations, or other social events without disguising the gender of their partner. Nevertheless, national surveys have documented a clear decline in the level of homophobia and increased support for same-sex marriage in the United States in recent years, particularly among younger people.

A May 2013 Pew Research Center for the People & the Press poll found that for the first time more than half (51 percent) of Americans favored allowing gays and lesbians to marry legally. People younger than thirty supported gay marriage by a ratio of about two to one. Even among Republicans, support for legal agreements that give gays and lesbians rights similar to heterosexual married couples almost doubled in ten years (63 percent in 2013 in contrast to 34 percent a decade earlier). Compared to a 2004 *Los Angeles Times* poll that found that most (60 percent) Americans said that they would be upset if they had a child who told them that he or she was gay or lesbian, in 2013 that dropped to less than half (40 percent). Over the past ten years, the balance of favorable and unfavorable attitudes about gay men and lesbians has shifted from predominantly unfavorable to favorable (Pew Research Center for the People & the Press, 2013). Those groups that had the highest level of favorable attitudes toward both gay men and lesbians include liberal Democrats, white college-educated women, postgraduates, religiously unaffiliated, white Catholics, and 18- to 29-year olds. Those with the lowest level (less than 50 percent) of favorable views toward gay men include white evangelical Protestants, African Americans, conservative Republicans, and those with high school or less education. Individuals who know many LGBT people as acquaintances, close friends, or family members are more likely to favor same-sex marriage than those who do not. As more LGBT people "come out of the closet" and share their identity with family, friends, and neighbors, there is likely to be greater support for their civil rights.

Experiences of LGBT Youth

Homophobic prejudices may be particularly painful when they are experienced by adolescents who are gay or lesbian. In a 2011 study, more than 80 percent of LGBT students stated that they were called names or threatened because of their sexual orientation (Pearsall, 2014). Increasing numbers of schools are establishing Gay Straight Alliance (GSA) organizations to help protect and promote the rights of sexual minority students;

at the end of the 2005–2006 school year, there were over 3,000 GSAs in the United States (Kilman, 2007). As of 2014 at least thirty-seven states had a GSA network. Eighteen states and the District of Columbia have laws that prohibit discrimination, harassment, and bullying of students based on sexual orientation and sixteen states have similar laws for discrimination or harassment on the basis of gender identity (Family Equality Council, n.d.).

Overall, suicide is the third leading cause of death among youth aged 15 to 24 years, and lesbian, gay and bisexual youth are more likely to attempt suicide compared with their heterosexual peers (Suicide Prevention Resource Center, 2008). A study by Hatzenbuehler (2011) found that LGBT students in the state of Oregon living in "unsupportive" environments were 20 percent more likely to attempt suicide. Supportive (county-level) environments were identified through a composite index that included the proportion of same-sex couples, the proportion of registered Democrats, the presence of gay-straight alliances in schools, and nondiscrimination and antibullying school policies that specifically supported LGBT students.

Hate Crimes

Of more serious concern than simple harassment is physical violence against gays. As of August 2008, thirty-one states and the District of Columbia had laws that addressed hate or bias crimes based on sexual orientation (Human Rights Campaign, 2009). The Southern Poverty Law Center examined hate crime statistics from 1995 through 2008 and found a total of 15,351 antihomosexual hate crimes offenses during those years or 17.4 percent of the total number of hate crimes for that time period (Potok, 2010). The figures show that homosexuals are 2.4 times more likely to suffer a violent hate crime attack than Jews, 2.6 times more likely to be attacked than blacks, 4.4 times more likely than Muslims, 13.8 times more likely than Latinos, and 41.5 times more likely than whites, according to the FBI figures.

The Fight for Civil Rights

In May 1953 President Dwight Eisenhower's Executive Order 10450 went into effect, banning anyone engaged in "sexual perversion" from federal employment, and thousands of LGBT civil servants lost their jobs (Engardio, 2013). A handful fought back, sparking the beginning of the long march to equality that was enhanced by the 1969 Stonewall riots and the efforts of gay pioneers such as Harvey Milk, the member of the San Francisco Board of Supervisors who was assassinated as a result of his activism.

LGBT people continue to experience a wide range of discriminatory practices, but there have been significant recent successes in the promotion of equality. These include repeal of Don't Ask, Don't Tell, some gains in fair employment, and a Supreme Court ruling on same-sex marriage.

Don't Ask, Don't Tell (DADT) was the law prohibiting gay and lesbian people from serving openly in the military, which went into effect in 1994. DADT was a compromise measure that protected homosexual and bisexual members of the military from discrimination and harassment as long as they did not disclose their sexual orientation. At the end of 2010, Congress repealed DADT and the repeal went into effect in September 2011. This meant that LGBT individuals could, for the first time, serve openly in the military.

LGBT people have also made progress in the area of employment discrimination. Twenty-one states, the District of Columbia, and several hundred municipalities and counties have legal protections in place for lesbian, gay, and bisexual public and private employees, and seventeen states have protections for transgendered individuals (Herwitt, 2013).

In late June 2013, the United States Supreme Court handed down a landmark ruling on same-sex marriage. Their 5-4 decision overturned the 1996 federal Defense of Marriage Act (DOMA). The act defined marriage as being between a man and a woman. Those who argued against DOMA put it in the same category as interracial-marriage bans, noting that religious beliefs and moral disapproval cannot be used to legitimize discrimination against vulnerable minority groups (Americans United for Separation of Church and State, 2013). As of February 2014, same-sex marriage was legal in eighteen states and the District of Columbia. Massachusetts was the first to legalize same-sex marriage in 2003. Same-sex marriage is legal in all of the New England states, plus Delaware, New Jersey, Washington, California, Hawaii, Illinois, Iowa, Minnesota, and

New Mexico. Thirty states have amended their constitutions to ban gay marriage and several others have statutory bans. The federal court's ruling on DOMA paved the way for legal challenges to restrictive state marriage laws across the country. In fact, no state or federal judge has opposed same-sex marriage since the Supreme Court decision was announced. According to multiple news sources, as of mid-May 2014, U.S. district courts had overruled state bans in Arkansas, Idaho, Kentucky, Ohio, Oklahoma, Texas, Utah, and Virginia, concluding that they violate the Constitution's promise of equal treatment under the law, but the orders were stayed pending appeal. Litigants in more than three dozen cases are challenging same-sex marriage bans in additional states (Murphy & McCombs, 2014). The Human Rights Campaign website (www.hrc.org) has the most current information on LGBT legal issues.

At the federal level, marriage brings with it more than a thousand recognized legal benefits, including the ability to file joint income taxes, receive Social Security benefits, inherit shared assets after a spouse's death, enjoy joint parenting rights such as access to children's school records, and receive bereavement leave upon the death of a spouse, have rights to shared property, child support, and alimony after a divorce, and receive veterans' discounts based on a spouse's armed forces status.

Adoption by Same-Sex Couples

The determination of adoption is made on a case-by-case basis and it is a judicial decision whether to grant adoption petitions. According to the Human Rights Campaign organization (2009), in many states the status of parenting laws for LGBT people is unclear and the laws governing adoption vary widely. As of 2013, there were twenty-one states and the District of Columbia where same-sex couples could jointly petition to adopt (Human Rights Campaign, 2013). In 2009, about 19 percent of same-sex couples who had children reported that one or more was adopted, up from just 8 percent in 2000 (Tavernise, 2011).

Scouting and LGBT Issues

In June 2000, in Boy Scouts of America v. Dale, the U.S. Supreme Court ruled that, as a private organization, the Boy Scouts of America (BSA) could not be compelled to accept a member whose activities and beliefs were inconsistent with its values. It reversed a state court ruling that public accommodations law required the BSA to readmit an assistant scoutmaster who had made his homosexuality public. In spring 2013, in response to protests, public pressure, and loss of corporate sponsorships, the organization decided to admit gay scouts, but to continue its ban on adult leaders who are open homosexuals ("An old knot, untied?" 2013). The response of religious groups that sponsor troops varied, with support from the Church of Jesus Christ of Latter-Day Saints, and rejection from the Southern Baptist Convention and the Assemblies of God (Dias, 2013). The Girls Scouts, Boys and Girls Clubs, and 4-H Clubs welcome gay members ("An old knot, untied?" 2013).

The Business Community and Support for LGBT Employees

Every year the Human Rights Campaign foundation scores large businesses on their treatment of LGBT employees using their "Corporate Equality Index," a benchmarking report on corporate America's adoption of LGBT-inclusive policies, benefits, and practices (Fidas & Cooper, 2012). In 2002, only thirteen businesses achieved a top score of 100 percent. In 2012, 252 of 688 participating businesses achieved this top rating. Among the benefits counted are domestic partner health-care coverage, an employee resource group, and transgender-inclusive health-care coverage. Expedia, Google, Starbucks, Nike, Xerox, Nordstrom, Amazon, and eBay were among those cited as being on record in support of same-sex state marriage laws.

Gay Rights in a Global Perspective

Persecution in Other Countries

Attitudes towards homosexuality vary greatly around the world. According to a 2013 survey of more than 37,000 respondents in thirty-nine countries conducted by the Pew Research Center's Global Attitudes Project, there is broad acceptance of homosexuality in North America, the European Union, and much of Latin America; however, rejection of homosexuality is widespread in Muslim nations, in sub-Saharan Africa, parts of

Asia, and Russia. There is a strong correlation between high levels of religiosity in a country and negative opinions about homosexuality.

In many countries around the world, LGBT people are not only discriminated against but actively persecuted by their governments. There is widespread condemnation of homosexuality in Belize, Honduras, India, Iran, Jamaica, Jordan, Nigeria, Pakistan, Palestinian territory, Russia, Saudi Arabia, Senegal, Sudan, and Uganda, Zimbabwe, and other countries (Beirich, 2013; Strasser, 2014).

During the 2014 Winter Olympics in Sochi, the host country Russia received widespread condemnation for its violations of the civil rights of its LGBT citizens. In recent years, Russian authorities have routinely intimidated and arrested LGBT activists and condoned anti-LGBT statements by government officials (Council for Global Equality, 2013).

In 2014 Nigeria and Uganda passed laws calling for lengthy jail sentences for gay sex between consenting adults (Muhumuza, 2014). The Southern Poverty Law Center reports that several "hard-line, U.S. religious right" groups are aiding anti-LGBT forces abroad where anti-gay attitudes are strong and violence against the LGBT community is common ("U.S. Groups working to keep LGBT sex illegal in Caribbean," 2013). Such groups coordinate, fund, and litigate legal cases, including those that criminalize homosexual acts (Beirich, 2013).

Same-Sex Marriage in Other Countries

The legal definition of marriage is in flux, particularly in the developed world, as governments reexamine what long seemed to be a well-established aspect of civil law. Beginning legal efforts on behalf of same-sex couples originated in 1989 when Denmark instituted "registered partnerships" that extended property and inheritance rights (Lozano-Bielat, Masci, & Ralston, 2009; Vestal, 2008). In December 2000, the Netherlands became the first country to legalize same-sex marriage (Lozano-Bielat, Masci, & Ralston, 2009). As of November 2013, same-sex marriage was recognized by fifteen other countries: Belgium (2003), Spain (2005), Canada (2005), South Africa (2006), Norway (2008), Sweden (2009), Portugal (2010), Iceland (2010), Argentina (2010), Denmark (2012), Brazil (2013), France (2013), Uruguay (2013), and New Zealand

(2013); Great Britain will allow same sex citizens to marry in 2014 (Freedom to Marry, 2013). More than a dozen other nations in Europe, South America, and elsewhere offer broad protections or some spousal rights for same-sex couples (Freedom to Marry, 2013).

DISABILITY

According to Cornell University's Employment and Disability Institute (Erickson & von Schrader, 2013), in 2011 there were 37.3 million Americans with one or more physical or mental disabilities (excluding those living in institutions); nearly one in eight citizens has a disability. The most common type of disability is mobility-related, with 6.9 percent of citizens reporting a disability in that category. West Virginia has the highest disability rate, at 18.8 percent of its population, followed by Kentucky at 17.1 percent, Arkansas at 16.6 percent, and Mississippi at 16.3 percent. Among racial groups, Native Americans and Alaska Natives ranked the highest, with 16.5 percent, followed by African Americans with 13.9 percent. Whites averaged 12.5 percent and Hispanics 7.7 percent. Females are a little more likely to report having a disability than males (12.4 percent versus 11.9 percent). About one in five veterans (19.1 percent) reported a VA service-connected disability. More than one in five Americans aged 21 to 64 without a high school education reports having a disability. More than one-fifth (20.7 percent) of people between the ages of 21 and 64 with a disability were employed full-time/full-year in 2011. Almost three in ten (27.8 percent) of those in the same age range with disabilities were living below the poverty line.

The number of people with disabilities continues to rise. One reason for this is that the workforce is getting older and with age comes more disabilities. On the other hand, Joffe-Walt (2013, p. 9) has argued that disability insurance has become "a de facto welfare program for people without job skills and without a lot of education." With new restrictions on TANF and a bleak job market, many people have few other options, particularly if their health is compromised. According to data from the Bureau of Labor Statistics, applications for disability rise and fall with the unemployment rate. Disability pays slightly less than minimum wage, but it includes full health care coverage. "But in most cases, going on disability means that you will not work, you will not get a raise, you will not get whatever meaning people get from work. Going on disability means, assuming you rely only on those disability payments, you will be poor for the rest of your life. That's the deal" (Joffe-Walt, 2013, p. 9).

One example of a population with a disability whose involvement in society has changed dramatically in the past generation is people with Down syndrome. There are more than 400,000 people living with Down syndrome in the United States (National Down Syndrome Society [NDSS], n.d.]). The prevalence rate for Down syndrome is approximately one out of 691 births (Centers for Disease Control and Prevention, 2012). At one time, parents were encouraged to institutionalize their Down syndrome children because of anticipated cognitive impairments, but although all people with Down syndrome experience some cognitive delays, the effect is usually mild to moderate. According to the NDSS "quality educational programs, a stimulating home environment, good health care, and positive support from family, friends and the community enable people with Down syndrome to develop their full potential and lead fulfilling lives." The average expected life span of people with Down syndrome has increased from 25 years in 1983 to 60 years today (NDSS, n.d.). This creates a different kind of risk. Because federal policy fails to provide a coherent network of community services and support, many families are the sole providers for their adult children with Down syndrome. Recent data indicate that 715,000 people with cognitive impairments of all kinds were living with caregivers aged 60 or older (Bauer, 2008). When adults with Down syndrome remain living at home, their primary caregivers may be parents in their 70s, 80s, or 90s, unless this role is shifted to other family members such as siblings or cousins (NDSS, n.d.)

An entirely different kind of problem results from the development of prenatal screening tests that identify Down syndrome very early in the gestational cycle. A bill, the Prenatally and Postnatally Diagnosed Conditions Awareness Act, was passed by Congress in September 2008. The law would require giving families who learn that their child may be born with or is born with a disability facts about the condition and information on the many options and support services available on caring for children with disabilities. The legislation also provides for the further development of peer-support groups and of a national clearinghouse on information for parents of disabled children. In addition, the bill creates a national registry of families who are willing to adopt children with diagnosed disabilities. Practice guidelines for genetic counselors recommend a "neutral, nondirective, and nonjudgmental manner . . . which includes [discussion of options of] continuing the pregnancy and either raising the child or creating an adoption plan for the child, or terminating the pregnancy" (Sheets et al., 2011, p. 438).

People with Down syndrome are born with their disability. The vast majority of individuals with disabilities, however, were not born that way, but were injured in an accident or war, or suffer from the effects of an illness. Another reason the number of persons with disabilities is greater now than in previous decades is because of advances in medical technology that keep at-risk infants and accident victims alive and allow people to live longer.

Many of the troops serving in the recent wars in Iraq and Afghanistan suffered serious injuries that led to permanent disabilities. Veterans are returning with blindness (Zoroya, 2007), loss of limbs (Ellison, 2008), and traumatic brain injuries (Emery, 2007). In fact, traumatic brain injury (TBI) has been called the "signature wound" of the Iraq War. From 2000 through mid-2013, 280,784 service members have received traumatic brain injuries, both in and out of combat (Defense and Veterans Brain Injury Center, 2013). Lingering effects of TBI include headaches, sleep disorders, memory loss and information-processing problems, sensory-processing issues, sensitivity to light or noise, irritability, depression, anxiety, personality changes, aggression, and social inappropriateness (Okie, 2005; Zoroya, 2005).

In the past two decades, there has been a dramatic change in the way that people with disabilities are perceived. The view has changed from one based on charity to one based on human rights (United Nations, n.d.). People with disabilities are no longer content to be considered objects of pity, but prefer to be viewed as individuals who are capable of responding to the challenges they face and participating fully in the larger society. Another aspect of a more enlightened perspective is the emphasis on focusing on the person first rather than the disability (for example "people who have a mental illness" rather than "the mentally ill"). Known as "person first language," it makes "the presence of a disability a character-istic, not the individual's sole identity" (National Association of Social Workers, 2012, p. 248). "Although people with disabilities may be handi-capped by environmental or individual or societal attitudes, they are not 'disabled' or 'handicapped' people" (NASW, 2012, p. 248).

While there are many definitions of disability, they essentially fall into two major categories: (1) those that locate disability as internal to the individual and (2) those that situate the problem in the interaction between the person with a disability and the social environment. The first category is the one that social workers are most likely to encounter in their dealings with other human service and health care professionals. According to the 1990 Americans with Disabilities Act, disability means "with respect to an individual, a physical or mental impairment that substantially limits one or more of the major life activities of such individuals, a record of such an impairment, or being regarded as having such an impairment." With this definition, professionals are looking for a cure, or at least a way to rehabilitate the individual. These professionals may expect the person with the disability to take on the role of patient or client and be compliant and passive.

The second category of definitions establishes disability not just as a personal problem but also as a challenge to society to change attitudes and remove barriers (Karger & Stoesz, 2010, p. 94). This latter view sees the person's inability to function as the result of a handicapped environ-ment, and disability as an element of human diversity (Gilson & DePoy, 2002). This is the perspective usually adopted by social workers.

Disability as Community and Culture

All who consider themselves disabled are potential members of the dis-ability community. According to Linton (1998), "we (disabled people) are bound together, not by . . . (a) list of our collective symptoms but by the social and political circumstances that have forged us as a group. We have found one another and found the voice to express not despair at our fate but outrage at our social positioning" (p. 4). Linton (1998) goes on to describe "the cultural stuff of the disability community" as being "the creative response to atypical experience, the adaptive maneuvers through a world configured for nondisabled persons. The material that binds us is the art of finding one another, of identifying and naming disability in a world reluctant to discuss it, and of unearthing historically and culturally significant material that relates to our experience" (p. 3).

The construction of disability as a community and culture constitutes a range of understandings. One noteworthy position on this continuum is that of the deaf community.[1] People in the deaf community perceive deafness not as a disability, but as a minority culture (Luey, Glass, & Elliott, 1995; Padden & Humphries, 2005). Perhaps because deaf children are routinely separated from their families to attend special residential schools for the deaf at an early age, they are more likely to develop a unique or bicultural orientation to the world than are people with other kinds of disabilities. Among communities of disabled persons, the deaf community stands alone in having its own language, American Sign Language (ASL). ASL is usually dominant in residential schools; fluency in ASL has the effect of cementing the culture and creating a different worldview, particularly for those who grow up with it (Luey, Glass, & Elliott, 1995). According to the National Association of the Deaf (NAD, n.d.), deaf and hard of hearing people feel that the words *deaf* and *hard of hearing* are not negative in any way. Instead, they view "hearing-impaired" as negative, because the label focuses on what they cannot do.

Understanding Social Stratification and Disability

Functionalist Perspective

The functionalist perspective uses a medical model to explain the role of disability in society. The medical model uses the first category of definition, discussed earlier, which suggests that pathology resides within the individual. From a functionalist perspective, people with disabilities are restricted to the role of chronic patient. They are perceived as being unable to work, or at least unable to work as productively as the able-bodied.

---

[1] *Deaf culture* is a term applied to the social movement that holds deafness to be a difference in human experience rather than a disability. When used in the cultural sense, the word *Deaf* is very often capitalized in writing, and referred to as "big D Deaf" in speech (Mackelprang & Salsgiver, 2009, pp. 23, 211; Padden & Humphries, 2005, p. 5.

Conflict Perspective

Conflict theorists argue that people with disabilities belong to a minority group that is kept in a subservient position and exploited by the health care industry (Albrecht, 1992). People with disabilities are treated as second-class citizens. Categorizing them as "deserving poor" and giving them subsistence-level grants does little to bring them to full inclusion in society. Restrictions of opportunities for schooling, employment, public transportation, and housing continue to limit their options.

A caste system is a form of social stratification in which one's status is lifelong and unchangeable. Szymanski and Trueba (1994) argue that "the difficulties faced by persons with disabilities are not the result of functional impairments related to the disability, but rather are the result of a castification process embedded in societal institutions for rehabilitation and education that are enforced by well-meaning professionals" (p. 12).

For example, federal policy related to disability benefits forces recipients to choose between a limited grant and Medicaid, versus accepting a job with an income that will threaten their eligibility for health care coverage. Biased professionals also keep persons with disabilities locked into their low status by referring them to sources of employment such as dishwashing and custodial work that they believe are most suitable to their perceived limitations (Mackelprang & Salsgiver, 2009).

Constructionist Perspective

The social construction of disability is a process that has for the most part marginalized people with disabilities. People with disabilities are sometimes perceived as dangerous, especially persons with cognitive impairments or mental illness, when there is a proposal to move them into a group home in a residential neighborhood. They are more often thought of as helpless, dependent, incompetent, and tragic figures or even as "perpetual children" (Mackelprang & Salsgiver, 2009, p. 10). The response to this construction is a patronizing stance that may result in their exclusion from activities or places that are considered to be suitable only for adults, including those arenas where they could effectively advocate for themselves.

When not perceived as victims, people with severe disabilities are sometimes portrayed as heroes who miraculously overcome all obstacles to lead a "normal" life. Members of the disability community sometimes refer to such individuals as "supercrips" (people with severe disabilities who seem to excel and receive lots of media coverage) (Shapiro, 1993). This image is also misleading. Linton points out that persons with disabilities are

> not only the high-toned, wheel chair athletes seen in recent television ads, but the gangly, pudgy, lumpy, and bumpy of us, declaring that shame will no longer structure our wardrobe or our discourse. We are everywhere these days, wheeling and loping down the street, tapping our canes, sucking on our breathing tubes, following our guide dogs, puffing and sipping on the mouth sticks that propel our motorized chairs. . . . Our symptoms, though sometimes painful, scary, unpleasant, or difficult to manage, are nevertheless part of the dailiness of life. They exist and have existed in all communities throughout time. What we rail against are the strategies used to deprive us of rights, opportunities, and the pursuit of pleasure. (Linton, 1998, pp. 3–4)

American Society and the Experience of Inequity Related to Disability

The issue of ascribed status is an important one for people with disabilities. Sociologists use the term *master status* to describe a perceived social status that dominates all the other statuses a person holds. Historically, occupation has been a master status for many men, and the most common master status for a woman was her role in the family as wife or mother. Being very rich or poor can be a master status, as well as being a member of a minority race or ethnicity in a society where discrimination is the rule. For many individuals, disability becomes a master status. For example, when individuals must use wheelchairs, their disability may override all other statuses they might enjoy, such as educational achievement or occupational success. The master status concept is often apparent in the media. Many television portrayals of people with disabilities highlight the disability; television and film directors are reluctant to insert an individual with a physical disability into a minor role where the disability is irrelevant to the story. (See figure 7.1.)

FIGURE 7.1 CRITICAL THINKING ABOUT PORTRAYALS OF DISABILITIES
IN THE MOVIES

How is disability portrayed in contemporary films? Think about the challenges faced by fictional characters in *Rainman* (autism), *My Left Foot* (cerebral palsy), *Scent of a Woman* (blindness), *Madgascar: Escape 2 Africa* (deafness), *Forrest Gump* (intellectual disability), *As Good as It Gets*, (obsessive-compulsive disorder), *I Am Sam* (cognitive disability), *Girl Interrupted* (mental illness), *A Beautiful Mind* (schizophrenia), and *The Piano* (deafness and speech impairment). What are the qualities associated with the villains in the *Batman* series? What are the implications for contemporary culture?

The built environment is probably the most potent symbol of exclusion of people with disabilities from society. Mark Johnson, a disabilities activist (quoted in Shapiro, 1993, p. 128) notes that whereas African Americans fought for the right to sit at the front of the bus, persons with disabilities have had to fight for the right to *get on the bus.*

The current prevalence of "handicapped" parking places and bathroom stalls may lead the casual observer to believe that most public places are easily accessible to persons with mobility problems. Nevertheless, many amenities are inadequate or poorly designed or limited in their applicability. For example, trendy brick pavers may cause people using walkers to trip; sometimes a freight elevator at the back of the building may be the only available means of ascent. Public address announcements in airports are barely intelligible to people with normal hearing, much less to those who are hard of hearing. Most signs and signals in our built environment are purely visual; Braille labeling is provided in elevators but rarely in other public areas. The lack of convenient and accessible public transportation is a major impediment for many persons with disabilities. A Government Accountability Office report noted that in the 2008 election, 73 percent of polling places presented obstacles to voters with disabilities (Korte, 2012).

According to the National Council on Disability (2012), parents with disabilities are unique in their struggle to retain custody of their children. There are reportedly 4.1 million parents with disabilities in the United States, roughly 6.2 percent of all American parents with children under the age of eighteen. Children are at high risk of being removed from a home where a parent has a psychiatric or intellectual disability, and parents who are deaf or blind report extremely high rates of child removal and loss of parental rights. When a divorce occurs, parents with disabilities are more likely to lose custody of their children.

Organized political activity by people with disabilities and their families was rewarded in 1990 with the signing of the Americans with Disabilities Act (ADA). The ADA extends to disabled people civil rights similar to those made available on the basis of race and sex through the Civil Rights Act of 1964. Nevertheless, stigma and oppression are ongoing problems for people with disabilities. As long as disability is viewed as an individual affliction rather than as a deficit in the physical or social environment, people with disabilities will continue to be an oppressed minority. If one accepts the assumption that stigma is a major barrier to full citizenship for people with disabilities, then advocacy for civil rights, in addition to the provision of social services and income maintenance, is the appropriate response (Hahn, 1991).

Disability in a Global Context

In developed countries, the disabilities rights movement concerns itself with human rights to ensure full participation in society. Some people are concerned, however, that the greatest need for advocacy is in developing countries. In those nations, basic needs, such as accessibility, education, and employment are not being met.

According to the United Nations (n.d.), over 650 million people, or approximately 10 percent of the world's population, live with a disability of one form or another. Over 80 percent of them live in developing countries. In those countries, 90 percent of children with disabilities do not attend school.

The United Nations has been at the forefront of challenging oppressive treatment of disabled people around the globe. In 2007 the U.N. Convention on the Rights of Persons with Disabilities, the first comprehensive human rights treaty of the twenty-first century, was adopted with signatories from eighty-two countries. The Convention spells out general principles, including the "respect for inherent dignity, individual autonomy including the freedom to make one's own choices, and independence of persons" and the obligations of nations to "adopt all appropriate legislative, administrative and other measures for the implementation of the rights recognized in the present Convention; to take all appropriate measures, including legislation, to modify or abolish existing laws, regulations, customs and practices that constitute discrimination against persons with disabilities; and to take into account the protection and promotion of the human rights of persons with disabilities in all policies and programs" (United Nations Enable, 2006).

LOOKING AHEAD

The chapters in Part III addressed social structure and its impact on vulnerable populations. In Part IV, we discuss social settings as contexts for human behavior. Social justice issues will be a continuing theme.

REFERENCES

Albrecht, G. L. (1992). *The disability business: Rehabilitation in America.* Newbury Park, CA: Thousand Oaks.

American Psychological Association. (2010). General guidelines for reducing bias. *Publication Manual of the American Psychological Association* (6th ed., pp. 71–77). Washington, DC: American Psychological Association.

American Psychological Association. (2011). *Answers to your questions about transgender people, gender identity, and gender expression.* Retrieved from http://www.apa.org/topics/lgbt/transgender.aspx.

Americans United for Separation of Church and State. (2013, March 1). *Marriage law should not be based on theology, Americans United tells Supreme Court* (press release). Retrieved from https://au.org /media/press-releases/marriagemarriage-law-should-not-be-based -on-theology-americans-united-tells-supreme-court.

An Old Knot, Untied? (2013, February 11). *Time,* p. 10.

Andersen, M., & Taylor, H. (2013). *Sociology: The essentials* (7th ed.). Belmont, CA: Wadsworth.

Badgett, M. V., Durso, L. E., & Schneebaum, A. (2013). New patterns of poverty in the lesbian, gay, and bisexual community. Williams Institute. Retrieved from http://williamsinstitute.law.ucla.edu/research /census-lgbt-demographics-studies/lgbt-poverty-update-june-2013/.

Bailey, M. J., & Dawood, K. (1998). Behavioral genetics, sexual orientation, and the family. In C. J. Patterson & A. R. D. Augelli (Eds.), *Lesbian, gay, and bisexual identities in families: Psychological perspectives* (pp. 3–18). New York, NY: Oxford University Press.

Bauer, P. (2008, August 17). A movie, a word and my family's battle. *The Washington Post.* Retrieved from http://www.washingtonpost.com /wpdyn/content/article/2008/08/14.

Beirich, H. (2013). Dangerous liaisons. *SPLC Intelligence Report,* pp. 18–23.

Belec, H. M. (2014, winter). Coming out at work. *Outlook, The Magazine of AAUW* [American Association of University Women], pp. 6–9.

Bennett, J., Ellison, J., & Ball, S. (2010, March 29). Are we there yet? *Newsweek,* pp. 40–46.

Bernard, T. S. (2013, June 14). The unspoken stigma of workplace flexibility. *The New York Times.* Retrieved from http://www.nytimes.com /2013/06/15/your-money/the-unspoken-stigma-of-workplace-flexibil ity.html?_r = 0.

Bureau of Labor Statistics (2013a). *American time use survey.* Retrieved from http://www.bls.gov/news.release/atus.nr0.htm.

Bureau of Labor Statistics. (2013b). *Labor force statistics from the Current Population Survey: Employed persons by detailed occupation, sex, race, and Hispanic or Latino ethnicity.* Retrieved http://www.bls .gov/cps/cpsaat11.htm.

Cann, O. (2012). *Slow progress in closing global economic gender gap, new major study finds* (news release). World Economics Forum. Retrieved from http://www.weforum.org/news/slow-progress-in-clos ing-global-economic-gender-gap-new-major-study-finds.

Carothers, S. C. (1990). Catching sense: Learning from our mothers to be black and female. In F. Ginsberg & A. Lowenhaupt Tsing (Eds.), *Uncertain terms: Negotiating gender in American culture* (pp. 232–247). Boston, MA: Beacon Press.

Centers for Disease Control and Prevention. (2012). World Down syndrome day. Retrieved from http://www.cdc.gov/ncbddd/features/DownSyndromeWorldDay-2012.html [top].

Chandra, A., Mosher, W. D., Copen, C., & Sionean, C. (2011). *Sexual behavior, sexual attraction, and sexual identity in the United States: Data from the 2006–2008 National Survey of Family Growth.* National Health Statistics Reports. Retrieved from http://www.cdc.gov/nchs/data/nhsr/nhsr036.pdf.

Cherlin, A. J. (2008). *Public and private families: An introduction.* New York, NY: McGraw-Hill.

Council for Global Equality. (2013). *The facts on LGBT rights in Russia.* Retrieved from http://www.globalequality.org/newsroom/latest-news/1-in-the-news/186-the-facts-on-lgbt-rights-in-russia.

Cruikshank, M. (1992). *The gay and lesbian liberation movement.* New York, NY: Routledge.

Davidson, R. (2013, Winter). Graduating to a pay gap. *Outlook, The Magazine of AAUW* [American Association of University Women], pp. 8–11.

Defense and Veterans Brain Injury Center (2013). *Traumatic brain injury.* Retrieved from http://www.dcoe.mil/content/Navigation/Documents/About%20DVBIC.pdf.

Dias, E. (2013, June 10). Brave, clean, reverent . . . and split. *Time,* p. 14.

Duret, D. (2012, November 13). Partner abuse among teens grows. *The State* [Columbia, SC], p. A4.

Education for All Global Monitoring Report and UNESCO Institute for Statistics. (2013). *Literacy rates are rising, but women and girls continue to lag behind.* United Nations Education, Scientific and Cultural Organization. Retrieved from http://www.uis.unesco.org/literacy/pages/adult-youth-literacy-data-viz.aspx.

Ellison, J. (2008, December 15). A new grip on life. *Newsweek,* p. 64.

Emery, E. (2007, April 16). TBI: Hidden wounds plague Iraq War veterans. *The Denver Post.* Retrieved from http://www.veteransforcommonsense.org/articleid/7406.

Engardio, J. (2013, May 21). How Eisenhower's ban on gays backfired. *USA Today,* p. 9A.

Engels, F. (1902/1884). *The origin of the family*. Chicago, IL: Charles H. Kerr.

Erickson, W. L., & von Schrader, S. (2013). *Disability statistics from the 2011 American Community Survey* (ACS). Ithaca, NY: Cornell University Employment and Disability Institute. Retrieved from http://www.disabilitystatistics.org/reports.

Family Equality Council (n.d.). *Safer schools*. Retrieved from http://www.familyequality.org/get_informed/advocacy/safer_schools/our_safer_schools_work/.

Fidas, D., & Cooper, L. (2012, Fall). The new normal: How corporate America became a steadfast partner in equality. *Equality*, pp. 18–23.

Foucault, M. (1990). *The history of sexuality: An introduction*. (R. Hurley, Trans.). New York, NY: Vintage.

Freedom to Marry. (2013). The freedom to marry internationally. Retrieved from http://fredomtomarry.org/landscape/entry/c/international.

Gates, G. J., & Newport, F. (2012). *Special report: 3.4% of U.S. adults identify as LGBT*. Gallup. Retrieved from http://www.gallup.com/poll/158066/special-report-adults-identify-lgbt.aspx.

Gilson, S. F., & DePoy, E. (2002). Theoretical approaches to disability content in social work education. *Journal of Social Work Education, 37*, 153–165.

Gramick, J. (1983). Homophobia: A new challenge. *Social Work, 28*, 137–141.

Greenberg, D. F. (1988). *The construction of homosexuality*. Chicago, IL: University of Chicago Press.

Hahn, H. (1991). Alternate views of empowerment: Social services and civil rights. (Editorial). *The Journal of Rehabilitation, 57*(4), 17–20.

Hatzenbuehler, M. L. (2011). The social environment and suicide attempts in lesbian, gay, and bisexual youth. *Pediatrics, 127*(5), 896–903.

Henslin, J. M. (2014). *Sociology: A down-to-earth approach* (12th ed.). Boston, MA: Pearson Education.

Herman, D. (2001). The rape culture. In J. J. Macionis & N. V. Benokraitis (Eds.), *Seeing ourselves: Classic, contemporary, and cross-cultural readings in sociology* (5th ed.). Upper Saddle River, NJ: Prentice Hall.

Herwitt, A. (2013). *Breaking: ENDA vote next week.* Human Rights Campaign. Retrieved from http://hrc.org/blog/entry/breaking-enda-vote -next-week.

Hochschild, A. (1989). *The second shift: Working parents and the revolution at home.* New York, NY: Viking.

Human Rights Campaign. (n.d.). The HRC story. Retrieved from http:// www.hrc.org/the-hrc-story.

Human Rights Campaign. (2009). *About hate crimes.* Retrieved from http://www.hrc.org/issues/hate_crimes/5895.htm.

Human Rights Campaign. (2013). *Parenting laws: Joint adoption.* Retrieved from http://www.hrc.org/files/assets/resources/parenting _joint-adoption_062013.pdf.

Hymowitz, C., & Daurat, C. (2013, August 13). Best-paid women in S & P 500 settle for less remuneration. *Bloomberg News.* Retrieved from http://www.bloomberg.com/news/2013-08-13/best-paid-women-in-s -p-500-settle-for-less-with-18-gender-gap.html.

Institute for Women's Policy Research. (2013, May). Maternity, paternity, and adoption leave in the United States. Retrieved from www .iwpr.org.

Joffe-Walt, C. (2013). Unfit for work: The startling rise of disability in America. National Public Radio. Retrieved from http://apps.npr.org /unfit-for-work.

Karger, H. J., & Stoesz, D. (2010). *American social welfare policy* (6th ed.). Boston, MA: Pearson Education.

Kendall, D. (2013). *Sociology in our times* (9th ed.). Belmont, CA: Wadsworth.

Kilman, C. (2007, Spring). This is why we need a GSA. *Teaching Tolerance,* pp. 30–37.

Kimball, G. (2012). How third world feminism differs from first world feminism. Fem2pt0. Retrieved from http://www.fem2pt0.com/2012 /03/04/how-third-world-feminism-differs-from-first-world-feminism.

King, B. M. (2005). *Human sexuality today* (5th ed.). Upper Saddle River, NJ: Prentice Hall.

Kinsey, A. C. (1948). *Sexual behavior in the human male.* Philadelphia, PA: W. B. Saunders.

Kinsey, A. C. (1953). *Sexual behavior in the human female.* Philadelphia, PA: W. B. Saunders.

Korte, G. (2012, August 10). Study shows voters with disabilities face barriers. *USA Today*, p. 4A.

Krebs, C. P., Lindquist, C. H., Warner, T. D., Fisher, B. S., & Martin, S. L. (2007). College women's experiences with physically forced, alcohol- or other drug-enabled, and drug-facilitated sexual assault before and since entering college. *Journal of American College Health, 57*(6), 639–647.

Lambda Legal. (2013). Our mission. Retrieved from http://www.lambda legal.org/.

Linton, S. (1998). *Claiming disability: Knowledge and identity.* New York, NY: New York University Press.

Lippa, R. A., (2002). *Gender, nature, and nurture.* Mahwah, NJ: Lawrence Erlbaum.

Lozano-Bielat, H., Masci, D., & Ralston, M. (2009). *Same-sex marriage redefining marriage around the world.* Pew Forum. Retrieved from http://pewforum.org.

Luey, H. S., Glass, L., & Elliott, H. (1995). Hard-of-hearing or deaf: Issue of ears, language, culture, and identity. *Social Work, 40*, 177–182.

Lukes, C. A., & Land, H. (1990). Biculturality and homosexuality. *Social Work, 35*, 155–161.

Luscombe, B. (2010, November 22). The rise of the sheconomy. *Time*, pp. 58–61.

Macionis, J. J. (2014). *Sociology* (15th ed.). Boston, MA: Pearson Education.

Mackelprang, R. W., & Salsgiver, R. O. (2009). *Disability: A diversity model approach in human service practice* (2nd ed.). Chicago, IL: Lyceum.

Maternity leaves around the world: Worst and best countries for paid maternity leave. (2012, October 24). *Huffington Post.* Retrieved from http://huffingtonpost.ca/2012/05/22/maternity-leaves-around-the -world_n_1536120.

Muhumuza, R. (2014, February 23). Uganda president signs harsh anti-gay law. *The State* [Columbia, SC]. Retrieved from http://www.the state.com/2014/02/23/3287816/ugandas-president-to-sign-anti.html.

Murphy, S., & McCombs, B. (2014, January 16). Gay marriage rulings in Oklahoma and Utah build momentum. *The State* [Columbia, SC], p. A3.

National Association of Social Workers. (2012). *Social work speaks* (9th ed.). Washington, DC: NASW Press.

National Association of the Deaf. (n.d.). What is wrong with the use of these terms: "Deaf-mute," "deaf and dumb," or "hearing-impaired"? Retrieved from, http://www.nad.org/site/pp.aspx?c = foINKQMBF& b = 103786&printmode = 1.

National Center for Victims of Crime. (2004). *Spousal rape laws: 20 years later.* Retrieved from http://www.ncvc.org.

National Center for Victims of Crime. (2012). *Intimate partner violence.* Retrieved from http://www.victimsofcrime.org/library/crime-infor mation-and-statistics/intimate-partner-violence.

National Council on Disability. (2012). *Rocking the cradle: Ensuring the rights of parents with disabilities and their children.* Retrieved from http://www.ncd.gov/publications/2012/Sep272012.

National Down Syndrome Society (NDSS). (n.d.). *Down syndrome facts.* Retrieved from https://www.ndss.org/Down-Syndrome/Down-Syn dreme-Facts/.

National Human Trafficking Resource Center. (2013). *Sex trafficking in the U.S.* Retrieved from http://www.polarisproject.org/human-traf ficking/sex-trafficking-in-the-us.

Office of Refugee Resettlement. (2012). *Fact sheet: Sex trafficking.* Retrieved from http://acf.hhs.gov/programs/orr/resources/fact-sheet -sex-trafficking-english.

Okie, S. (2005, May 19). Traumatic brain injury in the war zone. *The New England Journal of Medicine, 352*(20), 2043–2047.

Padavic, I., & Reskin, B. (2002). *Women and men at work* (2nd ed.). Thousand Oaks, CA: Pine Forge Press.

Padden, C. L., & Humphries, T (2005). *Inside deaf culture.* Cambridge, MA: Harvard University Press.

Paglia, C. (2013, December 30). 2013: The year men became obsolete? *Time*, p. 26.

Parsons, T., & Bales, R. F. (Eds.). (1955). *Family, socialization and inter- action process.* New York, NY: Free Press.

Pearsall, B. (2014). Kids can be cruel: LGBT bullying in school. *Outlook, The Magazine of AAUW* [American Association of University Women], pp. 18–21.

Pew Research Center for the People & the Press (2013). *In gay marriage debate, both supporters and opponents see legal recognition as 'inevitable.'* Retrieved from http://www.people-press.org/files/legacy-pdf /06-06-13%20LGBT%20General%20Public%20Release.pdf.

Pew Research Global Attitudes Project. (2013). *The global divide on homosexuality.* Retrieved from http://www.pewglobal.org/2013/06 /04/theglobal-divide-on-homosexuality.

Potok, M. (2010, Winter). Anti-gay hate crimes: Doing the math. *Intelligence Report.* Southern Poverty Law Center. Retrieved from http:// splcenter.org/get-informed/intelligence-report/browse-all-issues/20 10/winter.

Queralt, M. (1996). *The social environment and human behavior: A diversity perspective.* Boston, MA: Allyn & Bacon.

Rape, Abuse and Incest National Network (RAINN). (2013a) *How often does sexual assault occur?* Retrieved from http://www.rainn.org/get -information/statistics/frequency-of-sexual-assault.

Rape, Abuse and Incest National Network (RAINN). (2013b). *Marital rape.* Retrieved from http://www.rainn.org/public-policy/sexual -assault-issues/marital-rape.

Shapiro, J. P. (1993). *No pity: People with disabilities forging a new civil rights movement.* New York, NY: Times/Random House.

Sheets, K. B., Crissman, B. G., Feist, C. D., Sell, S. L., Johnson, L. R., Donahue, K. C. . . . Brasington, C. K. (2011). Practice guidelines for communication of a prenatal or postnatal diagnosis of Down syndrome. Recommendations of the National Society of Genetic Counselors. *Journal of Genetic Counseling, 20,* 432–441.

South Carolina Coalition Against Domestic Violence and Sexual Assault. (2002). *Date rape on college campuses.* Retrieved from http://www .scadvasa.org.

Strasser, M. (2014, February 27). Top twelve most homophobic nations. *Newsweek.* Retrieved from http://www.newsweek.com/top-twelve -most-homophobic-nations-230348 .

Suicide Prevention Resource Center. (2008). *Suicide risk and prevention for lesbian, gay, bisexual, and transgender youth.* Retrieved from http://www.sprc.org/library/SPRC_LGBT_Youth.pdf.

Szymanski, E. M., & Trueba, H. T. (1994). Castification of people with disabilities: Potential disempowering aspects of classification in disabilities services. *The Journal of Rehabilitation, 60*(3), 12–21.

Taranto, A. (2014). Same-sex intimate partner violence: Current barriers to service and future goals for community agencies. Council on Crime and Justice. Retrieved from http://www.crimeandjustice.org /councilinfo.cfm?pid = 60.

Tavernise, S. (2011, June 13). Adoptions by gay couples rise, despite barriers. *The New York Times.* Retrieved from http://www.nytimes.com /2011/06/14/us/14adoption.html?pagewanted = all&_r = 0 .

United Nations. (n.d.). *Persons with disabilities.* Retrieved from http:// www.un.org/en/globalissues/disabilities/index.shtml.

United Nations Educational, Scientific and Cultural Organization, Institute for Statistics. (2013, June). *Schooling for millions of children jeopardised by reductions in aid.* Retrieved from http://www.uis .unesco.org/Library/Documents/fs-25-schooling-millions-children -jeopardised-reductions-in-aid-2013-en.pdf.

United Nations Enable. (2006). Convention on the rights of persons with disabilities. Retrieved from http://www.un.org/disabilities/conven tion/conventionfull.shtml.

U.S. Equal Employment Opportunity Commission. (2008). *Facts about pregnancy discrimination.* Retrieved from http://www.eeoc.gov/facts /fs-preg.html.

U.S. groups working to keep LGBT sex illegal in Caribbean. (2013, July 26). *SPLC* [Southern Poverty Law Center] *Report.* Retrieved from http://www.splcenter.org/get-informed/news/splc-report-us-groups -working-to-keep-criminal-statutes-barring-lgbt.

Vestal, C. (2008, March 2008). Gay marriage decisions in California, Connecticut. Retrieved from http://www.stateline.org.

Wang, W., Parker, K., & Taylor, P. (2013). *Breadwinner moms.* Pew Research Social & Demographic Trends. Retrieved from http://www .pewsocialtrends.org/2013/05/29/breadwinner-moms/.

World Health Organization. (2012). *Trends in maternal mortality: 1990-2010.* Retrieved from http://www.who.int/reproductivehealth/publica tions/monitoring/978 9241503631/.

World Health Organization. (2013). *Female genital mutilation.* Retrieved from http://www.who.int/mediacentre/factsheets/fs241/en/index.html.

Yen, H. (2011, April 26). In a first, women surpass men in advanced degrees. Retrieved from http://abcnews.go.com/us/wirestory?id = 13 45935&singlepage = true .

Zaino, J. (2013, July 25). New moms in Britain get royal treatment: In U.S., paid maternity leave lags far behind. *USA Today*, p. 9A.

Zoroya, G. (2005, March 3). Key Iraq wound: Brain trauma. *USA Today.* Retrieved from http://www.usatoday.com/news/nation/2005-03-03 -brain-trauma-lede_x.htm.

Zoroya, G. (2007, November 13). Blinded by war: Injuries send troops into darkness. *USA Today.* Retrieved from http://www.usatoday.com /news/military/2007-11-3-eyeinjuries_N.htm.

Social Settings

Drawing upon an ecosystems perspective, in part III we discussed various niches, or social statuses, in the social environment. In contrast, in part IV, we discuss habitats.

> The physical and social settings of community, workplace, school, and so on constitute the habitat [of human beings]. . . . Physical settings such as dwellings, buildings, rural villages, and urban layouts must support the social settings of family life, interpersonal life, work life, spiritual life, and so on in ways that fit the lifestyles, age, gender, and cultural patterns of the residents. (Germain, 1991, p. 45)

Traditionally, social work texts have not paid much attention to aspects of the physical environment, but that is changing gradually with the awareness of how environmental issues affect individuals and communities. On the other hand, "It is the understanding of *the person as a social being* [italics in original] that constitutes the main area for the contribution of the social work profession" (Chess & Norlin, 1991, p. 26). Thus social systems and social settings (e.g., families, groups, organizations, and communities, and so forth) have long been the focus of attention of social work curricula. These social systems are studied both as entities per se within a larger environment and as contexts for smaller systems.

In chapter 8, we discuss communities as geopolitical systems, that is, physical and social entities and settings (in contrast to the identificational communities described in chapters 6 and 7). We look at the reasons for the decline of central cities and the accompanying growth of suburbs and the implications for community well-being. In chapter 9, we draw on the large body of literature on organizational theories and assess their applicability to human service agencies and to the workplace as a social setting. In chapter 10, we discuss a special type of organization, residential institutions. We provide an overview of the history of institutional care in this country and discuss the impact of institutional settings on the people who live in them.

Oppression of vulnerable populations occurs not only in residential institutions, but in organizations and communities as well. The profession's commitment to social justice suggests that oppression should be an area of concern (Council on Social Work Education, 2008, p. 6; National Association of Social Workers, 2012). In addition to being the contexts for understanding human behavior, communities, organizations, and institutions also are settings for social work practice. Knowledge of how these collectivities operate will contribute to your professional effectiveness.

REFERENCES

Chess, W. A., & Norlin, J. M. (1991). *Human behavior and the social environment: A social systems model* (2nd ed.). Boston, MA: Allyn and Bacon.

Council on Social Work Education. (2008). *Educational policy and accreditation standards*. Alexandria, VA: Council on Social Work Education.

Germain, C. B. (1991). *Human behavior in the social environment: An ecological view*. New York, NY: Columbia University Press.

National Association of Social Workers (2012). *Social work speaks* (9th ed). Washington, DC: NASW Press.

C H A P T E R   **8**   E I G H T

Locational Communities

Social Workers and Communities
Looking Ahead
References

The profession of social work has its roots in community practice. Social workers in settlement houses adopted communities as the arena for their interventions. These early social workers worked to improve housing and neighborhood conditions, and to establish day-care centers, educational programs, recreational opportunities, and job training and referral services. Community context continues to be critical for certain vulnerable groups, particularly for those who cannot move about easily, such as children, older adults, people with physical disabilities, and often poor families. Knowledge of community is essential for good social work at any system level, and community practice reflects the profession's commitment to social and economic justice.

DEFINING COMMUNITY

Even within social work, the term *community* is often used to mean different things. In chapter 6, we introduced the concept of identificational communities; here we restrict the use of the term to mean locational or geopolitical communities. There are three essential elements of locational community: geographical area, social interaction, and common ties (Hillery, 1955). Locational community is where person and environment meet. Community residents interact with each other, share common interests, use many of the same resources, and access many of the same services. This interdependence among residents, and between residents and their community environment, is basic to the concerns of social work.

Communities are also social systems. Unlike organizations, which we will discuss in the next chapter, the relationships in communities are not based on formal, contractual expectations, but rather on mutual benefits. Communities usually do not have formal goals, but goals can be identified by examining the common needs and problems of people who share the same geographical space.

TYPES OF COMMUNITIES

Types of communities are defined in relation to population size and/or location and/or function. A *metropolis*, for example, is a city of 50,000 or more people. A *suburb* is a residential urban area beyond the political boundaries of a city; historically, some of these were small towns in their own right, but they have become connected to a larger city through the development of interstate highways and suburban sprawl. Many suburbs, called bedroom communities, are primarily residential and their inhabitants commute elsewhere to work during the day. An edge city is a business center some distance from the downtown but close to the intersection of major highways; typically it is a mix of corporate office buildings, medical centers, shopping malls, fast-food franchises, hotels, and entertainment complexes. The occupancy of bedroom communities peaks at night, while the occupancy of the edge city peaks during the day. Another term is *megalopolis,* which refers to one or more cities and their surrounding suburbs whose boundaries have converged; an example is the Boston to Washington, DC, corridor. Another example is California's coastal area from San Francisco to San Diego and beyond into Tijuana and its suburbs in Mexico.

Neighborhoods are important subsystems of cities or other incorporated areas. Fellin (2001, p. 128) notes that the prominent feature of most neighborhoods is private residences. In addition, many neighborhoods include amenities such as gardens, parks, or other recreational facilities, as well as schools, places of worship, grocery stores, dry cleaners, laundromats, cafes, and other small businesses, and service facilities (police and fire stations). The boundaries of a neighborhood may be politically set, as with voting wards, school districts, or church parishes. Social factors may also be used in the definition of neighborhoods. For example, the *Social Work Dictionary* says neighborhood inhabitants "share certain characteristics, values, mutual interests, or styles of living" (Barker, 2003, p. 292). Often neighborhoods are occupied by people of the same racial or ethnic background or sexual orientation, similar social class, or by families who are in the same stage of the family life cycle. Examples of mutual interests or styles of living might be found in a "university neighborhood," an "Italian neighborhood," or a "singles neighborhood." Slums, ghettos, and barrios are special types of neighborhood. These terms are often associated with high-poverty neighborhoods in large urban areas. *Slum* implies an area of extreme poverty, with deteriorated and abandoned structures. Although often used interchangeably with slum, the terms *ghetto* and *barrio* refer to neighborhoods with distinct racial or ethnic cultures that often are, but are not necessarily, poor. There are features of strong resident identification and positive social interaction within their boundaries, but few links with the larger community (Fellin, 2001, p. 145).

ISSUES AND TRENDS

Cities and Suburbs

The number of large U.S. cities continues to grow. In 1990, the census recorded 199 cities with populations over 100,000; in 2000, there were 243 cities with populations of this size or greater (Wright, 2007), and in 2010, there were 282 (U.S. Census Bureau, 2011). Most of the large cities in the United States can be classified as "postindustrial"—that is, their economies are dominated by "light" industry, information processing services, educational complexes, medical centers, convention and entertainment centers, and shopping malls (Kendall, 2013, p. 579). In 1950, nine of the ten largest cities were in the "snowbelt" (North) and in 2004, seven of the top ten were in the "sunbelt" (South) (Macionis, 2014).

Two significant trends of the last half-century that have implications for communities are the decline of central cities and the growth of suburbs. Several factors have contributed to these interrelated trends. These include a period of economic prosperity beginning at the end of World War II, increasing reliance on automobiles for transportation, government policies that penalize central cities and support suburbs, political fragmentation that prevents effective regional planning, and the loss of blue-collar jobs due to the relocation of industries. These factors are discussed in more detail next.

Between 1945 and 1960, per capita income in America increased by 35 percent (Coontz, 1992). This made it possible for working-class and middle-class people to purchase single-family homes. Eighty-five percent of the new homes in this period were built in the suburbs (Mason, 1982).

When workers bought automobiles, they no longer needed to live close to jobs or public transportation systems. Even though President Eisenhower's new interstate highway system was promoted to serve important military functions, the primary beneficiaries were suburbanites who used it for commuting back and forth to work (Jackson, 1985).

Although in the past few years more communities are taking a critical look at the effects of outward growth, by and large suburbs were, and continue to be, designed and built around the needs of cars (Cieslewicz, 2001).

The government subsidizes suburban commuters by failing to collect in gasoline or other taxes the full cost of road construction and maintenance, patrol and rescue services, and environmental damage. Other subsidies come to the suburbs in municipal outlays for extensions of electric power, water, and sewage lines. Perhaps the greatest impact of government policy results from national tax and economic policies directly related to housing. In the 1950s, almost half of the housing built in the suburbs depended on federal financing (Coontz, 1992; Duany, Plater-Zyberk, & Speck, 2000). The federal government provided insurance to lenders, and mortgages to families through the G.I. Bill and Veterans Administration, the Federal Housing Authority, the Federal National Mortgage Association ("Fannie Mae"), and the Government National Mortgage Association ("Ginnie Mae"). In the post–World War II period, millions of Americans received mortgage loans with artificially low interest rates (2 to 3 percent) and down payments of as little as 5 to 10 percent (or even just a single dollar when borrowing from the Veterans Administration) (Lee, 1986).

National tax and economic policies continue to favor wealthy suburban dwellers. The mortgage interest deduction is considered a "tax expenditure" or "tax subsidy" because it provides a benefit to a particular group of taxpayers; it is the most costly itemized deduction and among the largest tax expenditures. It is estimated that the mortgage deduction will reduce tax revenues by $70 billion in 2013 and by $379 billion over the five years from 2013 to 2017 (Fischer & Huang, 2013). This is much more than is spent on low-income housing. Homeowners currently can deduct their interest payments on home mortgage balances up to $1 million from their taxable income. They also can deduct interest on home equity loans of up to $100,000. Within these caps, taxpayers can claim deductions on up to two homes. Because high-income earners have more valuable homes, they make higher interest payments on their mortgages; the result was that in 2012, 77 percent of home mortgage interest deductions were claimed by taxpayers with adjusted gross incomes over

$100,000 and about 35 percent of the benefits went to homeowners with incomes above $200,000 (Fischer & Huang, 2013). Some critics of this policy call the various federal tax deductions "mansion subsidies" (Lazare, 2001). Urban advocates suggest that government subsidies that go to suburban homeowners might be more wisely spent in cities for mass transportation or infrastructure maintenance. Low-income taxpayers, especially those who are younger and live in urban areas, are less likely to own homes and thus less likely to itemize; therefore, they do not benefit from home mortgage interest deductions. Additionally, many low-income retirees tend to have less interest outstanding on home loans—that is, their home mortgages are paid off; this eliminates the tax benefit of the home mortgage interest deduction to them.

The political fragmentation of large metropolitan areas has resulted in lack of regional planning and less support for central cities. Although many suburbanites rely on the nearby city for employment, entertainment, air travel hubs, specialized medical care, and various public services, they pay their local property taxes only to suburban governments. Because suburbanites are able to use the resources of the city without contributing to its maintenance costs, they have little motivation to assume any responsibility for solving city problems.

The last factor contributing to the decline of central cities is the decrease in real opportunity brought about by the loss of blue-collar jobs due to deindustrialization and the suburbanization of employment (Wilson, 1987). Heavy industries have moved out of cities to rural areas, or even other countries, where space and labor costs are lower. Light industries and service businesses have moved to edge cities where land is cheaper, and utility rates and property taxes are lower.

The Minority Urban Experience

As discussed here, structural factors—particularly economic changes— affect all communities. In the "rust belt" of the upper Midwest, African Americans suffered most from the decline of central cities. A logical response to repressive conditions was the migration of middle- and working-class African Americans out of the inner city into areas with more favorable economic conditions. The result was that there was an increased concentration of the very poor in the central city. Middle-class urban residents continue to leave cities and those who remain behind are at opposite ends of the income spectrum—either very rich or very poor. Well-known sociologist William Julius Wilson (1987, 1996) argued that the social life of poor inner-city neighborhoods declined because of the intensification of poverty and the accompanying isolation from mainstream institutions and role models.

While Wilson (1987, 1996) focused on the mass "out-migration" of middle-class blacks from inner-city Chicago, Latino communities have experienced only gradual out-migration of successful residents and at the same time welcomed vast waves of energetic and hopeful new immigrants. A result of this pattern was that well-established Latino families could be found living next door to new immigrants and relationships across social class were developed and maintained (Valdez, 1993; White, 1988). This meant that local institutions, such as churches, might have changed, but they were not abandoned. In the case of Central American immigrants in Los Angeles, new small businesses—stores, markets, restaurants, and street vendors—continually appear, contributing "to the bustling street life and ethnic identity of the neighborhood" (Chinchilla, Hamilton, & Loucky, 1993, p. 55).

Like inner-city African Americans, Latinos suffered from economic restructuring. Since most Latinos lived in areas other than large Midwestern cities, however, their experience of economic change was shaped according to location. Historically, Latino barrios in the Southwest were scattered throughout the metropolitan areas so social isolation was not as much of a problem. Latinos live in neighborhoods where houses are both closer to job opportunities and cheaper. One factor contributing to their affordability is the contribution of in-kind assistance. For example, in Albuquerque, not only do many Mexican American carpenters and laborers build their own homes, but they also help in the construction and repair of the homes of their friends and relatives (Gonzales, 1993). In addition, Latinos are unlikely to experience the level of housing discrimination that plagues African Americans (Kochhar, Gonzalez-Barrera, & Dockterman, 2009). Half of adult Latinos own their own home (Lopez, Livingtson, & Kochhar, 2009). Among foreign-born Hispanic heads of households who arrived before 1990, almost six in ten (59.7 percent) were homeowners in 2011 (Motel & Patten, 2013). This contributes to neighborhood stability and pride.

Obviously there is great diversity within ethnic groups. A combination of ethnic/racial identity and social class may affect housing arrangements and locations (Fellin, 2001). For example, Cubans are more likely to be found in suburbs and Puerto Ricans in central cities. Filipinos, Koreans, and Indians, because they are more likely to be of a higher social class than other Asian groups, are less likely to live in segregated inner-city areas and more likely to live in suburban neighborhoods. Many Native Americans reside in inner-city neighborhoods, although these neighborhoods usually include other ethnic minorities.

Like the Latino communities discussed above, urban Chinatown communities, particularly in San Francisco, Los Angeles, and New York, have been reinvigorated by an influx of new refugees who created new demands for food, goods, services, and entertainment (Gold, 1999; Portes & Rumbaut, 2006; Yung, 1999). Vietnamese and other Indochinese refugees have established enclaves adjacent to Chinatowns, or in new locations, notably in the California cities of Westminster, Long Beach, San Diego, Santa Ana, Garden Grove, and San Jose (Min, 1995). Southeast Asian refugees developed a large number of voluntary associations that serve myriad functions and helped to build organized communities. The development and unification of Southeast Asian communities has been supported by an active media which produces newspapers, magazines, and radio and cable television programs (Gold, 1999, p. 518). More recently, many Somali refugees have resettled in the Twin Cities area in Minnesota; there are three Somali malls and Minneapolis is home to more Somalis than any other city in the United States (World Relief Minnesota, n.d.).

According to a feature article in *The New York Times* (Semple, 2013), in the last forty years the population of foreign-born New Yorkers has more than doubled. These immigrants make up about 37 percent of the city's total population. As noted earlier for other immigrant groups, many of these newcomers have settled near others from their homeland. There are now settlements of Arabs in in Brooklyn, Bangladeshis in Queens and the Bronx, Ecuadorians in Queens, Ghanaians in the Bronx, Guyanese in Brooklyn, and Sri Lankans on Staten Island, in addition to Chinese,

Korean, Mexican, and Polish neighborhoods in the New York area. All boast flourishing entrepreneurial enterprises, such as restaurants, bars, grocery stores and supermarkets, beauty salons, banks, malls, language and music schools, neighborhood newspapers, and businesses offering financial, travel, legal and other professional services.

Another minority population that has had a relatively positive urban experience is the gay community. In the 1970s, many lesbians and gay men gravitated to specific neighborhoods in large cities that were known to be accepting. Among the most prominent of these geographically bounded areas are the West Village in New York City, the Castro District in San Francisco, the South End in Boston, the Dupont Circle area in Washington, DC, New Town in Chicago, and West Hollywood in Los Angeles (Garnets & D'Augelli, 1994).

Suburban Sprawl and New Urbanism

While there is a general understanding that central cities are often inhospitable environments (Helling, 2002; Lazare, 2001; Wilson, 1987, 1996), suburbs generally do not carry similar negative connotations. In fact, suburbanites are significantly more satisfied with their communities than are residents of cities, small towns, or rural areas, according to a national survey (Morin & Taylor, 2009). Nevertheless, some urban designers describe the character of modern American suburbs as "soulless subdivisions, residential 'communities' utterly lacking in communal life; strip shopping centers, 'big box' chain stores, and artificially festive malls set within barren seas of parking; antiseptic office parks, ghost towns after 6 p.m.; and mile upon mile of clogged collector roads" (Duany, Plater-Zyberk, & Speck, 2000, p. 5). Since each piece of suburbia serves exclusively one type of activity (e.g., residential, commercial, office, recreation, industrial), residents must spend much of their time getting from one place to another, usually driving alone in a private automobile because walking, bicycling, and public transportation are rarely options.

FIGURE 8.1　CRITICAL THINKING ABOUT COMMUNITY LIFE

Interview your grandparents about their childhood neighborhood. How many facilities (school(s), houses of worship, grocery stores, drugstores, barbershops/beauty salons, hardware stores, and so forth) were located within walking distance of their home? How many were local businesses rather than national chains? What changes in community design have occurred over the past two generations?

The result of continuous, unplanned outward growth (called *suburban sprawl*) is the abandonment of existing, more centrally located neighborhoods. Squires (2001) suggests that suburban sprawl detracts not only from connectedness to place but also from a sense of community. Schneider (1992) asserts that the major attraction of suburbs is privatization: backyard patios or decks instead of front porches, private cars instead of buses, streaming movies onto smartphones or computers instead of going to theaters, and privately owned malls instead of town squares. The increasing segregation and homogeneity of neighborhoods, too much time devoted to commuting and too little time available for civic engagement, and the separation of home and work result in both physical and social fragmentation (Putnam, 2000).

In a relatively recent approach to urban planning, a small group of developers is applying what they have learned about the flaws of modern subdivisions and the relative benefits of traditional neighborhoods to build model communities such as Seaside and Celebration (in Florida), Laguna West (in California), Harbortown (in Tennessee), and Middleton Hills (in Wisconsin). Following the prescriptions of new urbanism, these towns offer streets laid out in a grid pattern, front porches instead of large lawns, small shops and offices within walking distance of homes—or even attached to homes—and many small shared green areas (Duany, Plater-Zyberk, & Speck, 2000; Hampson, 2012; New Urbanism, n.d.; Penn, 1998). These efforts at a more logical construction of communities have not been widely copied. On the other hand, some existing commuter suburbs are working on major transformations to develop resident-friendly city-style downtowns that include shopping, high-end restaurants, arts centers, grocery stores, and transit centers in walking distance. Among the cities experimenting with this new approach are Carmel, Indiana (just north of Indianapolis), Homewood, Alabama (at the southern edge of Birmingham), West Jordan, Utah (south of Salt Lake City), Lakewood, Colorado (in the Denver metropolitan area), and South Lake, Texas (outside

Fort Worth and Dallas) (El Nasser, 2012). Overall, the trends of the last half-century clearly do not reflect a history of successful community development or maintenance. The major barriers to implementing new urbanism are restrictive zoning codes (e.g., minimum lot size and restrictions on commercial use) currently in force in most municipalities and the ongoing investment in roads (New Urbanism, n.d.).

Rural Communities

At the time of the American Revolution, nine in ten colonists were farmers; that number dropped to one in five in the 1930s and today stands at one in 150 (or one in 500 if one counts only full-time farmers) (Grunwald, 2007). Currently, 46.2 million people (15 percent of the U.S. population) reside in rural counties spread across 72 percent of the U.S. land area (Cromartie, 2013). The Bureau of the Census defines *rural* (also called "nonmetropolitan areas") as a county or group of counties without a large central city (i.e., a city having a population of at least 50,000). Three major characteristics of rural communities are small-scale, low-density settlement; distance from large urban centers; and a specialized, non-diverse, rural economy (Deavers, 1992). In contrast to urban communities, rural communities have less adequate public services, such as schools, fire protection, road maintenance, health care, and recreation and entertainment facilities (Copeland, 2008; Ginsberg, 1993). Unemployment rates are also likely to be higher.

The most rural state in the country is Vermont, where more than 61.8 percent of residents live in rural areas; other rural states include Maine, with 59.8 percent and West Virginia, with 55.9 percent (Henslin, 2014). The most urban states are California and New Jersey, where fewer than 6 percent live in rural areas (Henslin, 2014). Rural areas contain both the most ethnically homogenous and ethnically diverse communities in the United States, depending on the region of the country (Flora, Flora, & Houdek, 1992).

Historically, it was not unusual for rural communities to depend on industries related to natural resources (e.g., agriculture, forestry, fishing, mining) to sustain their economy. Although farming and mining still dominate the local economy of many rural counties, those areas are losing population. In some agricultural areas, family farms have been replaced by large-scale meat and poultry processors (Johnson, 1999). The contemporary economic base of many rural counties is dependent on government funding (payrolls) for military bases, prisons, and state universities (Flora et al., 1992; Huling, 2002). In the 1970s, lower wages in rural areas made it profitable for companies to move production facilities out of cities, but beginning in the 1980s the trend shifted to moving plants overseas, where labor was even cheaper. In rural areas, many shutdowns devastated "company towns" with long-established ties to a single manufacturer (Geller, 2003).

Most of the counties with the highest poverty rates in the United States are rural; at 16 percent, rural poverty rates are higher than the national average of 15 percent (Henslin, 2014). Child poverty rates in America tend to be highest in Appalachia, the Mississippi delta, along the Mexican border, and in states with many American Indian reservations. Compared to urban Americans, the rural poor are less educated and employment opportunities available to them pay less than similar jobs in urban areas (Arsneault, 2006).

Although declining population has been a common problem in rural counties in the past, during the decade of the 1970s, more than 80 percent of rural counties gained population (Johnson, 1999). This trend slowed in the 1980s, but returned in the 1990s, when 71 percent of rural counties gained population. Sociologists call this trend a rural rebound (Henslin, 2014; Macionis, 2014). New arrivals in rural communities include blue-collar workers (who comprise 30 percent of the workforce in rural areas), disenchanted city dwellers, and many older adults. Wealthy retirees are attracted to the forested lake counties of Minnesota, Wisconsin, and Michigan, winter sports areas in California, Nevada, Wyoming, and Utah, coastal areas of California, South Carolina, and Florida, and the foothills of the Ozark Mountains in Arkansas and of the Appalachian Mountains in Virginia, Kentucky, North Carolina, and Tennessee (Johnson, 1999). When rich former city dwellers purchase or build vacation or retirement homes in rural areas, they drive up the cost of housing, but they may at the same time produce a demand for workers in construction, retail, service, and other local businesses, providing new employment opportunities. Between 2000 and 2010 the rural rebound pattern faded (Macionis,

2014) and the population in rural counties has been declining steadily since 2006 (Cromartie, 2013).

UNDERSTANDING COMMUNITIES

Ecosystems Perspective

As noted in chapter 1, the ecosystems perspective views person and environment as integrated, interdependent systems. Often concerns about habitat (meaning, in this case, the natural home of an organism) are expressed in discussions about the degradation of wetlands or rain forests and the loss of wildlife. To view community as habitat is a useful way to understand the individual in his or her environment. This perspective should lead social workers to consider the physical aspects of the environment such as crowding, noise levels, air pollution, sanitation, and access to transportation. Habitats are especially important for some populations. For example, both young children and older adults are more dependent on their local environments than other age groups that have more independent mobility.

Naturally occurring retirement communities (NORCs) are neighborhoods or building complexes where a large proportion of the residents are older adults who have "aged in place." Gerontologists believe that NORCs provide an opportunity to deliver elder services effectively; such services might include assessment and crisis prevention, health promotion, community improvement initiatives, and other supportive services (Jewish Federation of North America, 2013).

Mismatch theory is a hypothesis that explains high rates of depression and anxiety in modern life as the result of humans living in habitats quite different from those for which natural selection shaped their hominid ancestors (Wright, 1995). Not only is the physical setting of large buildings and paved streets different from the forests and savannahs of humans' ancestral Africa, but the resulting social environment is very different too. Primitive humans lived in small bands of related individuals who interacted almost continuously. In today's society, social isolation is a result of the physical structure of communities, particularly for stay-at-home suburban mothers. Even in cities, loneliness can occur in a crowd of strangers, where interactions tend to be economic rather than social.

The ecosystems perspective also encourages an examination of the fit between a community and its larger environment. Communities that are unable to obtain needed resources experience entropy, which means decline or breakdown. This occurs whenever a system uses up more energy than it takes in. Thus when a city spends more on infrastructure, and police and fire protection than it receives in taxes the community experiences entropy. People who drive through central cities with boarded-up storefronts and garbage-filled streets have witnessed the results of the process of entropy.

Another ecological term that can be applied to communities is succession. In the natural environment, succession occurs when one species is displaced by another, such as when African killer bees drive out local populations of native honeybees. In the community, succession directs us to look at the process of neighborhood change when one population replaces another. One example is when one ethnic group is replaced by another, such as when Mexican Americans replaced the Lithuanians in the Marquette Park area of Chicago in the mid-1980s. Another example of succession is when a low-income population is replaced by young, upper-middle-class individuals through the process of gentrification. Gentrification is the renovation or replacement of older homes in desirable areas with upscale residences. Gentrification often results in the removal of poor and elderly residents for whom affordable replacement housing is scarce.

Functionalist Perspective

In part II, we discussed social institutions and the functions that they perform in society. These functions are usually carried out on the local level. They include production, distribution, and consumption of goods and services; planning and decision making; law enforcement, public safety, and social control; education and socialization; provision of health care and social welfare; and information dissemination. Warren (1978, p. 9) defined community as "that combination of social units and systems that perform the major social functions having locality relevance." Thus communities provide the settings for the local components of major social institutions: businesses, local governments, schools, places of worship, clinics and hospitals, social service agencies, media outlets, and other organizations.

Communities are the interface between individuals or families, and social institutions. Healthy communities provide necessary supports and resources that enhance the functioning of smaller social systems. At an informal level and on a spontaneous basis, communities provide opportunities for social participation and mutual aid and support. An example would be the way that neighbors organize multifamily garage sales or share tasks like transporting children to and from after-school events. Another informal function of communities is the provision of a base for political action.

Breakdown in the functioning of one subsystem in a community requires that another subsystem step in. For example, if there is not adequate planning for recreation, bored adolescents are more likely to get into trouble, requiring extra police patrols. Or, if the economic system falters and there are massive layoffs, local food banks may be called upon to fill the gap in the provision of nutrition basics.

Conflict Perspective

Conflict theorists argue that community life reflects the inequalities of wealth and power in American society. Community viability is influenced by investment decisions made by the political and economic elite who entertain little input from local residents. The societal oppression of poor people and people of color is readily apparent in American communities. This is seen most clearly in patterns of segregation and environmental injustice, topics which are discussed in depth under the section "How Communities Deter Well-Being" later in this chapter.

Rational/Social Exchange Perspective

An important premise of the rationalist perspective is that individuals act in their own self-interest. "Rational" does not mean that people get together to determine what would bring the greatest good to society as a whole, or even to large numbers of people in the community, but only to themselves and their immediate family.

This idea of self-interest is particularly evident in the pattern of automobile dependence in our society. Hart and Spivak (1993) explain that Americans do not seek alternatives to use of the private automobile because it is a "free good"; in other words, they pay only a fraction of the actual cost. If motorists were required to absorb the true expense of building roads, paving parking lots, cleaning up pollution, and providing emergency medical care for accident victims, the cost of gasoline would increase by four to ten dollars a gallon (Hart & Spivak, 1993; Holtzclaw, 1993; Korb, 1996). In real dollars, Americans are paying about half as much in gas taxes now as they did in 1975 ("Tax truth: We need to raise the levy on gasoline," 2010). Because gas taxes are kept artificially low, others must shoulder the costs of suburban sprawl. As confirmed individualists, Americans prefer to go where they want, when they want, without taking into account the needs of others. Only when mass transit alternatives are readily available and the cost of driving and parking is prohibitive, will Americans give up traveling in their own private cars. New York, where the cost of parking is extravagant, is the only American city in which the majority of households don't own one or more automobiles (Seabrook, 2002). Recent census data show that most commuters continue to travel solo on a daily basis; 71 percent drive alone while 18 percent use public transportation and 9 percent carpool (Ponce, 2013).

Constructionist Perspective

A constructionist perspective would emphasize the different meanings that people give to the term *community*. Sociologist Ferdinand Tonnies (1963/1887) used the terms *gemeinschaft* and *gesellschaft* to describe the ways that people related to each other in their communities. *Gemeinschaft* is found in communities where residents share traditions, know each other well, and are eager to offer mutual support. *Gesellschaft* describes communities where relationships are impersonal and contractual. Tonnies believed that communities could exhibit both characteristics, but that usually one was predominant. Tonnies suggested that as society became more urban and industrialized, communities would exhibit more features of *gesellschaft* than *gemeinschaft*. Despite his predictions, many Americans would still describe their community experience as *gemeinschaft*, reflecting on their involvement in neighborhood associations, shared interests and responsibilities for local children, participation in holiday or ethnic celebrations, support for school or city sports teams, and socializing in local taverns and restaurants (Fellin, 2001; Oldenburg, 2001).

PREFERRED PERSPECTIVES

Descriptions of communities often focus on deficits, particularly in relation to communities of people of color. Despite obvious challenges in many poor and minority communities, the strengths perspective promotes the assumption that all communities have assets. There are many kinds of community assets: natural beauty, a pleasant climate, strategic location, thriving industries, skilled leaders, and strong social institutions. Distinct from these is the idea of social capital (Bourdieu, 1986; Coleman, 1988; Putnam, 2000; Warren, Thompson, & Saegert, 2001). In this text, *social capital* is defined as "the set of resources that inhere in relationships of trust and cooperation between people. . . . Social capital is a collective asset, a feature of communities, rather than the property of an individual. As such, individuals both contribute to it and use it, but they cannot own it" (Warren, Thompson, & Saegert, 2001, p. 1). Stolle and Rochon (2001, pp. 145–146) include in their list of "indicators" of social capital such factors as participation and engagement in "politics generally and in the community specifically," generalized trust that fosters "norms of reciprocity" within the community, trust toward public officials and institutions, individual willingness "to do one's share in collective endeavors," and optimism about the future in relation to social and political relationships.

One type of social capital is bonding within communities. Strong community institutions, such as schools, places of worship, parent/teacher groups, fraternal organizations, and small business associations are essential for creating an environment where social capital can develop (Warren, Thompson, & Saegert, 2001). Bonding capital tends to occur among people who are similar; if there is only bonding capital, a community will be segregated into mutually exclusive groups (Putnam & Feldstein, 2003). Another type of social capital is *bridging* across groups or populations. Bridging capital is harder to build than bonding capital, but it is essential for fostering healthy communities in a diverse society (Putnam & Feldstein, 2003).

Historically and currently, immigrants and refugees, and ethnic enclaves (see chapter 6) have been a constructive force in many cities. These areas of concentrated entrepreneurship rely on three conditions: the presence of a number of immigrants with substantial business expertise acquired in their homeland, access to a small amount of capital, and labor (Portes & Rumbaut, 2006, pp. 28–29). Typically the labor requirement is found in family members initially and later in more recent immigrants. In addition to the economic vitality of immigrant-serving businesses, traditional social controls are revived, networks are strengthened, and old community institutions are changed or new community institutions emerge to meet the needs of new residents (Gold, 1999; Moore & Pinderhughes, 1993; Padilla, 1993; Wysocki, 1991). Mutual aid linked to strong extended family networks is a characteristic of many immigrant groups.

In poor communities, social capital is a critically important factor for survival when other forms of capital (e.g., financial capital) are missing. The use of social capital is often the only factor that allows community residents to cope. Poor communities are more likely to have religious institutions whose missions may include more than just the spiritual life of its members. African Americans develop and maintain some of the strongest forms of social capital, stemming from a tradition of high rates of church membership and participation (Lincoln & Mamiya, 1990). Even the much-maligned public housing projects at one time provided a positive home and close-knit community for many inner-city African American residents. In describing her experiences growing up in the Ida B. Wells Homes in Chicago in the 1950s, newspaper columnist Leanita McClain spoke of

> lives as full of personal cheer as anyone else—birthday parties, graduation celebrations, block club parties . . . There were dance classes and sewing classes and charm classes, when we weren't roller skating or bicycling. There was a corner soda shop, Doc's, that made the best malts in our limited world. People raised money to pay the rent by selling baked goods or chicken dinners. Every Sunday there was a parade of scrubbed Sunday school children. . . . And there were fathers who were fathers to those without them, and plenty of working people, factory workers and

domestics whose rush hour began long before dawn. (1986, pp. 141–142)

Nevertheless, even high levels of social capital cannot withstand the overwhelming negative forces found in oppressive economic and political systems. Wuthnow notes that a significant share of the decline in social capital in the United States over the past two decades has occurred among marginalized groups: "People need to feel entitled in order to take part in the political process, and they need to feel that their participation will make a difference. Part of the decline is also due to the fact that people need other resources in order to create social capital, not the least of which are adequate incomes, sufficient safety to venture out of their homes, and such amenities as child care and transportation" (2002, p. 101).

THE IMPACT OF COMMUNITIES ON INDIVIDUALS AND FAMILIES

How Communities Deter Well-Being

Negative Impacts on Childhood

In his studies of concentrated poverty, Jargowsky (1997) noted that where you live clearly affects how you grow up. Some groups of people in particular are affected by neighborhood deficits: these categories include people living in extreme poverty, older adults, and children. They are trapped in the sense that they cannot move and many do not even leave the neighborhood regularly because they lack access to transportation or are too frightened to go out.

When they enter school, children encounter the world beyond their family and home. Schools that are prepared to deliver sound educational services to children and their families are critical in communities that are economically deprived (Garbarino, 1992). Unfortunately, it is the poorest communities that are most likely to have schools that are only marginally able to meet the needs of students (Kozol, 1991).

Growing children also need safe areas for play and exercise. A study found that inner-city children who lived in neighborhoods with parks gained about 13 percent less weight over a two-year period than children who lived with less green space (Gupta, 2008). Heavily trafficked streets, alleys strewn with litter and used drug paraphernalia, playgrounds with broken equipment, and dark stairwells and hallways limit children's access to healthy physical activity. Heavy auto traffic also produces high levels of ozone. Children are thought to be particularly at risk from the effects of ozone. According to the School Health Profile report from the Centers for Disease Control (2010), asthma is disproportionately higher among low-income populations, racial and ethnic minorities, and children in inner cities.

Childhood safety is also threatened by community violence. A thirteen-year-old describes his life on the South Side of Chicago:

> If you act like a little kid in this neighborhood, you're not gonna last too long. 'Cause if you play childish games in the ghetto, you're gonna find a childish bullet in your childish brain. If you live in the ghetto, when you're ten you know everything you're not supposed to know. When I was ten I knew where drugs came from. I knew about every different kind of gun. I knew about sex. I was a kid in my age but my mind had the reality of a grown-up, 'cause I seen these things every day! (Jones & Newman, 2000, p. 116)

The experience of this child is not uncommon.

This child's perspective demonstrates how blighted neighborhoods present not only physical threats, but psychological ones as well. As cognitive powers develop and children are able to make social comparisons, they become aware of the discrepancies between their home neighborhood and more affluent ones. Kozol records how a fifteen-year-old Harlem resident views her environment: " 'It's not like being in jail,' she says, 'It's more like being "hidden." It's as if you have been put in a garage where, if they don't have room for something but aren't sure if they should throw it out, they put it there where they don't need to think of it again' " (1995, pp. 38–39).

Another negative community factor that may detract from the well-being of children is the lack of social density. Social density measures "the degree to which an environment contains a diversity of roles for children to learn from and for parents to draw upon" (Garbarino, Galambos, Plantz, & Kostelny, 1992, p. 208). Poor neighborhoods that lack such diversity impoverish the experiences of the children living there. Children are enriched when they can observe different occupational, kinship, and acquaintance roles. A neighborhood made up exclusively of mother-headed families, with no adult male role models and no consistent male disciplinary presence leaves boys to "learn about manhood on the streets, where the temptation is strong to demonstrate prowess through lawbreaking, violence, and fathering a child" (Schorr, 1989, p. 20). McClain (1986) speaks of a "poverty of the spirit" that differentiates such neighborhoods from "poverty of the pocket." Lack of social density is also apparent in new residential suburbs where children are likely to grow up surrounded by young families in similar middle-class circumstances. The only adult roles these children encounter in their neighborhoods are those of parents, joggers, dog walkers, and the ice cream vendor. They don't have regular interaction with shopkeepers, mechanics, retirees, or even extended family members.

Environmental Racism

Environmental racism is the term used to describe the pattern whereby environmental hazards are located near poor people of color (Bullard, 1990; Bullard, 2005; Hoff & Rogge, 1996; Mohai & Saha, 2007; Wolcott & Milligan, 1992). Racial and ethnic minority groups are disproportionately exposed to the dangers associated with environmental degradation (Bullard, 2004). For example, Hoff and Rogge (1996) noted that just three communities, all of them more than 78 percent minority, hold 40 percent of the landfill capacity of the entire country. Lipsitz (2002, pp. 67–68) summarizes a number of reports documenting the inequitable distribution of risks; among them, in Houston, Texas, African Americans make up 25 percent of the population but 75 percent of the municipal garbage incinerators and 100 percent of the city-owned garbage dumps are located in black neighborhoods; penalties for violating federal environmental laws regulating air, water, and waste pollution were 46 percent lower in minority communities than in white communities; and across the nation, 60 percent of African Americans and Latinos live in communities with uncontrolled toxic waste sites. For young people, local environmental hazards have been associated with high rates of stunted growth and lead poisoning, and residents of all ages are susceptible to asthma, various types of cancer, and other serious illnesses (Lipsitz, 2002).

Interventions also may differ depending on the race of those affected. An article published in the *Washington Post* (Duke, 2007) chronicled the story of one African American family living in rural Tennessee whose well water was contaminated by trichloroethylene (TCE), a carcinogen, leaking from a nearby county landfill. Records indicate that when state environmental and water officials became concerned about potential TCE leaks, they hastily tested the wells of nearby white families but waited nine years to test the well of the African American family. Ten of their relatives, who live near each other and the landfill, were diagnosed with various kinds of cancer.

Conflict theory suggests that it is more difficult for marginalized populations to keep their communities free of environmental degradation. Poor communities without other choices may accept environmentally hazardous industries and/or commercial waste operations in their neighborhoods in order to create jobs in the local economy (Beasley, 1990; Bullard & Wright, 1986; Monk & Fretwell, 2008). The relationship between poverty and environmental threats is clear "in polluted inner city neighborhoods where children of color suffer from high rates of asthma; in crop lands where poor migrant workers carry agricultural pesticides home to their families on their work clothes; in low-income Louisiana parishes along the industrial 'Cancer Alley' stretch of the Mississippi River; and in the unsanitary, crowded, hastily and poorly constructed *maquiladoras* that house Mexican plant workers along the U.S.-Mexico border" (National Association of Social Workers, 2012, p. 124).

The pattern exists on the international level as well. The imbalance of power among nations is reflected in the movement of toxic chemicals from industrialized to developing countries (Rogge & Darkwa, 1996). Between 60 and 80 percent of electronic waste (e.g., discarded cell phones and computers parts) is shipped overseas, mostly to China, India, and Pakistan where poor laborers, wearing no protective gear, "scratch for precious metals in pools of toxic muck" (Royte, 2005, p. 84). Waste is dumped into fields and streams where hazardous chemicals accumulate in the soil and water and contribute to high rates of birth defects, infant mortality, blood diseases, and severe respiratory problems.

In the United States, violations of Native people's land provide the most graphic and poignant illustrations of environmental racism (Hoff & Rogge, 1996, p. 45). For example, the Goshute reservation in Utah is surrounded by a magnesium plant on the north, a stockpile of chemical weapons on the east, an army testing ground for exposure to nerve gas on the south, and a bombing range and hazardous waste incinerator on the west (Wolfson, 2000). In order to secure donations for a cultural center and desperately needed jobs, the tribal chairman agreed to let eight power companies from California, New York, Minnesota, Wisconsin, Michigan, Georgia, Pennsylvania, Florida, and Alabama use a part of the reservation as a nuclear waste dump. Corporations and even the federal government "systematically target Native American reservations when looking for locations for hazardous waste incinerators, solid waste landfills, and nuclear waste storage facilities" (Lipsitz, 2002, p. 68).

Environmental racism is considered a human rights issue. Litigation is typically brought using the principles of two different laws: Title VI of the Civil Rights Act of 1964 and the National Environmental Policy Act of 1969 (Bullard, 2005). The first prohibits discriminatory practices in programs receiving federal funds, and the second ensures that environmental factors are weighted equally when compared to other factors in the decision-making process before major development projects can proceed. Impetus for the movement to oppose environmental racism did not come from regulatory agencies, but rather from grassroots and national environmental and civil rights leaders (Bullard, 2005, p. 30).

Segregation by Class

In America, a limited number of financial institutions and developers finance and construct most suburban housing and large city projects. Given the dynamics of the capitalist system, their motivation rests not in benefiting the community, but in making a profit. Developers are seldom called upon to think about, much less pay for, the impact of their development on surrounding areas in terms of traffic congestion, pollution, excessive demands on infrastructure (schools, utilities, water, and sewer), or destruction of existing neighborhoods. Typically, it is people of color and the lower social classes who pay disproportionately for these developments even though they derive little direct benefit from them.

Prior to the 1960s, although many neighborhoods were segregated by race and ethnicity, most were integrated by socioeconomic class, both in large cities and small towns (Fellin, 2001, p. 152). Historically in America, gulfs between classes were not reflected in physical distances; even in cities with terrible slums, the middle class lived with or very near the poor (Coontz, 1988). As whites and middle-class blacks and other minorities moved to the suburbs, center cities became more homogenous by race and class, and poverty and deprivation become increasingly more concentrated (Jargowsky, 2002; Powell, 2002; Wilson, 1987). Between 1970 and 1990, the number of poor persons living in high-poverty neighborhoods almost doubled (Jargowsky, 1997). (High-poverty neighborhoods are defined as census tracts with poverty rates of 40 percent or higher.)

Census data confirm that between 1970 and 2000, there was a 32 percent increase in the residential separation of high-income Americans from all other Americans (Taylor & Morin, 2008). Since the Great Recession and housing crisis, spatial concentration of poverty has surged. Using data from three waves of the American Community Survey five-year census tract files to examine the resurgence of concentrated poverty in detail, Jargowsky (2013) found three important differences in patterns from earlier decades. First, the concentration of poverty has increased faster in smaller metropolitan areas than in central cities (p. 4). Second, although the concentration of poverty among non-Hispanic whites remains much lower than for minority groups, it increased faster; the number of non-Hispanic white people living in high-poverty neighborhoods more than doubled between 2000 and 2007–2011 (pp. 4, 5). Third, whereas two-thirds of high-poverty neighborhoods were dominated by a single race or ethnic group in 1990, in 2007–2011 only about half of high-poverty neighborhoods were described this way (p. 5). Seldom are developers interested in building affordable or low-income housing in new suburbs. Instead, they concentrate on upscale, high-profit neighborhoods. Adding insult to injury, many of the most exclusive new neighborhoods are literally walled off from the rest of the community. Duany, Plater-Zyberk, and Speck (2000) note that it is not the walls per se that threaten social unity, but the homogeneity and exclusivity of the people living behind them. The residents of these private, gated communities are uniform in terms of both race and class. They have little regular contact with people at the lower end of the socioeconomic ladder—with the exception of the cleaning ladies and yardmen who show up to do the tasks that wealthy residents prefer to hire out.

Suburbs are rarely zoned for multifamily dwellings or other forms of affordable housing. Codes that restrict the building of houses in a new development that do not meet minimum cost or square footage requirements are used to separate even the very rich from the very, very rich. For the first time in our history, "we are now experiencing ruthless segregation by minute gradations of income. . . . To prove this point, one need only to attempt to build a $200,000 house on an empty lot in the $350,000 cluster; the homeowners' association will immediately sue. . . . The real estate business caters to this elitism so relentlessly that even some mobile home parks are marketed in this way" (Duany et al., 2000, pp. 43–44).

Wealthy and powerful community residents use building codes and zoning ordinances not only to insulate themselves from their poorer neighbors, but also to exclude people with disabilities. Persons with mental illness or cognitive impairments, for example, who are able to live in a group home in the community are often shut out of upscale neighborhoods by property holders who assert "I think it's great to have halfway houses for people like that, just not here!" Such N.I.M.B.Y. ("not in my backyard") attitudes often result in needed facilities being clustered in older transitional neighborhoods bordering on retail or industrial areas where public transportation is available, houses are relatively large, and political power is small.

While suburban areas focus on segregation by class, center cities struggle with a lack of affordable and structurally sound housing. During the 1950s and 1960s, while the Federal Housing Authority (FHA) provided subsidies for suburban housing, the federal government built large, high-rise housing projects in major cities. Because tenant selection procedures were done without resident input, urban renewal projects had the effect of destroying important social networks that had existed in the poor neighborhoods that were razed, and instead promoted anonymity and social isolation (Goering, Kamely, & Richardson, 1997). Ninety percent of the low-income housing units removed during the urban renewal programs were never replaced (Lipsitz, 2002, p. 65). Even the construction of interstate highways was detrimental to those living in the central city. Overpasses destroyed or devalued urban neighborhoods and limited access roads were used as physical barriers between neighborhoods, separating different racial and ethnic communities. For example, the Dan Ryan Expressway in Chicago established a barrier between African American neighborhoods to the east and white ethnic neighborhoods to the west. Many stable racial minority communities were destroyed; more than 60 percent of those displaced by urban renewal projects were people of color (Jackson, 1985; Zarembka, 1990).

Segregation by Race and Ethnicity

Although housing segregation by class is a new and growing concern, segregation by race has a long history in this country. It was and is fostered by different mechanisms. As southern blacks migrated to northern industrial centers, and especially after desegregation laws made it harder to avoid contact with African Americans, whites moved to outlying areas. (This pattern is called white flight.) Although it might appear at first that patterns of residential segregation can be attributed solely to the personal choices of individual white homeowners, Powell (2002) explains how the government was significantly involved in the segregation of people of color into less desirable neighborhoods. Beginning in the 1920s and extending through the post–World War II period, government housing authorities instituted policies that were specifically designed to discriminate against minorities in mortgage loans and insurance. These government agencies assessed neighborhoods in which people of color lived in the lowest value category, without consideration of the actual worth of the housing stock. On FHA maps, these neighborhoods were marked in red ink. The term *redlining* thus came to refer to the practice of identifying minority neighborhoods to be excluded from consideration for granting mortgage funding. While federal programs denied home ownership to minorities, the same policies encouraged investment in white-only suburbs. A third mechanism of racial discrimination against minority individuals is mortgage lending. As discussed in chapter 6, more than half of African Americans and almost half of Latinos pay a higher-than-typical interest rate for home mortgages compared to less than 20 percent of whites (Aversa, 2006). A final mechanism is racial steering. This occurs when real-estate agents take people of color to see houses in some neighborhoods and direct white people to others.

A recent analysis of neighborhood-level census data (Glaeser & Vigdor, 2012) shows that American cities are now more integrated than they have been since 1910. Levels of racial segregation that peaked dramatically with black migration to cities in the mid-twentieth century have been entirely erased by integration since the 1960s. The study also found that "all-white neighborhoods are effectively extinct": African-American residents can be found in 199 out of every 200 neighborhoods nationwide. The remaining neighborhoods are mostly in remote rural areas or in cities with few black residents. Other sociologists have expressed caution, however, noting that "we're nowhere near the end of segregation" (El Nasser, 2012, p. 1A). Chicago remains the most segregated city in the country, with Philadelphia and New York following (Glaeser & Vigdor, 2012).

Regardless of the actual patterns of segregation in the country, the Pew Research Center (Taylor & Morin, 2008) reports that 65 percent of Americans say they prefer to reside in a racially mixed community, while 20 percent say they would prefer to live in a community made up only of members of their own race. Blacks (83 percent) are more likely than whites (60 percent) to say they prefer a diverse community and younger adults are more likely to prefer diverse communities than are older adults. People in the Midwest demonstrate the least support for racially diverse communities, but even among Midwesterners, diversity is preferred by a margin of more than two to one.

How Communities Promote Well-Being

Communities promote well-being at three levels: formal service organizations, small businesses that meet a service need, and families and individuals acting as neighbors. Various formal local organizations provide services to community residents. These include neighborhood centers, Boys and Girls Clubs, schools, places of worship, and VFW halls. Some of the services and settings that are offered include day-care centers and preschools, recreation opportunities, food pantries, health services (e.g., flu shots, blood pressure screening), and space for organizations ranging from Scouts to Alcoholics Anonymous and Weight Watchers. Such activities are not limited to white, middle-class communities. Solomon (1976, p. 220) reported that, contrary to common perceptions, voluntary associations "abound" in black communities. These include church-related organizations; veterans groups; political clubs; professional, business and service groups; sports and athletic clubs; civil rights or social action groups; and social clubs. In Latino communities, Catholic churches and Protestant evangelical churches may provide a range of social services (Chinchilla et al., 1993; Moore & Vigil, 1993). Concrete services might include help finding an apartment or procuring food and furniture; providing literacy training and English-as-a-second-language classes; assistance in locating jobs; and counseling and legal assistance regarding immigration, and filling out forms for permanent resident visas. Services might also include advocacy on behalf of neighborhood residents for a supermarket chain to improve the quality of its products, for an insurance company to lower exorbitant rates, for local politicians to improve transportation services, or for a corporate office park to provide jobs.

Particularly in minority communities, small businesses may fulfill both commercial and social service roles. For example, African American barbershops and beauty parlors are not only a forum for the exchange of ideas, but also sources of information on how to prevent death from breast and prostrate cancer (Halebar, 2002). Studies of Latina-owned businesses have documented their provision of social services (Delgado, 1998). They also provide financial services (e.g., check-cashing, loans)—assistance made necessary by the absence of banks and automated teller machines in many Latino neighborhoods (Levitt, 1995). Latina business owners report that they have both an obligation and a God-given gift to be of help to their communities (Delgado, 1998; Lazzari, Ford, & Haughey, 1996). Many small businesses (e.g., bookstores, theaters, and restaurants) in lesbian and gay neighborhoods foster a powerful psychological sense of community and encourage information exchanges among different social networks (Garnets & D'Augelli, 1994). During the 1980s, urban gay communities in New York, San Francisco, and Los Angeles responded to the challenge of the HIV/AIDS crisis by constructing entire caring systems (Garnets & D'Augelli, 1994).

In addition to formal helping organizations and local businesses, families and individuals in communities also offer services to each other. These may involve a network of neighbors, such as those in Neighborhood Watch Associations or babysitting exchange groups. On an individual level, neighbors take in mail while others go on vacation, share tools, help look for lost pets, swap plant cuttings, mow yards or shovel walks for neighbors who are elderly or sick, and provide food when there is a death in the family. "Neighboring" also can include "watching out" for each other, such as checking on older adults when the weather is extreme. These forms of mutual aid improve the quality of residents' lives.

SOCIAL WORKERS AND COMMUNITIES

The lives of the most vulnerable populations are inextricably linked to the condition of the communities within which they reside. Because communities both promote and deter the well-being of clients, social workers who are engaged in direct practice with individuals and families view the community as both a resource for clients and as a possible source of client problems.

The client system for other social workers is the community per se. These macro social workers engage in community planning and development, working in partnership with community members and groups to create a more positive social environment (Brueggemann, 2013). Macro social work practitioners should be prepared to view the community as possessing assets and solutions to problems, and to see partnership with community members and groups as a way to create a more positive social environment.

In small or rural communities, social workers are more likely to have a broad range of responsibilities and engage in practice at several systems levels. They may use their generalist skills not only as direct service workers, but also as administrators, organizers, planners, and consultants (Ginsberg, 2005).

LOOKING AHEAD

In the next chapter, we examine the role of organizations in communities and society. We also examine the influence of organizations on the lives of those who work there or receive services.

REFERENCES

Arsneault, S. (2006). Implementing welfare reform in rural and urban communities: Why place matters. *American Review of Public Administration, 36*, 173–188.

Aversa, J. (2006, September 9). Loan study finds inequality. *The State* [Columbia, SC], p. B9.

Barker, R. L. (2003). *The social work dictionary* (5th ed.). Washington, DC: NASW Press.

Beasley, C., Jr. (1990). Of pollution and poverty, part 3: Deadly threat on native lands. *Buzzworm, 2*(5), 39–45.

Bourdieu, P. (1986). The forms of capital. In J. Richardson (Ed.), *Handbook of theory and research for the sociology of education* (pp. 241–258). New York, NY: Greenwood Press.

Brueggemann, W. G. (2013). *The practice of macro social work* (4th ed.). Belmont, CA: Brooks/Cole.

Bullard, R. D. (1990). *Dumping in Dixie: Race, class, and environmental quality.* Boulder, CO: Westview Press.

Bullard, R. D. (2004). Environmental racism. In J. H. Skolnick & E. Currie (Eds.), *Crisis in American institutions* (pp. 237–244). Boston, MA: Pearson.

Bullard, R. D. (2005). *The quest for environmental justice: Human rights and the politics of pollution.* San Francisco, CA: Sierra Club Books.

Bullard, R. D., & Wright, B. H. (1986). The politics of pollution: Implications for the black community. *Phylon, 68*(1), 71–78.

Centers for Disease Control. (2010). *School health profile 2010.* Retrieved from http://www.cdc.gov/healthyyouth/profiles/2010/profiles_narrative.pdf.

Chess, W. A., & Norlin, J. M. (1991). *Human behavior and the social environment: A social systems model* (2nd ed). Boston, MA: Allyn and Bacon.

Chinchilla, N., Hamilton, N., & Loucky, J. (1993). Central Americans in Los Angeles: An immigrant community in transition. In J. Moore and R. Pinderhughes (Eds.), *In the barrios: Latinos and the underclass debate* (pp. 51–78). New York, NY: Russell Sage Foundation.

Cieslewicz, D. J. (2001). The environmental impacts of sprawl. In G. D. Squires (Ed.), *Urban sprawl: Causes, consequences & policy responses* (pp. 23–38). Washington, DC: Urban Institute.

Coleman, J. S. (1988). Social capital in the creation of human capital. *American Journal of Sociology (supplement) 94,* S95–S120.

Coontz, S. (1988). *The social origins of private life: A history of American families 1600–1900.* New York, NY: Verso.

Coontz, S. (1992). *The way we never were: American families and the nostalgia trap: The myth of the traditional family.* New York, NY: Basic Books.

Copeland, L. (2008, June 17). South's rural towns shrink as economic troubles grow. *USA Today,* pp. A1–A2.

Council on Social Work Education. (2008). *Educational policy and accreditation standards.* Alexandria, VA: Council on Social Work Education.

Cromartie, J. (2013, May 24). *How is rural America changing?* United States Department of Agriculture. Retrieved from http://www.census .gov/newsroom/cspan/rural_america/20130524_rural_america_slides .pdf.

Deavers, K. (1992). What is rural? *Policies Studies Journal, 20,* 183–189.

Delgado, M. (1998). Latina-owned businesses: Community resources for the prevention field. *Journal of Primary Prevention, 18,* 447–460.

Duany, A., Plater-Zyberk, E., & Speck, J. (2000). *Suburban nation: The rise of sprawl and the decline of the American dream.* New York, NY: North Point Press.

Duke, L. (2007, March 20). A well of pain. *The Washington Post.* Retrieved from http://www.washingtonpost.com.

El Nasser, H. (2012, January 31). Study finds black segregation in cities is lowest in century. *USA Today,* p. 1A.

Fellin, P. (2001). *The community and the social worker* (3rd ed.). Itasca, IL: F. E. Peacock.

Fischer, W., & Huang, C. C. (2013, June 25). *Mortgage interest deduction is ripe for reform: Conversion to tax credit could raise revenue and make subsidy more effective and fairer.* Center on Budget and Policy Priorities. Retrieved from http://www.cbpp.org/cms/?fa = view& amp;id = 3948.

Flora, J. L., Flora, C. B., & Houdek, E. (1992). *Rural communities: Legacy and change.* Boulder, CO: Westview Press.

Garbarino, J. (1992). *Children and families in the social environment* (2nd ed.). New York, NY: Aldine de Gruyter.

Garbarino, J., Galambos, N. L., Plantz, M. C., & Kostelny, K. (1992). The territory of childhood. In J. Garbarino (Ed.), *Children and families in the social environment* (2nd ed.). New York, NY: Aldine de Gruyter.

Garnets, L. D., & D'Augelli, A. R. (1994). Empowering lesbian and gay communities: A call for collaboration with community psychology. *American Journal of Community, 22,* 447–470.

Geller, A. (2003, August 10). Rural South reels as plants move out, ship jobs abroad. *The State* [Columbia, SC], pp. F1, F4.

Germain, C. B. (1991). *Human behavior in the social environment: An ecological view.* New York, NY: Columbia University Press.

Ginsberg, L. H. (1993). *Social work in rural communities* (2nd ed.) Alexandria, VA: Council on Social Work Education.

Ginsberg, L. H. (2005). *Social work in rural communities* (4th ed.). Alexandria, VA: Council on Social Work Education.

Glaeser, E., & Vigdor, J. (2012, January). *The end of the segregated century: Racial separation in America's neighborhoods, 1890–2010.* Retrieved from http://www. Manhattan-institute.org/html/cr_66.htm.

Goering, J., Kamely, A., & Richardson, T. (1997). Recent research on racial segregation and poverty concentration in public housing in the United States. *The Urban Affairs Review, 32,* 723–745.

Gold, S. J. (1999). Southeast Asians. In E. R. Barkan (Ed.), *A nation of peoples: America's multicultural heritage* (pp. 505–519). Westport, CT: Greenwood Press.

Gonzales, P. B. (1993). Historical poverty, restructuring effects, and integrative ties: Mexican American neighborhoods in a peripheral sunbelt economy. In J. Moore and R. Pinderhughes (Eds.), *In the barrios: Latinos and the underclass debate* (pp. 149–171). New York, NY: Russell Sage Foundation.

Grunwald, M. (2007, November 12). Down on the farm. *Time*, pp. 26–36.

Gupta, S. (2008, December 8). Slender in the grass. *Time*, p. 60.

Halebar, J. (2002, September 9). Beauty shops offer breast cancer information. *The State* [Columbia, SC], p. B5.

Hampson, R. (2012, September 14). City living will feel like a blast from the past. *USA Today*, pp. 1F and 15F.

Hart, S., & Spivak, A. (1993) *The elephant in the bedroom: Automobile dependence and denial; impacts on the economy and environment.* Pasadena, CA: New Paradigm Books.

Helling, A. (2002). Transportation, land use, and the impacts of sprawl on poor children and families. In G. D. Squires (Ed.), *Urban sprawl: Causes, consequences & policy responses* (pp. 119–139). Washington, DC: Urban Institute.

Henslin, J. M. (2014). *Sociology: A down-to-earth approach* (12th ed.). Boston, MA: Pearson Education.

Hillery, G. (1955). Definitions of community: Areas of agreement. *Rural Sociology, 20*, 111–123.

Hoff, M. D., & Rogge, M. E. (1996). Everything that rises must converge: Developing a social work response to environmental injustice. *Journal of Progressive Human Services, 7*, 41–57.

Holtzclaw, J. (1993, Winter). America's autos on welfare: A summary of studies. *The Transportopia Bulletin*, p. 11.

Huling, T. (2002). Building a prison economy in rural America. In M. Mauer and M. Chesney-Lind (Eds.), *Invisible punishment: The collateral consequences of mass imprisonment* (pp. 197–213). New York, NY: New Press.

Jackson, K. (1985). *Crabgrass frontier: The suburbanization of the United States.* New York, NY: Oxford University Press.

Jargowsky, P. A. (1997). *Poverty and place: Ghettos, barrios and the American city.* New York, NY: Russell Sage Foundation.

Jargowsky, P. A. (2002). Sprawl, concentration of poverty, and urban inequality. In G. D. Squires (Ed.), *Urban sprawl: Causes, consequences & policy responses* (pp. 39–72). Washington, DC: Urban Institute.

Jargowsky, P. A. (2013). *Concentration of poverty in the new millennium.* Camden, NJ: Century Foundation and the Rutgers Center for Urban Research and Education.

Jewish Foundation of North America, Inc. (2013). *All about NORCs.* Retrieved from http://www.norcs.org/page.aspx?id = 119552.

Johnson, K. M. (1999). The rural rebound. *Reports on America, 1*(3), 1–21.

Jones, L., & Newman, L. (2000). Our America: Life and death on the south side of Chicago. In D. N. Sattler, G. P. Kramer, V. Shabatay, and D. A. Bernstein (Eds.), *Lifespan development in context: Voices and perspectives* (pp. 116–121). Boston, MA: Houghton Mifflin.

Kendall, D. (2013). *Sociology in our times* (9th ed.). Belmont, CA: Wadsworth.

Kochhar, R., Gonzalez-Barrera, A., and Dockterman, D. (2009). *Minorities, immigrants, and home ownership: Through boom and bust.* Pew Research Hispanic Trends Project. Retrieved from http://www.pew hispanic.org/2009/05/12/through-boom-and-bust/.

Korb, L. J. (1996, September 18). Holding the bag in the gulf. *The New York Times*, p. A21.

Kozol, J. (1991). *Savage inequalities: Children in America's schools.* New York, NY: Crown.

Kozol, J. (1995). *Amazing grace: The lives of children and the conscience of a nation.* New York, NY: Crown.

Lazare, D. (2001). *America's undeclared war: What's killing our cities and how we can stop it.* New York, NY: Harcourt.

Lazzari, M., Ford, H., & Haughey, K. J. (1996). Making a difference: Women of action in the community. *Social Work, 41,* 197–205,

Lee, D. (1986). Government policy and the distortions in family housing. In J. Peden & F. Glahe (Eds.), *The American family and the state* (p. 312.). San Francisco, CA: Pacific Research Institute for Public Policy.

Levitt, P. (1995). A todos les llamo primo (I call everyone cousin): The social basis for Latino small businesses. In M. Halter (Ed.), *New migrants in the marketplace: Boston's ethnic entrepreneurs* (pp. 120–140). Boston, MA: University of Massachusetts.

Lincoln, C. E., & Mamiya, L. H. (1990). *The black church in the African American experience.* Durham, NC: Duke University Press.

Lipsitz, G. (2002). The possessive investment in whiteness. In P. S. Rothenberg (Ed), *White privilege: Essential readings on the other side of racism*. New York, NY: Worth.

Lopez, M. H., Livingston, G., & Kochhar, R. (2009). *Hispanics and the economic downturn: Housing woes and remittance cuts*. Pew Research Hispanic Trends Project. Retrieved from http://www.pew hispanic.org/2009/01/08/hispanics-and-the-economic-downturn-hous ing-woes-and-remittance-cuts/.

Macionis, J. J. (2014). *Sociology* (15th ed.). Boston, MA: Pearson Education.

Mason, J. (1982). *History of housing in the U.S.* Houston, TX: Gulf.

McClain, L. (1986). More of a home to me now . . . In C. Page (Ed.), *A foot in each world: Essays and articles by Leanita McClain* (pp. 140–143). Evanston, IL: Northwestern University Press.

Min, P. G. (1995). Major issues relating to Asian American experiences. In P. G. Min (Ed.), *Asian Americans: Contemporary trends and issues* (pp. 38–57). Thousand Oaks, CA: Sage.

Mohai, P., & Saha, R. (2007). Racial inequality in the distribution of hazardous waste: A national-level reassessment. *Social Problems, 54*(3), 343–370.

Monk, J., & Fretwell, S. (2008, November 17). We are the pay toilet of the nation. *The State* [Columbia, SC], pp. A1, A6–A7.

Moore, J., & Pinderhughes, R. (Eds.). (1993). *In the barrios: Latinos and the underclass debate*. New York, NY: Russell Sage Foundation.

Moore, J., & Vigil, J. D. (1993). Barrios in transition. In J. Moore and R. Pinderhughes (Eds.), *In the barrios: Latinos and the underclass debate* (pp. 27–49). New York, NY: Russell Sage Foundation.

Morin, R., & Taylor, P. (2009, February 26). *Suburbs not most popular, but suburbanites most content*. Pew Center. Retrieved from http://pew socialtrends.org/pubs/727/content-in-american-suburbs.

Motel, S., & Patten, E. (2013*). Statistical portrait of Hispanics in the United States, 2011*. Pew Research Hispanic Trends Project. Retrieved from http://www.pewhispanic.org/2013/02/15/ statistical -portrait–of-hispanics-in-the-united-states.

National Association of Social Workers. (2012). Environmental policy. In *Social work speaks* (9th ed., pp. 123–128). Washington, DC: NASW Press.

New Urbanism. (n.d.). Principles of new urbanism. Author. Retrieved from http://www.newurbanism.org.

Oldenburg, R. (Ed.). (2001). *Celebrating the third place: Inspiring stories about the "great good places" at the heart of our communities.* New York, NY: Harlowe & Company.

Padilla, F. M. (1993). The quest for community: Puerto Ricans in Chicago. In J. Moore & R. Pinderhughes (Eds.), *In the barrios: Latinos and the underclass debate* (pp. 129–148). New York, NY: Russell Sage Foundation.

Penn, M. (1998, Winter). Taming the suburban wasteland. *In Wisconsin, 99*(6), 28–35.

Ponce, A. (2013, March 5). *Report: Illinois among top commuter states.* NBC Chicago. Retrieved from http://www.nbcchicago.com/traffic /transit/Report-Illinois-Among-Top-Commuter-States-195277951.html.

Portes, A., & Rumbaut, R. G. (2006). *Immigrant America* (3rd ed.). Berkeley, CA: University of California Press.

Powell, J. (2002). Sprawl, fragmentation, and the persistence of racial inequality: Limiting civil rights by fragmenting space. In G. D. Squires (Ed.), *Urban sprawl: Causes, consequences & policy responses* (pp. 73–118). Washington, DC: Urban Institute.

Putnam, R. D. (2000). *Bowling alone: The collapse and revival of American community.* New York, NY: Simon & Schuster.

Putnam, R. D., & Feldstein, L. M. (2003). *Better together: Restoring the American community.* New York, NY: Simon & Schuster.

Rogge, M. E., & Darkwa, O. K. (1996). Poverty and the environment: An international perspective for social work. *International Social Work, 39,* 395–405.

Royte, E. (2005, August). E-gad! *Smithsonion,* pp. 82–87.

Schneider, W. (1992, July). The suburban century begins. *The Atlantic Monthly,* pp. 33–44.

Schorr, L. B. (1989). *Within our reach: Breaking the cycle of disadvantage.* New York, NY: Anchor Books.

Seabrook, J. (2002, September 2). The slow lane: Can anyone solve the problem of traffic? *The New Yorker,* pp. 120–129.

Semple, K. (2013, June 8). Take the A train to little Guyana. *The New York Times.* Retrieved from http://www.nytimes.com/interactive/2013/06 /09/nyregion/new-york-citys-newest-immigrant-enclaves.html?_r = 0.

Solomon, B. B. (1976). *Black empowerment: Social work in oppressed communities.* New York, NY: Columbia University Press.

Squires, G. D. (2001). Urban sprawl and the uneven development of metropolitan American. In G. D. Squires (Ed.), *Urban sprawl: Causes, consequences & policy responses* (pp. 1–22). Washington, DC: Urban Institute.

Stolle, D., & Rochon, T. R. (2001). Are all associations alike? Member diversity, associational type, and the creation of social capital. In B. Edwards, M. W. Foley, & M. Diani (Eds.), *Beyond Tocqueville: Civil society and the social capital debate in comparative perspective* (pp. 143–156). Hanover, NH: University Press of New England.

Tax truth: We need to raise the levy on gasoline. (2010, July 8). *The Washington Post.* Retrieved from http://www.washingtonpost.com/wp-dyn/content/article/2010/07/07/AR2010070704480.html.

Taylor, P., & Morin, R. (2008). *Americans say they like diverse communities: Election, census trends suggest otherwise.* The Pew Center. Retrieved from http://pewsocialtrends.org/pubs.

Tonnies, F. (1963/1887). *Community and society.* New York, NY: Harper & Row.

U.S. Census Bureau. (2011). *Profile of general population and housing characteristics: 2010, 2010 Census summary file 1, Table DP-1.* Retrieved from http://www.census.gov/prod/cen2010/briefs/c2010br-01.pdf.

Valdez, A. (1993). Persistent poverty, crime, and drugs: U.S.-Mexican border region. In J. Moore & R. Pinderhughes (Eds.), *In the barrios: Latinos and the underclass debate* (pp. 173–220). New York: Russell Sage Foundation.

Warren, M. R., Thompson, J. P., & Saegert, S. (2001). The role of social capital in combating poverty. In S. Saegert, J. P. Thompson, & M. R. Warren (Eds.), *Social capital and poor communities* (pp. 1–28). New York, NY: Russell Sage Foundation.

Warren, R. L. (1978). *The community in America* (3rd ed.). Chicago, IL: Rand McNally.

White, M. J. (1988). *The segregation in residential assimilation of immigrants.* Washington, DC: Urban Institute.

Wilson, W. J. (1987). *The truly disadvantaged: The inner city, the underclass, and public policy.* Chicago, IL: University of Chicago Press.

Wilson, W. J. (1996). *When work disappears: The world of the new urban poor*. New York, NY: Alfred A. Knopf.

Wolcott, R. M., & Milligan, R. (1992). Findings and recommendations of EPA's Environmental Equity Workgroup. *EPA Journal, 18*, 21–22.

Wolfson, H. (2000, December 3). Tiny Indian tribe agrees to turn reservation into nuclear waste dump. *The State* [Columbia, SC], p. A4.

World Relief Minnesota. (n.d.). *Refugee populations in Minnesota.* Retrieved from http://www.worldreliefmn.org/about-refugees/refugee-populations-in-minnesota/.

Wright, J. W. (Ed.). (2007). *The New York Times almanac.* New York, NY: Penguin Books.

Wright, R. (1995, August 28). The evolution of despair. *Time*, pp. 50–54, 56–57.

Wuthnow, R. (2002). United States: Bridging the privileged and the marginalized? In R. D. Putnam (Ed.), *Democracies in flux: The evolution of social capital in contemporary society* (pp. 59–102). New York, NY: Oxford University Press.

Wysocki, B., Jr. (1991, January 15). Influx of Asians brings prosperity to Flushing, a place for newcomers. *The Wall Street Journal,* pp. A1, A8.

Yung, J. (1999). Chinese. In E. R. Barkan (Ed.), *A nation of peoples: America's multicultural heritage* (pp. 119–137). Westport, CT: Greenwood Press.

Zarembka, A. (1990). *The urban housing crisis: Social, economic, and legal issues and proposals.* Westport, CT: Greenwood Press.

CHAPTER NINE

Organizations

A large part of our daily lives, and the lives of our clients, occurs within the context of organizations: day-care centers, schools, and businesses. Social work students also must be concerned with organizations as providers of social services and as employers of social work practitioners. Organizations act in ways that affect not only individuals and families, but also other organizations, communities, and even entire societies. Some sociologists argue that large organizations are the key phenomenon of our time (see Perrow, 1991).

DEFINING ORGANIZATIONS

A *formal organization* is a social system that is deliberately established for the purpose of achieving specific goals. Most organizations have both official goals and operative goals (Perrow, 1961). Official goals are goals the organization acknowledges in its charter, mission statement, annual reports, and other public documents. Operative goals, on the other hand, reflect what the organization actually does from day to day, regardless of what the official goals are. These may or may not reflect similar purposes. For example, some for-profit psychiatric facilities may advertise their organizational mission as helping people suffering from mental illnesses, while their operative goal is to admit patients who have good insurance coverage.

Goals in organizations change over time. There are two types of changes: goal displacement and goal succession (Etzioni, 1964). "*Goal displacement* often occurs when the means to a goal becomes the goal itself" (Holland & Petchers, 1987, p. 208). An example of this would be in a health care setting when filling out charts takes priority over patient care. The process, rather than successful consumer outcomes, then becomes the organization's product.

When an agency's mission is achieved, it doesn't go out of business. Instead it shifts its attention to new goals. Goal succession involves the replacement of an accomplished goal with a new one. A classic and often-cited example is the March of Dimes, which began as an organization dedicated to raising money to fund research to eradicate polio. The disease ceased to be a major health problem when an effective vaccine was developed and the March of Dimes turned to raising money to combat birth defects instead.

Pfeffer (1997) suggests that defining organizations in terms of goal pursuit is problematic in that many employees either do not know the organization's goals or do not support them (p. 7). On the other hand, he notes that there is one goal that appears to be common to all organizations. Whether acknowledged or not, the goal is its own survival. Organizations are more likely than other social systems to hold this goal of self-perpetuation (Pfeffer, 1997, p. 9). An example is the Interstate Commerce Commission, a federal agency that survived for almost fifteen years after virtually all of its functions were removed (Sanger, 1996).

TYPES OF ORGANIZATIONS

For social work purposes, organizations can be divided into three basic types: (1) public/government, (2) private nonprofit/voluntary, and (3) private for-profit. Examples of public/government organizations include public universities, welfare offices, and police departments. Examples of private nonprofit/voluntary organizations are United Way agencies, the NAACP, and privately funded foundations such as the Children's Defense Fund. Other examples include the nongovernmental organizations (NGOs) discussed at the end of this chapter. Many social workers and their clients are employed by or otherwise affected by public and private/nonprofit organizations. Some for-profit organizations are owned by individuals or families; others are owned by stockholders who are paid dividends based on the profits the company earns. Examples of well-known private for-profit organizations are General Motors, Time-Warner, Olive Garden, and Target. Today, large numbers of health provider organizations (e.g., hospitals, nursing homes, psychiatric in-patient units) are part of large, for-profit corporations. Many nonprofit organizations have chosen to pursue for-profit activities, blurring the distinction between them and the for-profits. Both of these trends have led to concerns about who will serve the most needy (Salamon, 1993).

ISSUES AND TRENDS

Corporations as People

As noted in chapter 2, since 1886 the U.S. Supreme Court has repeatedly ruled that corporations have many rights similar to individuals. In January

2010 in the case of Citizens United v. Federal Election Commission, the court decided in a 5-4 ruling that corporations have a First Amendment right to spend unlimited amounts of money to support or oppose candidates for elected office (Liptak, 2010). Corporate contributors to broadcast ads are protected from having to disclose their sources of funding. This ruling gives corporations unprecedented influence over local, state, and national elections (Public Citizen, 2011). Critics of the decision worry that the ruling puts the economic and political interests of corporations ahead of the rights of ordinary American citizens (Barnes & Eggen, 2010) and furthermore note that some corporations (Chrysler, for example) are owned by non-Americans and some (IBM and GE, for example) have more non-American employees and customers than American (Reich, 2013).

More recently, Hobby Lobby, a retail crafts company owned and operated by the Green family, with more than 500 stores and roughly 13,000 employees, asked the Supreme Court to rule on its claim to a First Amendment "religious liberty right" to be exempted from providing insurance coverage to its employees for birth control as required by the Affordable Care Act (Alman, 2013; Schwartzman & Tebbe, 2013). Religious organizations and some religiously affiliated nonprofits are already excluded. The Obama administration is asking the Supreme Court to decide that for-profit corporations cannot deny their employees coverage for contraceptives to which the employees are otherwise entitled by federal law, based on the religious objections of the corporation's owners (Bailey, 2013). Critics argue that allowing private, for-profit businesses to decide what insurance coverage they will or will not provide their employees is an infringement of the employees' rights and, carried to extremes, might allow businesses to exclude other common medical treatments, such as blood transfusions or immunizations. The Court is expected to rule on the Sebelius v. Hobby Lobby Stores Inc. case in 2014.

Technology

Technology, and especially "commuting electronically," has made working at home a possibility for many people. Tasks that once required an office setting can now be done at home if the worker has a fax machine, computer, and access to the Internet. Whereas taking work tasks home used to be the province of executives and professionals, the present-day unlimited connectivity to the workplace has now intruded on the lives of many working couples and parents across social classes (Fraenkel & Capstick, 2012). Nevertheless, based on nationwide representative surveys of thousands of respondents, Noonan and Glass (2012) report that the proportion of workers who telecommute has been essentially flat between the mid-1990s and mid-2000s and the average hours spent telecommuting has remained steady at about six hours per week. Some people who work at home, however, may miss the opportunities to socialize that face-to-face contact with coworkers offers. The potential for, or reality of, friendships in the work setting is clearly an important factor in the decision to be committed to a particular job. Another problem for those who work outside of the home as well as those who are paid for work they do at home is that the line between work and home life is becoming more permeable. Even more so than the telephone, computer-mediated communication strengthens the expectation that workers will be available twenty-four hours a day, seven days a week. People have to use additional technology at home, such as caller ID, to shield themselves from work-related interruptions.

Accountability

Another trend is that human service agencies, like other organizations, are being asked to be accountable to their stakeholders, stockholders, and funding sources. Rather than just reporting activities or outputs (volume of work accomplished—such as how many clients were seen), they must measure and report on program outcomes (United Way of America, 1996). Outcomes are the actual benefits or changes experienced by individuals or client populations during or after participating in program activities; these might include new knowledge, increased skills, changed attitudes, modified behaviors, and improved conditions or altered statuses (United Way of America, 1996, pp. 2–3).

Criticism of Affirmative Action

Title IV of the Civil Rights Act of 1964 prohibits discrimination. *Affirmative action* goes beyond nondiscrimination to encourage special efforts to reach out to particular groups. It evolved over time from executive orders and court decisions. In practice, it is the explicit and intentional consideration of a person's group identity (race, ethnicity, gender) as a criterion in making selection decisions; among candidates who are qualified on other criteria, members of underrepresented groups are selected in preference to those from overrepresented groups. Thus affirmative action addresses two goals: equal opportunity to redress the results of past discrimination and promotion of diversity within the organization.

There are three common misconceptions about affirmative action that contribute to its negative image: that it requires the use of rigid quotas, that it results in the selection of unqualified individuals, and that it is essentially "reverse discrimination." Although broad goals and timetables may be used anywhere, specific quotas apply only in cases where a court has found evidence of past discrimination within an organization. Affirmative action requires that gender and/or race or ethnic background be counted only in reviewing the files of *qualified* candidates; those who don't meet minimum requirements need not be considered, regardless of their group identity. Lastly, if the use of affirmative action "is viewed in the context of overall employment opportunity and the history of opportunity (both within the organization and within the society), then characterizing it as reverse discrimination seems inaccurate" (Cox, 1993, p. 249). In the opinion of many, American society has yet to establish the "level playing field" that would make affirmative action programs obsolete.

Nevertheless, critics of affirmative action argue that it promotes diversity at a special cost to some (white males) who cannot logically be held responsible for patterns of past discrimination. In both education and employment settings, many of those who protest most vocally are themselves the beneficiaries of another kind of insidious advantage—the legacy privilege that is accorded the relatives and friends of the rich, powerful, and well-connected (Kinsley, 2003).

Corporate Crime

Since the 1980s, corporate crime has emerged as a topic of concern with the general public. Corporate crime is sometimes confused with white-collar crime. *White-collar crimes* are those committed by high-status individuals within the context of their occupation (Sutherland, 1940). *Corporate crime* usually refers to organizational crime and includes offenses such as tax evasion, antitrust violations, food and drug violations, polluting the environment, knowingly selling faulty or dangerous products, bribery, fraud, and obstruction of justice, where the purpose is to increase profits at the expense of consumers, competitors, and the general public (Center for Corporate Policy, 2005). Reiman and Leighton (2013, p. 71) state that tax cheating and fraud and consumer deception cost the public more money than all of the property crimes in the FBI index combined. Corporate criminal recklessness leads to the deaths of many Americans who perish on the job or from occupational diseases such as black lung or asbestosis; tens of thousands more fall victim to pollution, contaminated foods, hazardous consumer products, and hospital malpractice (Mokhiber, 2007).

Corporate crime is underprosecuted by a factor of about 100; for example, for every company convicted of health care fraud there are hundreds of others that get away with ripping off Medicare and Medicaid (Mokhiber, 2007). Unfortunately, the annual Justice Department "Crime in the United States" report covers only street crime, not corporate crime; there has been no comprehensive study of corporate crime in twenty-five years (Center for Corporate Policy, 2012). Generally, reports of corporate crime do not appear on the evening news and those who commit it are not brought before criminal courts. Instead, these perpetrators appear before regulatory agencies that have no power to imprison (Henslin, 2014). It is unlikely that these crimes will be significantly punished and if they are punished, the price will be so small that it is considered part of the normal cost of doing business. For example, serious violations of the Occupational Safety and Health Administration Act (OSHA) carry an average fine of about $910, and often corporations can take tax deductions for that amount, meaning that taxpayers are picking up the tab (Center for Corporate Policy, 2012). Since 1972, when OSHA was passed, over 200,000 workplace deaths have been reported; of these, just 151 cases have been referred to the U.S. Justice Department and federal prosecutors decided not to act on more than half of those referrals (Barstow & Bergman, 2003).

The last time a major American corporation was faced with homicide charges was in 1978. Indiana state prosecutors charged that the Ford Motor Company engaged in criminally reckless conduct in the design of the gas tank in the Pinto model after three teenage girls were burned to death when their car was rear-ended. A jury found Ford not guilty. Altogether twenty-seven people died before Ford recalled 1.5 million Pintos in 1978; an internal memo showed that Ford executives had delayed after weighing the cost of the recall ($121 million) against the estimated cost of lawsuits ($50 million) (Phillips, 2010).

In late 2008, many Americans were shocked to learn that a favorite food was contaminated with salmonella. The Peanut Corporation of America processed and shipped batches of peanut products while allegedly knowing that they were contaminated with the bacteria. The Centers for Disease Control and Prevention tied 654 illnesses to the salmonella outbreak, and it is believed to have caused nine deaths. More than 2,000 products were recalled that contained peanuts, peanut butter, or peanut paste from the company (Martin, 2009).

An explosion at the Massey Energy Company's Upper Big Branch mine in Raleigh County, West Virginia, occurred on April 5, 2010. Twenty-nine out of thirty-one miners at the site were killed, making it the worst coal mine disaster in forty years. A former Massey Energy executive was sentenced to forty-two months in prison for conspiracy to violate mine health and safety standards (Berkes, 2013). Others convicted include a security chief who lied to investigators and attempted to destroy evidence, and a superintendent who disabled a methane monitor, which is designed to prevent explosions (Berkes, 2013)

On April 20, 2010, a large oil rig operated by BP exploded forty-two miles off the coast of Louisiana in the Gulf of Mexico, killing eleven workers. According to the Smithsonian Ocean Portal Team, by the time the well was capped off eighty-seven days later, almost five million barrels of oil had leaked into the water (Ocean Portal Team, 2013). A government official stated that "the explosion of the rig was a disaster that resulted from BP's culture of privileging profit over prudence" (Muskal & White, 2012).

Another large industrial accident occurred on April 17, 2013, when a fertilizer plant exploded in West, Texas, killing fifteen people and destroying a nearby middle school and nursing home. The plant had 2,700 tons of ammonium nitrate, 1,350 times the amount that should have required a report to the Department of Homeland Security (Swanson & Tarrant, 2013). OSHA had not inspected the business for worker safety since

1985. Eight months later the accident was still under investigation and the state fire marshal had not ruled out arson as a possible cause (Swanson & Tarrant, 2013).

In July 2013 a train derailment and fire involving spilled crude oil in Lac-Mégantic, Quebec, killed forty-seven people and destroyed a large part of the downtown area (Woods, 2014). The company had been described as being in "repeated violation" of Canadian railway regulations and responsible for 129 accidents in the previous ten years. Criminal negligence charges were filed in May 2014.

According to multiple news sources, on January 9, 2014, a coal-cleaning chemical from a 35,000-gallon storage tank in West Virginia leaked into the Elk River, which supplies water for nine counties, affecting 300,000 residents. The contaminated water was not only unsafe to drink, but also could not be used for washing dishes, bathing, or even doing laundry. The do-not-drink water ban was lifted after five days, but four weeks later Charleston city schools were again closed after teachers and students reported experiencing symptoms related to exposure to the chemical, and seven weeks later there was still uncertainty about the safety of drinking water across seven counties in West Virginia.

On February 2, 2014, coal ash from one of Duke Energy's coal ash ponds started spilling into the Dan River near Eden, North Carolina, polluting seventy miles of the river with toxic sludge that contained arsenic, mercury, and lead. Duke, the nation's largest electric company, had a history of polluting groundwater with leaky, unlined coal ash dumps at its fourteen coal-fired power plants across the state (Biesecker & Weiss, 2014). Federal prosecutors launched an investigation into the state's lax oversight of Duke's practices.

In March 2014, the CEO of General Motors was brought before Congress to answer questions about why GM waited ten years to alert customers and recall automobiles to repair an ignition switch that was blamed for at least thirteen deaths. The faulty part costs less than $10 and the repair takes less than an hour (Fletcher & Mufson, 2014).

Some people find it distressing that there appear to be two systems of justice in America, one for corporations and one for everyone else. The Reuters news agency (Mokhiber, 2013) reports that the U.S. Justice Department employs several weak strategies for dealing with allegations of corporate crime. One is deferred and nonprosecution agreements; in this action the company is criminally charged, but after a period of time the criminal charges will be dropped if the company pays a fine, appoints a monitor, and enhances the company's compliance program. A second course of action is a nonprosecution agreement; under this strategy there is no criminal charge but the company agrees to pay a fine, appoint a monitor, and enhance the compliance program. A third approach is declination; these are somewhat murky situations because they are not made public. Basically, the government agrees not to prosecute. The overall result is that corporations neither admit nor deny wrongdoing, and they are in no danger of losing their government contracts. And "almost universally, when a corporate crime case is settled, the [value of the] stock in the company goes up" (Mokhiber, 2007).

UNDERSTANDING ORGANIZATIONS

Throughout most of human history, most people lived and worked within small groups of relatives, friends, and neighbors. Only a few categories of organizations existed prior to industrialization; these included armies and religious orders, and in some societies, government bureaucracies created to collect taxes and build large structures, such as temples and fortifications. With industrialization, formal organizations became common and they are now a central feature of contemporary society.

Ecosystems Perspective

The environmental context in which an organization exists is critically important to the organization's ability to survive. Scientists who study organizational ecology (using what is called the population-ecology model) have applied Darwinian principles to organizational analysis (see Aldrich, 1979; Hannan & Freeman, 1977). The population-ecology model emphasizes resource scarcity and competition.

As Darwin and other evolutionists pointed out, the evolution of natural species occurs through change in individuals. Population ecologists argue, on the other hand, that evolutionary dynamics must be studied at the level of the population. Thus analysis moves from explaining how individual organizations adapt to their environment to understanding how different "species" (types of organizations) or whole industries rise and fall (Morgan, 1986, p. 67).

In a series of studies, population ecologists Hannan and Carroll (1992) found a common pattern across many kinds of organizations. The first appearance of a new type of organization (such as life insurance companies or beer breweries) is followed by a gradual and then dramatic increase in numbers. Just as natural environments can support only so many individual organisms, the business environment can support only so many organizations of the same type. The organizations must compete with each other and only those that are most "fit" survive. Eventually the density falls to a level that can be supported by the environment and there is relative stability in numbers. Within these numbers, however, individual organizations come and go as some are better able to adapt to changing environmental resources and demands.

From an ecosystems perspective, it is important for an organization to establish a good fit between itself and its environment. Important aspects of the environment include economic and political trends, population patterns and the available workforce, and other organizations (Macionis, 2014, p. 191). Local demographics, for example, will determine the available workforce and the market for an organization's products or services.

Applying this theory to human service agencies, one might note that they depend on outside sources of funding; those that receive income from a variety of sources are in a better position to make independent decisions regarding their future. Human service organizations also compete for clients. They have learned from the business world how to market themselves, both through public relations efforts and through making their services more appealing and "user-friendly"—offering evening and weekend appointments, for example.

Rapid changes in society mean that organizations must remain flexible. For example, an agency that has received government funding in an era of relative prosperity must be ready to seek alternative revenue sources when there are budget cutbacks. An agency that has provided counseling to a middle-class clientele may find that as lower-income people move into the surrounding neighborhood, client demands change from psychotherapy to concrete services, such as provision of day care or a food pantry.

Functionalist Perspective

From a functionalist perspective, members of organizations come together to cooperate in achieving a common goal efficiently. Their focus is on technical competence and task completion rather than in fostering positive ongoing personal relationships. Whereas a family might be able to operate a small restaurant, retail store, or repair shop, economy of scale and the need for uniformity and technical competence often favors large organizations.

Organizations are functional for society in that they epitomize productive efficiency. Large corporations are an important source of employment for people around the world. They tend to pay employees better than smaller firms and they usually have more formalized and objective hiring procedures, thus equalizing individual opportunities.

A number of systems terms can be explained and easily understood in the context of organizations. All social systems perform a variety of functions; these categories of functions occur in families, groups, and communities, as well as in organizations. In a human service organization, goal-directed functions are those activities that directly address the purpose of the organization. Examples might include counseling clients or licensing foster homes. Integrative functions are those activities that are directed at maintaining peace and harmony among members of the system; in a human service organization, this might mean holding regular staff meetings. Maintenance functions are those activities that meet the needs of the organization; these might include staff training or strategic planning. (Effective organizations attend to their own needs as well as consumer needs.) *The adaptation function* refers to those activities involved in responding to changes in the environment; in an organization, these might include developing new services to accommodate changing client demographics.

As organizations grow and change, they become more complex and the units within them become more *specialized*. In other words, there is a division of labor. For example, in a small agency, the director might handle staff recruitment and hiring, public relations, fund-raising, and budget preparation. A large agency not only has more personnel, but each person is likely to have a more specialized role. In fact, there may be whole departments with special functions, such as human resources or accounting. Small isolated human service agencies are more likely to need generalist practitioners, while large, multifunction agencies are more able to hire practitioners with expertise in one or two areas.

Conflict Perspective

In the view of conflict theorists, the history of organizations is a history of asymmetrical power relations that result in the majority working to support the interests of the few. Whether the organization has as its goal the building of pyramids, the establishment of trade routes, or the manufacturing of personal computers, the "pursuit of the goals of the few through the work and labor of the many continues. Organization, in this view, is best understood as a process of domination" (Morgan, 1986, p. 275).

Individuals' interests may be abused not only by the forces of societal oppression, but also by the normal functioning of impersonal organizations (Scott, 1981). The many ways in which workers in organizations may suffer is detailed later in the section on how organizations obstruct well-being.

Sources of power in organizations include (among others) formal authority, control of scarce resources, control of information, and interpersonal alliances (Morgan, 1986, p. 159). Formal authority is related to one's position. There is also power associated with the resources that an individual or unit can bring and whether those resources are available through other means. Thus, a social worker who sees sliding-scale clients may have less power in a counseling agency than a psychiatrist who sees third-party-pay clients. The effectiveness of a strike by unionized workers (and hence their relative power) depends on the availability of other workers ("scabs") who might be hired to fill their positions. Some individuals can favor their own interests by withholding information or slowing its dissemination. Through various kinds of interlocking networks, some people in organizations are able to access mentors and other friends in high places. Politically astute workers build and cultivate informal alliances and coalitions, trading current support for the potential of future assistance in a ritual of mutually beneficial exchange.

Robert Michels (1949/1911) suggested that eventually all formal organizations, as they get bigger, replace the goals of meeting the needs of their customers or clients and the needs of the organization with serving the interests of a small number of individuals who have gained power within the organization. This theory is called the iron law of oligarchy. Although Michels studied political parties and labor unions, an excellent business example that supports his hypothesis would be the wave of 2002 corporate scandals (e.g., AOL Time Warner, Arthur Andersen, Enron, Haliburton, Tyco), in which top executives made themselves rich through unethical practices while their companies suffered, investors lost millions of dollars, and employees lost their pension funds and/or their jobs (Patsuris, 2002).

Rational/Social Exchange Perspective

The rational/social exchange perspective in organizations emphasizes efficiency. Programs are evaluated on the basis of the ratio of costs to benefits (Holland, 1995). If costs outweigh benefits, managers will look for ways to reduce costs or even cut programs. The rationalist perspective is also used to explain the relationship between management and employees. Using this perspective, managers act on the assumption that employees will put their own interests before those of the company. Equity theory suggests that if employees think they invest more in their work than they get back in wages and benefits, they will act to reduce the imbalance, perhaps by working less or taking company resources for personal use (Adams, 1963). An example would be using company computers and work time for personal purposes, a practice known as cyberslacking (Henslin, 2014, p. 189). Examples include downloading music, browsing online catalogs, visiting travel sites, and tweeting. Organizations respond by setting up systems to monitor employees' time and use of resources.

Controlling employee behavior through close supervision of workers is one of several themes of scientific management theory, whose focus is maximum productivity (Taylor, 1911). Frederick Taylor was particularly interested in increasing the efficiency of factory workers. One way he did this was to conduct "time and motion" studies to determine the most efficient way of designing each job or task.

In common usage, bureaucracy has come to be associated with inefficiency and "red tape," particularly in public administration. Max Weber (1978/1922), however, originally assigned the term *bureaucracy* to organizations that employ strictly rational methods to maximize efficiency. In addition to a hierarchy of authority that ensures that each worker is closely supervised, Weber listed several other characteristics of an ideal bureaucracy: specialization, rules and regulations, written communications and records, qualification-based employment, and impersonality. Specialization means that each employee is responsible for a specific and limited number of tasks. Formal (usually written) and standardized rules and regulations guide the day-to-day operation of the organization. Written communication (e.g., memos) and records are used to track what is said and done. Qualification-based employment means that people are hired and retained based on their ability to perform the functions of their job, rather than on any personal relationships or other factors not directly related to job performance. Impersonality refers to treating everyone the same, regardless of any special circumstances that fall outside of procedural guidelines.

Bounded rationality is a term coined by March and Simon (1958) to describe the limits on logical decision making in organizations imposed by incomplete information and the inability (due to limited resources, including time) to identify and explore all of the possible alternatives available. The result is an outcome called satisficing (March & Simon, 1958), or settling for a satisfactory solution rather than seeking an ideal one. An example would be sending only supervisors to receive training in a new clinical technique rather than sending front-line social workers. Another quasi-rational approach to decision making in organizations is incrementalism (Hickson, 1987), or making shifts in small steps to avoid conflict and limit irreversible commitment to a major change. In a school, this might mean using temporary portable classrooms rather than building a permanent addition.

Organizational rationality in the early twenty-first century represents a continuation of the scientific management approaches of Frederick Taylor. According to Ritzer (2000), the methods used by McDonald's restaurants have become the current model of rationality. McDonaldization is "the process by which the principles of the fast-food industry are coming to dominate more and more sectors of American society as well as the rest of the world" (Ritzer, 2000, p. 1). Organizations everywhere of every type (e.g., beauty parlors, hospitals and clinics, retail stores, universities, travel agencies, and car maintenance shops) are adopting the principles of McDonaldization: efficiency, calculability, predictability, and increased control through automation. For example, customers may experience efficiency as getting an entire breakfast by simply going through the McDonald's drive-thru and ordering an Egg McMuffin and coffee. Efficiency is also enhanced by having restaurant customers themselves place their orders, pick up their food, refill their drinks, and bus their tables. Ritzer explains calculability as an emphasis on the quantitative aspects of products (e.g., the Quarter Pounder) and the time it takes to deliver them ("ready in three minutes or it's free"). Predictability is the result of a highly rational approach that prescribes every ingredient and every step of the process. Predictability ensures that a Big Mac purchased in Los Angeles next year will be identical to one purchased in New York last year. At McDonald's, employees are trained to do a limited number of tasks in precisely the way they are told to do them. Managers make sure the workers follow the prescribed routine. But because human beings are not always predictable or controllable, the restaurant replaces them with machines, such as drink dispensers that shut off automatically when the cup is full or French fry machines that lift the basket out of the oil when the fries are crisp.

Constructionist Perspective

The constructionist perspective is implicit in the study of organizational culture. *Organizational culture* is "the constellation of values, beliefs, assumptions and expectations" that shape the behavior of members of an organization (Holland, 1995, p. 1789). "Shared meaning, shared understanding, and shared sense making" are different ways of describing organizational culture (Morgan, 1986, p. 128). Organizational cultures reflect larger, national cultures as well as regional cultures in a country as large and diverse as the United States. An American automobile manufacturing plant would have different expectations than a plant in Germany, and one in Michigan may have a different culture than one in Alabama or South Carolina.

Within a given workplace, organizational culture is the product of a stable social unit with a significant shared history—that means there may be several (sub)cultures operating, including a managerial culture, various occupationally based cultures, and group cultures based on locational proximity (Schein, 1985). For example, in a hospital one might encounter nursing, social work, and accounting subcultures, as well as subcultures related to the intensive care unit, the emergency room, the pediatric wing, and outpatient services. In analyzing an organization's culture, one must acknowledge the process of reality construction. Like some other types of culture, organizational culture operates largely outside of the conscious awareness of group members.

If an organization has only a weak culture, employees with different perspectives, norms, and values are freer to act on their individual inclinations. In a human service agency, a weak culture can result in inconsistencies in the provision of client services. When norms and values are clearly laid out and enforced, an organization is said to possess a strong culture. In such organizations, the culture provides a behavioral standard to which everyone subscribes. Organizations with strong cultures may also have informal penalties for nonconformity. For example, in an agency that has a cultural norm that prescribes that workers remain in the building at lunchtime so that they can be available for clients, a new worker who goes out to eat may be greeted by sarcastic comments from peers when he or she returns.

Edgar Schein (1985, p. 2) suggests "the only thing of real importance that [organizational] leaders do is to create and manage culture and that the unique talent of leaders is their ability to work with culture." Among the ways the leaders can reinforce organizational culture are through what they pay attention to, measure, and control; reactions to critical incidents; criteria for the allocation of rewards and status; criteria for recruitment, selection, promotion, and "excommunication" of employees; and deliberate role modeling, teaching, and coaching (Schein, 1985, pp. 224–225). For example, a manager who values group process can support that kind of organizational culture not only by creating many different committees and advisory groups, but also by attending their meetings.

The physical design of an organization also reflects its cultural values. The number, location, size and furnishings of private offices; the presence of conference rooms and break rooms; and the ambience of waiting areas (including the provision of comfortable seating, current magazines, a television, fish tank, or toys) speak volumes about the organization's regard for employees and clients. For example, "welfare clients in a drab, unattractive waiting room, sitting on hard benches, are being given an unequivocal message of their inferior status in the welfare system, if not in society" (Seabury, 1971, pp. 47–48).

In addition to organizational culture, the constructionist perspective also frames theories about management styles and employee motivation. Three names often associated with these topics are Douglas McGregor, Frederick Herzberg, and Elton Mayo.

Noting the importance of subjective assumptions, McGregor (1960) identified two management styles that he labeled "Theory X" and "Theory Y." Theory X managers view workers as motivated only by rewards or by threats of punishment; these managers respond by providing much structure and close supervision. Theory Y managers view employees as wanting to grow and develop, and being motivated by internal rewards; they respond by giving their workers new challenges and responsibilities.

Theory Y is consistent with Herzberg's classic theory of employee motivation. Herzberg (1968/1986) identified hygiene factors—such as pay, benefits, status, job security, and working conditions—that keep employees from being dissatisfied but do not motivate them. Truly motivating factors include opportunities for challenge, responsibility, advancement, recognition, or achievement.

Mayo conducted research at the Hawthorne Plant of the Western Electric Company in Chicago between 1927 and 1932 (Homans, 1986). Although his goal was to investigate the effects of physical conditions such as lighting, humidity, equipment, and worker fatigue on performance, he discovered that productivity increased regardless of changes in the physical environment or working hours. He concluded that psychological and social factors were as important as other work conditions. The attention given the workers in the experiment and their interpretation of this attention was a crucial factor in their increased productivity. This reaction has been dubbed the Hawthorne effect. The implication of this finding is that workers should be invited to participate in decisions that affect their work. In this and other experiments, Mayo also found that informal work group norms have a significant effect on worker output; production rates above or below the informal norms resulted in social pressure to conform. This emphasis on understanding and using psychological and social variables is part of the human relations model of organizational administration (Mayo, 1933). Interest in the human relations model led to further research on small groups and the development or refinement of concepts such as group norms, roles, leadership, and decision making. An understanding of organizational life is often dependent on an appreciation of the small groups that function within organizations.

DIVERSITY IN ORGANIZATIONS

An alternative to more traditional management styles is one often manifested by female managers (although there may be small differences between the sexes and wide variations within a gender group) (Alvesson & Billing, 2009). One characteristic of this style is a manner of communication that values sharing and willingness to ask questions in order to gain a fuller understanding of the situation (Helgesen, 1990; Tannen, 1994). This is in contrast to a "male" style of communication that is task-focused and concerned about how asking questions will affect the questioner's image (Tannen, 1994). A second characteristic of women's management style is their relationship with subordinates. Women are less hierarchical and tend to offer greater autonomy to their subordinates (Helgesen, 1990; Rosener, 1990). This more egalitarian style of management is often misunderstood as a weakness (Tannen, 1994). It is likely that these differences in style are the result of the cultural socialization of females that leads them to recognize the "value of supporting and nurturing others, of protecting long-term . . . relationships, of seeking solutions in which everyone wins, and wherever possible, of forging a mutuality of interests. As a result of women's intensive socialization for their likely role in the family, they have often been taught to be responsive to others' needs, to seek mutually acceptable and equitable solutions, to support others, and to share information" (Rothschild & Davies, 1994, p. 588).

Over the years, the workforce of human service organizations has gradually become more diverse, particularly with respect to race, ethnicity, gender, and age (Mor Barak & Travis, 2010). On the other hand, the proportion of African American and Latino social workers in this work-force has lagged behind their numbers in the U.S. population. The presence of a diverse workforce may make an organization more capable of serving clients from diverse backgrounds, but unless women and members of minority groups are truly integrated both structurally and informally into the organization and its culture, service effectiveness may be limited (Cox, 1993; Mor Barak & Travis, 2010). The literature suggests that the full participation of members of different backgrounds in an organization promotes job satisfaction, employee well-being, organizational commitment, creativity, flexibility, and problem solving (Cox, 1993; Mor Barak & Travis, 2010).

Lack of diversity and the resulting omission of minority points of view may encourage groupthink, a tendency to suppress dissent, often in an effort to promote consensus (Janis, 1972; Miranda, 1994). Groupthink can result in errors in decision making and such errors lead to poor outcomes. According to Janis (1982), some factors that contribute to groupthink include groups composed of persons of similar backgrounds and ideologies, a high level of group cohesiveness, and group members who have weak ties with or awareness of external groups. An example of groupthink in an organization is the sex abuse scandal in the Catholic Church that was exposed in 2002. Primarily celibate older white men made decisions to protect the organization at the expense of vulnerable children. Critics of the church have argued that if a more diverse group shared leadership roles, the abusive practices would not have been tolerated.

A more recent but similar example of groupthink is the child sex abuse scandal at Penn State, where a former football assistant coach was convicted in 2012 of sexually abusing at least ten boys over a fifteen-year period. A number of athletic and university administrators, as well as law enforcement personnel, were implicated in a long-term cover-up, where the apparent goal was to protect the football program rather than the children (Chappell, 2012).

On the other hand, if diversity is not well managed, communication problems may increase and morale may suffer. Given the changing demographics of the workforce, workplace diversity is inevitable in most sectors. Social workers need to draw upon their values and skills to help make workplace diversity a positive feature of organizational life.

THE IMPACT OF ORGANIZATIONS ON INDIVIDUALS AND FAMILIES

How Organizations Deter Well-Being

Labor history and literature suggest that organizational settings are sources of oppression and health hazards for many people. This section documents the ongoing negative effects of organizations on today's workforce.

Discrimination

When a particular category of people (such as affluent white males) dominates the hierarchy of most organizations, the result is barriers against people in other categories, such as women and people of color. Even though discrimination based on race and sex has been against the law for some time, there still exist many examples of unfair treatment, as evidenced in the limited number of women and minorities in high-level positions, restricted access to authority even when they are in managerial jobs, and lower salaries for women and people of color when compared to white males with similar credentials and experience (Andersen & Taylor, 2013; Padavic & Reskin, 2002).

The nature of racial discrimination in organizations has changed. Although there are still instances of overt discrimination (Padavic & Reskin, 2002), usually the oppression of racial minorities is not so apparent. Today, blatant racism may affect profitability, so "companies must promote diversity—or at least pretend to" (Henslin, 2008, p. 192). The presence of people of color in the organization satisfies equal opportunity requirements and affirmative action goals. Sometimes people of color are hired or promoted in mostly white organizations to be used as tokens, or high-profile representatives of their race. Tokenism results in surplus visibility (Patai, 1991), or focused attention on the token individual whose achievements or mistakes are then viewed as a reflection on his or her whole race. The presence of a small handful of minorities also enhances contrast effects, or an exaggeration of the differences between groups and of the similarities within groups. Even if they are a significant part of a company's workforce, people of color are routinely channeled to support positions or departments where they are limited to dealing with other people of color who are customers or employees: their job assignments are comprised of affirmative action, community relations, and minority affairs (Collins, 1989, 1993; Cose, 1993; Padavic & Reskin, 2002). Despite important-sounding titles, these positions are unlikely to prepare the employee for advancement to more powerful positions in the organization.

Sometimes lateral moves to areas from which executives are promoted are blocked; the resulting barriers are called glass walls (Schaefer, 2012, p. 79). Scholars have identified certain factors that account for the concentration of people of color in entry-level or peripheral positions. Bernheide (1992) called this phenomenon the sticky floor. These factors include lack of mentors and role models, exclusion from informal communication networks, limited access to training, and early "tracking" into less challenging assignments (Cose, 1993; Feagin, 1991; Kanter, 1993/ 1977; Simon & Akabas, 1993).

Many of the same factors are cited to explain why women appear to perform more poorly than men in organizations. Surplus visibility, contrast effects, negative stereotypes, exclusion from informal networks, lack of mentors, limited training opportunities, and in addition, ill-fitting clothing or equipment designed for male bodies, inadequate bathroom facilities, and a climate of sexual harassment make some work environments more hostile for women (Simon & Akabas, 1993). Because women continue to carry major responsibilities for meeting family needs, they may be forced to take jobs that have short or flexible hours so that they can accommodate the schedules of their husbands and children. The Pregnancy Discrimination Act of 1978 requires that employers treat pregnant workers the same as other employees with temporary medical disabilities and also forbids employers from discrimination against pregnant women by forcing them to take pregnancy leave (U.S. Equal Employment Opportunity Commission, n.d.). The Family and Medical Leave Act of 1993 protects the job security of women and men who need to take time off work to care for a newborn, adopted, or foster child, or a dependent family member with a serious health condition, but it does not require that the employer provide paid leave.

According to the Institute for Women's Policy Research (IWPR) (2013), the United States is the only high-income country that does not require paid maternity leave for employees. Only one out of eight employees in the United States has access to paid leave for any care of dependent family members (newborns, adopted children, or ill children or adults) (IWPR, 2013). Even among the *Working Mother* magazine's "100 Best Companies," less than 30 percent provide nine or more weeks of paid maternity leave. Leave for adoptive parents and birth fathers tends to be less generous. Women who take extended breaks from employment to deal with family needs may be penalized by missing opportunities for promotion or losing seniority.

Women's advancement in corporate leadership continues to stagnate, with virtually no growth seen in women's share of top positions in recent years. In 2013, women held 16.9 percent of board seats in the largest 500 American firms according to Catalyst, a New York-based women's advocacy group that collects the data annually; one-tenth of companies had no women serving on their boards and women of color held only 3.2 percent of board seats (Soares, Bartkiewicz, & Mulligan-Ferry, 2013). The *glass ceiling* is the label given to the mostly invisible barrier that keeps women from being promoted to the highest levels of an organization. In contrast, men who are employed in traditionally female occupations, such as social work, nursing, and elementary education encounter not a glass ceiling, but a "glass escalator" that provides an express ride to the top. Compared to their female coworkers, they are promoted to higher-level positions, given more desirable work assignments, and paid higher salaries (Williams, 1995). Another threat to women's career success, the glass cliff, has been documented. In a study of 100 companies, the researchers found that women's "leadership appointments are made in problematic organizational circumstances and hence are more precarious" (Ryan & Haslam, 2005, p. 87). In other words, they were appointed to senior positions only after a downturn in the company's fortunes had already occurred, leaving them standing on the edge of a glass cliff where they can easily be scapegoated if things continue to get worse.

Workplace Hazards and Other Forms of Exploitation of Employees

Social work students may have learned about the 1911 Triangle Shirt Waist factory fire in New York that created the impetus for federal involvement in setting and enforcing worker safety standards. Using data from the U.S. Department of Labor, Bureau of Labor Statistics, the AFL-CIO (2012) reported that in spite of government regulations that should protect them, 4,693 workers were killed on the job in 2011—an average of 13 workers every day—and an estimated 50,000 died from occupational diseases. Workers suffer an additional 7.6 million to 11.4 million job injuries and illnesses each year. The average fine imposed for "fatality inspection reports" nationwide in 2011 was $9,057. The federal OSHA and the state OSHA programs have a total of 1,938 inspectors (873 federal and 1,065 state inspectors) to cover the eight million workplaces under the OSHA Act's jurisdiction. Federal OSHA staff can inspect workplaces on average once every 131 years; the state OSHA employees can inspect them once every 76 years. The AFL-CIO suggests that the number of inspectors is "woefully inadequate" and OSHA penalties are too low to deter violations.

Parenti notes that injury on the job "is mostly due to inadequate safety standards and lax government enforcement of codes" (2011, p. 84). In 1991, eighty years after the Triangle Shirt Waist factory fire, a fire at the Imperial chicken plant in Hamlet, North Carolina, killed twenty-five people and injured forty-nine. Emergency exits had been chained shut. Company executives had ordered the doors locked "to keep employees from going outside for coffee breaks, or stealing chickens" (Wright, Cullen, & Blankenship, 1995). Most of those killed were African American women.

American companies are also complicit in ignoring hazardous working conditions in other countries. For example, Wal-Mart, JCPenney, Target, Sears, Calvin Klein, Tommy Hilfiger, and Gap are attracted to countries such as Bangladesh, Vietnam, Cambodia, Pakistan, India, China, and Guatemala, where workers labor for low wages and without the protection of American-style safety regulations. Garment firms make up 80 percent of Bangladesh's exports; they face pressure from foreign buyers to maintain the nation's chief selling point, "the cheapest place to make clothes" (MacLeod, 2013). Bangladeshi garment workers make twenty-one cents an hour (Bhasin, 2013). About 3.5 million Bangladeshis, the majority of them women, work in the sector. In November 2012, a textile factory fire in Dhaka, the capital of Bangladesh, killed 112 people.

In April 2013, 1,127 garment factory workers in a suburb of the same city died when the eight-story building they were working in collapsed. In April 2011 there was a meeting in Dhaka that brought together retailers, factory owners, government officials, and nongovernment organizations. As reported in the *New York Times* (Greenhouse, 2012), at that time Wal-Mart rejected proposals to raise prices so that factories could improve their electrical and fire safety. Since the tragedies, many European companies and some, but not all, American companies have responded by supporting new mandatory safety checks; others (e.g., Wal-Mart, Gap) continue to hold out for alternate plans (O'Donnell, 2013). Whereas consumers around the world give lip service to boycotting irresponsible companies, when they go shopping they pay more attention to name brand, fit, and especially price (Mayerowitz, 2012).

Meatpackers and poultry workers perform one of the most dangerous and physically demanding jobs in the United States; these workers are likely to suffer cuts, amputations, skin disease, herniated disks, permanent arm and shoulder damage, and even death (Compa & Fellner, 2005). OSHA does not have specific standards that allow it to cite employers for hazards relating to line speed and repetitive stress injuries. The workers in this industry are increasingly immigrants from Mexico and Central America. Companies are able to exploit them due to their limited English skills and uncertain legal status, and to block their attempts to unionize (Compa & Fellner, 2005). Latinos and immigrants from Sudan and Burma account for more than half of employees at one meat processing plant in Denison, Iowa (Zoroya & MacLeod, 2013). The plant was recently sold by its parent company, Smithfield, to a Chinese firm, Shuanghui—the largest-ever acquisition of a U.S. company by the Chinese. American workers fear that when their current contract runs out, the Chinese owners might cut pay or squeeze more productivity out of the workers. Shuanghui workers in China earn about $500 a month; they live in six-person dorm rooms on site and have two days off a month, a concession that factory management granted two years ago (Zoroya & MacLeod, 2013).

In addition to occupations that have obvious dangers, such as law enforcement or mining, workplace settings that expose workers to various hazardous materials include pest control and the paper, chemical, drug, and paint industries, as well as beauty shops, nail salons, and dry cleaners (Draper, 1993; Glausiusz, 2008).

Perhaps less alarming but more commonplace are the chronic physical and mental illnesses that result from psychological pressures in the workplace. These include cardiovascular diseases (high blood pressure, heart attacks, strokes), and other stress-related symptoms, such as headaches, fatigue, gastrointestinal issues, and feelings of irritability, anger, nervousness, anxiety, depression, and lack of motivation. Moody (cited in Ehrenreich, 2001, p. 35) argues that there is a new system of "'management by stress' in which workers in a variety of industries are being squeezed to extract maximum productivity to the detriment of their health." One-third of American workers say they are chronically overworked and 89 percent experience high levels of job pressure (Galinsky et al., 2005, pp. 2, 4). Job pressures can include multitasking, longer hours or demand for overtime, and expected contact with the workplace outside of normal working hours.

The need to assume the responsibilities of colleagues who have been downsized creates resentment toward employers and coworkers who appear to be slacking off (Galinsky et al, 2005, p. 16). McNeely (1992, p. 235) reports that the satisfaction of female human service workers was affected much more than that of their male coworkers by perceptions of excessive on-the-job pressure and of job performance expectations— perhaps because they were at the same time experiencing work-family conflict.

A term used to describe one type of reaction to job stress is *burnout*. Burnout has been defined as "psychological withdrawal from work in response to excessive stress or dissatisfaction" (Cherniss, 1980, p. 16). Professionals who must work in close personal contact with those whom they serve, often in stress-filled situations, are especially at risk; these include social workers, police officers, nurses, and teachers (Maslach & Leiter, 2008; Shirom, 2011). Dunn and Craig (2013) say that those "who suffer job burnout are idealistic, highly motivated, extremely competent workers who finally realize they cannot make the difference they once thought they could" (pp. 435). An example of symptoms of burnout in a human service agency might involve a social worker who does the bare minimum in terms of job requirements, complains of psychosomatic illnesses, and is frequently absent as she or he "counts down" the months to retirement. Dunn and Craig (2013) suggest that to avoid burnout, workers should be realistic in their goals, not take work troubles home with them, and develop interests outside of their jobs. Smaller caseloads, better pay, and other improvements in working conditions also would help alleviate burnout among human service workers.

In addition to threats to life and health, employees at the bottom of the organization are also subjected to exploitation in other forms. For example, waitresses, retail workers, and fast-food restaurant managers may be required to be available to be called in which may prevent them from holding a second job or attending classes. Also, companies can avoid paying overtime by labeling certain low-level employees "managers" who then become exempt from wage and hour regulations (and thus ineligible for overtime pay), or by hiring people for less than full-time schedules, or as contract workers, so that the company doesn't have to provide benefits such as health insurance or paid time off.

Worker Responses

Although workplace conditions and family-related policies may be addressed by government or company directives, any hope for change has to take into account the unequal status of employee and employer; overall, working people have limited power to change the workplace to better accommodate their needs (Draper, 1993). This is especially true for people from lower socioeconomic classes who have limited finances and limited alternatives. Employees are not passive victims of their work environments, however. Workers may respond to problematic situations by resistance, slowdowns, or strikes, and collective bargaining. Labor unions have contributed significantly to the forty-hour workweek standard, health and retirement benefits, and workplace safety, and union workers typically earn higher wages than do nonunion workers in comparable jobs. (See chapter 2.)

Effects on Consumers

In addition to the ways organizations obstruct the well-being of their employees, they may use their considerable power to inhibit the well-being of others who come into contact with them. An example that many people encounter is *red tape*, or a bureaucratic preoccupation with rules and procedures that get in the way of meeting the needs of customers and clients. Other frustrations occur when a company or agency puts its own needs ahead of those of consumers. Nearly everyone has experienced the frustration of dealing with an organization's ineffective phone answering system that was purportedly designed to "serve you better" but instead only replaces direct telephone contact with the organization's staff with a series of irrelevant tape-recorded messages.

FIGURE 9.1 CRITICAL THINKING ABOUT BUREAUCRACY

The brother of one of the authors supplied the following story, which serves to illustrate the workings of a large bureaucracy:

"Our friend's wedding invitation was returned to her. When she checked with us we confirmed that she had our address correct ("E456 S4722 Lake View Lane"). Someone at the post office had circled the S and written "5?" above it. Ours is the only house on Lake View Lane. Why do they need a nine-digit number to deliver the mail? Where else on Lake View Lane did they think it might go?"

Often bureaucracies work smoothly and deliver products and services efficiently. An example would be the processing of millions of Social Security checks every month. At other times, some bureaucracies are plagued by inefficiency and "red tape" as in the example presented above. Can you think of an example of when a bureaucratic agency worked well for you? Can you think of an example of when a bureaucratic agency did not work well?

On a more significant level, some organizations have chosen to put profits before the health and safety needs of consumers. One example is the ongoing promotion of cigarettes which contributes to the illness and deaths of many consumers despite a 1997 court ruling that regulated the sale of tobacco. This industry targets adolescents, women in their early twenties, blue-collar men, African Americans and Latinos, and people in undeveloped countries. Reynolds Tobacco even developed candy- and fruit-flavored cigarettes aimed at the 12- to 13-year-old market, aware that 90 percent of adult smokers become addicted as children (Califano & Sullivan, 2006).

Lobbyists for American gun manufacturers—mostly the National Rifle Association (NRA)—have used many of the strategies pioneered by the tobacco industry. The tactics include "suppressing information, blocking research, and pushing for state laws that prohibit cities and counties from passing their own gun control measures" (Szabo & Hoyer, 2013). The NRA takes in more than $200 million a year from gun manufacturers and sellers (Collins, 2012). It promotes fear and paranoia in order to help them market their products, particularly military-style assault weapons that have no use for hunting or marksmanship practice, but fuel the fantasies of those who dream of shooting burglars—or agents of a federal government run amuck. The NRA response to the tragic school shooting at Newtown, Connecticut, in December 2012 was to recommend that more people arm themselves.

Some manufacturers also market guns sized specifically for young children—such as blue and pink .22-caliber "Cricket" and "Chipmunk" rifles made by the Pennsylvania-based Keystone Sporting Arms Company (Wolfson, 2013). In 2013, a five-year-old boy in Kentucky accidentally shot and killed his two-year-old sister while playing with the Cricket rifle he had received for his birthday six months earlier. According to news reports, members of the rural community where he lived saw nothing unusual about giving a gun to such a young child (Wolfson, 2013).

How Organizations Promote Well-Being

Of course not all businesses are driven solely by profit motives. For example, the drugstore chain CVS announced in February 2014 that it would stop selling cigarettes and other tobacco products at its 7,600 store locations. The decision will cut about $2 billion—1.6 percent—of the company's annual revenue. The CEO of CVS said it is "the right thing for us to do for our customers and our company to help people on their path to better health" (Memmott, 2014).

In May 2013 General Mills ran a thirty-second ad for Cheerios featuring an interracial family. The ad made headlines when General Mills chose to shut down the comments section on the YouTube version because of the number of racist remarks that were posted (Nudd, 2014). The company ran a sequel using the same family during the 2014 Super Bowl, demonstrating its commitment to diversity.

Early in 2014 the Arizona state legislature passed a bill protecting businesses that might discriminate against same-sex couples. The business community, as well as national corporations such as Apple, American Airlines, and Delta, succeeded in pressuring the Arizona governor to veto the bill (Collins, 2014).

Many traditional organizations contribute to the well-being of employees through a variety of measures. In addition to the obvious advantages of salaries, benefits, on-the-job training, and job satisfaction, these may include flextime and on-site day care to help with family responsibilities, employee assistance organizations to help with personal problems, on-site gyms to keep employees healthy, and employee stock ownership plans.

Every October *Working Mother* magazine identifies the "ten best places to work" based on support for employees and their families. Some of the more unusual benefits noted were on-site auto maintenance, take-home dinners, on-site hairstyling, and a gradual "phase-back" program to reintegrate new moms and dads into the workplace after taking family leave. Some companies, in an effort to retain valuable employees offer other kinds of perks, including the option to telecommute, bringing pets to work, a lax dress code, shorter hours on summer Fridays, and child care subsidies (Malcolm, 2013). While these companies are notable, the reality is that they represent but a small portion of American employers.

As noted in chapter 7, many organizations have taken a leadership role in providing benefits for LGBT employees. Private corporations have led the way in promoting equal treatment of gay men and lesbians. According to the Human Rights Campaign (2013), 88 percent of the Fortune 500 companies prohibit discrimination on the basis of sexual orientation and more than half (57 percent) prohibit discrimination based on gender identity. The majority of the total Fortune 500—67 percent—offer equivalent medical benefits for spouses and partners (up from 25 percent in 2000).

Many corporations also make substantial contributions to charities and foundations. It should be understood, however, that this generosity allows these corporations to place their resources with nonprofits that benefit their employees and their communities at the same time that they enhance their public image and save on taxes.

ORGANIZATIONS AS PROVIDERS OF SOCIAL SERVICES AND AS EMPLOYERS OF SOCIAL WORKERS

Social workers are employed in a variety of organizations. In many, social workers are directly involved in meeting the primary goals of the organization. Examples would include agencies that provide child protection services, mental health or family counseling, and battered women's shelters. In others, called host organizations, social workers provide ancillary services. Examples of host organizations are schools, hospitals, and prisons. It is not uncommon for social workers in host settings to be called upon to work with clients' families, and to locate and arrange for services or funding from other agencies. These social workers also may be called upon to present, explain, and defend social work values and to advocate for clients. In addition to providing social services per se, many social workers in various organizations supervise support staff, paraprofessionals, and volunteers.

Social service agencies and host organizations are subject to the same economic trends as other companies. In difficult economic times, staff are likely to be asked to do more with less, to live with threats of being "downsized," or to focus services on clients who can pay full fees themselves or have adequate insurance coverage. These situations present barriers to optimal services as well as ethical dilemmas.

LOOKING AHEAD

In chapter 10, we address a special kind of organization, residential institutions. These are not the social institutions we discussed in part II, but rather the settings and facilities that house individuals who pose a threat to society or have very special needs that cannot be met in the community.

REFERENCES

Adams, J. S. (1963). Toward an understanding of inequity. *Journal of Abnormal and Social Psychology, 67,* 422–436.

AFL-CIO. (2012). *Death on the job: The toll of neglect.* Author. Retrieved from http://www.aflcio.org/content/download/22781/259751/DOTJ 2012nobugFINAL.pdf.

Aldrich, H. (1979). *Organizations and environments.* Englewood Cliffs, NJ: Prentice Hall.

Alman, A. (2013, October 21). Hobby Lobby asks Supreme Court to take up case against contraception mandate. *The Huffington Post.* Retrieved from http://www.huffingtonpost.com/2013/10/21/hobby-lobby-supreme-court_n_4139356.html.

Alvesson, M., & Billing, Y. D. (2009). *Understanding gender and organizations* (2nd ed.). London, UK: Sage.

Andersen, M., & Taylor, H. (2013). *Sociology: The essentials* (7th ed.). Belmont, CA: Wadsworth.

Bailey, S. P. (2013, September 20). U.S. asks Supreme Court to review Hobby Lobby's birth control mandate challenge. Religion News Service. Retrieved from http://www.religionnews.com/2013/09/20/u-s-asks-supreme-court-review-hobby-lobbys-birth-control-mandate-challenge/.

Barnes, R., & Eggen, D. (2010, January 21). Supreme Court rejects limits on corporate spending in electoral campaigns. *The Washington Post.* Retrieved from http://www.washingtonpost.com/wp-dyn/content/article/2010/01/21.

Barstow, D., & Bergman, L. (2003, January 10). Deaths on the job, slaps on the wrist. *The New York Times.* Retrieved from http://www.nytimes.com/2003/01/10/us/deaths-on-the-job-slaps-on-the-wrist.html.

Berkes, H. (2013, September 10). Former Massey exec gets 42 months in mine disaster case. National Public Radio. Retrieved from http://www.npr.org/blogs/thetwo-way/2013/09/10/221161240/former-massey-exec-gets-42-months-in-mine-disaster-case.

Bernheide, C. W. (1992, Fall). Women still "stuck" in low level jobs. *Women in Public Services: A Bulletin for the Center for Women in Government,* p. 3.

Bhasin, K. (2013, May 7). American-made clothing companies find ways to survive as others chase cheap labor abroad. *The Huffington Post.* Retrieved from http://www.huffingtonpost.com/2013/05/07/american-made-clothing en_3225899.html.

Biesecker, M., & Weiss, M. (2014, April 17). Duke: Coal ash spill won't affect bottom line. *News and Observer* [Charlotte, NC]. Retrieved from http://www.newsobserver.com/2014/04/17/3791988/nc-govs-proposal-doesnt-address.html.

Califano, J. A., & Sullivan, L. W. (2006, June 29). The flavor of marketing to kids. *The Washington Post.* Retrieved from http://www.washington .com.

Center for Corporate Policy. (2005). *Corporate crime and abuse: Tracking the problem.* Retrieved from, http://www.corporatepolicy.org /issues/crimedata.htm.

Center for Corporate Policy. (2012). *Cracking down on corporate crime.* Retrieved from http://www.corporatepolicy.org/2012/03/26/cracking -down-on-corporate-crime/.

Chappell, B. (2012, June 21). Penn State child abuse scandal: A guide and timeline. National Public Radio. Retrieved from http://www.npr.org /2011/11/08/142111804/penn-state-abuse-scandal-a-guide-and-time line.

Cherniss, C. (1980). *Staff burnout: Job stress in the human services.* Beverly Hills, CA: Sage.

Collins, G. (2012, March 25). Pity the poor gun lobby. *USA Today,* p. D3.

Collins, G. (2014, February 25). The Arizona business community's stand. *The State* [Columbia, SC], p. A13.

Collins, S. (1989). The marginalization of black executives. *Social Problems, 36,* 317–331.

Collins, S. (1993). Blacks on the bubble: The vulnerability of black executives in white corporations. *Sociological Quarterly, 34,* 429–448.

Compa, L., & Fellner, J. (2005, August 3). Meatpacking's human toll. *The Washington Post.* Retrieved from http://www.washingtonpost.com.

Cose, E. (1993). *The rage of a privileged class.* New York, NY: HarperCollins.

Cox, T. H. (1993). *Cultural diversity in organizations: Theory, research, and practice.* San Francisco, CA: Berrett-Koehler.

Draper, E. (1993). Fetal exclusion policies and gendered constructions of suitable work. *Social Problems, 40,* 90–107.

Dunn, W. L., & Craig, G. J. (2013). *Understanding human development* (3rd ed.). Boston, MA: Pearson.

Ehrenreich, B. (2001). *Nickel and dimed: On (not) getting by in America.* New York, NY: Metropolitan Books.

Etzioni, A. (1964). *Modern organizations.* Englewood Cliffs, NJ: Prentice Hall.

Feagin, J. R. (1991). The continuing significance of race: Antiblack discrimination in public places. *American Sociological Review, 56,* 101–116.

Fletcher, M. A., & Mufson, S. (2014, March 30). Why did GM take so long to respond to deadly defect? Corporate culture may hold the answer. *The Washington Post.* Retrieved from http://www.washingtonpost.com/business/economy/why-did-gm-take-so-long-to-respond-to-deadly-defect-corporate-culture-may-hold-answer/2014/03/30/5c366f6c-b691-11e3-b84e-897d3d12b816_story.html.

Fraenkel, P., & Capstick, C. (2012). Contemporary two-parent families: Navigating work and family challenges. In F. Walsh (Ed.), *Normal family processes: Growing diversity and complexity* (4th ed., pp. 78–101). New York, NY: Guilford Press.

Galinsky, E., Bond, J. T., Kim, S. S., Bacon, L., Brownfield, E., & Sakai, K. (2005). *Overwork in America: When the way we work becomes too much.* New York, NY: Families & Work Institute.

Glausiusz, J. (2008, Winter). Dying for a manicure? *On Earth,* p. 16.

Greenhouse, S. (2012, December 5). Documents indicate Walmart blocked safety push in Bangladesh. *The New York Times.* Retrieved from http://www.nytimes.com/2012/12/06/world/asia/3-walmart-suppliers-made-goods-in-bangladeshi-factory-where-112-died-in-fire.html?ref=asia.

Hannan, M. T., & Carroll, G. R. (1992). *Dynamics of organizational populations: Density, legitimation, and competition.* New York, NY: Oxford University Press.

Hannan, M. T., & Freeman, J. H. (1977). The population ecology model of organizations. *American Journal of Sociology, 82,* 929–964.

Helgesen, S. (1990). *The female advantage: Women's ways of leadership.* New York, NY: Doubleday.

Henslin, J. M. (2008). *Sociology: A down-to-earth approach* (9th ed.). Boston, MA: Allyn & Bacon.

Henslin, J. M. (2014). *Sociology: A down-to-earth approach* (12th ed.). Boston, MA: Pearson.

Herzberg, F. (1986/1968). One more time: How do you motivate employees? In M. T. Matteson & J. M. Ivancevich (Eds.), *Management classics* (3rd ed., pp. 282–297). Plano, TX: Business Publications.

Hickson, D. J. (1987). Decision-making at the top of organizations. *Annual Review of Sociology, 131,* 165–192.

Holland, T. P. (1995). Organizations: Context for social service delivery. In R. L Edwards and J. G. Hopps (Eds.), *Encyclopedia of social work* (19th ed., Vol. 2, pp. 1787–1794). Washington, DC: NASW Press.

Holland, T. P., & Petchers, M. K. (1987). Organizations: Context for social service delivery. In A. Minahan et al. (Eds.), *Encyclopedia of social work* (18th ed., Vol. 2, pp. 204–215). Silver Spring, MD: National Association of Social Workers.

Homans, G. C. (1986/1941). The Western Electric researches. In M. T. Matteson and J. M. Ivancevich (Eds.), *Management classics* (3rd ed., pp. 35–43). Plano, TX: Business Publications.

Human Rights Campaign. (2013) *LGBT equality at the Fortune 500.* Retrieved from https://www.hrc.org/resources/entry/lgbt-equality-at -the-fortune-500.

Institute for Women's Policy Research. (2013, May). *Maternity, paternity, and adoption leave in the United States.* Retrieved from www .iwpr.org.

Janis, I. L. (1972). *Victims of groupthink.* Boston, MA: Houghton Mifflin.

Janis, I. L. (1982). *Groupthink: Psychological studies of foreign policy decisions and fiascoes* (2nd ed.). Boston, MA: Houghton Mifflin.

Kanter, R. M. (1993/1977). *Men and women of the corporation.* New York, NY: Basic Books.

Kinsley, M. (2003, January 27). How affirmative action helped George W. *Time,* p. 70.

Liptak, A. (2010, January 21). Justices, 5-4, reject corporate spending limit. *The New York Times.* Retrieved from http://www.nytimes.com /2010/01/22/us/politics/22scotus.html?pagewanted = all&_r = 0?.

Macionis, J. J. (2014). *Sociology* (15th ed.). Boston, MA: Pearson.

MacLeod, C. (2013, May 17). Will 1,127 deaths move the needle for U.S. shoppers? *USA Today,* p. 1A.

Malcolm, H. (2013, April 30). Unlimited way-k? I want to work here. *USA Today,* p. 5B.

March, J., & Simon, H. (1958). *Organizations.* New York, NY: Wiley.

Martin, A. (2009, February 14). Peanut Corporation of America to liquidate. *The New York Times.* Retrieved from http://wwwnytimes.com.

Maslach, C., & Leiter, M. P. (2008). Early predictors of job burnout and engagement. *Journal of Applied Psychology, 93*(3), 498–512.

Mayerowitz, S. (2012, December 9). Even after fatal fire, shoppers don't think of where products come from. *The State* [Columbia, SC], pp. D1, D4.

Mayo, E. (1933). *The human problems of industrial civilization*. New York, NY: McMillan.

McGregor, D. (1960). *The human side of enterprise*. New York, NY: McGraw Hill.

McNeely, R. L. (1992). Job satisfaction in the public social services: Perspectives on structure, situational factors, gender, and ethnicity. In Y. Hasenfeld (Ed.), *Human services as complex organizations* (pp. 224–255). Newbury Park, CA: Sage.

Memmott, M. (2014, February 5). CVS to stop selling tobacco products. National Public Radio. Retrieved from http://www.npr.org/blogs /thetwo-way/2014/02/05/271906167/cvs-to-stop-selling-tobacco-pro ducts.

Michels, R. (1949/1911). *Political parties*. Glencoe, IL: Free Press.

Miranda, S. M. (1994). Avoidance of groupthink. *Small Group Research, 25,* 105–136.

Mokhiber, R. (2007). Twenty things you should know about corporate crime. *Corporate Crime Reporter.* Retrieved from http://www.corpo ratecrimereporter.com/news/200/2007/06/.

Mokhiber, R. (2013, April 30). The failure to prosecute corporate crime undermines U.S. justice. Retrieved from http://blogs.reuters.com /great-debate/2013/04/30/the-failure-to-prosecute-corporate-crime -undermines-u-s-justice/.

Mor Barak, M. E., & Travis, D. J. (2010). Diversity and organizational performance. In Y. Hasenfeld (Ed.), *Human services as complex organizations* (2nd ed., pp. 341–378). Los Angeles, CA: Sage.

Morgan, G. (1986). *Images of organization*. Beverly Hills, CA: Sage.

Muskal, M., & White, R. D. (2012, November 15). BP fined, charged in oil spill. *Los Angeles Times.* Retrieved from http://articles.latimes .com/2012/nov/15/nation/la-na-nn-holder-bp-oil-spill-settlement-20 121115.

Noonan, M. C., & Glass, J. L. (2012, June). The hard truth about telecommuting. *Monthly Labor Review Online, 135*(6), 38–45.

Nudd, T. (2014, January 29). Ad of the day: Cheerios brings back its famous interracial family for the Super Bowl. *Adweek*. Retrieved from http://www.adweek.com/news/advertising-branding/ad-day -cheerios-brings-back-its-famous-interracial-family-super-bowl-155 302.

Ocean Portal Team. (2013). Gulf oil spill. Retrieved from http://ocean.si .edu/gulf-oil-spill?gclid = CJnppngutbwcfzbj7aoduzwajg.

O'Donnell, J. (2013, May 23). Treat workers well, or kiss our cash goodbye. *USA Today*, p. 5B.

Padavic, I., & Reskin, B. (2002). *Women and men at work* (2nd ed.). Thousand Oaks, CA: Pine Forge Press.

Parenti, M. (2011). *Democracy for the few* (9th ed.). Boston, MA: Wadsworth.

Patai, D. (1991). Minority status and the stigma of "surplus visibility." *Chronicle of Higher Education, 38*(10), p. A52.

Patsuris, P. (2002, August 26). The corporate scandal sheet. *Forbes*. Retrieved from http://www.forbes.com/2002/07/25/accountingtrack er.html.

Perrow, C. (1961). The analysis of goals in complex organizations. *American Sociological Review, 26*, 856–866.

Perrow, C. (1991). A society of organizations. *Theory and Society, 20*, 725–762.

Pfeffer, J. (1997). *New directions for organization theory*. New York, NY: Oxford University Press.

Phillips, M. (2010, March 15). Can we really forgive and forget? *Newsweek*, p. 56.

Public Citizen. (2011.). *Citizens United v. Federal Election Commission: Questions and answers* (brochure). Public Citizen, 1600 20th Street, NW, Washington, DC, 20009.

Reich, R. (2013, February 6). The real debate over American citizenship. *Nation of Change*. Retrieved from http://www.nationofchange.org /print/36214.

Reiman, J., & Leighton, P. (2013). *The rich get richer and the poor get prison* (10th ed.). Boston, MA: Pearson.

Ritzer, G. (2000). *MacDonaldizaton of society*. Thousand Oaks, CA: Pine Forge Press.

Rosener, J. B. (1990). The ways women lead. *Harvard Business Review, 68*, 119–125.

Rothschild, J., & Davies, C. (1994). Organizations through the lens of gender. *Human Relations, 47*, 583–590.

Ryan, M. K., & Haslam, S. A. (2005). The glass cliff: Evidence that women are over-represented in precarious leadership positions. *British Journal of Management, 16*, 81–90.

Salamon, L. M. (1993). The marketization of welfare: Changing nonprofit and for-profit roles in the American welfare state. *Social Service Review, 67*, 16–39.

Sanger, D. E. (1996, January 1). A U.S. agency, once powerful, is dead at 108. *The New York Times*, pp. 1, 9.

Schaefer, R. T. (2012). *Racial and ethnic groups* (13th ed.). Boston, MA: Pearson Education.

Schein, E. H. (1985). *Organizational culture and leadership*. San Francisco, CA: Jossey-Bass.

Schwartzman, M., & Tebbe, N. (2013, November 26). Obamacare and religion and arguing off the wall. *The Slate*. Retrieved from http://www.slate.com/articles/news_and_politics/jurisprudence/2013/11/obamacare_birth_control_mandate_lawsuit_how_a_radicaleargument_went_mainstream.html.

Scott, W. R. (1981). *Organizations: Rational, natural, and open systems*. Englewood Cliffs, NJ: Prentice Hall.

Seabury, B. A. (1971). Arrangement of physical space in social work settings. *Social Work, 16*, 43–49.

Shirom, A. (2011). Job-related burnout: A review of major research foci and challenges. In J. C. Quick and L. E. Petrick (Eds.), *Handbook of occupational health psychology* (2nd ed., pp. 223–241). Washington, DC: American Psychological Association.

Simon, B. L., & Akabas, S. H. (1993). Women workers in high-risk public service: Tokens under stress. In P. A. Kurzman and S. H. Akabas (Eds.), *Work and well-being: The occupational social work advantage* (pp. 297–315). Washington, DC: NASW Press.

Soares, R., Bartkiewicz, M., & Mulligan-Ferry, L. (2013, December 10). *2013 catalyst census: Fortune 500 women board directors*. Catalyst. Retrieved from http://www.catalyst.org/knowledge/2013-catalyst-census-fortune-500-women-board-directors.

Sutherland, E. H. (1940). White collar criminality. *American Sociological Review, 5*, 1–12.

Swanson, D. J., & Tarrant, D. (2013, December 14). It could happen again. *The Dallas Morning News.* Retrieved from http://res.dallas news.com/interactives/2013_December/westretrospective/1215_west retrospective.html.

Szabo, L., & Hoyer, M. (2013, February 1). Similar paths for tobacco, gun lobby? *USA Today*, p. 9B.

Tannen, D. (1994). *Talking from 9 to 5: How women and men's conversational styles affect who gets heard, who gets credit, and what gets done at work.* New York, NY: Morrow.

Taylor, F. W. (1911). *Scientific management.* New York, NY: Harper.

United Way of America (1996). *Measuring program outcomes: A practical approach.* Alexandria, VA: Author.

U.S. Equal Employment Opportunity Commission. (n.d.). *Facts about pregnancy discrimination.* Retrieved from http://www.eeoc.gov/facts /fs-preg.html.

Weber, M. (1978/1922). *Economy and society,* G. Roth and C. Wittich (Eds.). Berkeley, CA: University of California Press.

Williams, C. (1995). *Still a man's world: Men who do women's work.* Berkeley, CA: University of California Press.

Wolfson, A. (2013, May 2). Rifle used by Ky. boy in sister's death made for kids. *USA Today.* Retrieved from http://www.usatoday.com/story/ news/nation/2013/05/02/boy-shoots-s ister-my-firs t-rifle/2128573/.

Woods, A. (2014, May 12). Criminal negligence charges filed in Lac-Mégantic train crash. *The Star* [Montreal, Canada]. Retrieved from http://www.thestar.com/news/canada/2014/05/12/criminal_negli gence_charges_filed_in_deadly_lacmgantic_train_crash.html.

Wright, J. P., Cullen, F. T., & Blankenship, M. B. (1995). The social construction of corporate violence: Media coverage of the Imperial Food Products fire. *Crime & Delinquency, 41*(1), 23–24.

Zoroya, G., & MacLeod, C. (2013, June 26). A world apart, meat workers share a bond. *USA Today*, pp. 1B–2B.

Residential Institutions

Institutions in Other Countries
Social Work in Institutions
References

The role of institutions in America has changed dramatically in the past two centuries. For example, "jails and prisons have increasingly become America's social agency of first resort for coping with the deepening problems of a society in perennial crisis" (Currie, 1998, p. 34). Many social workers are or will be employed in large group care settings (Ginsberg, 2001).

DEFINING INSTITUTIONS

Institutions are organizational settings where residents exercise little or no choice about their participation, have virtually no input into how they are treated, and cannot leave without being officially released or discharged. Moore and Starkes (1992) identified three kinds of institutional settings: those that are medically oriented, those that are residential and service-oriented, and those that are custodial and/or correctional. "All provide some mix of custody and treatment," they note, and the total milieu is considered to be part of the service delivery process. This total milieu idea was emphasized by Trieschman, Whittaker, and Brentro in their book about residential treatment centers for children, *The Other 23 Hours* (1969). They pointed out that what happens in the hours outside of the therapy session may have more of an impact than what happens in it, and that the cook or the groundskeeper, not to mention the recreation therapist and the child-care staff, may play as important a role in the youths' treatment as their therapists.

Erving Goffman (1961) perceived the defining characteristic of an institution to be the inability of residents to leave at will. Wolf Wolfensberger (1972), on the other hand, believed that it was the features of *de-individuation* that make institutions different from other organizations and residences. These features include numbers of residents distinctly larger than might be found in a large family, a high level of regimentation, a physical or social environment that aims at a low common denominator, and a place in which all or most of the transactions of daily life are carried out under one roof or on one "campus" (Wolfensberger, 1972, pp. 28–29). For example, a traditional children's residential treatment center might have dozens or even hundreds of residents; it certainly would not be mistaken for a typical single family home even if it were located in a residential neighborhood. Residents all eat breakfast at 7 a.m. and dinner at 5:30 p.m. whether they are hungry or not; there are craft activities on Wednesday evenings and movies on Fridays; group therapy is offered on Tuesdays and Thursdays. If the neediest resident cannot manage an outing to the mall, then no one can go to the mall. Most residents sleep, eat, socialize, attend classes, study, play, exercise, watch TV, and receive counseling on the same campus, if not in the same buildings, day after day.

At a less coercive level on the continuum are institutional settings where people live for extended periods of time, but are not so isolated from society. These include assisted living centers, halfway houses, group homes, and other community-based facilities. Residents living in these facilities often participate in the same activities, at the same locations, as other community members. For example, children living in a community-based group home are likely to attend a public school and swim at the local Y. At the other end of the continuum are total institutions (Goffman, 1961), those organizations that isolate residents (sometimes called inmates in these settings) from the rest of society and put them under the control of the officials who run the institution. Usually total institutions attempt to resocialize the residents to become more compliant and accepting of institutional and societal norms. Rewards (or more commonly punishments) are used to encourage conformity (Johnson, 1999). The success of total institutions in rehabilitating and preparing their clients for reintegration into society has been strongly and widely challenged.

A BRIEF HISTORY OF INSTITUTIONS

In the mid-nineteenth century, there appeared a well-intentioned effort to provide a new kind of help for at least some at-risk populations. Originally conceived as sanctuaries, asylums were established in the countryside with the intention of resocializing and rehabilitating inmates (including not only prisoners, but also people with mental illness, cognitive impairment, and dependent children) in a wholesome environment far from the chaos, temptations, and exploitations of the city (Rothman,

1971). Physical separation of the asylum from the community was consistently practiced.

At the turn of the century, what began as efforts toward reform had been transformed into a system of custodial and/or punitive care. By the 1950s public attention was brought to bear on the deplorable conditions that existed in asylums. Exposés such as Goffman's *Asylums* (1961) pointed out the deleterious effects of institutions on the lives of inmates who were given minimal custodial care without treatment (a process called warehousing). At the same time, the growing costs of institutional care, advances in pharmacology, and changes in public assistance policies supported a drive for deinstitutionalization. The term *deinstitutionalization* refers to preventing inappropriate admissions to institutions and developing appropriate alternatives in the community.

The Civil Rights Movement in the United States provided fertile ground for legal action on behalf of institutionalized persons. Reflecting the "due process clause" of the Fourteenth Amendment to the Constitution, several court cases that were heard during the 1970s and early 1980s, augmented by federal and state statutes, public licensing, and private accreditation standards, affirmed the basic rights of institutionalized people (see figure 10.1).

FIGURE 10.1   THE RIGHTS OF INSTITUTIONALIZED PEOPLE

The following are the basic rights of institutionalized people.[1] These include:
  • to be housed in the least restrictive setting;
  • to receive minimally adequate, reasonable, appropriate, and humane treatment, rehabilitation, or training in the least restrictive manner (e.g., without the unnecessary or excessive use of physical restraints or isolation);
  • to receive adequate medical care, or care that generally meets a "community standard";
  • to refuse treatment;
  • to refuse to participate in involuntary or uncompensated work for non-therapeutic reasons;
  • to be assured of confidentiality of records and privacy in treatment;
  • to have personal property (within reason) and to wear their own clothes;

- to live without supervision in the community if they pose no threat to themselves or others.

[1] Although prisoners must be treated humanely, many of these rights do not apply to them. On the other hand, unnecessary restraints and excessive use of seclusion in prisons also have also been ruled unconstitutional.
Sources: The Pew Center on the States, (2008); Saltzman, & Proch, (1990).

Unfortunately, the implementation of deinstitutionalization policies often resulted in the precipitous discharge of residents without concurrent development of family support and community resources (DiNitto, 2011). Thus, many patients with chronic mental illnesses became homeless "street people," while others ended up in places smaller but no less "institutional" than their previous setting, or worse yet, in local jails. This pattern of moving from one institution to another is called trans-institutionalization (Segal, 2008).

ISSUES AND TRENDS

Privatization

A recent trend in institutional care is the privatization of facilities. Large private, for-profit corporations have developed nursing homes, psychiatric treatment centers, and prisons (Karger & Stoesz, 2010). The trend toward privatization in prisons was presented in more detail in chapter 3.

"Revolving Door" Care

The term *revolving door* refers to a pattern of institutional care that involves repeated admissions and discharges. Although the term also is used currently to refer to the problem of the rehospitalization of elderly patients (Robert Wood Johnson Foundation, 2013), it has been particularly problematic in the case of people with chronic mental illnesses. Although the push for deinstitutionalization has prevented unnecessary, long-term custodial care, it also has encouraged premature discharges and repeated readmissions (Segal, 2008). In general, patterns of mental health admission to institutions now are periodic, temporary, frequent, and short-term (Moore & Starkes, 1992, p. 173). The term can also be applied to other institutionalized populations. More than half of released offenders return to prison within three years, either after being convicted of a new offense or for probation violations (Pew Center on the States, 2008). (The percentage of convicts who are rearrested is called the recidivism rate.)

Moore and Starkes (1992, p. 173) also note that concern now seems to have turned away from the location of care to issues of continuity of care. The continuity-of-care perspective views institutionalization as only one aspect of treatment and assumes that professionals will develop and implement a plan for working with significant others in the clients' lives and for appropriate aftercare and follow-up after discharge.

Other trends in institutional care in America vary by population. Some of these patterns have been well publicized, while others are less well known. They are discussed next.

Offenders

There has been extensive press coverage of the explosion in the prison population in this country, thanks in part to data collected by the nonprofit watchdog group the Sentencing Project (www.sentencingproject.org). The United States is the world's leader in incarceration with 1.57 million people currently in the nation's prisons or jails. Prison overcrowding continues and state governments are overwhelmed by the burden of funding their penal systems. The Sentencing Project (Mauer & King, 2007) reported that as of 2003, 20 percent of inmate populations at the state level, and 55 percent in the federal system, were drug offenders. Of all persons meeting the criteria as drug abusers or drug-dependent, less than half in state or federal prisons received *any* treatment or programming since admission.

The exploding inmate population just referenced necessitated a boom in federal and state prison construction. Much of the prison boom has been concentrated in small towns and rural areas. A PBS documentary, *Prison Town, USA* (Galloway & Kutchins, 2007), reported that 350 rural counties saw prisons open between 1980 and 2001. The possibilities of employment and a boost for local businesses were often part of the campaign to bring prisons to such localities.

The promised benefits, however, were not always realized. Many local workers were not qualified for some positions, such as corrections officer, and those positions were filled by people living outside of the community. Some jobs for which locals were qualified, both inside and outside the prison walls, were performed instead by prison labor (Huling, 2002). Often secondary benefits, such as contracts with local businesses to provide goods or services to the prison, were lost as prison management chose to renegotiate contracts or outsource aspects of the work. A 2003 study of prisons sited in rural communities found that there was no overall effect on local employment, per capita income, or consumer spending, three leading indicators of economic vitality (Galloway & Kutchins, 2007). Other problems include the many incidents of racism that have been documented in prisons in rural areas where correctional officers are predominantly white and prisoners are predominantly people of color (Huling, 2002).

Again, according to the Sentencing Project (Porter, 2012), overall state prison populations declined for the third consecutive year in 2011. Reasons for this decline include state sentencing reforms (e.g., relaxing mandatory minimums, and reducing the length of sentences for possession of crack cocaine) and changes in parole revocation policies. It is unclear whether this pattern will be sustained.

Although prison overcrowding is an ongoing concern, *jails* currently represent one of the most problematic aspects of institutional care. Jails serve a "catch-all function," holding individuals pending arraignment or trial, convicted offenders serving short-term sentences, convicted offenders awaiting transfer to prison, probation and parole violators, vagrants, drunks, people who are mentally ill or homeless, and increasingly, juveniles. In addition to being overcrowded, many jails are old and unsanitary, and inadequately staffed (Territo, Halsted, & Bromley, 2004). Problems result from the limited and unstable nature of local taxes, a general lack of public support for jail reform, rapid rates of inmate turnover that make it difficult to develop and coordinate programs, and the immense diversity of risks and needs found among inmates (Bohm & Haley, 2014). Jails are the "revolving door" of the justice system (Siegel & Worrall, 2014, p. 498), but like the prison population, the jail population has also been declining in in recent years.

Older Adults

Older adults who were confined to public mental hospitals were the principal beneficiaries of policies of deinstitutionalization. Older adults need long-term care because of disability, chronic illness, or dementia (National Association of Social Workers, 2012a). According to the Centers for Medicare and Medicaid Services (2012), more than 1.4 million U.S. residents were living in nursing homes on December 31, 2011, corresponding to 2.9 percent of the over-65 population and 10.7 percent of the over-85 population. (See table 10.1.)

According to an AARP Public Policy fact sheet (Houser, 2007), even as the number of older adults has continued to increase, the *number of nursing home residents* has remained constant since 1985; that means the proportion of the population likely to need long-term care has actually decreased. Because of the increased use of nursing homes for short-term post-acute care, however, the *number of stays* has increased.

In a study ordered by Congress (Fleck, 2002), it was reported that more than 90 percent of the nation's nursing homes are inadequately staffed, putting residents at risk for bedsores, blood-borne infections, dehydration, malnutrition, and pneumonia. A *Consumer Reports* investigation ("Nursing Homes," 2006) found that not-for-profit facilities employ more staff and do a better job of providing good care. The same analysis showed that independently run homes provide better care than

TABLE 10.1
Characteristics of Nursing Home Residents

Over age 65	85%
Female	67.2%
Non-Hispanic white	78.9%
Impairments in ADLs*	80%
Severely incontinent	35.6%
On anti-psychotic medication**	30%

Sources: Centers for Medicare and Medicaid Services (2012); Avitzur (2013).
*Activities of daily living (ADLs) include bed mobility, transferring, dressing, eating, and toileting.
**One-third of these had no identified indication for use of the medication.

do chains. The nursing home industry blames low rates of reimbursement under federal Medicaid and Medicare programs. Critics counter that government rates more than doubled between 1992 and 1998, and nursing homes chose to use the money to boost profits or to finance takeovers rather than to increase staffing (Fleck, 2002, p. 16).

The *Consumer Reports* ("Nursing Homes," 2006) investigation found that state officials responsible for overseeing nursing home care have often failed to correct problems. The most usual remedy for violations of standards in nursing home care is a "plan of correction." In this situation, the nursing homes acknowledge the problem and promise to address it within a specified period. Often the problem is corrected, but it soon resurfaces, a phenomenon regulators call yo-yo compliance, and fines tend to be "absurdly" low ("Nursing Homes," 2006).

Residential care facilities (RCFs) were developed to provide an innovative and humane alternative to nursing homes. They include assisted living facilities and personal care homes and have become a million-dollar industry. The Centers for Disease Control reported that there were 31,100 RCFs in 2010 with 971,900 beds nationwide (Park-Lee et al., 2011). RCFs serve primarily a private-pay adult population, but the use of Medicaid financing has gradually increased in recent years. About half of RCFs are small facilities with four to ten beds. More than three-quarters are private, for-profit facilities, and about 38 percent are chain-affiliated.

In 2013 PBS, *Frontline*, and ProPublica (Thompson & Jones, 2013) examined the conditions in assisted living facilities in America and came up with some disturbing findings. There are no federal-level standards, and state regulations vary widely; for example, in fourteen states administrators do not need to have high school diplomas and in other states there is no requirement for a licensed nurse to be on staff. Only fourteen states set staff-to-patient ratios; in California facilities housing as many as 200 seniors need no more than two workers on the overnight shift and only one of those needs to be awake. Compared to nursing homes, assisted living facilities receive little outside monitoring. In six states there are no regular inspections and there are few consequences for lapses in care. In California facilities pay as little as $150 in penalties in cases where a resident has died as a result of poor care. The jumble of state laws governing assisted living facilities reflects, in part, the industry's efforts to fight off tighter regulation.

People with Mental Illness

"The mental health system [in the United States] is fragmented, not welcoming, overburdened, and extremely difficult to navigate, especially by someone who is not thinking clearly," observed a Virginia state senator who tried in vain to find a psychiatric hospital to take his mentally ill son (Earley, 2013, p. 10a). The son stabbed him multiple times and then killed himself.

According to a report from the Treatment Advocacy Center (Torrey, Entsminger, Geller, Stanley, & Jaffe, 2008), experts suggest that fifty public psychiatric beds per 100,000 people is a minimum number required for adequate services. In 2005, forty-two states had less than half the minimum number recommended. In 1955 there were 340 public psychiatric beds available per 100,000 population; this dropped to 17 per 100,000 in 2005. Because psychiatric beds are not profitable, many HMOs have closed mental health inpatient facilities in favor of more lucrative surgical clinics (Earley, 2013). At the same time, states cut funding for about 4,500 public psychiatric beds, 10 percent of the total, between 2009 and 2012 (Szabo, 2014). The consequences of the lack of an adequate number of public psychiatric facilities include homelessness, inappropriate incarceration, and local emergency rooms filled with patients waiting for a psychiatric bed.

With the absence of community-based alternatives, care of people with mental illness has shifted to detention centers, jails, and prisons (Szabo, 2014); "jail becomes a default mental-health facility because there are no resources to provide care" (Torrey, Kennard, Eslinger, Lamb, & Pavle, 2010, p. 4). According to Bureau of Justice statistics, about two-thirds of jail inmates report having a mental health problem, and 15 percent of all state prisoners and 24 percent of jail inmates suffer from psychosis (Szabo, 2014).

The National Center on Institutions and Alternatives released a major study on jail inmate suicide in 2011. They reported that while jail suicide rates have been declining, suicide is still the single leading cause of unnatural deaths in local jails, and rates are still approximately three times greater than that in the general population. Among jail suicide victims, 38 percent had a history of mental illness and 34 percent had a history of suicidal behavior.

Most mentally ill offenders are arrested for minor offenses such as trespassing, vagrancy, urinating in public, or shoplifting at the corner convenience store. Many of them also have substance abuse problems, but cannot get into drug- and alcohol-treatment programs because of their mental illnesses.

People with Developmental Disabilities

Before deinstitutionalization, many people with developmental disabilities lived in the same institutions as people with mental illnesses. Only those with severe disabilities are now likely to live in other long-term care facilities, but nursing home employees often are not adequately trained to meet their special needs (National Association of Social Workers, 2012a). People with disabilities, however, have been successful in obtaining political support and financial resources due to strong lobbies and a public perception of worthiness (Segal, 2008). Contemporary practice emphasizes habilitation and rehabilitation training, and consumer-driven, highly individualized supports. Most people with cognitive disabilities live with their families or reside in community-based facilities, including intermediate-care facilities, foster homes, group homes, boarding homes, and supervised apartments (Segal, 2008).

Children and Youth

In the United States, the number of children living in institutions reached a low in 1960 and then more than doubled in the 1980s and 1990s, leveling off in 2000 at 144,981 (Segal, 2008). In the last twenty years, child welfare policy has heavily favored placing children in need of care with family-of-origin or kin-based alternatives, thus reducing government funding for residential treatment (Butler, 2006). Some residential centers, particularly unlicensed, unregulated private facilities, have been associated with reports of exploitation and mistreatment of children (U.S. Government Accountability Office, 2007). A study conducted by the American Bar Association found that thousands of children were placed by their parents in privately run, unregulated residential facilities (Behar, Friedman, Pinto, Katz-Leavy, & Jones, 2007). Seductive advertisements, particularly on the Internet, aim their messages at parents who are struggling to find help for their problematic children. Many of these programs do not require a professional assessment prior to admission and severely limit parental contact.

On the other hand, reputable and accredited residential treatment centers that provide the basic components of a therapeutic milieu (a multidisciplinary care team, deliberate client supervision, intense staff supervision and training, and consistent clinical/administrative oversight) continue to provide a much-needed service for many children and families (Butler, 2006).

Currently there are about 6,000 children under the age of twenty-one living in nursing homes in the United States, because their parents cannot manage the special demands of the care required by their physical and mental disabilities ("Disabled kids living isolated lives in institutions," 2012). Alternatives to nursing home placement include group homes or the provision of trained aides in their own family home, but waiting lists are lengthy.

UNDERSTANDING INSTITUTIONS

Ecosystems Perspective

Because they cannot voluntarily leave, institutional residents are more affected by the physical characteristics of their environment than people who can come and go at will. Historically, most institutions were immense buildings with high ceilings, long corridors, and large sleeping wards. The recognition of the importance of architectural design in promoting healthier social functioning created an impetus for new institutional facilities. Hutchinson (2008) has summarized the recent history of innovative institutional design in America (see for example Osmond, 1957, 1959, 1966; Sommer, 1969), and several research studies (see for example Cherulnik, 1993; Friedman, 1976; Holahan & Saegert, 1973; Sommer & Ross, 1958; Wener, Frazier, & Farbstein, 1985) documenting the effectiveness of more consumer-centered arrangements in psychiatric hospitals, large medical hospitals, correctional settings, and facilities for people with cognitive disabilities. Large wards were replaced with individual rooms and the furniture in day rooms was rearranged (for example, putting chairs around small tables in the middle of the room rather than placing chairs and couches around the walls with patients sitting shoulder to shoulder). An example of another innovation in institutional design is the use of enclosed outdoor patio pathways that allow patients with dementia to "go for walks" without getting lost or wandering away from the facility.

The general concept of person-environment fit was discussed in chapter 1. Lawton (1982) and others (see Cavanaugh & Blanchard-Fields, 2014; Lawton & Nahemow, 1973) have suggested that one way of examining the person-environment fit is to look at the individual's level of competence (his or her capacity to function across several dimensions) and environmental press (the demands of the environment). If competence and press are in balance, there is adaptation. If there are too many demands and too little competence, the result is maladaptive behavior and negative affect. And if there are too few demands and excess competence, the result is still maladaptive behavior and negative affect. This latter condition is applicable to many institutional settings where there is little in the daily routine that might offer a challenge or opportunity for growth to residents. For example, many nursing home staff members assume a lower level of functioning for residents than they are capable of and make decisions for them, causing residents to appear to be even more dependent than they are (Baltes, 1994; Wahl, 1991; Zarit, Dolan, & Leitsch, 1999). When researchers introduced decision-making options for residents, they not only demonstrated higher activity levels and greater well-being, but also lower mortality rates (Langer & Rodin, 1976; Rodin & Langer, 1977; Schulz & Hanusa, 1979).

Functionalist Perspective

Functionalists recognize several societal benefits of institutions. Some inmates are in institutions because they represent an immediate threat to society. In removing "deviants" from the community and punishing them, institutions help to reinforce a greater commitment on the part of the conforming majority to conventional norms and behaviors (Henslin, 2014).

A latent function of institutions is providing employment. An example would be a new prison built in a rural area that lacks other kinds of industries. Functionalists would hold that the employment opportunities and economic growth that result are a positive contribution to the well-being of an area that extends beyond the manifest functions of the institution itself. Studies have shown, however, that the actual outcomes are less encouraging (see chapter 8).

Rational/Social Exchange Perspective

Institutions are a special type of organization, called coercive organizations by many sociologists because, for the most part, residents are there against their will. As organizations, institutions are designed using a bureaucratic model (see chapter 9). That means that they have a hierarchical structure, a complex division of labor, and many rules and regulations that apply to staff as well as residents. One of the major complaints that are made about many nursing homes, for example, is that their programs serve to meet the needs of the institution rather than the needs of residents. Regimented scheduling is valued by such facilities despite arguments by gerontologists that such routines are detrimental to residents' well-being (Langer & Rodin, 1976).

On an individual level, the rationalist perspective underlies the deterrence theory of imprisonment (see chapter 3). Deterrence theory suggests that harsh prison settings will cause individuals to decide to refrain from engaging in criminal activity.

On a societal level, a cost-benefit analysis of institutional care suggests that not much rational thought has gone into planning. The same amount of money invested in preventive programs and community-based care would improve the lives not only of those who end up in institutions but others as well.

Conflict Perspective

From a conflict perspective, institutions satisfy the need to remove those who are unable to comply with the demands and expectations of the powerful in society. These would include those who are too old to work, those who are chronically ill, and/or those who are a danger to themselves or others. Spitzer (1980) stated it more strongly, saying that institutions are an instrument of social control, used to warehouse the surplus labor population that fails to contribute to capital accumulation.

In institutions, differences in power are everywhere. For residents, freedom of movement is restricted, contact with staff and outsiders is limited, and personal privacy is minimal. Although they are monitored almost continuously, residents have so little power that they may be treated as if they are invisible. Rosenhan (1973, p. 256), for example, reported incidents of ward attendants abusing mental patients in front of other patients, and of a nurse who "unbuttoned her uniform to adjust her brassiere in the presence of an entire ward of viewing men" as if they weren't there. Although in the past few decades laws and regulations have been put in place to protect the basic rights of many institutionalized adults, the reality is that they are still among the most oppressed of our society's citizens.

Given the current social climate, the mistreatment of inmates in American prisons and jails is often ignored or even condoned. There is a general attitude that convicted and incarcerated felons have forfeited their rights to be treated as human beings (Stringfellow, 1990/1991); thus the potential for human rights abuses at both large "supermax" facilities and at smaller, overcrowded facilities is great.

Constructionist Perspective

According to labeling theory, labels such as *patient* or *criminal* may result in institutional residents accepting and internalizing the attributes of those roles (Goffman, 1961). The impact of labeling is not limited to the label recipient but extends to those with whom she or he interacts. For example, once a person is labeled a psychiatric patient, staff may interpret even normal behaviors as symptoms of mental illness (Rosenhan, 1973).

Preferred Perspectives

Along with deinstitutionalization came a movement for institutional reform called normalization. In simple terms, *normalization* means making available to institutionalized people living arrangements that closely resemble those enjoyed by other citizens (Nirje, 1976; Wolfensberger, 1972). This approach suggests that facilities should be small (i.e., designed for no more than six to eight residents). They should resemble valued homes in the community—there should be no signs in front (or on the program vehicle) that identify the residents inside as different from other citizens. Facilities should be integrated into the community so residents can walk or use public transportation to get to the library, shopping mall, movie theaters, coffee shop, and so forth. Residents should work and receive services away from the facility. There should be a continuum of options available, but residents should not have to move simply because their needs change; instead, services should be adapted so that residents can experience a sense of permanence and security in their living arrangement.

A more recent effort to reform institutions is called the *Eden Alternative*. This approach was a response to the sterile, pathology-based, treatment orientation of nursing homes that results in loneliness, helplessness, and boredom. Eden Alternative founder William Thomas enumerates three fundamental principles of this new kind of care: acknowledging each resident's capacity for growth, focusing on the needs of the residents rather than the needs of the institution, and emphasizing quality long-term nurturing care while providing short-term treatment as needed (Thomas, 1994). This new philosophy of care involves "aesthetically transforming the physical environment of facilities with the addition of pets, plants, and children, creating a 'human habitat'; placing maximum possible decision-making authority in the hands of residents and those who care for them; de-emphasizing program activities by encouraging resident involvement in the 'human habitat'; and de-emphasizing the use of prescription drugs" (see "Long-Term Care Paradise," 1999). In contrast to the usual hierarchical, bureaucratic, department-based organizational design of most nursing homes, in the Eden Alternative facilities, staff members form multidisciplinary work teams that assume responsibility for an area, and make their own schedules and work assignments. Thus, a cooperative work environment is cultivated and staff feel empowered.

Calkins (2011) has summarized other trends in elder care in the past decade or two. These include elimination of the nursing stations and med carts; the "household model" of eight- to eighteen-bed residential facilities; and "intentional elder-friendly communities" that have houses that encourage "aging in place"—that is, at least one no-threshold entry, an accessible bathroom, a kitchen and bedroom on the main level, and doorways/hallways wide enough to accommodate a wheelchair.

THE IMPACT OF INSTITUTIONS ON INDIVIDUALS AND FAMILIES
How Institutions Deter Well-Being

Erving Goffman was a well-known early critic of psychiatric hospitals and other "total institutions," such as prisons and concentration camps. In his groundbreaking ethnographic work, *Asylums: Essays on the Social Situation of Mental Patients and Other Inmates*, Goffman argued that institutionalization was a traumatic and "mortifying" experience brought on by isolation, invasion of privacy, regimentation, and labeling (1961, pp. 13–14). Deegan (1993) echoes this sentiment in describing psychiatric hospitalization as the "radically dehumanizing and devaluing transformation from being a person to being an illness" (p. 7).

Conditions in some long-term care facilities continue to raise concerns. For example, overuse of physical restraints and psychotropic drugs for people with chronic mental illness, cognitive impairments or developmental disabilities, and those who exhibit behavioral symptoms of dementia have been reported in many nursing homes (National Association of Social Workers, 2012a).

Even when facilities are well run, most people dread living in an institutional setting because of the expected loss of freedom, control, and privacy. The powerlessness and deindividuation associated with most institutions leads members of many vulnerable populations, such as the aged and those with chronic physical or mental illnesses, to choose marginally adequate living arrangements in the community or even homelessness over inpatient status.

The regimentation of most institutions results in residents becoming institutionalized. *Institutionalization* is a syndrome characterized by apathy, withdrawal, submissiveness, and a reluctance to leave the institutional setting (Johnson & Rhodes, 2007). In other words, residents are resocialized to become compliant and dependent. In learning to adapt to the institutional environment, they lose the skills and attitudes—such as self-care and independent decision making, assertiveness, and self-confidence—they need to reenter and function successfully in the outside world. Wirt (1999) suggests "the restrictive environment of institutional settings coupled with oppressive staff [are] capable of producing institutionalism in almost any person regardless of diagnosis, predispositions, or personality" (p. 260). Prolonged isolation in prisons can even provoke severe symptoms of mental illness, such as anxiety, depression, despair, paranoia, rage, obsessive thoughts, claustrophobia, and hallucinations (Human Rights Watch, 2012; Metzner & Fellner, 2010). Solitary confinement can be unendurable for some prisoners, as is evident from the high number of suicides that take place (Metzner & Fellner, 2010). According to the nonprofit organization Human Rights Watch (2012), human rights law does not prohibit solitary confinement in all cases. Nevertheless, prolonged solitary confinement can violate the prohibition on cruel, inhuman, or degrading treatment.

In some institutional settings, particularly those designed for offenders, a *deviant subculture* develops and imposes its values and patterns on the residents, regardless of what goes on in the rest of the institution (Polsky, 1962; Sykes, 1958). Sometimes called the convict code, inmate subculture, inmate social code, or deprivation model in corrections settings, this theory suggests that an environment of shared deprivation gives inmates a basis for solidarity (Siegel & Worrall, 2014). The subculture represents a functional, collective adaptation of inmates to their environment. Norms of the convict code include not informing the staff about the illicit activities of other prisoners, skill in "conning" and manipulation of staff, and an ability to show strength, courage, and toughness. Criminologists say that there probably no longer exists one overriding inmate subculture, but rather several subcultures that are divided along racial and ethnic lines (Cole et al., 2013; Siegel & Worrall, 2014).

One might ask whether the funds used for institutional care might be put to better use in prevention or community-based services. "The money spent on prisons is money taken from the parts of the public sector that educate, train, socialize, treat, nurture and house the population—particularly the children of the poor" (Currie, 1998, p. 35).

How Institutions Promote Well-Being

For small numbers of individuals, institutional placement is the most appropriate alternative both for them and for the rest of society. Some people pose a clear danger to themselves or others and need a protective, structured environment. Institutions do have a place in a modern, democratic society. Problems occur when they are overcrowded, underfunded and understaffed, poorly designed, and used by default rather than by plan.

INSTITUTIONS IN OTHER COUNTRIES

In other countries, institutions are still used for purposes that are no longer common in the United States. Despite research that shows that institutional care of very young children is harmful to their development, an estimated minimum of 44,000 children under three years of age are officially recorded as living in institutional care for more than three months within forty-seven countries in the European region (Browne, 2009). "At least nine out of ten children in residential care have one living parent, and are mostly placed in institutions for social and economic reasons in transition countries, and for reasons of abuse and neglect in economically developed countries" (Browne, 2009).

There are investigations that document deplorable conditions in institutions in other places. Recently, for example, Disabilities Rights International, a U.S.-based human rights group, issued a report on the abuse of patients with cognitive disabilities housed in Mexico's psychiatric hospitals (Rosenthal, Jehn, & Galvan, 2011). Some children have disappeared and may have been subjected to sex trafficking and forced labor. Over the past decade, the same group has documented abuses in institutions in Vietnam, Serbia, Argentina, Romania, Turkey, Peru, and Kosovo (Disability Rights International, 2013).

Couples who adopt from abroad may pick up their babies in orphanages in Russia, Romania, China, or Guatemala. Most of these facilities are clean and well run and now in many countries, babies and young children waiting for adoption are placed with foster families.

SOCIAL WORK IN INSTITUTIONS

Ginsberg (2001) summarizes the many tasks that social workers perform in institutional settings. In hospitals, they work on discharge planning and help patients arrange for financial support. They not only provide social services in long-term care facilities for older adults, but also provide consultation around licensing issues. In prisons, they may be called upon to provide individual counseling and group therapy sessions and to help inmates stay in contact with their families.

Because most clients in institutional settings are involuntary, social workers have a special ethical responsibility to them. Social workers play an important role of advocacy for appropriate, culturally competent, quality care for those in long-term care facilities (National Association of Social Workers, 2012a). Often "it is social workers who must inform those who have been institutionalized or who face institutionalization of their rights or interpret their rights for them. Many times only social workers are available to act as advocates for those who are institutionalized, insuring that their rights are recognized and respected" (Saltzman & Proch, 1990, p. 360). In a corrections context in particular, and in other institutional settings as well, social workers must be prepared to advocate "for safe, humane, and equitable treatment" (National Association of Social Workers, 2012b, p. 324).

REFERENCES

Baltes, M. M. (1994). Aging well and institutional living: A paradox? In R. P. Abeles, H. C. Gift, & M. G. Ory (Eds.), *Aging and quality of life* (pp. 185–201). New York, NY: Springer.

Behar, L., Friedman, R., Pinto, A., Katz-Leavy, J., & Jones, J. G. (2007). Protecting youth placed in unlicensed, unregulated residential "treatment" facilities. *Family Court Review 45*, 399–413.

Bohm, R. M., & Haley, K. N. (2014). *Introduction to criminal justice* (8th ed.). New York, NY: McGraw-Hill.

Browne, K. (2009). *The risk of harm to young children in institutional care.* The Better Care Network. Retrieved from http://www.crin.org /docs/the_risk_of_harm.pdf.

Butler, L. S. (2006, December 20). Is residential treatment misunderstood? Springer Science + Business Media. Retrieved from http://link .springer.com/article/10.1007%2Fs10826-006-9101-6#page-1.

Calkins, M. P. (2011, March 1). Ten senior living design innovations. *Long Term Living.* Retrieved from http://www.ltlmagazine.com/print /article/ten-senior-living-design-innovations.

Cavanaugh, J. C., & Blanchard-Fields, F. (2014). *Adult development and aging* (7th ed.). Stamford, CT: Cengage.

Centers for Medicare and Medicaid Services. (2012). *Nursing home data compendium: 2012 edition.* Retrieved from https://www.cms.gov /Medicare/Provider-Enrollment-and-certification/Certificationand Complianc/downloads/nursinghomedatacompendium_508.pdf.

Cherulnik, P. (1993). *Applications of environment-behavior research: Case studies and analysis.* New York, NY: Cambridge University Press.

Cole, G. F., Smith, C. E., & DeJong, C. (2013). *The American system of criminal justice* (13th ed.). Belmont, CA: Wadsworth.

Currie, E. (1998). *Crime and punishment in America.* New York, NY: Metropolitan Books.

Deegan, P. E. (1993). Recovering our sense of value after being labeled mentally ill. *Journal of Psychosocial Nursing, 15,* 3–19.

DiNitto, D. M. (2011). *Social welfare: Politics and public policy* (7th ed.). Boston, MA: Allyn and Bacon.

Disabled kids living isolated lives in institutions. (2012, October 16). National Public Radio. Retrieved from http://www.npr.org/2012/10 /16/163018620/disabled-kids-living-isolated-lives-in-institutions.

Disability Rights International (2013). Our work. Retrieved from http:// www.disabilityrightsintl.org/work/.

Earley, P. (2013, November 21). Deeds attack shows that our system is a mess. *USA Today,* p. 10A.

Fleck, C. (2002, April). Nursing home care is found wanting. *AARP Bulletin, 43*(4), 3, 16–17.

Friedman, A. (1976, September). On politics and design. *Contract,* pp. 6, 10, 12.

Galloway, K., & Kutchins, P. (2007). *Prison town, USA.* Public Broadcasting System. Retrieved from http://www.pbs.org/pov/pov2007/ prisontown/for.html.

Ginsberg, L. H. (2001). *Careers in social work* (2nd ed.). Boston, MA: Allyn & Bacon.

Goffman, E. (1961). *Asylums: Essays on the social situation of mental patients and other inmates.* Chicago, IL: Aldine.

Henslin, J. M. (2014). *Sociology: A down-to-earth approach* (12th ed.). Boston, MA: Pearson .

Holahan, C., & Saegert, S. (1973). Behavioral and attitudinal effects of large-scale variation in the physical environment of psychiatric wards. *Journal of Abnormal Psychology, 82,* 454–462.

Houser, A. N. (2007). *Nursing homes.* Retrieved from http://www.aarp .org/research/longtermcare/nursinghomes/fs10r_homes.html.

Huling, T. (2002). Building a prison economy in rural America. In M. Mauer and M. Chesney-Lind (Eds.), *Invisible punishment: The collateral consequences of mass imprisonment* (pp. 197–213). New York, NY: New Press.

Human Rights Watch. (2012, June 18). *US: Look critically at widespread use of solitary confinement.* Retrieved from http://www.hrw.org/news /2012/06/18/us-look-critically-widespread-use-solitary-confinement.

Hutchison, E. D. (2008). *Dimensions of human behavior: Person and environment* (3rd ed.). Thousand Oaks, CA: Sage.

Johnson, M. M. (1999). Managing perceptions: A new paradigm for residential group care. *Child and Youth Care Forum, 28*(3), 165–179.

Johnson, M. M., & Rhodes, R. (2007). Institutionalization: A theory of human behavior and the social environment. *Advances in Social Work, 8,* 219–236.

Karger, H. J., & Stoesz, D. (2010). *American social welfare policy* (6th ed.). Boston, MA: Pearson.

Langer, E. J., & Rodin, J. (1976). The effects of choice and enhanced personal responsibility for the aged: A field experiment in an institutional setting. *Journal of Personality and Social Psychology, 34,* 191–198.

Lawton, M. P. (1982). Competence, environmental press, and the adaptation of old people. In M. P. Lawton, P. G. Windley, & T. O. Byerts (Eds.), *Aging and the environment: Theoretical approaches* (pp. 33–59). New York, NY: Springer.

Lawton, M. P., & Nahemow, L. (1973). Ecology of the aging process. In C. Eisdorfer and M. P. Lawton (Eds.), *The psychology of adult development and aging* (pp. 619–674). Washington, DC: American Psychological Association.

Long-term care paradise. (1999, September). In *Executive Solutions for Healthcare Management,* pp. 13–16. Available from Capitol Publishing Group, a division of Aspen Publishers Inc., 1101 King Street, Suite 444, Alexandria, VA 22314.

Mauer, M., & King, R. S. (2007, September). *A 25-year quagmire: The war on drugs and its impact on American society.* Retrieved from http://www.sentencingproject.org/doc/publications/dp_25yearquagmire.pdf.

Metzner, J. L., & Fellner, J. (2010). Solitary confinement and mental illness in U.S. prisons: A challenge for medical ethics. *The Journal of the American Academy of Psychiatry and the Law, 38.* Retrieved from http://www.hrw.org/news/2010/03/22/solitary-confinement-and-mental-illness-us-prisons.

Moore, E. E., & Starkes, A. J. (1992). The group-in-institution as the unit of attention: Recapturing and refining a social work tradition. *Social Work with Groups, 15,* 171–192.

National Association of Social Workers. (2012a). Long-term care. In *Social work speaks: National Association of Social Workers policy statements, 2012–2014* (9th ed., pp. 224–229). Washington, DC: NASW Press.

National Association of Social Workers. (2012b). Social work in the criminal justice system. In *Social work speaks: National Association of Social Workers policy statements, 2012–2014* (9th ed., pp. 321–326). Washington, DC: NASW Press.

National Center on Institutions and Alternatives, Inc. (n.d.). *National study of jail suicide.* Retrieved from http://www.ncianet.org/services/suicide-prevention-in-custody/national-study-of-jail-suicides/.

Nirje, B. (1976). The normalization principle. In R. B. Kugel & A. Sheerer (Eds.), *Changing patterns in residential services for the mentally retarded* (pp. 179–195). Washington, DC: President's Committee on Mental Retardation.

Nursing homes: Business as usual. (2006). *Consumer Reports.* Retrieved from http://www.consumerreports.org.

Osmond, H. (1957). Function as the basis of psychiatric ward design. *Mental Hospitals, 8,* 23–29.

Osmond, H. (1959). The relationship between architect and psychiatrist. In C. Goshen (Ed.), *Psychiatric architecture* (pp. 16–20). Washington, DC: American Psychiatric Association.

Osmond, H. (1966). Some psychiatric aspects of design. In L. B. Holland (Ed.), *Who designs America?* (pp. 281–318). Garden City, NY: Anchor.

Park-Lee, E., Caffrey, C., Sengupta, M., Moss, A. J., Rosenoff, E., & Harris-Kojetin, L. D. (2011, December). *Residential care facilities: A key sector in the spectrum of long-term care providers in the United States.* Centers for Disease Control and Prevention. Retrieved from http://www.cdc.gov/nchs/data/databriefs/db78.htm.

Pew Center on the States. (2008). *One in 100: Behind bars in America 2008.* Retrieved from http://www.pewcenteronthestates.org/report _detail.aspx?id = 35904.

Polsky, H. W. (1962). *Cottage six: The social system of delinquent boys in residential treatment.* New York, NY: Russell Sage Foundation.

Porter, N. D. (2012, December). On the chopping block 2012: State prison closings. Retrieved from http://sentencingproject.org/doc/publica tions/OntheChoppingBlock2012.pdf.

Robert Wood Johnson Foundation. (2013, February). *The revolving door: A report on U.S. hospital readmissions.* Retrieved from http://www .rwjf.org/en/research-publications/find-rwjf-research/2013/02/the -revolving-door--a-report-on-u-s--hospital-readmissions.html.

Rodin, J., & Langer, E. J. (1977). Long-term effects of a control-relevant intervention with the institutionalized aged. *Journal of Personality and Social Psychology, 35,* 897–902.

Rosenhan, D. L. (1973). On being sane in insane places. *Science, 179,* 250–258.

Rosenthal, E., Jehn, E., & Galvan, S. (2011, June). *Abandoned and disappeared: Mexico's segregation and abuse of children and adults with disabilities.* Retrieved from http://www.disabilityrightsintl.org/word press/wp-content/uploads/Mex-Report-English-Nov30-finalpdf.pdf.

Rothman, D. J. (1971). *The discovery of the asylum.* Boston, MA: Little, Brown.

Saltzman, A., & Proch, K. (1990). The rights of institutionalized adults. In A. Salzman & K. Proch, *Law in social work practice* (pp. 359–373). Chicago, IL: Nelson-Hall.

Schulz , R., & Hanusa, B. H. (1979). Environmental influences on the effectiveness of control- and competence-enhancing interventions. In L. C. Permuter & R. A. Monty (Eds.), *Choice and perceived control* (pp. 315–337). Hillsdale, NJ: Erlbaum.

Segal, S. P. (2008). Deinstitutionalization. In T. Mizrahi and L. E. Davis (Eds.), *Encyclopedia of social work* (20th ed., Vol. 2, pp. 10–20). Washington, DC: NASW Press.

Siegel, L. J., & Worrall, J. L. (2014). *Introduction to criminal justice* (14th ed.). Belmont, CA: Wadsworth.

Sommer, R. (1969). *Personal space: The behavioral basis of design.* Englewood Cliffs, NJ: Prentice Hall.

Sommer, R., & Ross, H. (1958). Social interaction on a geriatrics ward. *International Journal of Social Psychiatry, 4,* 128–133.

Spitzer, S. (1980). Toward a Marxian theory of deviance. In D. H. Kelly (Ed.), *Criminal behavior: Readings in criminology* (pp. 175–191). New York, NY: St. Martin's Press.

Stringfellow, F. X. (Autumn 1990/Spring 1991). Society's rejection of the incarcerated. *Journal of Prisoners on Prisons, 3,* 1–2.

Sykes, G. M. (1958). *The society of captives.* Princeton, NJ: Princeton University Press.

Szabo, L. (2014, May 13). Mental illness: The cost of not caring. *USA Today,* pp. 1A, 5A.

Territo, L., Halsted, J. B., & Bromley, M. L. (2004). *Crime and justice in America: A human perspective.* Boston, MA: Pearson.

Thomas, W. H. (1994). *The Eden Alternative: Nature, hope, and nursing homes.* Sherburne, NY: Eden Alternative Foundation.

Thompson, A. E., & Jones, J. (2013, July). *Life and death in assisted living.* Public Broadcasting Service. Retrieved from http://www.pbs .org/wgbh/pages/frontline/life-and-death-in-assisted-living/.

Torrey, E. F., Entsminger, K., Geller, J., Stanley, J., & Jaffe, D. J. (2008). *The shortage of public hospital beds for mentally ill persons.* Treatment Advocacy Center. Retrieved from http://www.treatmentadvoca cycenter.org/storage/documents/the_shortage_ofepublichospital_beds .pdf.

Torrey, E. F., Kennard, A. D., Eslinger, D., Lamb, R., & Pavle, J. (2010). *More mentally ill persons are in jails and prisons than hospitals: A survey of the states*. Treatment Advocacy Center. Retrieved from http://www.treatmentadvocacycenter.org/storage/documents/final _jails_v_hospitals_study.pdf.

Trieschman, A., Whittaker, J. K., & Brentro, L. K. (1969). *The other 23 hours: Child care work in a therapeutic milieu*. Chicago, IL: Aldine.

U.S. Government Accountability Office. (2007). Preliminary observations on efforts to improve health care and disability evaluations for returning service members. GAO publication No. GAO-07-1256T.

Wahl, H. (1991). Dependence in the elderly from an interactional point of view: Verbal and observational data. *Adult Residential Care Journal, 5*, 113–129.

Wener, R., Frazier, W., & Farbstein, J. (1985). Three generations of evaluation and design of correctional facilities. *Environment and Behavior, 17*, 71–95.

Wirt, G. L. (1999). Causes of institutionalism: Patient and staff perspectives. *Issues in Mental Health Nursing, 20*, 259–274.

Wolfensberger, W. (1972). *The principle of normalization in human services*. Toronto, Canada: National Institute on Mental Retardation.

Zarit, S. H., Dolan, M. M., & Leitsch, S. A. (1999). Interventions in nursing homes and other alternative living settings. In I. H. Nordhus, G. R. VandenBos, S. Berg, & P. Fromhold (Eds.), *Clinical geropsychology* (pp. 329–343). Washington, DC: American Psychological Association.

Conclusion

In this book we have explored the ways in which large systems both promote and deter the well-being of individuals and families. We have suggested that using different perspectives provides conceptual frameworks that are useful in understanding social institutions, social structure, and social settings. It is clear that large systems influence the lives and affect the daily experiences of individuals and families. Given the events of the first decade of this century, it is difficult to predict how these systems may change over the next few years. For example, as this book goes to press, the country still has not fully recovered from the Great Recession, the wealth gap not only endures but increases, and the acrimonious national debate over the implementation of health care reform continues. More so than many other professionals, social workers embrace the idea that people cannot be understood apart from the social environments in which they live. This person-in-environment approach is dependent upon up-to-date information about local, state, national, and global trends. As you complete your formal education, we encourage you to continue to become more knowledgeable about emerging societal trends and changing environmental contexts in order to provide informed and appropriate interventions at all levels of practice, and to promote social and economic justice.

This text could lead students to be pessimistic about the immense power associated with the larger social environment and the potential of social workers to achieve positive change. The reality is that individuals, in connection with other like-minded souls, have the capacity within them to make change occur. When we say we are powerless, we give power away. When we believe we can make a difference, the strengths perspective is realized within ourselves, our colleagues, and those whom we seek to support. As Margaret Mead said, "Never doubt that a small group of thoughtful, committed individuals can change the world: indeed it is the only thing that ever has."

Index

About the Authors

Miriam McNown Johnson (BA in social work; MS in educational psychology, University of Wisconsin-Madison; MSW and PhD, University of Alabama) is associate professor and associate dean for academic and student affairs at the College of Social Work, University of South Carolina. She has more than twenty years of social work practice experience, working mostly with children in out-of-home care and their families, and almost twenty years' experience teaching human behavior and the social environment classes. She has published multiple journal articles on many topics and has presented papers at national and international social work education conferences.

Rita Rhodes (BA, DePaul University; MA and PhD, University of Illinois, Chicago; MSW, University of South Carolina) is professor emeritus at the College of Social Work, University of South Carolina. She has a research and practice interest in women's issues including depression, addiction, domestic violence, and incarceration. She has written a book on Irish women. Rhodes has chaired the HBSE sequence at the College for the past ten years. She has published many journal articles on a variety of topics and has presented papers at national and international social work education conferences.